FROM MOUNT VERNON
TO CRAWFORD

FROM MOUNT VERNON
TO CRAWFORD

A History of the Presidents and Their Retreats

KENNETH T. WALSH

CHIEF WHITE HOUSE CORRESPONDENT
U.S. News & World Report

HYPERION

NEW YORK

Library of Congress Cataloging-in-Publication Data

Walsh, Kenneth T.
  From Mount Vernon to Crawford : a history of the presidents and their retreats / by Kenneth T. Walsh.—1st ed.
    p. cm.
  Includes bibliographical references and index.
  ISBN 1-4013-0121-5
    1. Presidents—Homes and haunts—United States. 2. Dwellings—United States. 3. United States—History, Local. 4. Presidents—United States—Biography—Miscellanea. I. Title.

E176.1.W285 2005
813'.54—dc22   2004059242

Hyperion books are available for special promotions and premiums. For details contact Michael Rentas, Assistant Director, Inventory Operations, Hyperion, 77 West 66th Street, 11th floor, New York, New York 10023, or call 212-456-0133.

FIRST EDITION

10 9 8 7 6 5 4 3 2 1

For Barclay
and Gloria

CONTENTS

ACKNOWLEDGMENTS

ONE OF THE MOST important aspects of my research for this book was a series of interviews with five of the men who served as president during some of the most turbulent periods in the past half century.

President George W. Bush was generous with his time and gave me a lengthy tour of his ranch in central Texas. With the president at the wheel of his beat-up white pickup truck and Barney, his frenetic black Scottie, on the seat between us, Bush proved to be an informative and enthusiastic tour guide. Similarly, First Lady Laura Bush was helpful and gracious.

Bill Clinton offered his thoughts about how every president needs to get away from Washington and how he found respites at Martha's Vineyard, Massachusetts, and the official presidential retreat at Camp David, Maryland.

George Herbert Walker Bush and Barbara Bush were happy to share their time and recollections, and provided insight and anecdotes about their many days at Kennebunkport, Maine, and Camp David.

Jimmy Carter offered a revealing look into his commitment to Plains, Georgia, and explained how his peanut farm gave him a haven from the political storms of Washington. Carter also reviewed his experiences at Camp David, where he negotiated a historic peace agreement between Egypt and Israel.

Gerald Ford reminisced about his service as president, the harsh choices that he faced, and his use of retreats in Vail, Colorado; Palm Springs, California; and Camp David.

Senator Edward Kennedy, brother of the late President John F. Kennedy, regaled me with stories about JFK at the family compound in Hyannisport, Massachusetts, and gave an eloquent account of his brother's love for the sea.

I also drew on interviews with scores of presidential advisers and aides, historians, political scientists, and journalists; on archival records at the presidential libraries and homes; and on a large assortment of books written about the men who have led the United States over the course of our history.

I WOULD LIKE to thank Brian Duffy, editor of *U.S. News & World Report*, and Terry Atlas and Gordon Witkin, assistant managing editors at the magazine, for giving me the opportunity to complete this book while continuing my work as chief White House correspondent.

My thanks go to all the others who were so generous with their time and resources.

The staffs at the presidential libraries and museums were indispensable. In researching this book, I learned anew that the presidential library system is a wonderful repository of our national history.

Thanks specifically to Dan Ariail, Joe Bankovich, Dan Bartlett, Jean Becker, Mike Berman, Doug Brinkley, Nick Calio, Andy Card, Penny Circle, Deanna Congileo, Bob Dallek, Mike Deaver, Reed Dickens, Frank Donatelli, Ken Duberstein, Trent Duffy, Marlin Fitzwater, Ari Fleischer, Tom Frechette, Al From, Bill Galston, Geoff Garin, David Gergen, Mike Gerson, Georgia Godfrey, Stan Greenberg, Joe Hagin, Carol Hegeman, Ron Kaufman, Ken Khachigian, Nancy Konigsmark, Deborah Leff, Diane Lobb-Boyce, Joe Lockhart, Scott McClellan, Mike McCurry, Bill McInturff, Harry Middleton, Ron Nessen, Noam Neusner, Anna Perez, John Podesta, Roman Popadiuk, Noelia Rodriguez, Karl Rove, Dave Schafer, Susan Stein, Amy Verone, and Bob Wolz.

I would like to express my gratitude to my editor, Mark Chait, and to Will Schwalbe at Hyperion, and to my agent, Jillian Manus, all of whom saw the value of this book and believed in it from the beginning.

Of course I am most grateful to my wife, Barclay Walsh, who provided invaluable research, suggestions, and encouragement all along the way. She is my partner in work and in life, and she is simply the best.

Kenneth T. Walsh
Bethesda, Maryland

NOTE TO READERS

THIS BOOK AIMS TO add a new dimension to presidential biography by examining the private world of America's chief executives at their retreats, hideaways, and homes—the places where they could be themselves.

I have concentrated on 18 presidents who spent large amounts of time away from the White House and whose lives provide insight into important periods of our history or are interesting in their own right. They include the five men whom historians consider our greatest leaders: George Washington, Thomas Jefferson, Abraham Lincoln, Theodore Roosevelt, and Franklin D. Roosevelt. Because they are significant, fascinating, and familiar to today's Americans, I also look closely at John Adams and John Quincy Adams and at all 11 presidents from Harry Truman to the present.

The final chapter peeks behind the scenes at Camp David, the permanent presidential retreat in Maryland's Catoctin Mountains that has played a key role in the lives of the presidents for more than 60 years.

Since I began working as a full-time White House correspondent in 1986, I have become familiar with the retreats of the four presidents I have covered: Ronald Reagan, George Herbert Walker Bush, Bill Clinton, and George W. Bush. This personal insight has supplemented my research for the book. Occasionally I will enter the narrative as an eyewitness to the events I describe.

K.T.W.

FROM MOUNT VERNON
TO CRAWFORD

CHAPTER ONE

―∞∞∞―

THE IMPORTANCE OF PRESIDENTIAL RETREATS

PRESIDENTS HAVE COMPLAINED about the burdens of office from the beginning of the Republic.

George Washington fretted about "the magnitude and difficulty of the trust to which the voice of my country called me." Thomas Jefferson described the presidency as "a place of splendid misery." Andrew Jackson saw the office as "dignified slavery." Warren Harding said, "It's Hell! No other word to describe it." Harry Truman called the White House "the great white jail." John F. Kennedy told Dwight Eisenhower, his predecessor, "No one knows how tough this job is until after he has been in it for a few months." Ike readily agreed. Lyndon Johnson complained, "The presidency has made every man who occupied it, no matter how small, bigger than he was; and no matter how big, not big enough for its demands." George W. Bush remarked, "Whatever shortcomings you have, people are going to notice them, and whatever strengths you have, you're going to need them."

Yet the burdens of the presidency are manageable, and each chief executive finds his own ways to ease the stress. It turns out that the most common means of coping is for a president to escape from the confines, protocols, routines, and pressures of the White House altogether, to a retreat, hideaway, or personal home. Many of the presidents were wealthy individuals who had their own estates; others borrowed or rented the homes of rich friends or supporters or stayed at hotels or resorts.

In each case, these havens have conveyed the distinctive personalities and character of America's leaders, from George Washington to George W. Bush.

LIKE SO MANY ordinary Americans, presidents find that getting away from the job is a way to rejuvenate themselves and to connect with what is real and truly important in their lives. In fact, one irony of presidential life is that our leaders try so hard to reach the White House, and then, once they win the right to live there, they try equally hard to escape its confines.

"I loved the White House," Bill Clinton told me. "But even so, once in a while you just need to physically get out of Washington and get back into America and kind of clear your head. . . . It's one of the reasons that taking regular vacations is so important."

The extent to which presidents have taken these "sanity breaks" and created their own habitats is one of the enduring but largely unexamined facets of American government. Washington and Jefferson got away to their estates in Virginia for weeks at a time. John Adams spent five to seven months annually at his home in Quincy, Massachusetts. James Madison fled to his central Virginia estate at Montpelier for three to four months every summer and fall. Abraham Lincoln lived at the Soldiers' Home, a residence for injured soldiers during the Civil War, and commuted three miles to his office at the White House for one-quarter of his presidency. Theodore Roosevelt spent most of his presidential summers at Sagamore Hill, on Long Island, New York, mixing work and play in pursuit of "the strenuous life."

Franklin Roosevelt made 134 trips home, encompassing more than 500 days at Hyde Park, New York, and spent many additional weeks at a health resort in Warm Springs, Georgia, where he received treatments for polio. Dwight Eisenhower and Ronald Reagan each spent a year of their eight-year terms at their private getaways—Ike at his Gettysburg, Pennsylvania, farm and Reagan at his ranch in Santa Barbara, California. After taking office in January 2001, George W. Bush enjoyed nine months of his first four-year term at his ranch in Crawford, Texas.

To examine the lives of the presidents at their retreats is to see each man as he really was, without the façades that so many of them created to obscure their private selves. What emerges is a series of portraits of real human beings, subject to self-doubt and overconfidence, physical afflictions and exhaustion, sorrow and heartache, depression and melancholy, self-indulgence and laziness—in short, all the weaknesses and problems that affect the rest of us.

. . .

A SENIOR AIDE recalls strolling on the South Lawn of the White House with George W. Bush one evening a few weeks after his inauguration. It was a clear, crisp February night; the Washington Monument glowed majestically across the Mall, and the White House was illuminated in all its glamour. But Bush longed for escape. He took in the panorama of official Washington, shook his head, and said, "Fifteen years ago I never would have imagined living here. . . . But it's like living in a museum. You can't really go out." The grounds are heavily protected, he explained, and people are constantly peering through the wrought-iron fences hoping to catch a glimpse of the president or the First Lady. Inside, there are grim-faced armed guards in nearly every corridor. Even walking the dog or taking a jog becomes a spectator sport, and a president can't go out for dinner and a movie or visit a hardware store without bringing along an entourage of Secret Service agents, military aides, reporters, and photographers.

Reflecting on his new life, Bush said he needed to get back to Crawford, Texas, and his Prairie Chapel Ranch as soon as he could, to put things into better perspective. A few weeks later, he started what would become a ritual, conducted every few weeks during his presidency: visiting his ranch for some R & R. In an interview for this book conducted at his main ranch house in December 2003, Bush told me, "In Washington, which is an exciting place to be, life is hectic and it's full and there's a lot of decision making. And then I can come out here and, although you know you're still the president and there's daily briefs and occasionally there's decisions to be made, you're able to get a perspective about the job, the current events. I mean, one of the things that's very important for a president is to maintain a vision and see where the world is headed. This helps me maintain perspective. . . . I love to be outdoors [and] I spend a lot of time outdoors here. . . . You need to get your batteries recharged."

After spending many summers at his parents' capacious home on the cool, rocky coast of Maine, Bush purchased his own spread in 1999. It was in a completely different setting that reflected his self-perception and the image he wanted to project. The 1,600-acre property on the rolling prairie of central Texas is a beautiful tract in its own right but an acquired taste for many Americans, who might not take kindly to the overwhelming summer heat and the isolation of the place. As historian Doug Brinkley points out, the ranch, located in the tiny town of Crawford not far from Waco, is in the heart of the Bible Belt and reflects the conservative, small-town values that Bush feels he embodies and that he wants voters to identify him with. Bush wishes to reinforce perceptions that he is a rough-hewn Texan who enjoys manual labor. Seeing the grinning president in a sweat-soaked shirt cutting cedar on a 100-degree August afternoon leaves no doubt that his delight in ranch pursuits is genuine.

THOSE WHO HAVE seen the presidents up close understand the dynamic of breaking away from the West Wing. "Washington is not real," says Stan Greenberg, a Democratic pollster and former adviser to Bill Clinton. "I assume leaders are better for their ability to escape it."

"It tells you about their personality and character," says presidential historian Robert Dallek. "And it gives you a sense of their roots."

Each president tends to go to a place that is "an extension of themselves," observes Brinkley. "These retreats will eventually be national historic sites and interpretive centers for the way the presidents really lived."

Adds Geoff Garin, a Washington pollster and former adviser to Clinton's White House: "You can learn a lot about a president by how he relaxes. Just think of Kennedy on his sailboat. It helped burnish him as hale and hearty, and a family man. . . . You got some really great pictures of Ronald Reagan at his ranch, clearing brush, riding horses, etc. For Bill Clinton, there was a sort of a salon quality to his vacations."

Clinton went so far as to analyze polls to help determine where to go. Dick Morris, his public-opinion analyst, found that visiting a national park would be more acceptable to middle Americans than vacationing with the rich and famous on Martha's Vineyard, Massachusetts, which Clinton preferred. The result: Clinton went to Jackson Hole, Wyoming, near Yellowstone and Grand Teton National Parks during the summer in both 1995 and 1996, his reelection year. Because Clinton didn't have a home of his own—he never had the money to invest in one during his many years as Arkansas governor—he was forced to borrow the often opulent residences of friends for his escapes. This gave his vacations a rambling and rootless quality.

In contrast, even though Lyndon Johnson was a Washington insider and former Senate Democratic leader, as president he emphasized his Texas background with frequent trips to his ranch on the Pedernales River. LBJ wanted voters to know he had roots outside the capital.

Similarly, Jimmy Carter used his peanut farm in Plains, Georgia, to present a down-to-earth, non-Washington image and to reconnect with his past. While he was in office, Carter criticized Washington as an island "isolated from the mainstream of our nation's life."

Ronald Reagan also cultivated his reputation as a Washington outsider. He tried to recreate the lifestyle of an independent Western landman at his Santa Barbara, California, ranch, where he would, famously, ride horses, chop wood, and clear brush. "It was open space and freedom and contact with reality," observes Ken Khachigian, former speechwriter for both Reagan and Richard Nixon. "It was analogous to people who do weekend gardening. It was relaxing. It was mindless—and I'm not being critical. It wasn't anything you had to do a lot of thinking about. It was the adult equivalent of shooting hoops or throwing a ball around. It was also the exercise. Some presidents, like Reagan, did it for physical upkeep."

IN THEIR GETAWAY habits, our presidents have been in tune with larger trends among the American people. "Think, for a moment," writes historian Cindy S. Aron, "of the range of vacations that we indulge in today: the grueling week-long backpacking trek, the trip to Disney World, the quiet week at a rented seashore cottage, the European tour, the hunting and camping expedition, the splurge at a posh resort, the visit to relatives in another part of the country, the golfing holiday, the road trip in the Winnebago, the time at a health spa. Vacations announce much about the vacationer—not only class status and economic standing but personal aspirations and private goals. More than just yearly rituals in which we connect with friends and family, vacations are also exercises in self-definition. In affording time away from the demands of everyday life, vacations disclose what people choose to do rather than are required to do."

For most of the early history of the United States, vacations were suspect for most Americans. It was only during the early decades of the 20th century that the practice of vacationing spread beyond the privileged classes to an increasingly prosperous Middle America and was seen as essential to health and well-being. And it was only during the Depression, in the 1930s, that most working-class Americans won the right to an annual paid summer vacation, even though few could afford to take a leisure trip. Aron calls this process the "democratization of vacationing."

. . .

PRESIDENTS ARE SOMETIMES criticized by their political adversaries for spending too much time away from the White House. George Herbert Walker Bush paid a political price, for example, for vacationing at his estate in Maine during a recession when many Americans were losing their jobs. "People were angry in 1992," says Greenberg. "And they saw the president on the golf course, etc. It reinforced the sense of him being out of touch." The Democrats helped to fuel this image by running ads featuring Bush in a golf cart.

But this was the exception. Says Republican pollster Bill McInturff: "People feel that the president lives a very different life than the rest of us do. People are not shocked that presidents have money and that they hang around with rich friends or go to Martha's Vineyard like Clinton did. If the country is going well, and people's lives are going well, it's okay. If things are bad and people feel that a president is not doing his job, that's a different story."

Democratic pollster Garin adds: "Americans believe everybody deserves a vacation, and they think the president brings 'the store' with him wherever he goes and he always lives above the store. People cut the president a helluva lot of slack."

OVER THE YEARS, America's major presidents, such as George Washington and Franklin Roosevelt, established most of the lasting traditions for getting away from the capital. But even the less historically significant chief executives set patterns that offered insight into their character and priorities.

James Madison, who served from 1809 to 1817, considered his estate at Montpelier in Virginia not only a refuge from the pressures of office but also a personal rehabilitation center. Madison was always fearful about his health, and felt that the federal city of Washington bred disease and lethargy with its swampy, humid climate in the summer, so he left the capital frequently. But he was also a workaholic and made some important decisions at his getaway, as most presidents do. In the summer of 1811, for example, Madison decided that another war with Great Britain was inevitable because of London's violations of U.S. maritime rights, including the seizing of American sailors.

Through the next two centuries, presidents experienced a common need to escape from the capital even if the journey home was arduous and time consuming. When he took office in 1829, Andrew Jackson planned to visit his thousand-acre estate at the Hermitage outside Nashville every other summer. He would use one of two routes, both difficult because of bad roads and frequent stormy weather—overland via Virginia and Tennessee, or through Maryland and West Virginia and then south over the Ohio and Cumberland Rivers. The trip covered a thousand miles and took three or four weeks each way, but Jackson still found the journey home worthwhile even though he was unable to visit as much as he intended.

James Garfield, a longtime Republican representative from Ohio, was preparing to take a vacation at the Jersey Shore about four months after he took office when, on July 2, 1881, he was shot by a deranged office seeker in the railroad station in Washington. Garfield remained close to death in the capital for two months, at which time his doctors decided to move him to the Shore, where they thought he might recuperate more rapidly. On September 6, 1881, he took a train from Washington to the beachfront home of Charles Francklyn in Long Branch, New Jersey. A special spur at Elberon had been constructed directly to the house to accommodate the critically ill president, but he developed an infection and died in Long Branch on September 19, 1881.

Chester Arthur, his successor, had expected to remain in relative obscurity as vice president and wasn't sure he was up to the job as the nation's 21st president. A New York lawyer who rose in the Republican party as a prodigious fund-raiser, he achieved relatively little. He suffered from what was then termed Bright's disease, a kidney disorder that causes headaches, fever, and fatigue, and he needed as much rest as he could get. As a result, his periodic trips out of the capital were mostly therapeutic. In 1882, he sought the cool breezes and leisurely pace of his rich friends' homes in Rhode Island. In the spring of 1883, he visited northern Florida, but the heat and humidity did not suit him. In fact, he developed a high fever and came close to death, which was kept secret. Several newspapers criticized him for laziness, but Arthur felt that revealing his health problems would be worse for his image than his reputation for indolence.

Grover Cleveland was the first president to be married at the White House, and his desire for privacy was acute. (He was also unusual because he was elected to two nonconsecutive terms, meaning that historians count him as president twice. The history books refer to 43 presidents, but there were actually only 42 men who held the title.) After Cleveland took Frances Folsom as his bride in 1886, the couple immediately left for a honeymoon at a secluded resort in the western Maryland countryside. Unfortunately for them, a trainload of reporters showed up and tried to invade their privacy. Cleveland referred to the correspondents as "animals and nuisances." The episode showed why presidents prefer to vacation or relax at their own estates, which can be more easily policed than resorts or other public places.

After his honeymoon, Cleveland worked at the White House but actually lived much of the time during his first term at a secluded house he owned on 23 acres in northern Washington. Frances named the estate Oak View. Reporters called it Red Top, for the color of the roof on the main house. "Oak View or Red Top, it was not intended as a summer or vacation getaway spot like Camp David and others frequented by twentieth-century presidents," writes author H. Paul Jeffers. "It was meant to be a year-round retreat. A safe haven from the nosy and noisome minions of the press, it would become a full-fledged farm with a cow named Grace. In due course Frances, an animal lover, assembled a menagerie of dogs, chickens, ducks, quail, foxes, kittens, and even some white rats. A coach house and a large kitchen garden were constructed. The stable and the one at the White House accommodated five horses. . . . More than a hundred years after the dream hideaway became a reality, Red Top claims a unique niche in the history of Cleveland's presidency. It was the only house in the nation's capital to be used by a president as a year-round alternative to living in the White House."

Woodrow Wilson had no home outside the White House during his presidency, and for his first summer, in 1913, he and his wife, Ellen, went with their daughters to an artists' colony, Haarlachen, in Cornish, New Hampshire. (Mrs. Wilson was a painter of some renown.) They stayed at Haarlachen for eight days in July. In other years, Wilson and his family went to Sea Girt, New Jersey; Long Branch, New Jersey; and Pass Christian, Mississippi.

Warren Harding, Wilson's successor, vacationed frequently during his two and a half years in office, and enjoyed railroad trips around the country. In July 1921, he went on a woodsy retreat to a Maryland spot called Nature's Laboratory. Harding's companions included industrialists Henry Ford and Harvey Firestone (who hosted the event) and inventor Thomas Edison.

Calvin Coolidge, who succeeded Harding after his predecessor's death in 1923, spent part of his presidential summers fishing and relaxing in Vermont, Massachusetts, the Adirondack Mountains of New York, the Black Hills of South Dakota, and Wisconsin. "In the pre-air-conditioning era, before the 1950s, Washington was a cesspool of heat and humidity and mosquitoes," historian Doug Brinkley said. "A president had to get away for his health and his sanity."

Herbert Hoover had a retreat built in Virginia's Blue Ridge Mountains in 1929, his first year as president. He paid for the land himself and called it Camp Rapidan. Hoover initially said he wanted a hideaway within 100 miles of the White House where the trout fishing was good. He had one other stipulation: The retreat needed to be at least 2,500 feet above sea level in order to reduce the mosquito population.

The land was cleared by the military and a dozen cabins were built, along with riding stables and barracks for the soldiers who would protect the commander in chief. The president's cabin was roomy, with a big stone fireplace in the living room, a dining area, two bedrooms, and a porch that overlooked trout streams. Hoover made the two-hour drive there as often as he could, mostly on weekends. He liked to fish alone, sometimes wearing a suit and tie with hip boots.

He envisioned the 164-acre property as a permanent retreat for presidents, and he donated it to the government when he left office after one disastrous term. It is now part of Shenandoah National Park. But its distance from the White House, nearly 100 miles to the southwest, was considered impractical, and subsequent presidents didn't like the area's heat and humidity or its association with the unpopular Hoover. Camp David, in Maryland's Catoctin Mountains, eventually came to serve as the official year-round hideaway that Hoover tried to create, and it has been the scene of many important decisions.

Yet it was at their private properties, each tailored to their individual needs and tastes, that America's presidents felt they could truly relax and be themselves. In addition, these refuges have played an important role in our history from the beginning of the Republic.

———∞∞∞———

CHAPTER TWO

GEORGE WASHINGTON AND MOUNT VERNON, VIRGINIA

GEORGE WASHINGTON WAS the pacesetter. He established precedents that most of his successors have followed to this day, in everything from resisting the concentration of federal power to his insistence on finding a respite from his official duties at regular intervals. As the first president, serving from 1789 to 1797, he made 15 visits to his beloved 8,000-acre estate at Mount Vernon over eight years, for periods ranging from several days to a few months.

The picture that emerges of Washington at home may surprise those familiar only with his historical image as a military and political leader. He actually considered himself primarily a Virginia planter, and he took pride in being recognized as one of the leading farmers of his time. "I think," he once wrote, ". . . that the life of a Husbandman of all others is the most delectable. It is honorable—It is amusing—and with Judicious management, it is profitable." His preoccupation with agriculture extended to the décor of his home. On the ceiling of his two-story dining room—the first room his guests would enter upon arrival—were plaster depictions of farm tools such as picks, shovels, and scythes.

"Washington designed Mount Vernon himself," writes historian Henry Wiencek. "The house and every foot of its gardens and ground present a view of the inner man and the workings of his mind. . . . It embodies a basic contradiction—Mount Vernon is not the humble abode of a democrat, but the manor house of a colonial potentate. Washington lived privately in some grandeur and rural pomp, with a decidedly British flavor, and yet he was the man who refused to be king, who infused the ceremonies of the republican government with plainness, who left a legacy of presidential modesty."

Washington made a sharp distinction between his private life and his public duties. At home he was master of all he surveyed and enjoyed many luxuries, including the finest foods and wines. More controversially, he embraced the aristocratic culture of the South and believed until late in his life that slaves were essential to running his plantation.

Yet in his public role, Washington knew that, as the most revered man in the nation, nearly everything he did would set a precedent, and he established a code of restraint. He sought out and listened to advice. He rejected imperial titles such as "Your Highness" in favor of "Mr. President" or "Mr. Washington." He used the presidential veto only once, rejecting the congressional reapportionment of 1792. As a rule, he deferred to the will of Congress. When he left office, exhausted, after eight years, he set still another precedent limiting a president to two terms, which lasted until Franklin Roosevelt's tenure in the mid-20th century.

WHAT WAS THE father of his country like as the squire of Mount Vernon? Benjamin Henry Latrobe reported visiting the president during his second term to deliver a letter from Bushrod Washington, the president's nephew and Latrobe's friend. "Having alighted, I sent in my letter of introduction, and walked into the portico next to the river," Latrobe recalled. "In about 10 minutes, the president came to me. He was dressed in a plain blue coat, his hair dressed and powdered. There was a reserve but no hauteur in his manner. He took me by the hand, said he was glad to see a friend of his nephew, drew a chair and desired me to sit down."

Washington, then 64, looked to his visitor younger than his years. He was physically impressive, standing at least six feet tall, making him tower over most men of his time, and his weight fluctuated between 175 and 200 pounds. Latrobe found him intense, with an air of reserve that caused him to keep silent for long periods. This resulted in an awkwardness that was felt by everyone in his presence. His answers to questions were "often short and sometimes approached to moroseness," Latrobe recalled, but he laughed at "a humorous observation, and made several himself." Latrobe concluded: "Washington has something uncommonly majestic and commanding in his walk, his address, his figure and his countenance."

On several occasions during Latrobe's visit, nothing animated the former general more than talking about agriculture. Latrobe said Washington struck him as "a respectable and opulent country gentleman." Washington wanted to know his guest's assessment of "the state of the crops about Richmond," and "he gave [Latrobe] a very minute account of the Hessian fly and its progress from Long Island where it first appeared through New York, Rhode Island, Connecticut, Delaware, part of Pennsylvania and Maryland." Washington then discussed his views on the cultivation of Indian corn, and the merits of different types of plows.

It was also clear that Washington's business instincts overruled whatever compassion he had for his slaves. In his discussions with Latrobe, for example, he analyzed the nutritional needs of the Africans on his plantation with the same detachment that he displayed in discussing the diet of his livestock. Evaluating the pros and cons of raising Indian corn, Latrobe wrote, "As food for the Negroes it was his opinion that it was infinitely preferable to Wheat bread in point of Nourishment. He had made the experiment upon his own Lands and had found that though the Negroes, while the Novelty lasted, seemed to prefer Wheat bread as being the food of their Masters, they soon grew tired of it. He conceived that should the Negroes be fed upon Wheat or Rye bread, they would, in order to be fit for the same labor, be obliged to have a considerable addition to their allowance of Meat."

WASHINGTON'S ROUTINE ON the farm was vigorous. He would rise each day at 4 A.M. (an hour earlier than his 5 A.M. rising time in the capital of Philadelphia, where he kept "city hours"). He would walk down a flight of stairs to his office, where he would put on his spectacles—kept on a small desk near the big globe of the world he had ordered from London—and begin his workday. Maps were strewn on the floor, and he would consult them regularly for his research and correspondence. He hated to be interrupted during this quiet time, when he would write letters, add to his diary, do official paperwork, or read at his desk. Breakfast was served at 7 A.M.

His favorite morning meal consisted of tea and hoe cakes, which were cornmeal pancakes drowning in honey and butter. Then he would ride around his property on horseback. His step-grandson, George Washington Parke Custis, once gave this description to a stranger inquiring how he might recognize the master of the house: "You will meet, sir, with an old gentleman riding alone, in plain drab clothes, a broad-brimmed white hat, a hickory switch in his hand, and carrying an umbrella with a long staff, which is attached to his saddle-bow—that person, sir, is General Washington!"

He would return at noon, do some more letter writing and reading, and preside over chores around the house. Lunch was served at 2 or 3 P.M., and was an elaborate affair in the tradition of British gentry. Washington expected his guests to dress in their finest clothes, and there were many courses: several meats, such as roast pig, boiled leg of lamb, roasted goose, or roast beef; plates of vegetables, such as peas, cucumbers, artichokes, cabbage, and onions; bread; and prepared dishes; followed by various pies, cakes, and other desserts; and finished off with plates of fruit and nuts accompanied by tea. Washington would generally have three glasses of Madeira wine (imported from Europe) with lunch or afterward, sometimes as he read the 10 newspapers he perused nearly every day.

After such a feast, often no evening meal was served. At 6 or 7 P.M., he might take tea with visitors and show them his gardens or other parts of his property. In the evening, he enjoyed games of cards (such as whist but also including loo and pharaoh, which involved gambling) or leading his guests in a series of guessing games in the parlor. Another activity was listening to his step-granddaughter, Nelly Custis, play the harpsichord and sing. He would sometimes read aloud from various newspapers to stimulate discussion and debate. He was particularly interested in reports of what the Virginia General Assembly was up to. On some occasions, when the Madeira had loosened his tongue, he would tell war stories and reminisce about how his armies had defeated the British only a few years earlier.

But if he didn't know visitors well, or if they displeased him, he would say only a few words, letting them know he was keeping company with them only out of a sense of courtesy. He would retire at 9 P.M. (In Philadelphia and New York, he would go to bed an hour later.)

WASHINGTON HAD A strong sense of decorum. He had loved dancing all his life, and he was very good at it, whether it was a minuet or a country jig. But after he became president, he rarely took to the dance floor. He thought it was unbecoming of a national leader and, besides, he didn't think he was as limber as he used to be. When dancing was on the agenda at Mount Vernon, he would limit himself to starting off the first minuet in the most stately way possible and then sit out the rest of the evening.

He was an avid horseman, widely recognized as one of the superior riders of his time. Yet once on a trip to nearby Great Falls, his mount almost slipped into some rapids and Washington lurched in an awkward way to avoid tumbling onto the rocks. He was in his 60s at the time, and badly wrenched his back. This didn't keep him from continuing his horseback riding, however.

He loved to entertain friends and family, but complained that strangers would drop in with little or no notice, simply to meet and greet the "father of the United States." On more than one occasion he lamented that Mount Vernon seemed to be turning into a tavern where travelers expected to find food, drink, and a place to stay for a night or two. He longed for the days when he and his wife, Martha, could sit by the fire and sip Madeira by themselves. This rarely happened. Such was his sense of decorum and responsibility that if visitors were people of stature or importance, he would not turn them away, especially if they had letters of introduction from friends or associates.

Of course Washington could not have handled his social life at all without his spouse. Plump and good-natured, she had an ability to make people feel comfortable in her home, and she was able to create the kind of relaxed, welcoming atmosphere that the old general could not have done himself. "She has something very charming about her," said Polish army officer Julian Niemcewicz in an observation typical of Mount Vernon's guests. Washington was out inspecting his properties so frequently, in fact, that it was Martha who often stayed at the house and entertained the visitors.

She generally left the operation of the lands and the renovation of the houses to her husband, but she did take an interest in other domestic matters, such as choosing the china and glasses for the dining room, supervising the making of the slaves' clothing, and overseeing the housecleaning and the preparation of meals.

Most of all, she tended to the children. She and the president had no offspring of their own, but, as a widow, she had two children from her first marriage, John "Jackie" and Patsy Custis. After Jackie died, the Washingtons adopted Jackie's two youngest children, George Washington Parke Custis and Eleanor Parke Custis, whom they raised at Mount Vernon. Washington never warmed to the grandchildren, however, apparently because they were not his own.

. . .

MOUNT VERNON GAVE Washington pleasure all his life. Even during the War of Independence, when he had rarely been able to spend time there, he often imagined himself at his imposing white mansion with the red roof and the distinctive cupola that commanded a wonderful view of the Potomac. "In the darkest days of the Revolution, that mental picture of Mount Vernon had provided Washington with a much-needed source of relief, a refuge from the trials that seemed to multiply around him constantly," write authors Robert F. Dalzell, Jr., and Lee Baldwin Dalzell. "It was to perform exactly the same function through the eight long years of his presidency. If the pressures and tensions of that time were different from those he had encountered as a commander in the field, in their own way they were just as harrowing."

His ideas about how to improve the estate were exhaustive and remarkable, considering that he was running the new Republic at the time and there was no shortage of political and civic problems to deal with. He was trying to balance the need for an energetic central government with his concerns about excessive federal power, and he was attempting, unsuccessfully, to heal a growing schism between Treasury Secretary Alexander Hamilton and his Federalists, who wanted government to encourage economic development, and Secretary of State Thomas Jefferson and his Republicans, who were leery of centralized power.

Just as important, Washington was attempting to keep the new nation solvent and at peace as he tried to steer clear of entanglements with the warring empires of Great Britain and France. And he faced considerable social unrest that led to his ending the Whiskey Rebellion, an anti-tax movement in western Pennsylvania, with armed troops. But virtually everyone in the country thought that Washington, the revered former war leader, was the only individual who could command some minimal amount of national unity.

It was at Mount Vernon that Washington agonized and finally decided to run for a second term. Particularly influential was the advice of Thomas Jefferson, who said the country was not stable or united enough to survive without Washington as its leader. The factionalism that the Founding Fathers greatly feared was coming to pass, with the nation becoming divided on the power of the federal government, relations with Europe, and many other issues. In the end, he reluctantly agreed to serve again—though he made clear that he would have preferred to return to Mount Vernon after four years.

When he ran for reelection in 1792, he had no competition and won all 132 votes cast in the electoral college.

DESPITE THE BURDENS of office, Washington continued to micro-manage his plantation and he saw fit to constantly look over the shoulders of his overseers and other subordinates. In the fall of 1792, for example, he wrote Anthony Whiting, his manager at Mount Vernon, with specific instructions on where to plant trees, which varieties he preferred, where to place ivy around an icehouse, how to care for sick slaves, the manner in which the staff was to spread gravel on the garden walkways, and much more. He devised a seven-year schedule of crop rotation, and was forever experimenting with basic farm techniques, such as which manures were most effective as fertilizers.

In December 1793, in the middle of his presidency, he made a list of some of his most important holdings. It was apparently an exercise in accounting that he enjoyed doing over the holidays. In his large, bold handwriting, he made a detailed drawing of the "Mansion house Farm," complete with the road up to the main house, carefully sketched trees, and the Potomac River, which bordered his property. Accompanying the map was a list of "Farms and Their Contents," in two neat columns under four headings: "Union Farm," "Dogue R.[Run] Farm," "Muddy hole Farm," and "River Farm." In all, he described 3,260 acres on the four farms, and he carefully enumerated lands devoted to "meadow," "clover," "fields," and "orchards."

He actually had five farms on 8,000 acres, and when he was in residence at his mansion, he would try to ride on inspection tours of his property every day, to make sure his orders were being carried out.

He had concluded that America's future was in farming and he observed that the open West offered nearly unlimited lands for Americans to settle on. He envisioned a canal system for transportation that would link the country together much as the interstate highway system does today. He always believed that each man was responsible for improving his property as much as possible.

To that end, President Washington spent many years designing his house and grounds, and by the time he became president it was basically the way he wanted it. The house was painted white on the outside, with the wooden walls—made of yellow pine—beveled to make them look like stone blocks.

The large dining room was one of his favorites. Painted in a muted verdigris—a mint green color—it was his showcase room, designed to demonstrate his status. The largest room in the house, it featured a large marble mantel over the fireplace and was where he received his most important visitors and conducted affairs of state.

It was, in fact, where he first got word that he was elected president. Washington, at 57, was chosen unanimously by the Electoral College in April 1789, and received official notification from Charles Thomson, secretary of Congress, who traveled from the nation's first capital in New York. The emissary read the announcement in formal style as he stood across from Washington in the huge dining room.

NEARLY HALF THE estate was woodland, and Washington wanted the property to be as close to self-sufficient as possible. He had acquired Mount Vernon from family members as a young man and wanted it to stay in the family forever. (He was actually born 65 miles south of Mount Vernon in the Northern Neck of Virginia in 1732.) The estate provided firewood and lumber for construction. It also provided entertainment and exercise, allowing Washington and his family and guests to ride horses, hunt, fish, and stroll among the tulip poplars, white ash, elm, locusts, and other trees, which he loved and had planted around the main house. Most basic of all, it provided food—meat of various kinds, wheat and corn, vegetables, and fruit, from peaches to apples.

In addition, Washington, as a member of the American gentry, wanted his estate to be impressive.

He designed it so it provided a magnificent view as a visitor approached from a distance, with the main house flanked by trees and a vast lawn, and behind it the Potomac River and the Virginia countryside rolling as far as the eye could see.

The spot that Washington most treasured—other than the large dining room—was the large piazza in the back, where he often sat in the afternoons, reading or chatting with family and friends, or just admiring the grand view of the Potomac. "I can truly say I had rather be at Mount Vernon with a friend or two about me, than to be attended at the seat of government by the officers of state and the representatives of every power of Europe," Washington wrote.

He was a stickler for maintaining standards and issuing rules. As historian Henry Wiencek observes, Washington was "practical, hardworking, and demanding of himself and others."

Even after Washington began presiding over the fledgling federal government in New York, he insisted on receiving weekly written reports from his overseers. These memoranda updated him on the planting of crops, the improvement of the property, and many other aspects of life on his land—and he made his wishes known in a long stream of his own memos back to Mount Vernon. He set aside several hours each Sunday to write these directives. He continued this practice after the capital was moved from New York to Philadelphia in November 1790, and for his entire presidency.

Throughout his two terms in office, Washington was in frequent correspondence with Andrew Young, an English agronomist; John Beale Bordley, an agronomist from Maryland; and Oliver Evans, a millwright from Delaware, who invented a system for automating grist mills to more efficiently grind wheat and corn for market and household use. He exchanged ideas about farm management with Thomas Jefferson, and he was a devotee of the agronomy books of English agricultural scientist Jethro Tull.

Washington, operating from his own moral code, felt that since he was wealthy, it was his responsibility to take risks with experimental practices, so that less fortunate farmers could learn from his experiences and he could set an example.

"Experiments must be made," he once wrote, "and the practice (of such of them as are useful) must be introduced by Gentlemen who have leisure and ability to devise and wherewithal to hazard something. The common farmer will not depart from the old road 'till the new one is made so plain and easy that he is sure it cannot be mistaken."

He followed Bordley's lead and experimented with crop rotation. Washington took particular interest in the use of trees for shade in pastureland, and the use of clover and timothy in rotating crops. He developed a seven-year plan for his Dogue Run Farm that included the planting of buckwheat, corn, clover, and potatoes and the use of manure.

He was one of the first Americans to buy and install Oliver Evans's system of elevators and conveyances to automate the processing of wheat and corn flour. The system enabled Washington to reduce the workers at his grist mill from six men to one millwright and an assistant. He also tried to promote the use of mules instead of horses or oxen for farmwork, since he believed mules were more sturdy and less subject to injury and disease than other animals.

While he was president, he found the time in 1792 to invent a new kind of barn for threshing and storing wheat, which didn't catch on with other farmers but served him well. Washington had noticed that sometimes the tools on his farm were broken or allowed to deteriorate by his slaves as a form of passive resistance or out of simple misuse. The threshing barn that he designed made use of horses instead of human labor, and it saved him money because it cut down on the disrepair of equipment.

It was actually a two-story, 16-sided circular barn that would allow farm animals to tread out wheat under cover from rain and wind, and keep the grain secure indoors from theft. He made sure the barn had bars on the lower-level windows and a solid lock on the door. In October 1792, Washington gave one of his managers a detailed design and a list of material needed to build such a barn on his Dogue Run Farm. Ever meticulous, he determined that the foundation and the first-floor walls of the barn would need 30,820 bricks.

On one of his visits home during his presidency, he complained that this barn was not being used according to his instructions. On October 16, 1793, the president told one of his supervisors that, despite having "one of the most convenient Barns in this, or perhaps any other Country, where 30 hands may with great ease be employed in threshing . . . notwithstanding, when I came home . . . I found a treading yard not 30 feet from the Barn door, the Wheat again brought out of the Barn and horses treading it out in an open exposure liable to the vicissitudes of weather."

Such concerns were remote from the matters of statecraft, finance, and politics that Washington faced as the first president of the American Republic. But he believed that focusing on his farm grounded him in real life and kept him from growing isolated. He was prescient in this, as with so many other things.

He also showed no reluctance to get into even the earthiest details. "When I speak of a knowing farmer, I mean . . . above all, Midas like, one who can convert everything he touches into manure, as the first transmutation towards Gold," Washington wrote. He used manure from his horses, cattle, mules, and sheep for fertilizer, along with fish heads and innards, and even mud that he had his slaves haul from the Potomac River. He sent orders to his farm manager to create a "dung repository" near the stables.

At the end of his life, he had accomplished one of his great missions. He had kept his financial affairs solvent, and protected his family from financial disaster.

MOST IMPORTANT, MOUNT Vernon illustrated Washington's uncomfortable relationship with slavery. In his will, he ordered that all his slaves be freed upon the death of his wife, Martha, and he added that the children of his slaves should be educated and trained so they could thrive as free adults. He was the only Founding Father to set all his slaves free. But he came to this decision after a lifetime in which slave labor was the cornerstone of his wealth and central to his life at Mount Vernon. In this respect, as in so many others, his life was filled with contradictions.

"If anything can take founders like Washington and Jefferson out of our present and place them back into the particular context of their time, it is this fact that they were slaveholders," writes history professor Gordon S. Wood. "Slavery is virtually inconceivable to us. We can scarcely imagine one person owning another for life. Seeing Washington and Jefferson as slaveholders, men who bought, sold and flogged slaves, has to change our conception of them. They don't belong to us today; they belong to the 18th century, to that coarse and brutal world that is so remote from our own."

Washington was pragmatic above all. He told friends he favored the abolition of slavery but felt that the only way to accomplish it was through "Legislative authority." As president, he feared losing political support in the South if he pushed in any way to end the institution, and he didn't try. He was a traditional Southern planter.

"Washington was not a cruel man," Wood says, "but relying as he did on slave labor made him act in a manner that to us can only seem cruel. To make his farm pay he worked his slaves hard, divided their families for efficiency, punished them by whipping or selling them and clothed and housed them as meagerly as possible. He, along with other planters, raffled off the slaves, including children, of bankrupt slaveholders who owed him money."

He made some efforts to minimize his own use of slaves, such as by the construction of the special round threshing barn, which emphasized horse power;

but that apparently was because he didn't think the bondsmen could be trusted to work as hard as the horses.

"There is a particular incident in Washington's slaveholding career that is hard to sugarcoat," writes Wiencek. "Some of his famous false teeth, celebrated in textbook lore, were yanked from the heads of his slaves and fitted into his dentures. Moreover, Washington apparently had slaves' teeth transplanted into his own jaw in 1784, in a procedure that did not succeed. At first, this seems to be the *ne plus ultra* of casual plantation cruelty; but Washington paid his slaves for the teeth, and the custom of the wealthy buying teeth from the poor was common in Europe." Still, it was an exploitative practice.

Washington worked his slaves hard at Mount Vernon. He expected them to get up before dawn so they could start their tasks by sunup. Breakfast would come later. This was the same routine practiced by the master himself. Everyone was expected to work from dawn to dusk, with a two-hour break for lunch and a rest, and then the slaves would walk home in the dark. In the summer, the slaves and everyone else worked 15- or 16-hour days, six days a week.

Washington authorized his white overseers to whip slaves when the managers felt it necessary, such as when a slave tried to escape or was found guilty of serious theft. Mount Vernon, as a slaveholding plantation, was not a pleasant place for the bondsmen and -women. There were many cases of slaves "misbehaving" and running away. And Washington often grew angry or frustrated when his slaves didn't work as hard as he wanted them to.

Some insight into Washington's acceptance of slavery as a necessary evil in his life came during the spring of 1791, after the capital had moved from New York to Philadelphia. He was well aware that Pennsylvania had passed a law under which slaves brought into the state became free after six months of residence. Not wanting to lose the handful of slaves he had brought with him, President Washington decided to evade the law, shuttling slaves back and forth from Philadelphia to Virginia within the six-month time frame, to avoid any legal problems. He also hoped that the slaves would not learn of the Pennsylvania emancipation law and then seek freedom by escaping from his control in that state. Washington wrote his assistant that "the idea of freedom might be too great a temptation for them to resist." In sending them back to Virginia to circumvent the law, Washington wrote, "I wish to have it accomplished under pretext that may deceive both them [the slaves] and the Public."

In 1796, he ordered the pursuit of Ona Judge, one of his slaves who escaped from his household in Philadelphia to New Hampshire, where slavery was legal but frowned upon. The president valued Ona's household skills as a seamstress and personal attendant for Mrs. Washington, who was apparently incensed at her attendant's "disloyalty" and "ingratitude." At Martha's insistence, Washington sought repeatedly to return her, by force if necessary, to servitude at Mount Vernon, even though she had married and had a child during her time of freedom. In the end, Washington's efforts were unsuccessful.

Historians still debate whether Washington consorted with slave women. One theory is that he slept with a slave named Venus at Mount Vernon and fathered a child named West Ford.

But there is no definitive evidence either way. My own belief, shared by Wiencek and other historians, is that Washington was such an advocate of discipline and self-control, and so protective of his image as a moral individual who was beyond reproach, that it is difficult to imagine such a lapse. But certainly the nature of slavery gave Washington and all other slave masters plentiful opportunities to rape and abuse their charges, and in every case gave the masters total control over other human beings' lives. This was partly why Washington, in the end, found slavery so repugnant. It corrupted everyone connected with it.

By the end of his life, he had rethought the slavery issue in fundamental terms. This caused him to order in his will the freedom of all his slaves—more than 300 of them—upon the death of his wife, Martha. This provision was vehemently opposed by his family and Martha's family.

AFTER HE DIED at Mount Vernon, on December 14, 1799, Martha Washington moved out of their bedroom on the second floor and into a much smaller bedroom on the third floor. It was a mourning custom at the time that surviving spouses temporarily would not sleep in the room that had been shared with the deceased. But Martha could not bear to return to the second-floor bedroom and the four-poster bed where her husband passed away, so she stayed in the spartan upstairs bedroom, which is where she herself died.

GEORGE WASHINGTON'S LIFE at Mount Vernon revealed his commitment to his farm and to agriculture, and underscored his style as a micro-manager who delved into virtually every detail of running his estate. He found that it was far easier to control his plantation and to solve problems there than it was to impose his will as president, and he took immense satisfaction in dealing with his property. Beyond this, Washington's life at Mount Vernon showed the contradictions of his approach to slavery. What emerges is a more complete picture of the Father of Our Country, blemishes and all.

CHAPTER THREE

JOHN ADAMS AND JOHN QUINCY ADAMS AND QUINCY, MASSACHUSETTS

JOHN ADAMS, THE nation's second president, didn't look like a commander in chief. Short and stout, with a prominent nose, bald pate, and double chin, he was derided by opponents as "His Rotundity," and he lacked the charisma of George Washington. Yet he was in many ways a brilliant thinker and certainly one of the most influential of the Founders.

He was plagued with innumerable problems as president and had considerable difficulty coping with them. Making matters worse, the ridicule he endured deeply wounded him and his wife, Abigail, and he had a more powerful need to escape from the hothouse of the capital than Washington had. He retreated to his home in Quincy, Massachusetts, with great frequency, and these stays enabled him to rejuvenate himself, although he was always a hardworking president who took his job very seriously.

AS HIS PUBLIC life unfolded, from his years as U.S. emissary to England to the vice presidency under Washington and his own presidency from 1797 to 1801, Adams adopted an aristocratic view of public service. "Popularity was never my mistress, nor was I ever, or shall I ever be a popular man," he wrote. "But one thing I know, a man must be sensible of the errors of the people and upon his guard against them, and must run the risk of their displeasure sometimes, or he will never do them any good in the long run." He stubbornly declared that he would "quarrel with both parties and every Individual in each, before I would subjugate my understanding, or prostitute my tongue or pen to either."

As president, he was attacked as a monarchist, "champion of kings, ranks, and titles," and a nepotist seeking to pave the way for his son, John Quincy Adams, to follow him as president, which in fact did happen some years later. And his tenure was plagued by controversies over states' rights, intensifying partisanship between Federalists and Republicans and among the Federalists themselves, the creation of a national monetary system and a national bank, the levying of import duties, and the power of the federal government versus that of the individual states. There was also the issue of possible war with France, which he managed to avoid despite French provocations and support for war among many Americans. He drew bitter Republican criticism for nepotism when he named John Quincy as minister to Prussia. Making matters worse for him, Thomas Jefferson, elected as his vice president, opposed many of his policies and emerged as a leader of the opposition, creating one of the most debilitating internal divisions of any administration in U.S. history.

"As president, Adams had to operate in the intense, superheated partisan politics of the 1790s, when the fate of the fragile new federal republic seemed to teeter on the brink of disaster," writes historian Alan Taylor. "Politicians of every stripe expected the worst of one another and of events. Such beliefs tended to become self-fulfilling prophecies as both Federalists and Republicans magnified every sign of opposition into a crisis that imperiled the nation. . . . Federalists saw the Republicans as libertines and anarchists eager to replicate the terror of the French Revolution. In turn, the Republicans depicted the Federalists as cryptomonarchists preparing to destroy the republic and to restore British domination."

NOT SURPRISINGLY, JOHN and Abigail were always eager to get away from Philadelphia's rancid atmosphere for as long as they could, and they returned to their home in Quincy, Massachusetts, after Congress adjourned each year. They remained there for extended periods, and Adams was criticized for having "absconded" from the capital and shirking his duties. Despite the attacks, he considered his retreat indispensable as a refuge.

At first, Abigail planned to remain for most of the year in Massachusetts. After only a few weeks in office, however, John found he couldn't run the presidential household without her, and pleaded for her to have a local family move onto their land and care for their farm so she could move to the capital immediately. After some difficulty finding the right people, Abigail did so and left Quincy at the end of April to join the new president. She took charge of their official residence— first in the temporary capital of Philadelphia and, starting in 1800, in the new City of Washington in the federal District of Columbia. She supervised the staff, organized an active social calendar, and ordered from New England her husband's favorite cheeses, bacon, white potatoes, and cider.

But Adams was struggling to maintain the brutal pace he felt his office required. He rose at 5 A.M., with breakfast at 8 and lunch at 3 P.M., and often didn't finish his duties until 8 at night. It was debilitating, made all the worse in the hot, humid weather that began in June and deteriorated with each passing week.

"The hot weather of July has weakened us all," Abigail wrote during their first presidential summer, in 1797, prior to their departure for Quincy. "Complaints of the bowels are very frequent and troublesome." She added: "The task of the President is very arduous, very perplexing, and very hazardous. I do not wonder Washington wished to retire from it or rejoiced in seeing an old oak [her affectionate term for her husband] in his place." In another letter written during his first year in office, she wrote, "The President really suffers for want of a journey, or rather for want of some relaxation."

Congress adjourned on July 10, and the couple began their two-week journey home to Peacefield, their home in Quincy, on July 19. The tensions of Philadelphia quickly faded as they took comfort in old friends and the fact that the cooler New England weather was a wonderful change from the sweltering summers in Philadelphia, where yellow fever epidemics posed a constant danger until cold weather arrived.

John conducted business from their home, which they called the Old House. He was following the precedent set by Washington, who had gone home to Mount Vernon whenever he could. But the first president had such stature that his critics muted their attacks, compared with what Adams faced.

He remained in Quincy until early October, a period of more than two months, when he returned to Philadelphia. But this extended stay was seized upon by his enemies. The *Aurora*, an anti-Federalist newspaper, berated Adams because public opinion was "exceedingly agitated" and his presence was needed in the capital.

Yet during his sojourn, there were no crises to deal with, no political flare-ups, no news from France that might bring war closer. As biographer David Mc-Cullough notes, "For Adams the pleasures of August and September at Peacefield had all the desired effect. By the time they were heading back to Philadelphia, he and Abigail were both rested and revived. Abigail wrote of feeling better than she had in years." There is little record of Adams's activities during this period. He apparently had little pressing business to attend to. He spent his days reading, taking walks with Abigail, and in the evenings had leisurely dinners with friends.

When the president and First Lady departed from Quincy the first week of October, they learned en route that another one of its periodic yellow fever epidemics was spreading through Philadelphia and they waited in East Chester, Pennsylvania, until it passed. They stayed there for a month with their daughter, Nabby, and her four children.

From then on, Adams followed Washington's pattern of going home during the hot, humid months as often as he could. This represented the first time a president used a "Summer White House."

But unlike Washington, who found that Mount Vernon was never far from his mind, Peacefield was rarely on Adams's mind, because of the press of business in the capital. "I have however almost forgotten my farm. . . . My whole time and Thoughts must be devoted to the Public," he wrote to Abigail in January 1797.

Yet like so many of the Founders, Adams always longed to return to his roots throughout his government service. His goal, he said, was "to lay fast of the town [of Quincy] and embrace it with both arms and all my might. There live, there to die, there to lay my bones, and there to plant one of my sons in the profession of law and the practices of agriculture, like his father."

THE ADAMS FAMILY'S roots in Quincy were strong. The town, in fact, was named after Col. John Quincy, Abigail's grandfather (after whom the couple's son, John Quincy Adams, was named).

Adams took considerable solace walking in his formal garden and the grounds surrounding the Old House. One thing that had attracted the couple to the property was this garden, which included a variety of fruit trees.

During the early years of their marriage, they had lived in a simple farmhouse in this same area, just outside Boston. While in London representing the new

American government as minister plenipotentiary in 1787, Adams arranged the long-distance purchase of what was called the Vassall-Borland place, which Adams had wanted to buy for years. The house had been built 50 years earlier, about 1731, as the summer villa of a rich sugar planter from the West Indies, Leonard Vassall. Throughout the War of Independence the house was empty, after Vassall's daughter, a loyalist to the British, moved to England. Adams paid 600 pounds for the house, farm buildings, and 80 acres.

In 1788, a year after the long-distance purchase, they returned to their new home after four years abroad for Abigail and ten years for John. It was not as grand as they remembered it—certainly it paled in comparison to the estates and mansions they had grown familiar with in Europe. Nor was the town of Quincy much to brag about. It had little more than a main road and a handful of connecting streets lined with wooden houses all painted white with window blinds of green. At the center of town was a meeting house and town hall and a tavern behind big elm trees. It was on a stagecoach route that ran between Boston and Plymouth. This modest farmhouse was where John Quincy Adams and his siblings were born.

Abigail brought from England a cutting of the red rose of Lancaster and one of the white rose of York, which she planted in the southwest corner of the front yard. She also planted three lilac bushes, which have survived to this day, and her husband added a horse chestnut tree nearby. It was the start of many years of Abigail's plantings, which included daffodils, nasturtiums, and delphiniums.

Adams used the house, which was on the site of a working farm of more than 100 acres, as his law office. Much later, while John was serving as president, Abigail added an east wing as a surprise, which her husband greatly appreciated. It was clear that she actually ran the place.

IN 1798, THE bitterness and divisions in the fledgling government got worse. Congress passed and Adams signed the infamous Alien and Sedition Acts. Adams regarded them as war measures, imposed because of informal hostilities with France, which was raiding American shipping and threatening an invasion. Many Americans feared that the thousands of French immigrants to the United States would foment rebellion. There was also fear that Irish radicals who had fled to America from their homeland would side with France in her war with Britain and foment violence in the United States against critics of France.

Among the unfortunate provisions of the new laws was one that gave the president the right to expel any foreigner he considered dangerous and another that increased the required period of residence to qualify for citizenship from five to fourteen years. Even more appalling, and clearly unconstitutional, the Sedition Act imposed fines and prison terms on anyone found to be writing or making "false, scandalous, and malicious" statements against the government, including Congress and the president. Complicating things immensely, Vice President Thomas Jefferson opposed the Alien and Sedition Acts and was promoting the idea that each state had the right to nullify federal actions it deemed unconstitutional.

Amid war fever and paranoia, Congress adjourned on July 16, and the Adamses began their second major journey to Quincy on July 25. As they left, a yellow fever epidemic was killing hundreds of Philadelphians every week. They arrived in Massachusetts on August 8, but this time their stay in Quincy was not what they sought. In fact, it was one of the most prolonged and agonizing periods that any president has endured while on "vacation."

Unlike Washington, who enjoyed almost universal respect, Adams felt besieged and wronged by all sides; he had few powerful friends in the capital, and was plagued by vituperative critics in the press. While Washington sought to return to Mount Vernon simply to reconnect with his roots and enjoy his estate, Adams, who was subject to bouts of depression, anxiety, irritability, and exhaustion, needed to restore his own emotional stability and physical health.

"The year 1798, the most difficult and consequential year of John Adams's presidency, was to provide him no respite," writes biographer David McCullough. "His stay at Quincy would be longer even than the year before, but the stress of the undeclared war—the Quasi-War, as it came to be known, or Half-War, as he called it—combined with the threatening ambitions of Alexander Hamilton and growing dissension within Adams's own cabinet, filled his days with frustration and worry. There was precious little peace at Peacefield in the summer of 1798, and especially so as Abigail fell so ill that she very nearly died."

The First Lady became sick during the journey home and was bedridden with fever, possibly caused by malaria, for eleven weeks. The president described it as "the most gloomy summer" he had ever experienced. Abigail would recover, but her sickness and frailty were constant weights on the president's mind. In addition, he was confronted almost daily with the problems of office, and he worked with great perseverance and energy. His days were consumed by the paperwork that arrived by rider from the capital in Philadelphia, by reports on the activities of the departments of government, by requests for spending on various items, including a lighthouse at Cape Hatteras, and by reports on the yellow fever epidemic in Philadelphia and outbreaks in Boston, New York, and Baltimore. By September, 40,000 people had fled Philadelphia alone; in the end, 3,000 people would die of the disease that year, including four of the servants at the President's House.

Things were going badly in his family, too. John Quincy had left his savings, about $2,000, in the custody of his brother Charles before he left on his foreign assignment, and Charles had lost nearly all of it in bad investments. This caused the president and First Lady no small amount of worry and embarrassment, because they had been so frugal and careful with their own money and expected the same of their children.

When Adams left for Philadelphia on November 12, in a horse-drawn coach accompanied by his nephew William Shaw, he had gained little of the rest and peace of mind he had hoped for. His teeth and gums ached, and one side of his face was for some reason badly swollen. But the weather was clear and crisp, and his two horses made good time, sometimes 30 miles a day. Better still, he was told along the way that a British fleet under Admiral Horatio Nelson had apparently destroyed a French fleet off the coast of Egypt. If true, this meant the chance of war with France had disappeared. He arrived in Philadelphia on November 24, where he learned for certain that the British had indeed won a great naval victory and ended the prospects of a French invasion of the United States.

In March 1799, Adams left Philadelphia again, to rejoin Abigail in Quincy. He remained away from the capital for eight months, more than twice as long as Washington's longest absence. This was partly to avoid the yellow fever epidemic that again struck Philadelphia. But Adams, as Washington before him, also wanted to go home to clear his head and gain a fresh perspective. Adams believed he could run the government just as well from behind his big oak desk at home in Quincy as he could from the nation's capital.

He was wrong. His self-imposed isolation loosened his grip on the government and allowed his enemies to nearly ruin his peace overtures to France. It was the possibility that they might succeed that finally brought him back to the capital in October. "Because it was a period of suspense and crisis in American domestic politics and foreign relations, Adams's prolonged absence aroused considerable comment and criticism," writes historian Alan Taylor. "And it enabled Hamilton's allies in the cabinet to govern with virtual independence." In the end, Adams managed to reassert his control and avoid war, but his hiatus had made matters worse.

Many Americans were outraged. "The public sentiment is very much against your being so much away from the seat of government," a supporter wrote him, fearing that his enemies might plot to overthrow him during his absence. "They did not elect your officers, nor do they . . . think them equal to govern without your presence and control. I speak the truth when I say that your real friends wish you to be with your officers because the public impression is that the government will be better conducted."

Adams told associates that George Washington, too, had spent long weeks at home in Mount Vernon (though never as long as Adams did). The important thing, he said, was to be in residence in the capital when Congress was in session. If he were unable to keep watch on the legislature, he said, he would resign.

It never came to that, of course. And his months on his farm affected him like a tonic. His health and Abigail's health improved, and at the end of his stay he was reported in "very good humor."

In 1800, his final year in office, Adams moved into the new President's House in Washington but still managed to spend four months in Quincy, from June 14 to October 13. It was a campaign year and Adams was standing for re-election, but he told friends he realized he had taken too many unpopular stands to win. He was correct. He was ousted by Thomas Jefferson. Embittered by his experiences, he left the President's House before dawn on inauguration day, March 4, 1801, rather than endure the humiliation of watching his successor take the oath of office.

JOHN QUINCY ADAMS, the second president's son, followed him into the nation's highest office, in 1825. "Quincy" lost the popular vote to Andrew Jackson, but neither received a majority in the electoral college. In a tumultuous showdown, the closely divided House of Representatives gave JQA the presidency. Jackson supporters condemned it as a "corrupt bargain" between Adams and fellow candidate Henry Clay, who released his supporters to Quincy and ended up as secretary of state.

John Quincy had been well prepared for the presidency, having served as U.S.

minister to the Netherlands and Prussia, U.S. senator, and secretary of state. But despite his impressive résumé and his personal integrity, he was bullheaded, prone to temper tantrums, and showed poor judgment in all manner of political and policy issues.

All these traits were evident from the time he was a small boy, living with his family in Boston and Braintree, Massachusetts, as his father tried to expand his legal practice and got increasingly involved in the revolutionary movement against the British. "His mother worried about how impatient he could be, how determined to have his way, and how sensitive he was to criticism," writes biographer Paul C. Nagel. "He clamored to tackle tasks that boys older than he might hesitate to accept. In part, this was because Johnny considered himself the man of the house during his father's long absences. Among the responsibilities he claimed before he was ten was riding horseback the several miles between Braintree and Boston in order to carry and fetch the mail."

JQA, as he called himself to avoid confusion with his famous father, would have an awful experience in his single term as chief executive. "His four years in the White House were misery for him and for his wife," writes Nagel. "All that he hoped to accomplish was thwarted by a hostile Congress. His opponents continually assailed him with what he claimed was the foulest slander. Consequently, while Adams sought reelection in 1828, he did so mostly from stubborn pride, and he actually looked impatiently toward his certain defeat by Andrew Jackson. For the remaining twenty years of his life, he reflected on his presidency with distaste, convinced that he had been the victim of evildoers. His administration was a hapless failure and best forgotten, save for the personal anguish it caused him."

To escape, Adams spent each summer in Quincy, as his father had done. What he found there were domestic problems to rival his political ones, which included bitter disagreements with members of Congress over his ideas about strengthening the federal government through higher tariffs and federal support for manufacturing, roads, and canals.

En route home on July 4, 1826, his father, John Adams, died, leaving JQA as the head of the extended family. He was shaken by the death of his model and mentor. He found that his father had specified in his will that the family mansion and farm not be sold, even though they were in poor condition and the farm was running at a loss, which he could never overcome. Making matters worse, JQA was named co-executor with his cousin Josiah Quincy, leaving him with many problems in deciding what to do with his father's estate.

He also was distressed throughout this period that his son George Adams was gambling, drinking, and amassing embarrassing debts in nearby Boston. JQA paid the debts off quietly, all the while urging his son to "spurn the deadly draft of pleasure." JQA's brother, Tom, was also drinking heavily. To acquire his father's estate from family members and to care for his extended family, JQA borrowed money and sold some of his father's lands.

He was weary when he returned to Washington later that summer, and his frustrations in the capital deepened throughout the following year. Some of his friends felt he was near collapse. He was unable to sleep well, endured stomach pains, indigestion, and loss of appetite, and fell into what he called "uncontrollable dejection of spirits." His doctor, according to Adams, told him to "doff the world aside and bid it pass; to cast off as much as possible all cares, public and private, and vegetate myself into a healthier condition." He was encouraged to return to Quincy during August and September 1827.

It had a salutary effect. He slept better and began to swim regularly, an exercise he enjoyed. He woke up at 5 A.M. each day, as he had in Washington, to read the Bible, peruse a number of newspapers, and take a walk or swim. He ate breakfast at 9 A.M., worked until late afternoon, and had supper at 5 P.M. or later. He found time to go fishing, work in the garden, and plant trees. He liked to chat with family members or play billiards with them. Then he worked in his study before retiring at 11 P.M. He got to know friends and neighbors, such as wealthy Boston businessman Peter Chardon Brooks, whose daughter was betrothed to the president's son Charles.

But his sour mood, bad health, and depression returned when he arrived in Washington in October. He could never shake off his problems, and the presidential campaign of 1828 was a nightmare for him. Andrew Jackson and his supporters had tried to undermine him at every turn, and Adams and his supporters grew bitter and nasty in return.

Adams's backers spread the story that Jackson and his beloved wife, Rachel, had committed adultery before Mrs. Jackson was divorced from her first husband. What the Adams faction didn't say was that Andrew and Rachel didn't know that her divorce proceedings were incomplete at the time they wed. Jackson never forgave

Adams for what he considered a vicious personal attack. Later, when Rachel died, Jackson believed her heart had been broken by the embarrassment of the campaign disclosures.

After his defeat, John Quincy found satisfaction and a measure of vindication as a member of Congress from Massachusetts—the only former president to serve in the House of Representatives after leaving the White House. He fought slavery and became a formidable elder statesman of American politics in his post-presidential years.

IN ALL, THE presidential pattern for John Adams and John Quincy Adams was similar. Hoping for relief from their extremely stressful work, each man got away from the capital as much as he could. John Adams, in fact, was the first president to be vilified for not being on the job, in some cases rightfully so. The son followed in his father's footsteps, but with fewer accomplishments.

—◦∞◦—

CHAPTER FOUR

THOMAS JEFFERSON AND MONTICELLO, VIRGINIA

L IKE GEORGE WASHINGTON, Thomas Jefferson considered himself above all a farmer. But unlike Washington, Jefferson was a man of the Enlightenment who enjoyed many other pursuits, such as architecture, viniculture, European history, literature, science, and gadgets and inventions of all kinds, and he was perfectly content to do so as a private citizen at his home in Monticello, Virginia.

"Many of the Founding Fathers were caught between a nagging realization that they must serve the nation they had wrought, and a longing for a calmer life at home—a home that very often was a plantation or farm," writes historian Donald Jackson. "It was almost routine for a man entering or reentering public life to assert dolefully that he did so with grave doubts and after long deliberation. Jefferson more than once expressed his own preference by saying he would rather be sick in bed at Monticello than hale and chipper anywhere else."

Jefferson once wrote, "Those who labour in the earth are the chosen people of God, if ever he had a chosen people, whose breasts he has made his peculiar deposit for substantial and genuine virtue. It is the focus in which he keeps alive that sacred fire, which otherwise might escape from the face of the earth."

Monticello, Jefferson's estate near Charlottesville, Virginia, was a refuge where he could be the center of love and deference from his family and friends without enduring the antagonisms and suspicions of public life. This is a feeling common to most presidents in regard to their home places.

As for the presidency itself, Jefferson believed that a man of his stature might stand for election as a civic duty, but he would never run for office overtly. That, he felt, would be beneath him. He might respond to a call to service but would never seek power on his own. Of course, in the end he gave up his quiet life in 1801 to serve as the third President of the United States, a post he held until 1809, after being reelected in 1804.

He was an advocate of limited government and strict construction of the Constitution, but he also showed amazing foresight. When an armistice was declared among European powers, the threat of America getting drawn into a war was greatly reduced and Jefferson made the most of it. He lowered taxes, cut federal employees, trimmed the national debt, and enabled many private citizens to acquire national lands. Perhaps his crowning achievement was the Louisiana Purchase in 1802, when he arranged for the government to buy a vast tract of land from France, which doubled the size of the United States.

JEFFERSON VISITED MONTICELLO about three months every year, on average, while he was president. It took him four or five days to get there by horseback or carriage from the President's House in Washington, depending on the weather—a distance of about 140 miles. He stayed overnight with friends and sometimes in taverns along the way. His visits took place in the summer months, when Congress wasn't in session and when he and many people in the capital couldn't endure the pestilential weather and the mosquitoes of the region.

His routine at Monticello while he served as president was active and engaged, and like so many other Southern gentlemen of his era, he mixed work with self-indulgence.

He woke up at dawn—as soon as he could make out the hands of the clock near his bed—and would make himself a fire during the cold months by taking wood out of a box in his room, doing the job himself rather than summoning a servant. He made a habit of immersing his feet in a pan of cold water as soon as he got up even when it was so cold there was frost on the floor of his bedroom. He believed the practice helped him avoid catching cold. (Whatever the reason, Jefferson rarely did catch cold throughout his adult life, which deepened his belief in foot-dunking.)

He enjoyed walking on his terrace and taking in the sunrise, and then would be ready for the day. About 9 A.M., he would have breakfast and then take a horseback ride unless the weather was particularly bad. He liked to bring an overseer or friend with him, and he either kept up a running commentary on what he was seeing and what he wanted done, or would hum a tune or sing to himself, obviously pleased to be outdoors and surveying his domain. At a slender six foot two, he cut an impressive figure in the saddle.

He had dinner served at 3:30 P.M., and his table was covered with the bounty of his farm, such as smoked meats and a form of macaroni and cheese, peas, corn, and other vegetables grown on his property. He enjoyed apple cider, produced on his estate, and wines from Europe and from his own vineyards. At 7 P.M., he had tea and light snacks such as cakes and pies.

He kept himself busy. He loved the world of ideas, and liked to read, especially the Bible, to write, talk with friends or associates, prepare some model or invention, or sketch plans for various projects at his mansion or on his estate. For thirty years, he pushed along a large construction program at Monticello, designing, among other things, a domed two-story house that would look like one story from the outside. "Jefferson did the designing, but his slaves did the work, ranging from making bricks and pulling down or putting up walls to skilled carpentry and furniture making," writes historian R. B. Bernstein.

After explorers Meriwether Lewis and William Clark returned in 1806 from their expedition to the American West, which Jefferson had arranged, the president decorated the Executive Mansion—today called the White House—and Monticello with animal and plant specimens they brought back. Among the artifacts in the main hall at Monticello were two pairs of huge antlers, one of an elk and the other of a moose; busts of a Native American man and woman; a painting on a buffalo pelt of a battle between Osage and Pani tribes; and the mounted heads of a buffalo, a deer, and a bighorn sheep. He also displayed the upper and lower jaws, thigh bone, and teeth of mastodons.

He had a "cannonball clock" built in the main foyer. By means of using cannonball weights that could sink below floor level, the clock showed the time of day and the day of the week according to markings on the walls. He put in a set of doors between the hall and the parlor that could open at a touch because of a hidden set of gears and chains. He installed a portable copying press in his study and also a primitive "copying machine" that made duplicates of letters and other handwritten documents by using two linked pens. And while it isn't clear whether Jefferson invented it or just employed it, he had a bookstand or music stand that allowed five separate books or packets of sheet music to be displayed at the same time.

HE RECORDED WEATHER observations in a diary, listing the temperature, precipitation, sky conditions, and other thoughts at least once a day. He kept daily records of his purchases, often extravagant, of everything from trees to fine wines from abroad. Sometimes he hunted squirrels and grouse, although he disliked fox hunting.

He always tried to be immaculately groomed, generally wearing short breeches and bright shoe buckles, and overalls when he took his horseback rides. He always cut a striking figure, "presidential" in every way. His posture was ramrod straight; he had striking blue eyes and clear skin, and was nearly always in good health.

(After he grew old and infirm, a servant would follow him around his plantation carrying a camp stool; Jefferson could then sit down while he was watching work being done or while he gave instructions. He had become too weak to remain on his feet for long periods of time.)

Edmund Bacon, who was Jefferson's chief overseer and business manager at Monticello for 20 years, once described some of his habits: "He did not use tobacco in any form. He never used a profane word or any thing like it. He never played cards. I never saw a card in the house at Monticello, and I had particular orders from him to suppress card-playing among the negroes, who, you know, are generally very fond of it. I never saw any dancing in his house, and if there had been any there during the twenty years I was with him I should certainly have known it."

Bacon also wrote, "He was never a great eater, but what he did eat he wanted to be very choice. He never eat [sic] much hog-meat. He often told me, as I was giving out meat for the servants, that what I gave one of them for a week would be more than he would use in six months. . . . I knew mighty well what suited him. He was especially fond of Guinea fowls; and for meat he preferred good beef, mutton, and lambs. . . . Merriweather [sic] Lewis' mother made very nice hams, and every year I used to get a few from her for his special use. He was very fond of vegetables and fruit, and raised every variety of them." Jefferson also was an early American connoisseur of ice cream and served it in hot pastry shells. He even came up with a recipe for the concoction: "2 bottles of good cream, 6 yolks of eggs, ½ pound of sugar."

HE HAD A soft spot for entreaties from the poor. Bacon reported that when he would return home from Washington, people who were down on their luck would find out and "come in crowds to Monticello to beg him. He would give them notes to me, directing me what to give them. I knew them all a great deal better than he did. Many of them I knew were not worthy—were just lazy, good-for-nothing people, and I would not give them any thing. When I saw Mr. Jefferson I told him who they were, and that he ought not to encourage them in their laziness. He told me that when they came to him and told him their pitiful tales, he could not refuse them, and he did not know what to do. I told him to send them to me. He did so, but they never would come. They knew what to expect."

DESPITE HIS APPARENT compassion toward poor people seeking help, Jefferson's relationship with his slaves was, as many historians have noted, complicated and hypocritical. Even though he has always been known as an eloquent advocate of the highest American ideals of human rights and independence, he owned more than 100 slaves at the start of his presidency. He considered them an indispensable part of his plantation and the economic system of the South, even if he detested the institution of slavery as a matter of personal philosophy and felt it could ruin the country because it was so divisive an issue.

Jefferson arranged to have as little direct contact with slavery as he could. He had dumbwaiters installed and shelves mounted on small casters, so house servants could wheel a dumbwaiter to the dining room, latch it to a rotating door, and then turn the door and send the food to Jefferson and his guests, who would serve themselves. There were wine dumbwaiters on either side of a fireplace in the dining room, in this case connecting to the wine cellar below. A slave would load wine into a box and raise it into the dining room using a pulley. Then Jefferson would open the door of the wine dumbwaiter and remove the drinks. Similarly, Monticello's covered walkways and plantings blocked the main house's view of the slave quarters.

In addition to keeping his distance personally, Jefferson mostly maintained a public silence on the issue of slavery. As historian Sean Wilentz points out, "Not only would attacks on slavery endanger both his party and the Union; but he had learned from hard personal experience in his younger days that antislavery sentiments would be politically disastrous in Virginia. Yet his circumspection was not purely self-protective and self-serving. He appears to have become genuinely pessimistic about the prospects of free blacks and whites living together in harmony. The long chain of abuses that was slavery, he feared, had so hardened the color line that nothing short of 'diffusion' (that is, spreading slavery out far and wide) or colonization would solve the problem."

Many of Jefferson's racial theories would make us cringe today. In a letter written in 1807, Jefferson said blacks were "as inferior to the rest of mankind as the mule is to the horse, and as made to carry burthens." In his *Notes on the State of Virginia*, which he wrote in 1781 and 1782 and had published in Paris in 1785, he condemned slavery as "a hideous evil" but said blacks were inherently inferior to whites in reasoning powers and imagination (though superior to whites in music, and equal in courage and the "moral sense"). Appallingly, Jefferson also wrote in *Notes* that black men lusted after white women because they found them more attractive than black women, just as an orangutan in the wild lusted for "the black women over those of his own species."

Jefferson's life at Monticello reflected his belief in blacks' racial inferiority. According to historian Donald Jackson, "Slaves were everywhere, more than a hundred, populating the house and grounds, some living in cabins on Mulberry Row not far from the mansion, others dispersed on farms at Shadwell and Lego across the Rivanna. Most had well-defined roles, and among themselves maintained a kind of class system based in part on their duties and partly on their seniority, proven loyalty, or sheer appeal to the Jefferson family. There were body servants, house servants, cooks, artisans, and, at the bottom of the scale, the field hands. There also was a special inner family of slaves, a matriarchy headed by mulatto Betty Hemings, which would eventually include twelve children. Betty had come to Monticello as part of Martha Jefferson's dowry, and apparently six of her offspring were sired by her former owner John Wayles, the father of Jefferson's late wife."

Sally Hemings, one of Betty's daughters, is thought to have had an affair with Jefferson and given birth to at least one of his children. Sally spent much of her adolescence serving Jefferson and his two daughters while he was U.S. envoy to France, and then, as a house servant and seamstress at Monticello, tended Jefferson's bedchamber and clothing and eventually received considerable authority in running the main house.

Historian R. B. Bernstein is among the scholars who have pointed out that Jefferson was in proximity to Sally Hemings nine months before the birth of each of her six children. Oral tradition among Hemings family members suggests that some were descended from Jefferson. All of Sally Hemings's children received names with links to the Jefferson family, which was not true of other slaves born at Monticello. Finally, when accusations about his adultery with Hemings surfaced in the press during his first term as president, Jefferson never specifically denied them.

Jefferson was relatively kind to his slaves, according to the standards of his day. Bacon reported that he would not let them be overworked and would "hardly ever" allow one of them to be whipped. He permitted some of his slaves to learn to read but not to write. He feared that the bondsmen might forge papers giving themselves freedom.

He was particularly interested in maintaining his mildly profitable nail factory, which sold nails to the surrounding community, and decided that it would be more humane to put slave boys, aged 10 to 16, to work there rather than make them work in the fields (although when they grew up, many were sent to the fields anyway).

All this was probably of little comfort to the slaves, who were, after all, still in bondage. But Jefferson appears to have been more lenient than other slave owners. Donald Jackson reports that he sometimes allowed his slaves to "escape" by walking off his plantation and disappearing permanently, and he rarely sold slaves, preferring to keep them with their families and friends under his care.

On one occasion, a slave named Jim Hubbard was accused of stealing several hundred pounds of nails from the nailery. Faced with the accusation in the presence of Jefferson, he began to weep and repeatedly asked his master for forgiveness. Jefferson turned to overseer Bacon and said, "Ah, sir, we can't punish him. He has suffered enough already." Instead of ordering him to be flogged—the common punishment for such an offense—Jefferson told him never to do such a thing again and sent him back to the nailery to work.

Soon thereafter, Jim Hubbard committed himself to religion and was soon baptized. "He was always a good servant afterwards," Bacon recalled.

Jefferson also bargained with at least one of his slaves to keep him at Monticello. When he was secretary of state in the temporary capital of Philadelphia, he brought with him James Hemings, who had lived with Jefferson in Paris and was trained at considerable expense to cook French food. Jefferson realized that Pennsylvania had a law emancipating blacks (the same law that Washington evaded under similar circumstances). He and other Virginia slave owners understood that any slaves they brought with them could easily escape and gain freedom in Pennsylvania, a strong antislavery state where many free blacks already lived.

"Jefferson, who had begun paying him [James Hemings] a salary in Paris [where slaves had been freed by an act of the French revolutionary government], continued to do so on their joint return to Monticello," wrote author Garry Wills. "Perhaps that was an inducement to keep him in service. But Philadelphia posed new and far more acute dangers. Hemings would find fellow blacks speaking English there, and a city with strong anti-slavery sentiment. The Abolition Society, if it learned of James' time in France, could legally declare him free. So Jefferson drew up an affidavit, properly witnessed, promising to free Hemings in the future if he stayed with him in Philadelphia and returned with him to Monticello."

In the end, Jefferson freed some of his slaves, but only after his death, according to his will, and he allowed many to remain in bondage. He didn't think they were "ready" for freedom during his lifetime, and didn't want to jeopardize the future of his debt-ridden plantation through a blanket emancipation.

THROUGHOUT HIS PRESIDENCY, indeed throughout his life, Jefferson issued a constant stream of letters and directives about the management of his estate to chief overseer Edmund Bacon. "Mr. Jefferson was very particular in the transaction of all his business," Bacon later wrote. "He kept an account of every thing. Nothing was too small for him to keep an account of. He knew exactly how much of every thing was raised at each plantation, and what became of it; how much was sold, and how much fed out." This caused no small amount of grumbling on the part of his staff, who felt he was too demanding and was what we would today call a micro-manager.

This tendency was reinforced when he returned to Monticello in January 1794 after serving as secretary of state. He was aghast at the sorry condition of his property and his house, and wrote George Washington in May that "a ten years' abandonment of them to the ravages of overseers, has brought on them a degree of degradation far beyond what I expected."

From then on, Jefferson would not relent in his attention to detail. During his presidency, he would send the overseers memos describing precisely how much grain each of 90 servants on the estate should be issued from October to July: 4½ barrels a week. His 70 hogs were to receive 1½ barrels apiece per week; his oxen, 6 gallons a day.

He also insisted on written contracts for his business transactions—such as in hiring mechanics, carpenters, or other workers—to make sure there were no misunderstandings later. He also preferred written agreements on purchases and sales, such as when his plantation supplied firewood for local families, at $5 per year, for what wood they would burn in a fireplace.

The president often sent Bacon trees and shrubs he admired and acquired from a nursery near Georgetown in Washington, and the president was familiar with nearly every tree on his property. "He always knew all about every thing in every part of his grounds and garden," Bacon wrote. "He knew the name of every tree, and just where one was dead or missing."

The president gave extraordinarily detailed instructions on the planting of vegetables and fruit, the management of his slaves, and many other aspects of his estate's operation. His official worries about matters of state did not keep him from giving considerable thought to the earthy specifics of farm life.

"If the weather is not open and soft when Davy arrives," he wrote Bacon from Washington in November 1807, "put the box of thorns into the cellar, where they may be entirely free from the influence of cold, until the weather becomes soft, when they must be planted in the places of those dead through the whole of the hedges which inclose the two orchards, so that the old and the new shall be complete, at 6 inches' distance from every plant. If any remain, plant them in the nursery of thorns. There are 2,000. I sent Mr. Maine's written instructions about them, which must be followed most minutely." He went on to order the precise method and location of planting four purple beeches, four red locusts, four prickly ash, six Spitzenberg apple trees, five peach trees, and 500 "October peach stones." He was even concerned about extending the "paling so as to include these [the peach stones], and make the whole secure against hares."

Despite the president's constant attention, Bacon observed that Jefferson's 10,000-acre farm, extending from Charlottesville five or six miles to beyond Milton, "was not a profitable estate; it was too uneven and hard to work." He added that it was neighbor (and future president) James Madison's plantation at Montpelier that was a profitable concern.

Still, there were regular if minimally successful attempts to increase productivity. Jefferson and Bacon gave "premiums" to the overseers, black or white, who grew the largest crops. The best crop of wheat earned an extra barrel of flour; the best crop of tobacco, a "fine Sunday suit"; the best supply of pork, an extra 150 pounds of bacon.

Typical of Jefferson's exhaustive memoranda to Bacon was a six-page description of the work that was to be done in the immediate future, from finishing construction of a mill to building a fence and a road, clearing a field and planting "Quarantine corn, which will be found in a tin canister in my closet. This corn is to be in drills 5 feet apart, and the stalks 18 inches asunder in the drills. The rest of the ground is to be sown in oats, and red clover sowed on the oats. All ploughing is to be done horizontally, in the manner Mr. Randolph does his."

JEFFERSON'S PENCHANT FOR innovation and experimentation was evident. He was the first farmer in his area of Virginia to import full-blooded Merino sheep, and he did so while he was president. He split the six animals between himself and his friend, Madison. Within a few years, after breeding their stock with that of neighbors, the flock expanded to several hundred sheep. He was less successful at breeding what Bacon called "large broad-tailed sheep." A group of four was unable to reproduce and they died within a few years. The estate also raised hogs, which thrived.

But it was horses that became one of Jefferson's passions, and he had very clear preferences. He insisted on riding only horses that were bay in color, and "would not ride or drive any thing but a high-bred horse," Bacon said. Whenever he traveled by carriage, he always had four horses for the carriage and a fifth for a servant who rode behind him.

He was an avid collector of books on agriculture, such as *Maison Rustique, The Countrie Farme*, and *The Practical Farmer*, published in 1793 by John Spurrier of Wilmington, Delaware. He tried a new approach to crop rotation in 1795, a seven-year cycle starting with wheat and turnips (for sheep feed); followed by corn and potatoes grown together and then in the fall by vetch, a beanlike crop he was experimenting with; peas or potatoes or both; wheat or rye sown with red clover; clover plowed under in the autumn and sown to vetch; vetch turned under, followed by buckwheat sown in the spring; and wheat in the fall, to restart the cycle.

Jefferson had borrowed this seven-year rotation from George Washington, but as was typical of him, he made it more complicated. Washington had only five types of crops in his plan. Jefferson had at least nine.

Like so many of his contemporaries, Jefferson loved apple cider, and set down strict rules for its production from his own orchards. He thought the best apples were Taliaferro and Red Hughes, and he insisted that no bruised fruit be used. Similarly, he loved peaches as his favorite crop above all.

He imported casks and bottles of wine from Italy and France, and began to plant Italian and French vines. His fascination with starting an American wine industry continued throughout his life, although he eventually realized that European vines would always have great difficulty thriving or even surviving in the hot, humid summers of southern Virginia. In the end, his experiments with grape growing were a disappointment.

The master of Monticello also imported cuttings of olive trees from Italy and France, hoping that they could be made a lucrative source of oil in America. He brought in rice that he thought might thrive in dry fields. (It didn't.)

He tried new kinds of farm machinery, such as a box for faster sowing of red clover seeds. He experimented with a new kind of ploughshare machinery that automatically flipped the soil over. He wanted no patent on it, hoping it could be made generally available and might be a boon to American farmers. None of these experiments resulted in any breakthroughs, however.

ONE EXAMPLE OF Jefferson's bad luck at business surrounded his construction of a flour mill. His neighbors wanted him to build it, believing that as president he had a large government salary and was better able than anyone else among them to invest the large sums necessary. And Jefferson intended that the four-story stone building would be used by the community, not him alone. But in 1807 a flood swept away the dam that provided water power for the mill, and all was lost.

Jefferson was undaunted, and immediately issued instructions on rebuilding it. But it was never a lucrative enterprise.

In fact, by the end of his life, Jefferson was debt-ridden and knew he could not pass Monticello on to his heirs free and clear.

. . .

HIS ESTATE AT Monticello was not the homey retreat of George Washington's Mount Vernon. While the first president's house looked lived-in and comfortable, Jefferson's seemed almost like a museum, formal and a bit austere. In fact, he referred to his entrance hall as the "museum" because it contained 18 paintings and statuary and other items designed to impress visitors with his erudition. All this reflected his formalized attitude toward his family. The grounds were a constant work in progress, as he always seemed to be building something, setting up a new planting, or removing an old one.

His wife, Martha, had died in 1782, before he became president, and he never married again. Four of their six children also passed away at early ages. Yet though Jefferson loved his surviving daughters, Martha and Maria, in order to challenge them and push them to make something of their lives, he treated them with stern discipline and imposed exacting standards on them. Maria married John W. Eppes, who later became a member of Congress. She died young and was buried at Monticello. She left a son, Frank Eppes, who stayed with his grandfather at Monticello on many occasions. Martha married Col. Thomas Mann Randolph, who became governor of Virginia. She and Randolph had six daughters and five sons.

Jefferson loved the role of paterfamilias. He liked to walk across his grounds and gardens with his grandchildren in tow. He often watched them play on the spacious lawn behind the house and presided over their footraces. He would order them to start and declare the winner in close contests. In one account of such games written by a visitor, as soon as Jefferson appeared on the terrace one afternoon, the children of his daughters and their friends "ran to him and immediately proposed a race; we seated ourselves on the steps of the Portico, and he after placing the children according to their size one before the other gave the word for starting and away they flew; the course round this back lawn was a qr. of a mile, the little girls were much tired by the time they returned to the spot from which they started and came panting and out of breath to throw themselves into their grandfather's arms, which were opened to receive them; he pressed them to his bosom and rewarded them with a kiss; he was sitting on the grass and they sat down by him until they were rested. . . ." When his visitor marveled at how much amusement the president took from the children, Jefferson replied, "Yes, it is only with them that a grave man can play the fool."

In another game, the children would divide themselves into two groups and place their coats, hats, and other valuables in piles. Then each party would try to "steal" the goods of the others. If caught, they were held prisoner. Jefferson would watch intently and laugh at their antics.

He once wrote a letter to his daughter, Martha, about her son Jeffy, who was staying temporarily at Monticello with his grandfather. The boy refused to wear shoes, even in winter, until his grandfather devised a plan to have him wear a pair of moccasins that could be laced on firmly. Still, Jefferson reported, the boy kept removing his footwear and using the shoes as a carryall. This frustrated the Founding Father to no end because he feared the boy would catch cold and learn bad habits.

As for Maria, his other surviving daughter, he badgered her with self-improvement advice all her life. When she was 11, for example, he told her not to go outside without a bonnet or she would freckle and "it will make you very ugly and then we should not love you so much." This tough love continued even after she married John Wayles Eppes and had two children of her own. She died in 1804.

He gave his grandchildren frequent advice, mostly urging them to find some sort of useful work to keep busy. On Saturdays, when they were not in school, he had them cut coal wood for the nailery and he would pay them 50 cents for a cord. He said they would be much happier if they were as productive as possible with their lives.

Once, Meriwether Lewis Randolph, one of his grandsons, objected when Jefferson praised some local boys for cutting down bushes in a field and earning $20. The boy said that if he worked like the others, his hands would get so sore that he couldn't hold his books, and in any case he didn't need to work so hard because he came from a rich family and would get a good education so he could associate with rich and intelligent people.

Jefferson was not pleased. "Those that expect to get through the world without industry, because they are rich, will be greatly mistaken," he said. "The people that *do* work will soon get possession of all their property." It was a good summary of his philosophy of life.

AFTER HE LEFT office in 1809 and returned full-time to Monticello, Jefferson found that the atmosphere had changed—much to his chagrin. As an ex-

president, he found the same thing that George Washington had found in his retirement, that there was no respite from fame. Americans considered their former
presidents and Founding Fathers to be public property, and they thought nothing
of dropping by and expecting to shake Jefferson's hand, chat, and perhaps stay for
a meal. He tried to accommodate all this, but it was a trial.

Monticello was so frequently packed with visitors that, Bacon said, "they almost ate him out of house and home." Jefferson, whose debts were mounting fast,
could scarcely bear the cost of supporting these multitudes, yet he felt an obliga-
tion as the former president of the new Republic to welcome them.

They came at all times of year, but especially in the spring and summer,
when whole families would sometimes show up unannounced to visit the former
commander in chief. Sometimes all the beds at Monticello were full because of
the guests, and Mrs. Martha Randolph, Jefferson's daughter who lived with him
after he returned from Washington, often borrowed spare beds from neighbors to
handle the overflow. "There was no tavern in all that country that had so much
company," Bacon wrote.

This was one reason why Jefferson built a house on his 5,000-acre estate 75
miles from Monticello, at Poplar Forest in Bedford County, Virginia. The former
tobacco plantation gave Jefferson a place in his retirement where he could escape
from Monticello in the summer "to get rid of entertaining so much company,"
Bacon said. Adds author Peter Hannaford: "At Poplar Forest, Jefferson could contemplate the state of the nation, work on his inventions, and pursue his interest in
architecture." In the end, he needed a sanctuary from his sanctuary.

When he died, his financial condition was terrible. For years, he had incurred
rising debts, since his estimates of the revenue he would earn from farming were
always too optimistic. He felt a need to keep up appearances as a leader of Virginia's planters and as a former president.

In March 1819, he agreed to co-sign a note for a close friend, Wilson Cary
Nicholas. When Nicholas could not pay, Jefferson was left with a debt that included $1,200 annually in interest, and this obligation continued for years. In
1825, there was a sharp decline in agricultural prices, the value of land pledged as
security for debts, and the value of paper money. Yet the demands of Jefferson's
creditors continued or increased.

He was forced to sell some of his lands, and when he died on July 4, 1826, at
age 83, he was nearly bankrupt, leaving behind a debt of $107,000. This was a

huge sum in 1826, and his heirs were forced to sell the houses, nearly 200 slaves, and some of his most prized possessions.

In addition to providing solace for Jefferson, Monticello also had a lasting impact on the country in another way. The British burned the President's House and part of Washington during the war of 1812, and in the process destroyed the library that had belonged to Congress. Jefferson sold Congress his own library, and sent 16 wagon loads of books to Washington. This became the basis for the vast collection known today as the Library of Congress.

JEFFERSON AT MONTICELLO showed his devotion to farming, as Washington had done at Mount Vernon. Each man was proud to be a Virginia planter who loved the land and built his livelihood on agriculture. Jefferson was a micromanager, as was Washington, but he didn't have his predecessor's ability as a businessman and allowed himself to go deeply into debt. Jefferson was also far more a man of ideas, with a penchant for innovation and experimentation that he freely indulged at his mountaintop estate.

Throughout his career, Jefferson wrote periodically and in strong terms condemning slavery, but it was an intellectual exercise. He never freed his slaves during his lifetime, and even after his passing he made clear in his will that most of his slaves must be kept in bondage.

—⊗⊗⊗—

CHAPTER FIVE

ABRAHAM LINCOLN AND THE SOLDIERS' HOME, WASHINGTON, D.C.

IF ANY PRESIDENT needed a retreat, it was Abraham Lincoln. Faced with the awesome problems of winning the Civil War and preserving the Union, he dealt with perhaps more stress than any other commander in chief, and was subject to severe bouts of melancholy and depression. Unknown to most Americans, Lincoln also endured intense grief over the death of a beloved son, and frustration and sadness over the mental instability of his wife. At the Soldiers' Home not far from the Executive Mansion, he found sanctuary from his tribulations.

Historians consider him probably America's greatest president because of the many challenges he overcame and because of the values that he espoused in such an eloquent and persuasive way. "Lincoln believed that the implications of this American Civil War reached beyond the United States to affect the 'family of man' and the future of self-government everywhere," writes historian Jean H. Baker. "He therefore provided stirring global claims to those caught in an internal, parochial war that seemingly would never end. The United States, as he put it in his message to Congress in December 1862 during the darkest days of the war, was the 'last, best hope of earth.'" His belief in America as a beacon of liberty and democracy has resonated through the years.

Little known to most Americans at the time or in the intervening years, Lincoln found solace at the Soldiers' Home, a three-story stucco house used as a residence for injured soldiers. It was located about three miles from the Executive

Mansion, now called the White House, in the northern section of Washington, a 30-minute ride by horse or carriage. For Lincoln, it became his favorite place for relaxation and contemplation. In fact, he finished a draft of the Emancipation Proclamation there. Local lore has it that he sat under a tree only a few yards from the house, polishing his words.

The hilltop cottage benefited from cooling breezes in summer, and Lincoln liked to sit on the spacious back porch, decorated with brown gingerbread, and look out at the commanding view to the south of the Capitol and the rising Washington Monument, then one-third completed. On a clear day he could see 20 miles, all the way to Alexandria, Virginia.

In 1842, banker George W. Riggs, Jr., had built a house on the site, and the Riggs family lived there until 1851. That's when the federal government bought the building and 320 leafy acres surrounding it as a retirement home for 150 enlisted men in the military (a function it still serves today) and a small complement of officers and administrators. Under federal control, a variety of other cottages and a main hall were built.

It was first used as a retreat and part-time residence by President James Buchanan, who said he slept better there than at the Executive Mansion, and it was Buchanan who recommended it to Lincoln, his successor. Lincoln agreed wholeheartedly, but there were so many military setbacks in the early part of the war, including the disastrous battle of Bull Run, that the new president didn't feel comfortable going to the retreat for a year. It wasn't until June 1862 that Lincoln moved his wife, Mary, and youngest son, Tad, to the Soldiers' Home.

The couple needed a break. Lincoln was exhausted and distressed about how badly the war was going, and he shared Mary's grief at the death of their beloved 12-year-old son, Willie, of either pneumonia or typhoid fever in February 1862. This loss, coupled with the sorrows of the war, made Lincoln more spiritual in the sense that it deepened his connection to God.

The setbacks in the war and in his personal life had the additional effect of intensifying Lincoln's existing depression or melancholy, which a friend once called "a cave of gloom." Historians argue that his depressions probably can be traced to a series of deaths during his childhood, including his newborn brother in about 1811, when Lincoln was about three years old; his mother in 1818 when he was nine; and his sister in 1828 when he was eighteen. He endured the death of Ann Rutledge, whom he was courting and with whom he was deeply in love, in 1835, when he was 26.

When he was president, he was grief-stricken by the seemingly endless losses suffered by Union troops under his command. In 1862, after Willie died, Lincoln, then 53, told a friend, "This is the hardest trial of my life. Why is it? Oh, why is it?" He was often reduced to convulsive weeping.

His depression would come and go, depending on how much bad news he was receiving at any given time. On some occasions, friends reported, he would laugh frequently, tell the humorous stories that endeared him to voters and associates, and enjoy life. At other times, he would sit alone and stare into space, and he had difficulty sleeping. He threw himself into his work. He became interested in sad poems and songs. One of his favorites was Oliver Wendell Holmes's "The Last Leaf," which contains these lines about a man mourning the death of a loved one:

> The mossy marbles rest
> On lips that he has pressed
> In their bloom;
> And the names he loved to hear
> Have been carved for many a year
> On the tomb.

As his presidency progressed and the pressures intensified, he lost weight, developed permanent dark circles under his eyes, and always seemed haggard and wraithlike. He was in his mid-50s during his presidential years, but at the end looked 20 years older.

Mary was in even worse condition. After losing Willie, she was almost incapacitated. For weeks she confined herself to bed and in her grief she sought the services of mediums to contact her dead son. "Spiritualism" led her to participate in séances and medium-led "circles." She held at least one circle at the Soldiers' Home with a medium named Charles J. Colchester. And she apparently held eight séances at the White House during the war.

Making matters worse was that the Executive Mansion in Washington was a public thoroughfare in addition to a residence. "Except for the family dining rooms, all the rooms on the first floor were open to all visitors, and anybody who wanted to could stroll in at any hour of the day and often late at night," writes historian David Herbert Donald. "A single elderly doorkeeper was supposed to prevent depredations, but often no one was on duty. On the second floor, nearly half of the rooms were also public; they were devoted to the business of the chief executive. . . . From early morning until dusk, these rooms were thronged with senators, congressmen, applicants for government jobs, candidates for military appointments, foreign dignitaries, and plain citizens who had favors to ask or who just wanted to shake the president's hand. . . . Lincoln found himself a prisoner in his own office; every time he stepped out into the corridor to go to the family quarters on the west end of the building, he was besieged with complaints and petitions." Lincoln had a partition built that allowed him to walk unobserved from his office to the family's private rooms, but it wasn't enough to allow privacy and foster a sense of calm.

The Soldiers' Home was a godsend. Lincoln, using the prerogative of the commander in chief, moved into the main house—the former Riggs residence—forcing the home's administrator to reside elsewhere on the grounds. President Buchanan, a bachelor who lived alone, had been content with one of the smaller cottages. The main level of what became known as "Lincoln cottage" had a library to the left of the front doorway with a big fireplace featuring a seven-foot marble mantel and a double-door cabinet on each side. There was a dining room with fireplace, and upstairs were separate bedrooms for the president and the First Lady—each with views of the grounds—and various servants' rooms. It wasn't posh or spacious, but it was comfortable and isolated from the city's bustle—an oasis of oak, chestnut, beech, maple, cedar, and cypress trees and 500 acres of rolling greensward.

IN ALL, LINCOLN spent one quarter of his presidency—13 out of his 49 months in office—in residence at the cottage, usually from early summer to late fall. In 1862, for example, he spent four months there, staying until October. In effect, he was a commuter who made the unpainted stucco home his seasonal retreat for three to five months every year, from June to November 1862, 1863, and 1864. It gave him a respite from the heat and humidity of central Washington, and a sanctuary from the awful pressures of his job.

Still, as with all presidents under crisis conditions, he could never fully divorce himself from his work. "My thoughts, my solicitude for this great country follow me where ever I go," he once told guests at the Soldiers' Home.

Strangely enough, safety was not an initial concern. "The president and his family had no formal protection of any kind," writes author Matthew Pinsker. "The question of presidential security had never really existed before the Civil War. A pistol-wielding maniac had once assaulted Andrew Jackson, but the disturbing incident was soon forgotten. Franklin Pierce briefly retained a bodyguard during the 1850s; otherwise nineteenth-century presidents typically traveled without protection."

After Lincoln moved to the Soldiers' Home in June 1862, he rode on horseback to and from the White House with only an aide or two, every day. And at first, Lincoln strongly resisted any change. "I cannot be shut up in an iron cage and guarded," he told a friend. But as the war intensified and emotions rose, Lincoln realized that there was good reason for the security. After one commute to the White House, Lincoln noticed that a bullet had pierced his hat. No one was sure whether it was a potential murderer or a stray round.

On September 2, 1862, after severe Union setbacks on the battlefield, Lincoln appointed General George McClellan as commander of the forces around Washington (overcoming his doubts about the stubborn general, whom he had relieved of an important command earlier—and would fire for the final time that November, after he became convinced that McClellan wasn't bold or aggressive enough). McClellan overcame his animosity toward Lincoln and ordered a military guard to protect the president and his family as a garrison at the Soldiers' Home. After some initial confusion, it was decided that about 100 men from Company K, 150th Pennsylvania regiment, would officially be assigned for this duty, which they retained for the rest of the war. Many of these men would befriend the president and his family, and Lincoln developed a particularly close relationship with Captain David V. Derickson of Company K, a 44-year-old businessman from Meadville, Pennsylvania, and a founder of the Republican party in Crawford County.

DESPITE THE MILITARY guards all around him, there were still security lapses at the Soldiers' Home. In September 1862, amid concern about the progress of a Confederate invasion of the North that would culminate in the Battle of Antietam September 17, the soldiers seized a man they believed was a spy who had made it all the way to the president's cottage as an official messenger. In mid-September, two horsemen approached the main gate and asked the sentry when Lincoln usually left the grounds. Then they disappeared. This made officials in Lincoln's entourage and family suspicious. Soon thereafter, at the insistence of the First Lady, a full cavalry escort rode with the president as he commuted to and from the Soldiers' Home.

At first, the job fell to 80 rather ordinary-looking horsemen from Company A of the 11th New York Cavalry regiment. In December 1863, influenced by lobbying from Ohio Gov. David Tod, Lincoln replaced the New Yorkers with the Union Light Guard from Ohio, a dashing unit that took over the responsibility for escorting the president whenever he left the grounds.

The arrival of these mounted troops agitated the president because he felt that, with the infantry already there, he was suffocating in security—a common feeling of presidents over the years—and now the cavalry was obliged to accompany him wherever he went. Sometimes Lincoln would enter his carriage and ride out of the Soldiers' Home earlier than scheduled, just so he could elude his minders. The cavalry detachment would show up, realize the president had left, and thunder through the streets of Washington to catch up with him.

Lincoln occasionally slipped out of the Soldiers' Home and left his minders behind completely, especially early in his tenure. On August 22, 1862, for example, he secretly left the compound with two friends and rode in a carriage after supper to the nearby U.S. Naval Observatory to look through its telescope at the moon and a star called Arcturus.

On September 13, 1862, Lincoln, apparently distracted, lost control of the horse he was riding at the Soldiers' Home and sprained his wrist. One of the problems that was on his mind was his consideration of the Emancipation Proclamation to free slaves in the Confederate states. He apparently was drafting the document both at the Soldiers' Home and the White House.

LINCOLN'S PATTERN IN his daily commute was to leave his retreat about 7:30 A.M. so he would arrive at the White House by 8, riding either on horseback or in a carriage, and then return to spend his evenings and overnight there. At the end of a day spent examining battle reports and counting up the casualties, coping with the incompetence of his generals, dealing with military setbacks, and overseeing what he considered the sacred trust of maintaining the Union, Lincoln was often near exhaustion when he left the White House at four or five o'clock. He would sit in his carriage, or occasionally ride on horseback, with a contingent of from a dozen to 30 federal troops in an early form of a presidential "motorcade." They would proceed at a brisk clip across Pennsylvania Avenue northward for the three-mile ride along the Seventh Street Turnpike to Rock Creek Road and onward to the Soldiers' Home.

Walt Whitman, the poet, resided on L Street along the route and he would frequently watch the president go by in the evening. "I see the President almost every day, as I happen to live where he passes to or from his lodgings out of town," Whitman wrote in his journal on August 12, 1863. ". . . I saw him this morning about 8 ½ coming in to business." Whitman said that when he got close enough to get a good look at Lincoln—they sometimes exchanged cordial bows—he noticed "deep-cut lines" in Lincoln's "dark brown face" and a "deep latent sadness" in the president's eyes.

The poet described Lincoln that morning as riding a "good-sized, easy-going gray horse," and dressed in black clothes and black hat, "somewhat rusty and dusty." He was escorted by 25 or 30 cavalry troops, all with sabers drawn and held over their shoulders as the entourage moved at a slow trot. On such occasions, Lincoln nearly always rode with a lieutenant at his left and a line of cavalry following two by two behind him in their yellow-striped blue jackets. Lincoln sometimes would ride in an open barouche, but the entourage had become so familiar by then that it was largely ignored by the neighbors.

Lincoln's entourage would rumble up the dirt driveway on the north side of the cottage, and he would clean his footwear on a metal boot scraper on a slab to the left of the front entrance. He would walk through a set of double doors at the main entrance and up a small enclosed flight of stairs to the main level of the house.

LINCOLN ENJOYED SIMPLE pleasures. He liked carriage rides with his wife, Mary, around the grounds of the Soldiers' Home. He conducted regular horseplay with Tad and the boy's friends, allowing them to pin him to the floor, sit on his stomach, or roll around with him on the lawn in wrestling matches.

He studied the Bible alone early each morning and sometimes late at night. "Take all of this book upon reason that you can, and the balance on faith, and you will live and die a happier and better man," Lincoln once told a friend.

He liked to read aloud to his friends and family in the parlor during the evenings, often from works of Shakespeare such as *Richard II* and *Richard III,* stories about a divided England. He also enjoyed the work of poet Alexander Pope and of humorists such as Artemus Ward and Petroleum V. Nasby. Occasionally, he regaled guests with down-home, humorous stories from his youth in Illinois.

And he seemed to seek out distractions that would temporarily divert him from running the war. He once helped to rescue several peacocks raised at the Soldiers' Home by the sons of Secretary of War Edwin Stanton. The birds had gotten tangled up in some trees, and the president, knowing how much the boys loved the peacocks, took a personal interest in making sure they weren't hurt.

The Lincolns found life at the Soldiers' Home more peaceful than what they experienced at the White House, but far from perfect. Visitors who discovered the location of his retreat showed up at all hours to ask for special favors or just to meet the president. Military bodyguards were never far from the cottage, and military transport wagons regularly and noisily hauled supplies along the nearby road. Sometimes the Lincolns could hear gunfire if the rebels were close to the city, as they were at some stages of the war.

The neighborhood had its problems, too. The roads were badly marked, and would-be visitors sometimes got lost at night. There were several taverns and a racetrack nearby, along with more than one house of prostitution. "Rode home in the dark amid a party of drunken gamblers & harlots," wrote John Hay, one of the president's advisers, in his diary after spending an evening with Lincoln at the Soldiers' Home. His matter-of-fact recounting suggested that such occurrences were routine.

En route to and from the retreat, Lincoln would stop at camps for "contrabands," or former slaves. "Aunt Mary" Dines, an escaped slave from Maryland, was the Lincoln family's cook at the summer retreat, and she lived at such a camp. The president would sometimes listen to Negro spirituals, such as "Nobody Knows What Trouble I See, but Jesus" and "Every Time I Feel the Spirit." It's possible that these plaintive songs intensified his sympathy for African Americans, and witnesses said he was often moved to tears.

Lincon's views on slavery and emancipation were central to his presidency and the course of American history. He never believed in equality or integration, but felt that slavery was an abominable institution for which God would punish America. This came to pass, he concluded, through the death and bloodshed of the Civil War. Yet even on this score, he was a supreme pragmatist. After his election in 1860, he didn't try to end slavery in states where it existed but instead attempted to prevent its spread to other states and territories while, above all, preserving the Union.

The secession of Southern states and the onset of the war forced his hand. Hoping to retain the support of the four key slaveholding Union states—Maryland, Missouri, Kentucky, and Delaware—he devised a policy for emancipating the slaves based on carefully calibrated stipulations: Emancipation must be gradual; slave owners must be compensated; their decision to free slaves must be voluntary. Doubtful that blacks and whites could ever live peacefully side by side in the South, he suggested that emancipated slaves might be shipped out of the United States or allowed to create a colony for themselves somewhere, preferably in Central America.

By 1862, with the war going badly and thousands upon thousands of Union casualties piling up, Lincoln's position on slavery hardened. Pushed by abolitionists in the North and in the Republican-controlled Congress, he changed course and decided that the emancipation of rebel-owned slaves was necessary to win the war and should be uncompensated and immediate. From then on, he used slavery as a moral issue to condemn the South, rally the North, and argue against European intervention on the side of the rebels. As part of his reconsideration, he concluded that freed slaves should be allowed to remain in the United States and should serve in the Union's armed forces along with freed blacks from the North.

THROUGH ALL HIS tribulations, Lincoln revealed himself at the Soldiers' Home as a human being with the same kind of frailties, failings, and quirks as anyone else. He padded around the house in heelless slippers, a loose-fitting shirt, and pants, and he carried a big palm-leaf fan when it was hot. More than one guest described him as disheveled and exhausted. Writes historian Pinsker: "There were probably hundreds who passed through the parlor during the first family's three seasons in residence, with a core group of about a dozen regulars and an unknown number of overnight guests. . . . They were Union generals and lower-ranking officers, cabinet members and mid-level political appointees, journalists and old Illinois friends, congressmen and their wives, Washington socialites, and foreign dignitaries. Most were friends but some were strangers. It was an eclectic assortment of human diversions for a family in sore need of distraction."

Lincoln also liked to play checkers with aides, friends, or bodyguards on the back porch, and spent time cavorting under the copper beech trees in front of the house with his son.

Just as important, the human scenes around him must have been heart-wrenching for the commander in chief. There was a national military cemetery on the grounds that was rapidly filling up with the remains of Union soldiers; eventually, 5,000 were buried there. Disabled veterans, some on crutches or with empty sleeves from lost limbs, made their way along the paths. Many of them had legitimate complaints about their treatment at the home, which was run in an authoritarian way and with few amenities. Many of them also had severe drinking problems, and there were frequent runaways.

Still, Lincoln gradually got to know the soldiers around him, both his body-guards and, to a lesser extent, the disabled veterans. He valued their company, especially during the many weeks when his own family was away and he got lonely. The soldiers gave him a sense of camaraderie, as did the presence of advisers and friends, including Secretary of War Edwin Stanton, who had a cottage at the Soldiers' Home.

The *New York Tribune* reported on July 8, 1862, that the president on the Fourth of July, "while on his way to his Summer Residence at Soldiers Home, meeting a train of ambulances conveying wounded men from the late battles to the hospitals just beyond the city limits, rode beside them for a considerable distance, conversing freely with the men, and seeming anxious to secure all the information possible with regard to the real condition of affairs on the Peninsula and the feeling among the troops from those who had borne the brunt of the fight."

Lincoln would often stroll along the edge of a grove that contained the soldiers' encampment and occasionally poked his head inside a tent or two to share a few words with the troops. "We always felt that the President took a personal interest in us," said Smith Stimmel of the Union Light Guard of Ohio. "He never spoke absent-mindedly, but talked to the men as if he were thinking of them." Added Robert McBride, another member of the company: "Occasionally, Mr. Lincoln would go among the men and chat familiarly with them. Mr. Lincoln's manner on such occasions was that of one having a genuine, kindly interest in the members of the company and a wish to learn how matters looked from their point of view. There was nothing patronizing about it, nor anything savoring of condescension or superciliousness."

Lincoln's 9-year-old son, Tad, found the soldiers delightful companions and mingled with them so often that the infantry guards gave him the title "third lieutenant." He often appeared at drill time on his pony, and would stand in line on many occasions when the dinner bell rang and draw his military rations as if he were really a member of the army. His parents didn't mind; they thought the soldiers were good companions for their son.

Sometimes the president would join the troops stationed nearby for coffee and a plate of beans. He enjoyed talking to the men and watching the ways they entertained themselves. One game was called the Trained Elephant, in which two men hunched over and were covered with a blanket. A plank wrapped in another blanket served as a trunk. The men then did a series of tricks, including standing on one leg.

In the summer of 1864, as he was returning with his guards from the White House, Lincoln passed a few grazing cows and ordered the entourage to divert off the Seventh Street Road so he could do a personal inspection. It turned out that he wanted to prove to the lieutenant traveling with him that the cow was, in Lincoln's words, "a lopsided animal," with one side higher than the other.

Lincoln's friendship with David Derickson, an officer from Meadville, Pennsylvania, deepened over the months, and Derickson even spent overnights at the cottage with Lincoln. Sometimes the young officer shared a bed with the president, wearing one of Lincoln's nightshirts, when Mrs. Lincoln was away. This has encouraged modern-day speculation by author C. A. Tripp and others that Lincoln was gay.

Yet the evidence to prove this assertion seems sketchy at best. Lincoln's relationship with Derickson was considered odd at the time, but not because the two slept in the same bed. Men routinely did that in those days, and it probably was platonic, according to Pinsker and other historians. What was considered odd was the fact that the commander in chief was violating protocol by socializing with a subordinate.

MARY LINCOLN HAD mixed feelings about the Soldiers' Home. She liked the country setting better than the White House, and in the summer of 1863, she moved her little family there along with 19 wagons filled with supplies and clothing. But she preferred to spend many weeks each year traveling to New York, New England, and other places where she could indulge her passion for buying clothes and furniture.

On July 2, 1863 (the second day of the three-day battle of Gettysburg, north of Washington in Pennsylvania), she jumped from a runaway carriage near the Soldiers' Home after her coachman was thrown to the ground and the horses bolted in fright. Mrs. Lincoln suffered various bruises and bumps and a serious wound on the back of her head that required stitches. Lincoln was preoccupied with urging his generals to pursue the Confederate army of Robert E. Lee after his defeat at Gettysburg, and didn't pay much attention to his wife's injuries, assuming they were not serious. But her wounds got infected and she nearly died. She associated the Soldiers' Home with this traumatic incident.

On the lighter side, Mrs. Lincoln also followed a pattern of many First Ladies and decided to redecorate her husband's retreat. In the spring of 1864, she hired John Alexander, a local upholsterer who had done some renovations at the White House, to refurbish the furnishings, upgrade the wallpaper, wash the floors and windows, repaint the interior, replace some of the curtains and carpeting, change the coverings on chairs and sofas, and move various items from room to room at her instruction. The project was completed by July, when the Lincolns began their third summer at the Soldiers' Home.

IN JULY 1864, rebel troops under Gen. Jubal Early raided the area around Frederick, Maryland, just north of Washington, and posed a threat to the city and to Lincoln. The capital was well protected with forts and troops but was far from impregnable. In fact, Early's forces defeated Union troops at the Battle of Monocacy on July 9, but the Federals managed to hold off the rebels long enough for reinforcements to back them up in defending the city.

Still, Early's men, benefiting from excellent information provided by spies, made it to a weak link in the Union lines. It was Fort Stevens on the Seventh Street turnpike, not far from Lincoln's retreat. On July 10, as Early's intentions and the size of his force remained unknown, Secretary of War Stanton rushed to the home about 11 P.M. and demanded that the president and his family return to the White House. They did so, just in case. The Confederates never got close enough to pose a real threat to the president, but the incident shows how vulnerable Lincoln was at the Soldiers' Home. If the rebels had mounted a serious effort to storm it, he could have been captured or killed.

There is also some evidence that Col. Bradley T. Johnson, a Confederate cavalry officer, had been told to develop a plan to capture Lincoln at the Soldiers'

Home in a lightning raid. But Johnson said he gave up his plan in June 1864 when he was ordered to support Early's forces in the Shenandoah Valley.

On July 12, as skirmishing continued nearby, Lincoln and his wife went to Fort Stevens, a few miles from the Soldiers' Home, and toured the fortifications. Standing on a parapet, he came under fire from unseen rebels in the distance, and a military surgeon was shot at his side. Union general Horatio Wright, who was present when the incident took place, later wrote, "When the surgeon was shot and after I had cleared the parapet of everyone else, [Lincoln] still maintained his ground till I told him I should have to remove him forcibly." The president then stepped down and sat behind the parapet, in a much safer position.

CONCERN ABOUT LINCOLN'S safety increased throughout 1864. One night at about 11 P.M. in August, a guard at one of the Soldiers' Home gates heard a rifle shot and saw a "bareheaded" president riding on horseback toward his cottage. When the guard asked the president what had happened, Lincoln replied that someone had accidentally fired a gun, which frightened the president's horse and resulted in his hat falling to the ground. The soldier later conducted a search and found the signature silk plug hat with a bullet hole through the crown. When he returned it, the president said the incident was just an accident and ordered him to make no further mention of it.

But military officials quickly increased his security. Lincoln was no longer given any latitude in deciding when he needed a military escort. (He sometimes rode between the Soldiers' Home and the War Department late at night, alone or with an aide or two. Often he would walk to government offices from the White House without any bodyguards.) In the fall of 1864, such laxity stopped. One bodyguard slept each night at the White House and at the Soldiers' Home, and by November, the War Department had assigned a former city police detective to accompany the president everywhere he went as his personal bodyguard. All this was particularly important because Lincoln often awakened in the middle of the night and took walks around the Soldiers' Home property.

Meanwhile, threatening letters continued to arrive at the Soldiers' Home. And historians now realize that there were several Confederate plots under way at the end of Lincoln's presidency to capture or kill him during his daily commute, similar to Bradley T. Johnson's plot that was called off during Jubal Early's raids on the Washington area.

Secessionist and actor John Wilkes Booth apparently was among those who considered abducting Lincoln, but he abandoned the idea in favor of a plan to shoot the president at a public event.

On April 14, 1865, Booth entered Lincoln's box at Ford's Theater in Washington and killed him.

LINCOLN FACED THE biggest challenges of any president. Making matters worse, the tragic events in his personal life and his susceptibility to depression intensified his need for a retreat. He was also the first president for whom security was a profoundly serious concern, and like so many of his successors, he felt suffocated by all the precautions taken to protect him at both the Executive Mansion and at the Soldiers' Home. Just as important, his time at his retreat gave him more than a respite from his duties. He enjoyed time with his wife and especially his son, and he appreciated the camaraderie of the soldiers who lived there, which probably deepened his empathy for the men whom he sent into harm's way.

CHAPTER SIX

THEODORE ROOSEVELT AND SAGAMORE HILL, NEW YORK

A S SOON AS visitors stepped onto the porch of Theodore Roosevelt's house at Sagamore Hill, New York, they were struck by TR's commitment to what he called "the strenuous life." It was a perfect reflection of his personality and approach to leadership.

The president, who watched their carriages or horses proceed up his long gravel driveway, would bound out to greet them, a wide grin on his face, and he would pronounce himself "dee-lighted" to see his guests. He would escort them briefly into the foyer, and then turn right into the library, where one got a good sense of the values and lifestyle of the 26th president. On the floor were the skins of two lions, each with head intact, mouths gaping, and fangs bared—mementoes of TR's many hunting trips. Guests would sometimes forget themselves and trample the heads or trip over them. A snarling stuffed badger, seemingly ready to pounce, stood near one of the massive bookcases that lined the walls. The shelves were filled with books, some of which were written by TR himself. A desk was piled with papers or even more books, and a spare pair of his trademark pince-nez.

The next stop would often be the North Room, at the other end of the house—designed by the president as his main reception area for dignitaries and people he particularly wanted to impress. Mounted heads of animals—including two buffalo at each side of a massive fireplace—stared from the walls in testament to the master of the house's hunting prowess. Gifts and trophies dominated every corner. There were samurai swords from the emperor of Japan, two huge elephant tusks presented by the emperor of Abyssinia, and TR's Rough Rider hat and saber, reminders of his military exploits in the Spanish American War. The hat and saber hung prominently from the antlers of an elk's head. The room itself was as massive as its owner's ego and as overwhelming as his personality—30 feet by 40 feet, with a high ceiling, black walnut columns, and walls of reddish brown American and Philippine wood. It reflected the essence of the man who dominated his political era as a domestic reformer and bold internationalist and who committed himself to a life of vigor and activism, both in private and in public.

Alice Roosevelt Longworth, TR's eldest child, clearly understood the president's craving for attention. "My father always wanted to be the corpse at every funeral, the bride at every wedding, and the baby at every christening," she once said. And that craving permeated everything TR did.

A CENTURY AGO, the extended escapes from the capital made by the early presidents were no longer considered acceptable. Vacations were one thing; as we have seen, many presidents left to get some rest and relaxation. But the trips had to be limited in duration or else the president appeared to be fleeing his responsibilities.

TR solved the problem by moving the functions of the executive branch out of the capital for several months every summer from 1902 through 1908. He generally left Washington in June and stayed at Sagamore Hill, on New York's Long Island, 35 miles from Manhattan, until the end of August, making the trip either by yacht or by train. A special rail spur was built near Sagamore Hill at Oyster Bay for his use.

Other presidents had taken vacations and brought along only a secretary and stenographer, but not TR. He was accompanied by several staff assistants and clerks, and had a steady stream of Cabinet members, other advisers, and political and civic leaders at his home to conduct presidential business.

During his first presidential summer there, in 1902, Roosevelt had the executive branch rent office space at the Oyster Bay Bank Building. Starting in May 1903 and for the remainder of his presidency, through 1908, the executive staff rented rooms in a new office building owned by James Moore. Special telegraph wires and telephone lines were installed at the Oyster Bay offices, allowing direct communication with the White House and the Departments of State and War.

This made it "possible to promptly inform the Chief Executive of any new events which might threaten to disturb the peace of the world," reported the *Brooklyn Standard Union* in May 1903.

Roosevelt understood that the newspapers of his day were important in fashioning a president's image, and he took full advantage. He rewarded reporters who gave him positive coverage, and shut out those who didn't. Partly as a result, positive coverage was the norm.

"One summer was like another at Sagamore, so far as the family life was concerned, even though the rambling house was the focus of eighty million pairs of eyes," writes author Hermann Hagedorn. "You rowed, you played tennis, you wrestled, you hiked, you chopped fire-wood, you swam, you shot at a target, and it did not much matter that you were President of the United States so long as the politicians and the reporters left you reasonably alone.

"The President's feeling about Sagamore was a good deal like his children's: he wanted to be free of the schoolmaster, Duty; free of the restrictions that hedged him round in a city and a city house—even the White House, particularly the White House. He wanted to get away from reporters and cameras, wear old clothes, old shoes, old hats, kick up his heels in the pasture, get a respite from the things he had been doing; for a few weeks, be a boy again."

TR wrote in his autobiography, "At Sagamore Hill we love a great many things—birds and trees and books, and all things beautiful, and horses and rifles and children and hard work and the joy of life."

On a typical day, he would get up at 6 or 7 A.M. and take a horseback ride or a hike or hit tennis balls with his kids or his guests. At 8 sharp, he would eat a big breakfast, often fried chicken or fried liver, or eggs and bacon, grits, and peaches drowning in cream, and spend an hour or two reading newspapers and magazines, often to see what they said about him. At 8:30 A.M. every weekday, a personal assistant would arrive with a leather bag filled with mail, which Roosevelt would inspect as he conducted official business in his library. This usually lasted until noon. He also kept in contact with Washington by using a telephone, which he had installed shortly after taking office in 1901. His number was Oyster Bay 67.

He sometimes summoned several staff members who worked in the second-floor office in Oyster Bay, a couple of miles away. Messages to and from the president would be carried by a messenger on a bicycle.

He would play a set of tennis or sit on the porch and hold forth for his family or friends from a rocking chair, then break for lunch with his advisers, his family, or with guests. Again, his portions were oversized, and he particularly enjoyed fried chicken, steaks, other roast meats, and rice, which he preferred over potatoes. He wasn't much of a drinker of alcohol, favoring iced tea, lemonade, and hot coffee, although for dinner he would serve his guests wine if they wanted it. He would put ice in his glass to dilute the wine, which horrified connoisseurs, though they never told him so.

On Sundays, TR would take his big family to one of the local houses of worship, such as Christ Episcopal Church in Oyster Bay, riding there in one or more surreys with two-seated buckboards.

On weekdays, the afternoon agendas varied but were almost always crammed with activities. The president might chop wood, one of his particular passions, or bale hay, or go horseback riding, rain or shine, at breakneck speed. It might be a picnic on the beach. It might be a nature walk with his kids, or a rowing expedition. It might be wrestling matches with his boys. It might be a ride on his dispatch boat, *Sylph*, or the presidential yacht, *Mayflower*. When he was particularly restless, Edith would encourage him to get out of the house and let off steam through exercise. He loved to chop wood at all hours, and told of once having the axe slip and slice into his leg. He had the wound bandaged but was soon outside chopping again. Or it might be some more meetings with advisers, business leaders, foreign dignitaries, members of Congress, or other politicians.

But at 4 P.M. nearly every day, Roosevelt called official business to a halt. One afternoon, TR was in his library with a visiting diplomat talking about Cuba policy when his sons, a few other relatives, and some of the local boys showed up at the door in old clothes and sneakers. "Cousin Theodore," one of them said gently, "it's after four."

The president declared, "By Jove, so it is! Why didn't you call me sooner? One of you boys get my rifle."

He turned to the diplomat and explained, "I must ask you to excuse me. We'll finish this talk some other time. I promised the boys I'd go shooting with them at four o'clock, and I never keep boys waiting. It's a hard trial for a boy to wait." With that, he went off with his young charges, whom he called "my little oysters." He enjoyed playtime as much as the children did.

Dinner was a bit more formal than other meals. One was expected to get cleaned up from the exertions of the day and wear nice clothes to the dining room. The boys, clad in jackets, were expected to stand when their parents or a fe-male entered the room. TR often had guests from the government, from politics, or from other fields, and his children were expected to hold their own in the con-versation and to treat everyone politely.

There were also quiet times. Roosevelt liked to sit on a low rail on his piazza and watch the sun set over the bay. He was equally fond of spending balmy eve-nings on the piazza in a rocking chair, with his wife, Edith, next to him, listening to the songs, screeches, and rustlings of nightbirds such as owls and whip-poor-wills. At other times of day, he listened for the cooing of mourning doves, the chattering of jays, the singing of wood thrushes and meadowlarks.

When he was in the mood for conversation, which was often, he enjoyed the company not only of his advisers and other politicians, but of foreign leaders and innumerable experts in various fields such as the Bible, ornithology, military his-tory, literature, and geography. His range of interests was immense.

"He stood at the divide between the nineteenth century and the twentieth," wrote historian Michael McGerr, "between the old presidency and the modern chief executive, between the old state and the new. Full of his own contradictions, this complicated man grappled with basic contradictions that define[d] the twentieth-century United States. He was both an architect of modern govern-mental regulation and a defender of Victorian individualism. He was a conserva-tive who promoted change. A fierce hunter, he was a pioneering conservationist. A war lover, he won the Nobel Peace Prize. An advocate of women's rights, he in-sisted women should do their duty as wives and mothers." Throughout his nearly eight years in office, he captured the nation's imagination as few other presidents have ever done.

WITH THE ASSASSINATION in September 1901 of William McKinley—TR's predecessor—fresh in everyone's mind, security was a constant concern. With good reason.

On one occasion, the president was reading in his library after the family had gone to bed when he heard a commotion outside. He rushed onto the porch, illuminated by light from the study, and found a man a hundred feet away hold-ing a loaded 32-caliber revolver. It turned out to be Henry Weilbrenner, a farmer from nearby Syosset who was a labor-movement zealot and was angry at the president for not aggressively representing the working class. This was Weilbrenner's third attempt to see the president that evening, and this time the Secret Service guards realized he might want to harm Roosevelt. When one of the guards asked what he wanted, Weilbrenner shouted, "None of your damned business," and at that moment, TR appeared on the porch. The interloper, riding in a buggy, urged his horse forward but an agent jumped aboard and wrestled him to the ground. Later, the farmer admitted he wanted to kill the president.

Mrs. Roosevelt chastised her husband for making himself so vulnerable to a possible attack. But TR replied, "But what would you have had me do? The Secret Service man was fighting my fight, and he was alone. Would you have had me hide—with him, perhaps, one against two or three?"

On another occasion, aides urgently needed the president's approval for a report on the construction of a Pacific cable, but he was nowhere to be found. A frantic hunt for him was begun. Finally, a friend of TR's who was a houseguest told the Secret Service that the president was okay, but the guest wasn't at liberty to disclose where he was. This persuaded the Service to call off the search.

The next morning, the president reappeared, very pleased with himself. He had gone camping on a beach several miles to the east with sons Ted and Kermit and their cousin Philip Roosevelt. The president had fried steaks with bacon in a big pan, and he had told the boys ghost stories and hunting tales around the campfire. The four had slept on Navajo blankets under the stars. There were no bodyguards. The story got out to the newspapers, and it reinforced the impression of many Americans that TR was fun to be with, and that he didn't take himself and his official duties so seriously that he neglected his sons. It might have made a difference to concerned Americans if they had realized that TR often carried a loaded pistol with him.

In still another situation, a stranger made his way onto the back porch, somehow eluding the president's bodyguards, and a butler chased him off. No one knew what the man wanted, but Mrs. Roosevelt was so unsettled that she insisted that the detail on duty be replaced.

Everyone knew that presidential safety was never guaranteed. On September 3, 1902, at the conclusion of a speaking tour of New England, Roosevelt's carriage was hit by a trolley car near Pittsfield, Massachusetts, and destroyed. A Secret Service agent was killed and the president was thrown 30 feet onto the pavement. He was cut and bruised but not seriously hurt and insisted on delivering his final speech of the tour that evening at Bridgeport, Connecticut. It was a close call. He returned to Sagamore Hill and resumed his normal activities.

ROOSEVELT HAD BEEN visiting Oyster Bay since he was 15 years old, when his father, Theodore, established a summer residence in what was becoming a family colony for the Roosevelts, who called that home "Tranquility." Relatives summering on Long Island included Cornelius Roosevelt, Jr., Hilbourne L. Roosevelt, Alfred Roosevelt, James Alfred Roosevelt, Emlen Roosevelt, and John E. Roosevelt. Young Theodore liked to ride horses, shoot and observe birds, hunt squirrels, and row on the bay and across Long Island Sound with his friends. While he was in college, he spent summer vacations on Oyster Bay, and after he married Alice Lee, daughter of a rich banker from Boston, he spent a two-week honeymoon at Tranquility in November 1880.

In 1880, about the time of his marriage to Alice Lee, he bought land in the same area, on a hill called Cove Neck, and had a house constructed there in 1884 and added to in 1895. He had one child, Alice, by his first wife, who died in 1884. Roosevelt was grief-stricken, but he eventually married Edith Carow in 1885, and together they had five children, Theodore, Jr., Kermit, Ethel, Archibald, and Quentin. "I love all these children and have great fun with them and am touched by the way in which they feel that I am their special friend, champion, and companion," TR once wrote.

He named his home Sagamore Hill in honor of Sagamore Mohannis, chief of a small Native American tribe that had lived in the area 200 years earlier. At first, it consisted of a barn on 155 acres. TR sold some of the land to relatives, and exchanged and acquired other parcels but kept about 90 acres for himself. Half was wooded and the other half landscaped or cultivated for growing vegetables and fruits, including potatoes, grapes, currants, strawberries, raspberries, gooseberries, asparagus, apples, peaches, and pears, which were consumed by the household. Likewise, the staff raised hogs, chickens, and turkeys for consumption by the family. There were generally about six cows and eight pigs on the property, along with five horses, a flock of chickens, and various turkeys.

But it was never a profitable commercial enterprise, and it strained the family finances over the years.

The 23-room Victorian house reflected his overwhelming personality. It was a sturdy brick-and-frame structure used year-round. It had eight fireplaces and two hot-air furnaces. On the first floor were a dining room, kitchen, center hall, a library that served as TR's private office, and the big North Room, which was added in 1905. On the second floor were family bedrooms, a nursery, and guest room. The top floor contained the Gun Room, which was TR's study, along with rooms for a cook and a maid, a sewing room, and a schoolroom where the children learned their lessons.

TR loved the North Room the most. He had it built after the 1904 election, when he won a full term in office, to serve as his main reception room.

The house was far more cluttered and simple than the palatial mansions of his wealthy Gold Coast neighbors overlooking Long Island Sound, especially the Vanderbilts down the road. In fact, it was considerably smaller than the norm in an area where houses were usually at least 25 rooms. TR usually had a full-time staff of about nine servants during his presidential years, compared with the average of 25 to 50 full-time servants on a 100-acre estate at that time.

Similarly, it was much less formal and seemed more "lived-in" than the stuffy residence of his distant cousins, the Franklin Roosevelts of Hyde Park. TR left his books, his papers, and other personal items lying around the house. He didn't want anyone touching them, for fear they would be misplaced or damaged. The president and his children would leave their clothes and shoes strewn about, and the servants were forever picking up after them.

Roosevelt was never a very good businessman. He had in fact lost nearly $85,000 in bad investments in cattle and land out West in his younger days. He let Edith, his second wife, run the farm and the house for him, and she actually gave him an allowance of about $20 per day. "Every morning Edie puts twenty dollars in my pocket," he once told a friend, "and to save my life I never can tell her afterward what I did with it!" He never cared very much about money, and it showed. More than once, TR and Edith discussed whether they could afford to maintain the house and farm, but in the end he considered it too important to his happiness, and they refused to sell.

His finances, largely family trusts that he and his wife regularly drew from, were so limited, compared to his neighbors and other country gentlemen of his day, that he couldn't indulge in one of his favorite pastimes—polo. He loved to ride and would have played polo seriously but he couldn't compete with his rich friends. He lacked the money to buy the requisite six to eight polo ponies and pay for their maintenance.

In fact, TR could be downright cheap. Once he went haying for a full day because his staff was a man short, and insisted on being paid the day's wage along with his other laborers.

He could also be down to earth and friendly. During haying, he would joke and chat with the men as they wielded their pitchforks, and he drank from the same water bucket and used the same wooden dipper as everyone else.

Yet he could be imperious. Edna T. Layton, born in 1906, grew up on a farm just south of Oyster Bay and recalled, "He had a habit of riding horseback for miles around. It was not uncommon for him to ride right across my grandfather's farm. He did not go around a field, but right across it, thus ruining whatever crops his horse stepped on. This made nearby farmers very angry. They did *not* like 'Teddy.' They said he was 'too big for his boots.' If Mr. Roosevelt saw a farmer, he might ride up and ask him questions with a superior air which did *not* please the farmers. I can remember his condescending to say a few words to me a couple of times when he rode over our farm. Looking back, some of the dislike of 'Teddy' might have been because the Laytons, like most of their neighbors, were staunch Democrats."

FOR TR, SAGAMORE Hill was a rollicking place that allowed him to indulge his love for the outdoors with his passionate commitment to his children. He would shout upstairs on many mornings to call his kids to breakfast in the big, formal dining room, and they would spill out at the last moment, sliding down the big, thick banister or thundering down the stairs. TR and his wife, Edith, had a rule: If a child was late, he or she would have to wait an hour and eat breakfast with the servants in a back room. But the children loved to dine with their father, and they tried to avoid tardiness at all costs.

For the rest of the day, the laughter, howls, and shouts of his children and numerous cousins who frequented the place made it all the more delightful for him.

He was an indulgent father. At the White House, his four sons and two daughters, ranging in age from 17 to 4 in 1901—the year, as the assassinated William McKinley's vice president, he succeeded to the presidency—were a favorite topic of the newspapers and the nation at large. "Quentin and his schoolmates formed the 'White House Gang' which rollicked through the mansion," writes historian Lewis L. Gould. "The ailing Archie became healthier when

Quentin used the White House elevator to bring his 350-pound calico pony, Algonquin, to Archie's second-floor sickroom. The president's residence housed a virtual zoo—from Archie's Josiah the Badger to Alice's snake, Emily Spinach, named after the First Lady's maiden sister. The president often acted as the largest child in Mrs. Roosevelt's brood."

TR was making up for the boyhood he missed. He had been sickly and asthmatic as a child, and spent many years building up his body. As an adult, he made sure his kids had plenty of freedom and fun. "The children do have an ideal time out here [at Sagamore Hill]," he wrote a friend, "and it is an ideal place for them. The three sets of cousins are always together. I am rather disconcerted by the fact that they persist in regarding me as a playmate. This afternoon, for instance, was rainy, and all of them came to get me to play with them in the old barn. They pled so hard that I finally gave in. . . . The barn is filled with hay, and of course meets every requirement for the most active species of hide-and-seek and the like."

Roosevelt jumped into the haystacks with them, offering the specter of a stout, elderly man rolling and pawing through the hay in playful pursuit of a tiny, squealing 9-year-old. He went rowing with the children, set off fireworks with them. He would get down on all fours for a pillow fight, and liked to play a game of "tickle" with his kids that ended in uproarious laughter and a knot of young children clinging to their dad.

He led them on point-to-point obstacle walks, in which everyone was expected to hike over or through whatever was in their way—streams, marshes, slime-covered ponds, shacks, briar patches, trees, bluffs—and never take the easy route by going around them. It was a test of resolve and ingenuity. He watched their theatrical productions, presented on a tennis court, and expressed admiration for their performances and their costumes, at one point writing with bemusement of "Quentin as Cupid in the scantiest of pink muslin tights and bodice."

He was particularly eager to inspire the boys to be men with an adventurous, can-do spirit—in other words, to be like him. He took them on daring horseback rides. Secretary of State John Hay gave an indication of just how adventurous TR was when he recounted an incident that had occurred in Washington. "The President came in this morning badly banged up about the head and face," Hay wrote in his diary on October 23, 1904. "His horse fell on him yesterday." A few days later, Hay wrote that the president had "landed . . . on his head, and his neck and shoulders were severely wrenched." If anything, the rides were even more vigorous at Sagamore Hill.

Roosevelt taught the boys marksmanship, instructed them how to hold a rifle when aiming at a grizzly that was bearing down on them, and offered the fine points of baiting a hook to catch a tasty snapper for dinner. On overnight camping trips, they looked up at the stars or watched the campfire blaze as he told stories of adventure in the woods, the mountains, the desert, the jungle—often tales of his own past.

The nation loved to read about these exploits, and Roosevelt's publicity-conscious staff fed reporters a steady diet of tales about the president cavorting with his young charges. Sometimes the president did the feeding himself.

Scores of reporters staked out the town of Oyster Bay, trying to pick up tidbits of information about the president and his family in any way they could, quizzing TR's guests as they passed through. Every few days, Roosevelt would ride his horse down East Main Street, along with a squad of children, to visit his in-town office, and the reporters would beg him to talk about his activities. Occasionally he obliged.

"I want you to know all the facts," he announced one day sarcastically, "so I shall give them to you at first hand. Teddy [Jr.] is now fishing for tadpoles, but really expects to land a whale. Archie shot three elephants this morning. Ethel at this moment is setting fire to the rear of the house; Kermit and the calico pony are having a wrestling match in the garret, and Quentin, four years old, is pulling down the windmill." If a reporter's coverage displeased him, he had no qualms about complaining to the writer's editor and demanding his removal. In at least one case, he succeeded.

But there was a downside to all the indulgence. The children were spoiled, and they sometimes became a burden to those around them, such as the Secret Service agents assigned to protect them, the household staff there to supervise them, and their mother, who had the real burden of raising them. It was sometimes too much for Edith, who would take to her bed with headaches.

ROOSEVELT SEEMED LARGER than life. The brawny, bespectacled New Yorker with the thick brown mustache was not only a hero of the Spanish American War who led his unit, the Rough Riders, up San Juan Hill in Cuba, he was a forceful exponent of the strenuous life in its every aspect. Contemptuous of the "idle rich," and a man who valued courage as the supreme virtue, he was a warrior, statesman, politician, writer, hunter, fisherman, runner, boater, tennis player, wrestler, boxer, and a voracious reader of books, newspapers, and magazines. Newspaper cartoonists loved to portray his summers at Oyster Bay not as vacations but as a remarkable series of physical and mental challenges that would exhaust a lesser mortal.

When TR went hunting in Mississippi in November 1902, a legend was born when he refused to shoot a small bear that had been brought in for him to kill. A cartoon depicted the incident, and toy makers began producing "Teddy's Bears," which became an enormous hit and were the forerunners of today's generic "teddy bears."

At the end of his first summer as president, he hosted a reception for his neighbors at Sagamore Hill. As many as ten thousand people showed up by carriage, surrey, farm wagon, train, steamboat, horseback, and on foot. Dressed in a frock coat and gray trousers, TR shook hands with the long line of guests for four hours, often at the very brisk rate of one person per second, and punctuated his greetings with an enthusiastic "Dee-lighted." The word had become his trademark.

His Secret Service bodyguards were understandably nervous, considering that President McKinley had been fatally shot in a similar receiving line only a few months earlier. In fact, McKinley's assassination had prompted Congress to establish the Secret Service to guard the president full-time. To protect TR, two agents stood watch every eight hours for days before the reception, sitting under a big maple tree in the president's yard. They scrutinized everyone who approached the house and refused to admit anyone who didn't have an appointment or proper credentials—a process that still exists at the White House today. The agents also watched all trains arriving at Oyster Bay, to check for suspicious characters.

As an added precaution for his reception, TR brought in eight New York City detectives that he knew from his days as police commissioner there. And the president's 14-year-old son, Theodore Jr., stood to his father's left during the reception and kept watch on every person who approached his dad, looking for weapons and signs of hostile intent. Not only did TR relish the experience, he allowed newspaper reporters to attend, and he received very positive coverage as a fearless man of the people.

. . .

EDITH PLAYED AN important role in his life, both at the White House and at Sagamore Hill. She tried, with occasional success, to smooth his rough edges. At dinners or other social occasions, when he would risk offending his guests, she would shush him with a "Now, Theodore," and sometimes he would back off. She was an excellent hostess, but more than anything else, she gave her husband a warm and loving environment to come home to.

She would scan newspapers for him and report on what the journalists were writing. A stern moralist, if she thought someone was an adulterer or immoral in some other way, that person would be stricken from invitation lists. She held receptions for women reporters, met with Cabinet wives, and gave her husband advice on art, music, culture, and historic preservation. She would advise him on appointments and a few political issues, although she did so sporadically. She lived at a time when domesticity was considered a woman's "place," and she arranged her life that way. She suffered from headaches apparently brought on by the pressures of keeping up with their social life, and the demands of six children, especially the rebellious Alice.

The president, candid as ever, made a habit of inspecting Edith's clothing and telling her she looked too much like a cook in her simple white skirts and shirtwaist blouses. He preferred her to dress in a more elegant way, in a manner he thought befitting a First Lady. Edith once wrote her sister, Emily, that Theodore "much prefers me thin." She worked hard to keep the weight off in order to please her portly husband.

EDITH GREW CONCERNED that the pressure of office was fraying her husband's nerves, making him more short-tempered and blustery than usual. In the spring of 1905, she spent her own money and bought a cramped three-room, two-story cabin she called Pine Knot, with a rough stone chimney, south of Charlottesville, Virginia, near the farms of friends. It had no toilet, running water, or electricity, but it had a grand view of the Blue Ridge Mountains from the porch and offered a seclusion that Edith treasured.

She insisted that her husband accompany her there as much as possible, to get away from work and the hectic pace of home life. TR much preferred Sagamore Hill, but he humored his wife at Pine Knot, where he set up a routine of chopping trees, hiking through the woods, hunting, and bird-watching to fill up his days, mainly as a favor to Edith, who insisted that he get his exercise.

Edith also was worried about his increasing weight, and hoped Pine Knot would inspire him to eat more healthy, less fattening foods. In this she was disappointed. On one overnight stay, he fried a huge portion of chicken for them over a kerosene stove for dinner, not exactly the kind of light dining she envisioned.

There was another problem. With labor strife rising around the country, with her husband the target of virulent anti-capitalist criticism from socialists, labor unions, and others, and with the memory of McKinley's assassination always in mind, Edith felt increasingly vulnerable at Pine Knot. She thought security was inadequate. Her husband, typically, said she was fretting too much and, besides, he carried a pistol and was perfectly capable of defending them. Things got worse when Theodore let her know that a radical named MacQueen had "preached my murder," and he'd had the Secret Service place the man under surveillance. From then on, whenever the couple tried to relax at Pine Knot, Edith "suffered terribly" and had trouble sleeping for fear of intruders. It was not the safe haven she had dreamed of.

IN ROOSEVELT'S NEARLY two terms in office, he faced no crisis that threatened the United States. But he became a reformer on domestic issues, seeking to restrain the power of corporate trusts and to preserve large tracts of wilderness and other federal land for public use. In foreign affairs, he managed to assert America's role in the world more than his predecessors.

One of the highlights of TR's presidency was his mediation of a war between Japan and Russia in 1905, and he did it at Oyster Bay.

At first, he didn't want to get involved. He didn't trust the corrupt Russian government and thought a treaty based on Japan's victories over Moscow on the battlefield and on the sea might threaten U.S. interests in the Pacific. Further, he wasn't sure he could do much good. But after receiving a private entreaty from the Japanese, he decided to give it a try. Both sides, exhausted from the conflict, couldn't see where it would all end, and when Tsar Nicholas II welcomed his interest in secret, Roosevelt proceeded to make the arrangements for peace talks.

In June, he invited Baron Kentaro Kaneko to Sagamore Hill for an advance chat. The baron was one of several Japanese envoys whom TR particularly respected and who would join the formal talks later at Portsmouth, New Hampshire. They took a walk and a swim and had dinner with Mrs. Roosevelt and 7-year-old Quentin. After the boy was sent to his room, the First Lady stayed a while, knitting beside a coal-oil lamp, then left the two men in the library with the announcement, "I am going to bed but I don't expect you to follow until you have straightened out the affairs of the world." She came back a few minutes later with two candlesticks, a tallow dip, and two boxes of matches. "Light yourselves to bed, gentlemen," she said, "and good night."

Roosevelt and his guest talked for another 90 minutes about the upcoming conference, the terms of a possible agreement, and the Harvard they had both attended in the 1870s. At 11 P.M., Roosevelt locked the windows, blew out the lamp, and put the dog out. The baron lit the candles that Mrs. Roosevelt had given them. Then the president led his visitor upstairs by the light of a tallow dip. TR's hospitality didn't end there. He fetched a blanket and gave it to the baron with a warning that even in July the nights could get breezy and cool on Oyster Bay. Kaneko never forgot the experience and later marveled at "what manner of country it was that produced such simple, genuine men as this soldier, traveler, statesman and citizen, whose creed was democracy in its finest form."

Roosevelt also met separately with other envoys for both sides at Sagamore Hill, but the first joint session of the delegations took place on the presidential yacht, *Mayflower*, for a ceremonial luncheon on August 5. It was a cloudless, hot day with a light breeze rustling the American, Russian, and Japanese flags flying from the many yachts, launches, and other vessels in the Oyster Bay harbor and from flagpoles at many residences along the shore. The guns of U.S. military vessels boomed salutes at intervals all day—21 guns for the president, 19 for each diplomat. Bands played the national anthems of the United States, Japan, and Russia. At TR's insistence, the pageantry was glorious.

The luncheon was a success, with everyone talking freely and seemingly in harmony. Then the delegations went on separate vessels to Portsmouth, New Hampshire, for the formal talks, which took place without TR's direct participation, although he did keep close track of what was going on and made many suggestions to both sides. He felt that Portsmouth would be an excellent venue. The weather would be cooler and more comfortable than Washington's; the town had sufficient hotel and meeting-room space for the conference; communications facilities were good; and it was relatively isolated so the negotiators would have "as much freedom from interruption as possible," Roosevelt wrote.

But the talks stalled and by August 18 they seemed about to collapse. TR intervened personally from Sagamore Hill. Through private discussions with each side and with the German kaiser—and after sending a cable directly to Tsar Nicholas of Russia in order to break the deadlock, which centered on Japanese demands for an indemnity and territorial concessions—he came up with a settlement.

During the most delicate phase of the talks, on Friday, August 25, TR did something typical of his leadership style: He took a break to ride a submarine and clear his head. Despite gale-velocity winds, he slipped out of Sagamore Hill and boarded a launch for a short but bumpy ride across the harbor, where he rendezvoused with *The Plunger*, one of the Navy's six new submarines. TR had ordered the vessel to Oyster Bay from Newport to make a personal inspection and assess the submarine's capabilities. The Navy men aboard assumed he just wanted to take a look, but the president said he wanted to take a ride, and the former assistant secretary of the Navy managed to squeeze his stout body through the 18-inch opening of the conning tower, took the ladder down, and emerged belowdecks.

Roosevelt peppered the captain and crew with questions as the vessel headed for the open water of Long Island Sound. For three hours aboard, he examined the equipment, especially the torpedo tubes, and took the controls himself. He kept the submarine motionless above the bottom, watched porpoises swim past the portholes, powered the ship forward and backward, and had a wonderful time. "I've had many a splendid day's time in my life," he said as he climbed out of the submarine, "but I can't remember ever having crowded so much of it into such a few hours."

It also gave him new energy for the final push toward the Russo-Japanese peace settlement, which was agreed upon on Tuesday, August 29.

TR was deluged with congratulations from around the world, and he received glowing reviews in the American press. As *The New York Times* reported on August 31, 1905:

OYSTER BAY, Aug. 30—Theodore Roosevelt, the peacemaker, to-day received his tribute from the world for the share he had had in ending the war between Russia and Japan and preventing further bloodshed in the Far East.

While the telegraph wires leading into this little village on the shores of the Sound, which has played such an important part in the history of the last few weeks, were humming with congratulatory messages from the mighty ones of the world, and while the instrument in the little telegraph room at the executive office was spelling out its ceaseless story of praise, the President might have been seen dressed in khaki and carrying an axe, striding down the wooded slope near his summer home. . . .

A treaty was signed in early September 1905, and in 1906, Roosevelt was awarded the Nobel Peace Prize for his mediation.

IT WAS AT Sagamore Hill that Roosevelt made a make-or-break decision on how to proceed with building the Panama Canal, one of the stellar achievements of his administration, which shortened the passage between the Atlantic and the Pacific by many weeks.

The problem was how to control the mosquitoes that were decimating the work crews by spreading yellow fever.

Roosevelt had appointed Theodore R. Shonts, a railroad builder, to take over the chairmanship of the Isthmian Canal Commission, which was in charge of the work. Shonts came to Sagamore Hill to request the dismissal of Col. William C. Gorgas, the chief sanitation officer for the project. Shonts said Gorgas was emphasizing Walter Reed's theories of eliminating yellow fever by oiling mosquito-infested pools and getting rid of stagnant water, but was doing little to clean up Colon and Panama City, which Shonts and other authorities believed were the real breeding grounds for disease.

Roosevelt brought in his old friend, widely respected physician "Alec" Lambert, for consultation at Sagamore Hill. Lambert wisely sided with Gorgas and told the president, "You are facing one of the greatest decisions of your career. You must choose between Shonts and Gorgas. If you fall back upon the old methods of sanitation, you will fail, just as the French failed. If you back up Gorgas and his ideas and let him pursue his campaign against the mosquitoes, you will get your canal. It is your canal, Mr. President, and you must choose tonight whether or not you are going to build it."

Roosevelt replied, "It's queer. I never appreciated before now how essential it was. But I do now. By George, I'll back up Gorgas and we'll see it through!"

LATE IN HIS second term, Roosevelt had some concerns about his hasty announcement shortly after his election in 1904 not to seek a third term. But in the end, it was the lure of Sagamore Hill that persuaded him to keep his pledge. "Sagamore is our own home," he wrote his son Kermit. "It is Sagamore that we love; and while we enjoy to the full the White House, and appreciate immensely what a privilege it is to be here, we shall have no regrets when we leave."

He would be proven wrong about that. In his post-White House years, he traveled widely and remained vigorous but became sad and embittered that he was no longer in power. He ran as head of the Progressive Party in 1912, but lost badly. He seemed too strident and extreme, and many Republicans considered him a traitor to the GOP and his upper class. He drew enough Republican votes to throw the election to Democrat Woodrow Wilson.

But as time passed, Roosevelt came back into fashion and he was widely expected to win the Republican nomination for president in 1920.

Yet the former commander in chief's health was failing. He was in severe pain much of the time from lumbago and other ailments, and it became very difficult for him to walk. He also remained heartbroken over the death of his beloved son Quentin, in World War I.

On January 5, 1919, he and Mrs. Roosevelt were alone at Sagamore Hill. Feeling weak, he stayed in bed that day in the northwest bedroom, reading aloud to his wife or listening to her read to him, writing letters, and working on several essays about reform in the wake of World War I. At dusk, he enjoyed a raging fire against the winter chill and spoke of how happy he was to be home. That evening, Mrs. Roosevelt was playing solitaire at a table beside him when he looked up from the book he was reading and said, "I wonder if you will ever know how I love Sagamore Hill."

He died in his sleep the next morning, January 6, after suffering a coronary embolism. He was barely 60 years old.

.   .   .

SAGAMORE HILL ALLOWED TR to indulge his passionate commitment to his children and his love for the outdoors. He was an active, vigorous man in private and in public. And unlike previous presidents, he didn't just go on vacation but moved much of the executive branch to his estate with him as he redefined the presidency as a full-time job. Roosevelt made history at Sagamore Hill, mediating between Russia and Japan to end a terrible war and making the decisions necessary for the construction of the Panama Canal, one of the world's most successful public works projects.

CHAPTER SEVEN

———— ∞∞ ————

FRANKLIN D. ROOSEVELT AND HYDE PARK, NEW YORK, AND WARM SPRINGS, GEORGIA

FDR ALWAYS CONSIDERED Hyde Park, New York, his home and an essential part of his life. "Franklin Delano Roosevelt's family owned land in and around Poughkeepsie and along the banks of the Hudson River for four generations," wrote his wife, Eleanor, "but even before that his Roosevelt ancestors lived just a bit farther down the Hudson River. . . . so the river in all of its aspects and the countryside as a whole were familiar and deeply rooted in my husband's consciousness."

Hyde Park, in short, was the center of his aristocratic world and the place that best reflected his close relationship with his domineering mother and his strange partnership with his strong-willed but insecure wife.

Roosevelt was born on January 30, 1882, in a second-floor bedroom of the "old house" owned by his parents at Hyde Park, and he spent much of his early childhood in the third-floor nursery. It was an idyllic life. "From the time he was a little boy he had a pony of his own," Eleanor said. "His father gave him his first gun and taught him how to shoot and how to carry it so as not to endanger anyone. He knew every tree, every rock and stream on the place, and never forgot the people who had worked there when he was small." He had a dog, tended a garden, took an interest in planting trees, and liked to build tree houses in the pines with the neighbors' children. He became a stamp collector, a hobby he continued all his life as a way to relax. He took an interest in building model sailboats and he raced some of them on the river with his friends.

As a young man, FDR described himself as a "Hudson River gentleman, yachtsman, philatelist and naval historian." What he meant was that he had inherited a family fortune and could do whatever he wanted. He had a substantial yearly income from a $100,000 trust fund controlled by his mother, and since he didn't have to earn a living he dabbled in various interests that caught his fancy, including stamp collecting, tree growing, naval history, investing, and politics. Few expected him to achieve great things.

One skill he always had was a breezy way of ingratiating himself with people, and he used this to good advantage all his life. FDR scored his first political victory when he ran an uphill race for the state senate as a Democrat in Republican Dutchess County in 1910. He won, becoming the first Democratic state senator from that area in 32 years, and was reelected 2 years later.

He served as assistant secretary of the Navy in the Woodrow Wilson administration in Washington, winning a reputation as a genial and smart political operative, popular among Democratic insiders. A robust man who stood 6 foot 2 and weighed 170 pounds, he was nominated by the Democrats for vice president in 1920 and campaigned vigorously across the country. But the ticket headed by James M. Cox was defeated. Roosevelt returned to New York, where he worked on Wall Street and accepted partnerships in several law firms that valued his name and connections.

He kept up his political pursuits, became governor of New York in 1928, and was easily reelected in 1930. In 1932, he won the presidency as the nation repudiated the conservative policies of Republican Herbert Hoover, who seemed heartless and ineffective in combating the Depression.

As president for 12 years, he invented a series of mammoth federal programs—including unemployment insurance, Social Security, federally provided jobs and works programs, and wage and hour laws—which he called the New Deal. His goal was to lift the country out of the worst economic catastrophe in U.S. history. He greatly expanded the federal role in national life because he believed that unprecedented measures were needed. "It is the government's first duty to keep people from starving," he said. Americans loved him for trying.

After America's entry into World War II in 1941, he proved himself a brilliant leader of the allied war effort against Germany and Japan, earning himself a place in history as one of America's greatest commanders in chief. But the pressures were enormous, and the 32nd president of the United States felt the need to escape regularly to Hyde Park.

FDR'S FREQUENT TRIPS to his home—134 visits during his 12-year presidency, for a total of 562 full or partial days—were logistical challenges for the hundreds of people involved. Not only did FDR's paralysis from polio complicate his travel arrangements but the onset of war in December 1941 heightened concerns about his security.

Depending on weather conditions, the trip from Washington took about 7 to 10 hours by train, which left from a railroad siding under the Bureau of Engraving and Printing on 14th Street, about five blocks from the White House. Employees of the railroad would walk along as much of the track from Washington to Hyde Park as they could, looking for cracks in the rails, obstacles, or other problems that might endanger or delay the president. This process took about six hours prior to departure, and train traffic was generally halted or diverted along the route during this time. Washington police removed parked vehicles from the streets near the tracks, in case assassins or spies lurked there. Security guards examined the food and drink before they were loaded in the dining car, to make sure they weren't poisoned or contaminated. The car in front of the president's car, which was heavily armored, was outfitted with typewriters and mimeograph machines in case the White House staff needed to work. Once he boarded the train, often late at night, FDR would have the blinds closed in his compartment and go to sleep.

Hyde Park was his refuge. "This was the place to which Roosevelt would regularly return when he needed sustenance and peace, the place where he could always relax no matter what was going on in the world," writes historian Doris Kearns Goodwin. "The unhurried pace was just what he needed to regenerate his energies and refocus his brain. Time and again, Roosevelt confounded his staff by the ease with which, even in the darkest hours, he managed to shake off the burdens of the presidency upon his arrival at Hyde Park, and emerged stronger and more confident in a matter of days."

FDR explained the healing effect after a recuperative stay at Hyde Park over a long weekend in 1943. In a letter to Winston Churchill, he wrote, "I think I picked up sleeping sickness or Gambia fever or some kindred bug in that hell hole of yours called Bathhurst [where his plane had refueled in British Gambia en route to a conference in Casablanca a few weeks earlier]. It laid me low—four days in bed—then a lot of sulphadiathole which cured the fever and left me feeling like a wet rag. I was no good after 2 P.M. and after standing it for a week or so, I went to Hyde Park for five days: got full of health in glorious zero weather—came back . . . and have been feeling like a fighting cock ever since."

Like many everyday Americans on holiday, he reveled in a leisurely schedule, sleeping late, often until 11 A.M. or noon, reading and doing paperwork, having a martini or two in the evenings, and receiving guests at a slower pace than in Washington. In the evenings, he liked to chat with friends and family, often over a Tom Collins made with extra gin.

Even though the property included a working farm with acreage reserved for growing corn and 20 cows for milk production, FDR never showed much interest in the commercial side of things. He left that to his farm manager, Moses Smith.

He especially enjoyed the Christmas holidays. Roosevelt would gather his extended family around him in his library on Christmas Eve, and sit in an easy chair to the right of a roaring fire and near a candlelit Christmas tree towering over a mountain of gaily wrapped gifts. The highlight was his annual reading of *A Christmas Carol*. His grandchildren would listen raptly as he spoke in the frail voice of Tiny Tim and the imperious manner of Ebenezer Scrooge.

He usually ended his campaigns in Hyde Park.

On election eve 1944, November 6, as he had on the three previous presidential election eves, he addressed the nation on the radio from his home. "As we sit quietly this evening in our home at Hyde Park," he said in his familiar nasal intonation, "our thoughts, like those of millions of other Americans, are most deeply concerned with the well-being of all our American fighting men. We are thinking of our own sons—all of them far away from home—and of our neighbors' sons and the sons of our friends. I do not want to talk to you tonight of partisan politics. The political battle is finished. Our task now is to face the future as a militant and a united people. . . . Twice in twenty-five years our people have had to put on a brave, smiling front as they have suffered the anxiety and agony of war. No one wants to endure that suffering again." He concluded with a prayer sent to him by bishop Angus Dun of Washington, declaring, "Enable us to guard for the least among us the freedom we covet for ourselves; make us ill-content with the inequalities of opportunity which still prevail among us. Preserve our union against all the divisions of race and class which threaten it."

On election night, he had a news ticker installed in his "smoking room," with bookshelves lining the walls, a fireplace, and a large set of antlers above the mantel. FDR tracked the returns in the adjacent dining room as he puffed on Camel cigarettes, and he ordered a Secret Service agent to keep everyone out. He was worried about the outcome and wanted to assess the early returns alone. But he relented as his lead widened, and he ended up celebrating with family and friends. Roosevelt won comfortably, 54.7 percent to 44.8 percent.

FDR DEVELOPED SOME important social policies at Hyde Park. One summer, he took a drive around the neighborhood and came upon a family of elderly siblings, all apparently in their eighties, who were trying to make a living on a modest farm. When he returned after the winter, he learned that one brother had died, possibly freezing to death between the barn and the house on his way back from milking cows. Another brother was in a home for the indigent. A sister was in what was described to FDR as an asylum. Roosevelt was unsettled at this turn of fortune and complained to Moses Smith, who managed his farm. "Moses, this thing can't go on," he said. "I'm going to plan some way or somehow to put over an old-age security so that the poor house in time will actually be done away with." Some of FDR's associates say this experience personalized his understanding of the living conditions of needy Americans, and informed his deliberations when he proposed and won enactment for the Social Security system.

PERHAPS THE MOST momentous events at Hyde Park occurred during British prime minister Winston Churchill's periodic visits. Those meetings illustrated FDR's blending of work and leisure, and his belief in personal diplomacy. He was convinced that bringing other leaders into his private world would promote mutual understanding and enable him to charm his counterparts one by one.

On June 19, 1942, FDR met Churchill at New Hackensack airport near Hyde Park. The president, whose legs were paralyzed from polio, was operating a blue Ford equipped with hand-controlled levers that enabled him to drive, and he raced around his estate to show off the property. Churchill was a bit unsettled when Roosevelt zoomed up to "the grass verges of the precipices over the Hudson" and he later admitted hoping that the brakes would hold. Yet as they drove, they talked about world affairs, and the British P.M. said "we made more progress than we might have done in formal conference."

What Churchill wanted was to persuade FDR that the Americans needed to take the lead in an invasion of France to drive the Nazis out as soon as possible. He didn't get his wish in 1942, as he desired, but he planted the seed, and the Normandy landing occurred successfully in 1944.

Even more far-reaching, the two leaders sat in FDR's small, book-lined study filled with nautical prints, looking out across the front porch, and talked about the future of the atomic bomb. The British called the project Tube Alloys.

Both FDR and Churchill had been briefed by their own advisers, separately, in 1939 about the potential for a "superbomb," and each man had authorized an aggressive research effort. Churchill now reported that the British were making progress, and it was time to start a research plant. He suggested that the two countries combine resources because the Germans were onto the idea, too. He expressed a fear that the Nazis might develop the bomb first, with catastrophic consequences for the Allies. FDR agreed, and the Manhattan Project was born. Churchill called it a "grave and fateful decision."

In August 1943, the two leaders met again at Hyde Park during an extensive Churchill visit to Quebec and the United States. They swam and picnicked at Val-Kill, Eleanor's cottage, dining on broiled hot dogs and watermelon. Churchill wore a huge Stetson that made him look small and quite ridiculous, and he sipped Scotch and brandy for much of the weekend.

Over cigars for Churchill and cigarettes for FDR, and liberal amounts of strong drink, the two made a variety of important decisions. Americans would command the cross-Channel invasion of France known as Overlord, and U.S. troops would make up the majority of the invading forces. They invited Soviet leader Josef Stalin to meet with them that fall. And following up on their June 1942 conversation at Hyde Park, they prepared a memorandum on the atomic bomb. In that document, they promised to share the results of the Manhattan Project with each other but to keep it secret from the rest of the world, including the Soviets. They formally agreed not to use the weapon against each other. And they agreed not to use it against anyone else without mutual consent. Churchill wanted reassurance that the Americans would not proceed without full consultation with him, and when he left Hyde Park he felt comforted that he wasn't being left out.

In September 1944, Franklin and Winston met in Quebec for talks about the final push against Germany, the possibilities for postwar Europe, and the strategy for defeating Japan in the Pacific. When their conference was over, Churchill and his wife accompanied FDR and Eleanor to Hyde Park for two days before return-ing to England. The leaders enjoyed picnics on the lawn, walks through the woods, and pleasant conversation, as among old friends, even though Eleanor viewed her role as that of a "glorified housekeeper" who had to make sure every-one was fed and happy 24 hours a day.

It was during Churchill's last night at Hyde Park that the conversation again turned to the atomic bomb. U.S. scientists were predicting that this new super-weapon would detonate with the force of 30,000 tons of TNT and would prob-ably be ready by August 1945. Roosevelt and Churchill felt that the war in Europe would be over by then and the superbomb could be used to end the con-flict with Japan.

Some scientists who were familiar with the project were arguing privately that the United States and Great Britain should tell the world what was about to hap-pen, because the superbomb was such a profound development in the history of warfare. But Roosevelt and Churchill rejected the idea. They endorsed a secret memo that said, "The suggestion that the world should be informed regarding Tube Alloys, with a view to international agreement regarding its control and use, is not accepted. The matter should continue to be regarded as of the utmost se-crecy; but when a 'bomb' is finally available, it might perhaps, after mature con-sideration, be used against the Japanese, who should be warned that this bombardment will be repeated until they surrender."

ON A PRIVATE level, Hyde Park served as the venue where the president and First Lady played out their unusual relationship. FDR had married Eleanor on March 17, 1905. She was the daughter of Elliott Roosevelt, President Theodore Roosevelt's younger brother, making her Franklin's distant cousin. President Theodore Roosevelt gave the bride away at the wedding.

Compared with the indulgent Franklin, Eleanor was a disciplinarian. She made sure her children were on time, whereas Franklin had a much looser attitude about punctuality. She believed fully in decorum and courtesy, only to find, again, that Franklin wasn't such a stickler for rules and could be swayed by the emotions of the moment.

She once punished their youngest son for losing his temper by sending him to his room. A bit later, she didn't find him there, and discovered the boy in the study "crying his heart out in his father's arms, with his head buried in his father's shirtfront. My husband sat tipped back in his desk chair looking entirely miserable and quite guilty because he knew he was not upholding discipline," she said. But he was gentle and tolerant with his kids, no matter how much Eleanor disapproved.

They bought their five children horses, which were kept in a stable, in addition to dogs, birds, and rabbits. When they traveled, Eleanor was responsible for bringing the smaller pets with them on many occasions.

The relationship between Eleanor and Franklin was deeply troubled. For one thing, Franklin had always enjoyed the company of other women. "Nothing is more pleasing to the eye," he once said, "than a good-looking lady, nothing more refreshing to the spirit than the company of one, nothing more flattering to the ego than the affection of one." Franklin was apparently eager for the kind of companionship, affection, and rapt attention that the aloof Eleanor seemed incapable of giving him. Among his companions during his presidency, for example, were Crown Princess Martha of Norway, living in the United States because her country had been overrun by the Nazis; and White House staff members Missy Le-Hand, Margaret "Daisy" Suckley, and Grace Tully.

But the real problem was elsewhere. In the winter of 1913–1914, Eleanor hired an attractive and engaging 22-year-old woman named Lucy Mercer as a social secretary, and Lucy became part of the household and saw Franklin nearly every day. They developed a strong mutual attraction.

In the autumn of 1918, when Franklin, then the father of five children and married 13 years, was bedridden with pneumonia at his mother's house in New York City, Eleanor found love letters from Lucy in Franklin's belongings. Eleanor apparently threatened him with divorce unless he cut short the affair. She never forgave him for his betrayal, which others in the family had long suspected. By early 1918, in fact, while he was assistant secretary of the Navy, "He had become less discreet about this love of Lucy," wrote his son Elliott. "They had been seen driving together by more people than his cousin, Alice Longworth, who invited them to her house for dinner, happy to plot against Mother. They had other gossiping friends who realized by now that something much more serious than a summer bachelor's flirtation had developed."

Franklin's mother, Sara, concerned with appearances and motivated by her sense of marital duty, helped persuade her son and Eleanor to stay together by offering her continued financial support and threatening to cut it off from both of them if there was a divorce. Eleanor made some harsh demands of her own, according to son Elliott: "This, she told him, meant that their marital relations could never be resumed. She was willing to have him as a partner in public life, not ever again as a husband."

From then on, Eleanor lived a life that was in basic ways separate from her husband's, devoting herself to liberal causes such as federal programs for the poor and building close friendships outside her husband's circle.

"At one level, the marriage was a shell, salvaged for the sake of the children and Franklin's political future," writes historian Mark H. Leff. "What remained of it? Not love, although in better times regard, affection, and even an emotional bond survived. Not trust; Eleanor would never forget or forgive. Instead, the marriage that emerged from this crisis paired a more tempered husband and a more self-directed wife in the most prominent and consequential political partnership of the century."

Franklin ended his affair with Lucy, who went on to marry Winthrop Rutherfurd, a wealthy businessman. Much later, and after Winthrop died, Franklin resumed a relationship with his Lucy, unknown to Eleanor. In fact, Lucy was with him at his retreat in Warm Springs, Georgia, the day he died—which came as a shock to Mrs. Roosevelt, who was away at the time.

THE ESTATE AT Hyde Park was actually run for many years by Franklin's formidable mother, the former Sara Delano. "Sara meant to dominate her son's married life in the way she had tried to dominate his childhood and youth," author Jon Meacham writes. "Her granddaughter Anna recalled Sara as 'the matriarch of the family,' and 'certainly the head of the household at Hyde Park,' which, in addition to the linked houses in Manhattan [with Sara in one home and her son and daughter-in-law in the other], was where Franklin and Eleanor raised their children." Eleanor lacked the self-confidence to stand up to her mother-in-law, and Franklin took little interest in the doings at home. He accepted Sara's dominance.

Sara had enjoyed a pleasant life with her husband, James Roosevelt, a widower, country squire, and her distant cousin, but she lavished most of her attention on Franklin, her only child. After her husband died in 1900, she lived for long periods on the estate and in a house on East 65th Street in New York City, and insisted on operating Hyde Park with an iron hand. Roosevelt had so many other interests that he didn't mind, so long as things ran smoothly and she consulted him on major decisions.

FDR's son Elliott wrote, "For good reason, Mother had no such attachment to the house which Granny owned and ruled, 'holding the fort,' as Father said. Mother felt that she was treated as a guest, not always a welcome one." FDR's mother apparently thought Eleanor was not a good match for her boy, not pretty, charming, or affectionate enough, and after he married against his mother's wishes, the old woman made life difficult for her daughter-in-law.

A case in point was the remodeling of the main house in 1915. FDR and his mother planned the renovations in close consultation, but with his mother's financing, which gave her the upper hand. The result was two huge bedrooms, one for Franklin and one for his mother, each with a fireplace, a splendid view, and an adjacent bathroom—and an embarrassingly small bedroom with no private bathroom and no fireplace for Eleanor.

As Elliott Roosevelt recalled in a memoir about his boyhood there, "If any of us had been old enough to realize the significance of the floor plan or to know about the ways of most other married people, we would have had a better understanding of the coldness which existed as a permanent condition between our parents."

In other parts of the renovations, FDR and his mother created a full third floor, expanding the three-story tower that had dominated the original clapboard structure. They resurfaced the exterior with brown and gray brick and stucco, and changed the architectural style from Italianate to neoclassical. They added two wings, a terrace, and a portico, and later constructed a cottage on the estate so Franklin could "get away from the show."

Sara made sure to serve the meals that her beloved son craved, even though Eleanor disapproved of the extravagance and poor nutrition such foods provided. For breakfast, for example, there were eggs and bacon, heaping plates of muffins and rolls, hot cereal or porridge, bowls of fresh strawberries drowning in sugar and cream. The eggs, fruits, and vegetables were from Granny's gardens or huge greenhouse, carefully maintained by her large staff and supervised by the elder Mrs. Roosevelt.

Grandmother Roosevelt would sit at one end of the table, Franklin at the other. Eleanor's place was halfway down one side of the table. Franklin would often arrive a bit late, but full of energy and good cheer.

Granny died in 1941, but her domineering presence for so many years resulted in Eleanor never feeling comfortable at the main house. She coped with it by having her own small cottage, called Val-Kill, built a few hundred yards from the mansion, and that's where she lived when Franklin wasn't home.

Family members and friends said Franklin was deeply upset by his mother's passing, which was brought home every time he returned to Hyde Park. He associated the estate with his mother and all the attention and affection she had lavished on him. After his mother died, FDR made a habit of looking through the boxes and crates filled with his mother's memorabilia, which were stored at Hyde Park, and it connected him to her in an almost visceral way as he reviewed their lives together.

AFTER THEY MOVED to the White House in early 1933, the 35-room main residence, which the family called Springwood, "became more of an official residence," Eleanor recalled, "and at times we brought extra people to help his mother's employees because of the large number of guests who followed the president and the extra staff that must come with him; but the manner of life changed very little." There was a regular staff of cook, kitchen maid, personal maid, house maid, waitress or butler, a houseman, laundress, coachman, and chauffeur. Sometimes there were also a governess, tutor, and nurse for the children.

Much of the furniture was mahogany with floral upholstery, and the Roosevelts always resisted suggestions that they update it. Eleanor admitted the furniture looked old-fashioned, but rejected making changes to accommodate "some whim of passing taste."

Many accommodations were made to FDR's physical condition. A closet-sized elevator, just large enough for him and his wheelchair, was installed near the main entrance hall so he could get to the upper floors, where his bedroom was located. With his legs paralyzed from polio, he could ascend and descend on his own by pulling special ropes on pulleys.

The house was crammed with family photos on the tables, on the walls, on the bookshelves. FDR and his mother always stood on the front porch to greet important guests, from senators and governors to the king and queen of England; it was where his mother met him when he arrived for a stay, and where friends and neighbors would congregate to congratulate him after he won each presidential nomination and every election night.

He had a phone on a table next to his bed, and another, a hotline directly linked to the White House, on the wall next to his headboard.

BUT THE MAIN house didn't give him enough privacy. Roosevelt decided he needed a place to "escape the mob" swirling around him. "I found that on my trips to Hyde Park from Washington it was almost impossible to have any time to myself in the big house," he wrote. "The trips were intended primarily for a holiday—a chance to read, to sort my books, and to make plans for roads, tree plantings, etc. This was seemingly impossible because of (a) visitors in the house; (b) telephone calls; (c) visits from Dutchess County neighbors; (d) visits from various people who, knowing I was going to be in Hyde Park, thought it an opportune time to seek some interview."

On July 1, 1938, he assembled a press conference on a wooded hilltop overlooking his mother's house and announced that he was planning to have a small, modest cottage built for himself there. He would have the walls constructed from fieldstone taken from the ancient walls that existed in the woods, but what he most loved about the location was the wonderful view of the wide Hudson River and the Catskill Mountains to the west of the property. He designed the place, which he called Top Cottage, with the assistance of professional architect Henry Toombs of Georgia.

Completed in 1939, it had two bedrooms, a large living room with a gorgeous view, and an open porch where he would entertain in good weather. It was wheelchair accessible. Everything was on one floor, with no threshold barriers in the doorways, and a ramp led up to the front door to accommodate his wheelchair. He had a servant set up a card table at teatime, and he toasted bread, buttered it, and handed it to his guests without help, in a declaration of his independence. There was no telephone and the only road was barely accessible to vehicular traffic. This bothered the Secret Service because the president could not be easily reached on the summit (which FDR intended all along) and because the agents would have trouble getting help if something happened.

The worst part for Franklin was his mother's disappointment that her son felt a need to have a retreat built apart from her. She made him promise never to spend a night there as long as she lived and he never did, even after her death in 1941.

He intended for the cottage to be his hideaway after he retired from the presidency, the place where he would write his memoirs. He told friends in the late 1930s that he didn't intend to seek a third term in 1940, but he changed his mind and was elected to that third term and then a fourth, in 1944.

Top Cottage was the scene of some vintage FDR moments. In 1939, he hosted King George VI and Queen Elizabeth of England during the first visit by British monarchs to the United States. The king and queen sat on the big flagstone patio overlooking the Hudson River Valley and were served their first hot dogs, which Eleanor provided to expose the British couple to America's comfort food. This shocked her straightlaced mother-in-law. The king asked for a second helping; the queen was not impressed and didn't eat.

A CONSTANT CHALLENGE for Roosevelt during most of his adult life was his disability. He had contracted polio in 1921, after his return to New York following the unsuccessful presidential campaign of 1920, when he was the Democratic vice presidential nominee.

He suffered permanent paralysis of his legs and even though he consulted with the best doctors and worked hard to rehabilitate himself for seven long years, nothing worked.

When he wasn't in bed, he wore harsh-looking, heavy steel braces on his legs from buttocks to feet, each one weighing more than five pounds. "Roosevelt never denied his polio," writes biographer Hugh Gregory Gallagher. "Although he minimized the extent of his impairment—to himself as well as to others—he always acknowledged it. He had a lifetime interest in the care and treatment of victims of the disease and in research into its cause and cure."

Until he contracted the disease, he had emulated his cousin Theodore in his love of the outdoors, of running, swimming, sailing, fishing, and cavorting with his children. The polio changed all that. At first, he was in great pain and completely helpless, unable to turn over in bed. His nurses and his wife, Eleanor, had to bathe and tend to his bodily functions, which must have mortified him.

Within a year, in 1922, he had strengthened his arms and upper body enough that he could get around, with great effort, on crutches. That October, he decided to see if he could return to work at an insurance company in Manhattan. A chauffeur drove him to the building, and he made his way on crutches with the driver's assistance into the lobby. Perspiring heavily, Roosevelt tried to walk to the elevators as a crowd gathered to watch, but he fell noisily to the polished marble floor. Displaying fierce determination, he struggled to a sitting position, but could not get to his feet even with the chauffeur's help. At that point Roosevelt looked around at the startled spectators, hailed them with a hand, and said calmly, "There's . . . nothing to worry about. We'll get out of this all right. Give me a hand there . . ." Others grabbed him under the arms and, at his direction—"All right now, all together!"—they got him back on his legs, and he made it to the elevators after all.

What made Roosevelt feel better was physical exercise and bathing in warm water. George Foster Peabody, a banker and family friend, told Roosevelt the story of Louis Joseph, a young man confined to a wheelchair by polio who had gained strength and the ability to walk with crutches after an exercise regimen and other therapies at a health spa in Warm Springs, Georgia. In October 1924, Roosevelt visited the resort at Warm Springs, which consisted of a ramshackle old hotel and other buildings built around a spring where water emerged from the ground at about 88 degrees, year-round.

In 1927, he acquired the property and then bought a 1,700-acre farm surrounding it, which he operated for the final 18 years of his life as a foundation and research center focused on the causes and treatment of polio and the care of its victims. These fund-raising efforts eventually became the March of Dimes, an immensely successful philanthropic effort to fight infantile paralysis. After he won the presidency in 1932, he had a simple pine-paneled house built for himself in Warm Springs. He called it the Little White House.

Roosevelt participated enthusiastically in the treatments offered at the spa, especially the exercises and the swimming that strengthened his heart and his upper body. He swam and exercised in the pool for at least an hour each morning and then took a sunbath; he repeated the regimen for two or more hours in the afternoon, then took another sunbath, wearing a floppy hat to guard against sunburn.

One game he played with special enthusiasm was "water football," in a new glass-enclosed pool that he had installed. With six players on a side, the goal was to get a sponge wrapped in oilskin from one end of the pool to the other.

FDR spent most Thanksgivings there, and marked the occasions with dinner and a speech for the patients and staff.

In all, during his presidency he made 16 trips to Warm Springs, often spending two or three weeks there. (It took an entire day to reach the area by train and car.) He didn't get there at all in 1942 because of the onset of World War II, but he went at least once a year for the remaining years of his presidency, for a total of 175 days. He did paperwork there and met with his advisers, but mostly he relaxed. It became even more important to him because he realized that his presence gave inspiration to hundreds of other patients who met him or heard of his own struggle with polio.

HIS COMMITMENT TO Warm Springs is one of the most remarkable stories in the annals of the presidency. Roosevelt could easily have afforded a more secluded facility, with upgraded amenities and creature comforts, but he insisted on mingling with the other polio patients in the rather Spartan atmosphere of the Georgia spa. Throughout his time there, they referred to him as "Doc Roosevelt," because he shared with fellow victims the exercises that seemed to work for him or regimens that seemed to help others.

Films taken of FDR at Warm Springs by staff members and friends show this poignant side of his life. He lowered his guard as he did nowhere else and seemed completely at ease in allowing everyone around him to see the extent of his disability. He wore a simple black bathing suit and lounged by the pool with his broomstick-thin legs clearly visible. He enthusiastically braced himself on the side of the pool while a physical therapist held him by the calves and pushed his legs up and down, hoping to spark some response in his muscles. It is remarkable to see the president of the United States so vulnerable, and FDR and his staff were careful to hide such images from the media and the public, which never realized the extent of his disability. But despite his courage and perseverance, he did develop one phobia: He became terrified of dying alone in a fire, and always insisted that someone be close by to rescue him.

He couldn't walk without canes, crutches, or the assistance of aides who held him by both arms, and he used a wheelchair. But he went to great lengths to camouflage his physical problems. The White House press corps went along with all this and most Americans never knew their leader had a serious disability. When a reporter once asked him how he coped with the problems of the presidency, he let some of his frustrations show. "If you had spent two years in bed trying to move your toes," FDR said, "you'd understand how easy the rest has been."

Warm Springs replaced FDR's frequent seagoing expeditions after the United States entered World War II. He loved getting out on the water, but the Secret Service and the military thought it was too dangerous for the president to ply the Atlantic, or even the Potomac and Chesapeake Bay, for most of the war. Therefore, he contented himself with landlocked pleasure trips.

At Warm Springs, he enjoyed picnics in the countryside. These were elaborate affairs with dishware and china, chairs or blankets to sit on, and martinis, cocktails, fried chicken, and many prepared dishes passed around by servants. On some occasions he would fasten his iron braces on the outside of his trouser legs, clearly visible to all around him, something he would never do in his public appearances. There was another addition during World War II: uniformed soldiers from Fort Benning who patrolled the woods with loaded rifles and sidearms.

For his meals at the Little White House, he would savor Brunswick stew, various meats such as chicken, squirrel, veal, or pork; corn and beans or onions in a thick tomato sauce. He learned to enjoy local specialties such as corn bread and turnip greens.

He would host local friends or his advisers from Washington at the Little White House for supper or go to neighbors' homes for the evening meal, swapping jokes and singing popular tunes such as "Home on the Range." Musical entertainment often featured Graham Jackson, an African-American accordion player and singer from Atlanta. FDR loved to mix and serve the drinks himself, with the remark, "How about another little sippy?"

His jokes were often silly and topical. He once teased Harry Hopkins, head of the Works Progress Administration, with this tale that made fun of WPA employees who didn't work hard enough:

"Harry, did you hear about the accident in Greenville today?"

"No, sir, Mr. President, I haven't heard. What happened?"

"Well, one of the WPA workers digging a ditch leaned on his shovel so long that the termites ate the handle out and he fell and broke his back."

Roosevelt roared with laughter and he shouted, "I love it! Don't you just love it!"

But he wouldn't make such jokes in public. He recognized that many Americans needed federally provided jobs to survive the Depression.

ELEANOR SAID HER husband learned "the greatest of all lessons—infinite patience and never-ending persistence" from his disability. He seemed "more aware of the feelings of people," and drew on reservoirs of "strength and courage he had not had before," she explained.

Adds biographer Hugh Gregory Gallagher: "Roosevelt's paralysis was his one and only major experience with failure. From it he learned about humiliation and loss." During a seven-year battle to regain use of his legs, from 1921 to 1928, he was out of public life and, Gallagher says, "had the time and the opportunity to meet, talk to, and become friends with people of a sort that he had never met before. Struggling on his braces and crutches down to the end of the driveway at Hyde Park, FDR came to meet the local citizens—the mailman, the delivery boys, neighboring tenants. He met them not as the lord of the manor passing in his limousine, but as a human being, visibly struggling with his problems as his neighbors struggled with theirs."

This leavening effect was particularly evident at Warm Springs. Prior to his election as governor of New York, he began to drive a hand-controlled Ford Model A or a Model T throughout the area to meet with neighbors and look around. The vehicles were modified so he could drive them with hand controls linked to the foot pedals. He continued this practice after he became governor, and then as president, only more sparingly because of security concerns. He would drive without bodyguards into the front yard of a farmer who had land for sale, and inquire about the price. His real mission was to get to know the community. He made frequent visits into the town of Warm Springs to have a soda, or to chat with whomever was around the drugstore or other shops.

After he became president, security became so tight that such casual solo visits became rare. But he had already gotten a strong sense of the region and the problems of the people who lived there, and he never forgot them. He apparently gained an appreciation of the nation's ills as felt by the everyday folks he knew around Warm Springs.

He once told a friend in his cottage, "Down here at Warm Springs I can't generalize the way a politician's supposed to. A national problem strikes me as simply people somewhere needing help. What people? Where? What kind of help? . . . The national farm problem? What about Ed Doyle up there on Pine Mountain? The bank? Well, what sort of trouble does Uncle Henry Kimbrough have with his little bank over there in Chipley?"

In a speech in Barnesville, Georgia, in 1938, Roosevelt said, "Fourteen years ago, a Democratic Yankee, a comparatively young man, came to a neighboring county in the State of Georgia, in search of a pool of warm water wherein he might swim his way back to health; and he found it. The place—Warm Springs—was at that time a rather dilapidated small summer resort. His new neighbors there extended to him the hand of genuine hospitality, welcomed him to their firesides and made him feel so much at home that he built himself a house, bought himself a farm, and has been coming back ever since. And he proposes to keep to that good custom. I intend coming back very often. . . . There was only one discordant note in that first stay of mine at Warm Springs; when the first of the month bills came in for electric light at my little cottage, I found that the charge was 18 cents per kilowatt hour—about four times as much as I paid in Hyde Park. That started my long study of proper utility charges for electricity and the whole subject of getting electricity into farm homes throughout the United States. So it can be said that a little cottage at Warm Springs, Georgia, was the birthplace of the Rural Electrification Administration."

He enjoyed looser security arrangements at Warm Springs, but even they became too much on occasion. As a gesture of independence, he sometimes tried to elude his ever-present Secret Service minders, which presidents have done for many years. Once, after a workout in the pool, he noticed that one agent who was supposed to be watching him was looking the other way, so he ducked his head and swam underwater through a canal-link channel to an adjacent pool. The agent and his colleagues grew understandably alarmed at the disappearance of the president, until they heard Roosevelt laughing in the nearby dressing room.

FDR also took an interest in farming and animal production. He concluded that cotton was overplanted, and used the land for more pasturage instead. He experimented with Concord grape plantings—varying from 2 to 12 acres over the years—and sales of the grapes at roadside stands and to an Atlanta winery were a modest success, no doubt partly because of the president's celebrity. His farm also raised peaches, spinach, peppers, eggplant, watermelon, cantaloupe, tomatoes, string beans, and other vegetables for sale at the roadside stands.

Roosevelt considered himself a conservationist, and he delighted particularly in his trees. He had firebreaks cut in his woods to protect against blazes, which could be very damaging in South Georgia, and other farmers followed his lead. He also had thousands of native pine seedlings planted on his property for reforestation.

But throughout FDR's presidency, the farm operated at a loss.

AS WORLD WAR II dragged on, Roosevelt lost energy and vitality. "And even at Warm Springs the nagging routines of great responsibility could not be laid aside," writes author Turnley Walker. "He had sanctuary in his cottage. . . . Sometimes he brought his cousins, Margaret 'Daisy' Suckley and Laura Delano, with him as house guests, knowing that they would keep the conversation light and nonpolitical. But outside, the military guards were everywhere around his house. The armored limousine, which the Secret Service men decreed he must use if he left the slope, weighed just short of eight tons. So many of the dear old roads were too narrow and too soft, and the beloved bridges were no longer safe."

By the end of 1944, FDR was in obvious decline, his cheeks hollow, even his once-powerful upper body frail, his effervescence waning, his fatigue nearly constant, his heart weakening inexorably. Eleanor refused to face up to his condition, but others around him realized the truth. His unmarried cousin Daisy Suckley was one, and she and other women in his orbit, including his daughter Anna, gave him the kind of unstinting devotion and affection that his wife couldn't provide.

Daisy observed that the president got very lonely when left by himself, so his little coterie of female aides and relatives tried to buoy him and comfort him at all times. "As soon as the door was closed, he relaxed completely, yawned and yawned," Daisy noted in her journal. "He said it was the greatest possible rest to be able to just be as he felt and not to have to talk and be the host. . . . It has apparently become the habit not to relax but to force himself to keep up the outward appearance of energy and force."

But Anna, in her effort to make her father's life as easy as possible, was keeping an important secret from her mother: FDR was seeing Lucy Mercer again.

Lucy Mercer Rutherfurd had married after her breakup with Franklin, but her husband had died in 1941, and she apparently had never lost her affection for the president. The feeling was mutual. "Lucy was the woman he turned to for companionship in the afterglow of a desire that had been frustrated by Mother more than a quarter of a century ago," Elliott recalled.

During the final year of his life, he visited the 51-year-old widow at her estate in northern New Jersey, and she visited him at the White House and at Warm Springs, all without Eleanor's knowledge. "Lucy cared for the ailing president in a way Eleanor never could," writes author Kati Marton. "His need of her reveals much about what he missed in his marriage. With Lucy, Franklin could be light-hearted, include his love of conversation for the sheer pleasure of it." One moment in 1944 serves to crystallize all that was missing between Eleanor and Franklin, while at the same time illuminating Lucy's role in his life. On December 2, FDR drove Lucy to his favorite hill in Georgia, Dowdell's Knob, near Warm Springs. Looking out on the lush sweep of Pine Mountain Valley, he spoke for an hour about his hopes for the postwar world, mingled with tales of the countryside around them. Lucy merely smiled and listened, happy to be in his company. Eleanor, for whom the day was never long enough, was "constitutionally incapable of sitting and listening to her husband for that long," according to Marton.

IN THE SPRING of 1945, FDR went to Warm Springs for the last time. At this point, not even Hyde Park could give him the solace and relaxation he needed. On March 29, he returned to the White House after four days at his New York home and was still deeply fatigued. When aide Grace Tully asked, "Did you get any rest at Hyde Park?" he replied, "Yes, child, but not nearly enough. I shall be glad to get down south." He left by train that afternoon for what was scheduled as a two-week vacation.

"Loneliness weighed as heavily on Father as did the responsibilities of being President and Commander in Chief," Elliott wrote. "What he missed more than anything was someone dear to him with whom he could talk over every problem late at night or the next morning. . . . Now, with his four sons away in uniform and Mother roaming the corners of the earth, his immediate family had been whittled down to Sis [Anna]. She delighted in the situation."

He arrived by train on March 30, 1945, looking ghastly, his complexion gray with dark pouches under his eyes. A Secret Service agent wheeled him to a blue Ford convertible—by this time, he no longer had the energy or the desire to walk using his leg braces, crutches, or canes—and he waved weakly to well-wishers who had gathered at the train station.

He was so weary that he stayed away from the swimming pool that had been a part of his routine there for so long. He wanted to minimize his workload but felt it necessary to write thoughtful letters to Churchill and Stalin outlining his concerns about Soviet intentions after the war. To relax him, his cousins Laura "Polly" Delano and Daisy Suckley took him on drives through the country, to admire the first signs of spring. He went to Easter services with them at the Warm Springs Chapel on April 1, and some of the churchgoers noticed that his hands trembled, and he dropped his prayer book once and his eyeglasses another time.

On Monday, April 9, Lucy Mercer Rutherfurd arrived and spent most of her time sitting with Franklin and listening to him talk. He was reading a new paperback mystery, *The Punch and Judy Murders,* and appeared to be enjoying it as an escape from his work. He also relished reading newspapers by a window in the warm sunshine, and perusing official war dispatches as he happily followed the progress of the Allied armies as they fought their way successfully through Europe and began a final push to Japan.

Gradually, Roosevelt seemed to be feeling better. He was getting plenty of rest; the gray pallor was gone; he was asking for second helpings at meals and at bedtime; and he was starting to increase his workload again.

He was even getting playful. Daisy Suckley wrote about an unusual, even bizarre, regression that she observed during this period. She wrote in her journal that on the evening of April 4, FDR's doctors and guests had departed, his valet had settled him in bed for the night, and his cousins decided to bring him a snack of the gruel his doctors had advised. "I get the gruel & Polly & I take it to him," Suckley wrote. "I sit on the edge of the bed & he 'puts on an act': he is too weak to raise his head, his hands are weak, he must be fed! So I proceed to feed him with a tea spoon & he loves it! Just to be able to turn from his world problems & behave like a complete nut for a few moments, with an appreciative audience laughing with him & at him, both!" The president "relapsed into babyhood" in this way almost nightly for the final few days of his life, Suckley reported.

On Thursday, April 12, FDR slept late and awoke with a headache. He read the previous day's newspapers in bed, propped up with two sofa pillows, as he waited for the latest editions to arrive from Atlanta. He changed into a gray suit, red tie, and a naval cape, and moved to an oval wooden card table in the living room, where he read official papers while an artist named Elizabeth Shoumatoff worked on a watercolor portrait of him. His cousin Daisy was crocheting on the sofa, and his cousin Polly left the living room to water some roses in her room. Lucy sat close by the president in case he wanted to chat. Just after 12:30 P.M., he stopped his reading, ate his doctor-prescribed lunch of gruel brought to him on a tray, and told the women around him: "We have fifteen minutes more to work" (before he would presumably take a nap).

At 1:15, Roosevelt raised his left hand to the back of his head and said, "I have a terrific pain in the back of my head," and slumped forward in his chair, unconscious. A valet and another member of the household staff carried him to his bedroom. He had suffered a cerebral hemorrhage. He died at 3:35 P.M.

FDR WANTED EVERYDAY Americans to see his home and the large collection of papers and memorabilia he had accumulated as president. To that end, he gave his estate at Hyde Park to the government to be converted into a presidential library and historic site. He was the first chief executive to do so.

ROOSEVELT'S INTERACTIONS WITH the poor and elderly at his retreats personalized his understanding of living conditions outside his own world of privilege and wealth. FDR's disability, sense of vulnerability, and connection with his fellow polio patients and others he met at Warm Springs made him a different, more caring person and shaped his presidency in fundamental ways. These experiences helped to inspire some of his most important policies, from his creation of the Social Security system to his commitment to using the federal government to assist those in need.

FDR also had contact with everyday people at Hyde Park, but to a lesser extent than at Warm Springs. His life at the family estate underscored his close— some would say excessively close—relationship with his mother and his strange partnership with his wife. But he made history there, such as when he and Churchill secretly established the U.S.–British policy for developing and using the atomic bomb, one of the 20th century's most far-reaching developments.

—∞∞∞—

CHAPTER EIGHT

HARRY TRUMAN AND INDEPENDENCE, MISSOURI, AND KEY WEST, FLORIDA

HARRY TRUMAN'S REPUTATION as the Everyman President was well founded. From the moment he succeeded to the job upon FDR's death in early 1945, there were questions about whether he could fill the massive shoes of his beloved predecessor. And if few Americans were sure that the former haberdasher was up to the task, they admired him for trying his best. After he was sworn in, he remarked humbly to reporters, "Boys, if you ever pray, pray for me now." But he had inner strength and a profound sense of duty, and he surprised nearly everyone by making sound decisions in extraordinarily difficult times, proving to many doubters that a regular citizen could become president and excel at it.

Truman's down-to-earth qualities were reflected in his choice of retreats, where he indulged in activities that most people could appreciate and which revealed him as the quintessential Middle American. He played tourist at Key West, Florida, donning a loud tropical shirt like so many other Midwesterners on holiday, and on one occasion losing his thick eyeglasses in the surf. He was sensitive about people taking photographs of his rotund belly. He regularly paid his respects to his hard-to-please mother-in-law at her home in Independence, Missouri, and was remarkably tolerant of her disdain for his leadership skills. He was devoted to his wife, Bess, and daughter, Margaret, and openly admitted that he got lonely in the White House or at his refuges when they were away. Americans could easily identify with him.

. . .

BORN IN LAMAR, Missouri, on May 8, 1884, Harry and his family didn't stay in one place for long. In 1887, they moved to the farm owned by his grandparents, near Grandview, Missouri, where Harry's father and grandfather were partners in raising cattle, mules, hogs, and sheep, and in growing wheat, corn, and hay. In December 1890, the family moved to Independence, where his father had bought a big house on South Crysler Avenue with several acres that included a garden and strawberry bed.

They moved again in 1896, to 909 West Waldo Avenue at North River Boulevard in Independence, and Truman described "wonderful times" in that neighborhood from 1896 to 1902, mostly revolving around chores and animals. "Usually there were goats, calves, two or three cows, my pony, and my father's horses to be taken care of," he said. "The cows had to be milked and the horses curried, watered, and fed every morning and evening. In the summertime the cows had to be taken to pasture a mile or so away after morning milking and returned the same evening. The goats and calves had to be taken to the big public spring at Blue Avenue and River, two blocks south of our house, for water."

There were several other moves while he was a boy, but they only deepened his attachment to the area that he loved. Likewise, the community's impact on Harry was unmistakable. Writes Truman biographer David McCullough: "Independence was southern in both spirit and pace—really more southern than midwestern—and very set in its ways." The town was clean and neat, with gardens tended carefully by the homeowners, and roosters crowing at dawn. Farmers came to town on Saturdays for haircuts and supplies. Everyone attended church on Sunday, then had their main meal at midday, often with fried chicken, mashed potatoes, gravy, peas, and biscuits. Blacks were clustered in what the whites called "Nigger Neck" northwest of the town square, and were denied use of public facilities that whites used.

This experience with prejudice didn't repel Truman. In fact, he showed little sensitivity to racial issues for most of his life and privately used epithets to describe African Americans. But he believed in playing fair and formed a task force on civil rights after he became president. This led to his executive order desegregating the armed forces and creating a civil rights division in the Justice Department. He made a distinction between legal rights and social equality, endorsing the former but remaining unenthusiastic about the latter.

More broadly, Harry learned a set of personal virtues in Missouri that he tried to abide by: Honesty is the best policy. . . . If at first you don't succeed, try, try again. . . . Never give up. . . . Make yourself useful. As historian David M. Oshinsky points out, "It was Martha Truman [Harry's mother] who encouraged Harry's love of reading, music, and history. . . . A product of rural Missouri, Harry Truman reflected both the certainties and prejudices of small-town, nineteenth-century America. His values were clear, fixed, traditional; his friendships lasted a lifetime. He possessed egalitarian instincts, remarkable courage, and a pioneer's faith that big things could come from small stakes."

After he married Bess Wallace, his home became the fourteen-room Victorian residence of his mother-in-law at 219 North Delaware Street, and he considered it so for the rest of his life, through his career in the senate, as vice president, as commander in chief, and in retirement.

FOR SUCH A devoted couple, it is difficult to understand how Bess could have left Harry behind in the White House for such long periods of time.

After less than a month living in the White House, the new First Lady, along with her mother, Madge Gates Wallace, and daughter, Margaret, took a train to Independence on Saturday, June 2. They stayed there all summer. Harry, meanwhile, occupied his time working in the Oval Office or, in the evenings, in his upstairs study in the residence. But he was lonely. "I sit here in this old house," he wrote Bess on June 12, 1945, "and work on foreign affairs, read reports, and work on speeches—all the while listening to the ghosts walk up and down the hallway and even right in here in the study. The floors pop and the drapes move back and forth—I can just imagine old Andy and Teddy having an argument over Franklin. Or James Buchanan and Franklin Pierce deciding which was the more useless to the country. And when Millard Fillmore and Chester Arthur join in for place and show the din is almost unbearable."

He wrote in his diary: "I'm always so lonesome when the family leaves. I have no one to raise a fuss over my neckties and my haircuts, my shoes and my clothes generally. I usually put on a terrible tie not even Bob Hannegan or Ed McKim would wear just to get a loud protest from Bess and Margie. When they are gone I have to put on the right ones and it's no fun."

Still, he enjoyed the presidency and as time went on felt he was getting quite good at the job. In keeping with his sense of duty, he believed that fate had placed him in the White House and he would commit himself to being the best president he could be.

But Bess hated the spotlight of being First Lady. Early on, she declared that she would hold no press conferences, departing from Eleanor Roosevelt's custom, for a simple reason: "I have nothing to say. I don't even think about public affairs." She also announced, "A woman's place in public is to sit beside her husband and be silent and be sure her hat is on straight."

Bess preferred living a quiet life with her mother in Independence where she played bridge with her friends and sat in the high-ceilinged parlor or the music room reading or listening to the radio. Bess's grandfather, George Porter Gates, had built the house at 219 North Delaware Street in 1867 and it had been renovated and expanded over the years. Bess was reared there, and after she married Harry, in 1919, they shared the place with Bess's widowed mother. The Trumans' daughter, Margaret, was born in an upstairs bedroom.

After Harry unexpectedly became the 33rd president, only 83 days after he took office as FDR's vice president in 1945, Bess returned to North Delaware Street again and again to be with her mother, a situation that lasted until the elderly woman died in late 1952, shortly before Truman left office. Bess barely tolerated being First Lady, with all its protocols and invasions of privacy, and didn't like living in the White House.

HARRY VISITED INDEPENDENCE often to be with his family, particularly over holidays such as Christmas, but also to get away from Washington. "I had learned that one of the hardest things for the President to do is to find time to take stock," Truman wrote in his memoirs. "I have always believed that the President's office ought to be open to as many citizens as he can find time to talk to; that is part of the job, to be available to the people, to listen to their troubles, to let them share the rich tradition of the White House. But it raises havoc with one's day, and even though I always got up early, usually was at work ahead of the staff, and would take papers home with me at night to read, there always seemed to be more than I could do.

"I do not know of any easy way to be President. It is more than a full-time job, and the relaxations are few. I used the presidential yacht, as well as the Little White House at Key West, less for holiday uses than as hideaways, and they were very useful when I wanted to catch up on my work and needed an opportunity to consult with my staff without interruptions."

But in Independence, he certainly wasn't treated as the lord of the manor, as Franklin Roosevelt had been at Hyde Park or as John F. Kennedy would be at Hyannisport. One problem was that the Truman home was actually the residence of Bess's mother, not Harry. And Madge Wallace never thought very highly of Harry's political career, even when he became president. Nor did Bess let Harry's exalted job inflate his ego. When Harry once arrived late for Christmas in Independence because of a snowstorm, an angry Bess sputtered, "I guess you couldn't think of any more reasons to stay away. As far as I'm concerned, you might as well have stayed in Washington."

She apparently took him down a few notches with great regularity. In one of his many letters to her, for example, he once wrote, "You can never appreciate what it means to come home as I did the other evening after doing at least one hundred things I didn't want to do and have the only person in the world whose approval and good opinion I value look at me like I'm something the cat dragged in."

Yet privately, Bess did serve as a sounding board for her husband. He consulted with her on matters ranging from increasing federal funding for mental health research to evaluating advisers who might not be serving him properly.

Harry appears to have visited Independence more to be with his wife and daughter than because he loved the modest, 14-room house. He often conducted business or stayed overnight at the Muehlenbach Hotel nearby, in Kansas City. Bess and Madge insisted that their home was for the family, and Harry shouldn't conduct business there or even play poker with his cronies.

One of Bess's and Madge's few concessions to his presidency was allowing the Secret Service to patrol close to the house. For months, curiosity seekers would walk within a few yards of the residence or drive by in their cars, hoping to catch a glimpse of the new president. The house was located at the corner of a busy intersection. They eventually agreed to let the Secret Service put up a fence.

They also permitted the installation of a secure telephone that scrambled Harry's official calls and made them unintelligible to outsiders. It was placed unobtrusively under the stairwell in the foyer.

Finally, the two women gave Harry the go-ahead to have the house painted white, instead of gray, to correspond with the White House in Washington. It was something he preferred as a sign of his new status, and they humored him.

ONE OF THE most dramatic moments in Truman's presidency occurred in Independence just after 10 P.M. on Saturday, June 24, 1950. He was spending the weekend with his family, sitting in the library of their home on North Delaware Street, when Secretary of State Dean Acheson telephoned. "Mr. President," Acheson said, "I have very serious news. The North Koreans have invaded South Korea." Acheson suggested asking the United Nations Security Council to immediately declare that the North Koreans had committed an act of aggression, and Truman agreed. He told Acheson to request a special meeting of the Security Council with utmost urgency. Truman briefly considered returning that afternoon to the White House but decided to wait until the situation on the ground was clearer.

The following morning, at about 11:30, Acheson called again, just as the president and his family were getting ready to sit down to an early Sunday dinner. The secretary of state said the situation was increasingly grave because the North Koreans showed no signs of slowing their attack, which seemed to be an all-out invasion, and the opposing forces were having great difficulty stopping them. Truman decided to fly back to Washington as soon as possible.

In less than an hour, the crew had his airplane ready, and he departed so quickly that he left two aides behind. Both at Independence and aboard the plane for the three-hour flight back to Washington, Truman had time to reflect. "In my generation, this was not the first occasion when the strong had attacked the weak," he recalled later. "I recalled some earlier instances: Manchuria, Ethiopia, Austria. I remembered how each time that the democracies failed to act it had encouraged the aggressors to keep going ahead. Communism was acting in Korea just as Hitler, Mussolini, and the Japanese had acted ten, fifteen, and twenty years earlier. I felt certain that if South Korea was allowed to fall, Communist leaders would be emboldened to override nations closer to our own shores. . . . If this was allowed to go unchallenged it would mean a third world war, just as similar incidents had brought on the second world war."

This reasoning set Truman on the path for America's bitter involvement in the Korean War.

George Washington is known to history as a military commander and the first U.S. president, but he considered himself primarily a Virginia planter. At home in Mount Vernon, he carefully kept track of all aspects of his farm — making inspection tours on horseback nearly every day when he was in residence — and gave orders to his overseers in meticulous detail. He revealed himself as pragmatic and demanding of himself and everyone around him.

Washington is known as the president who refused to be king, but at Mount Vernon he lived like a colonial potentate. He had slaves, enjoyed the luxuries of his day, and relished his role as master of all he surveyed.

As the second president, John Adams lacked Washington's stature and was harshly attacked for loafing during lengthy vacations at his home in Quincy, Massachusetts. Similar criticisms have been leveled at presidents ever since, but Americans generally don't mind if their leaders take time off to escape the pressures of the West Wing — as long as the country seems to be heading in the right direction.

Thomas Jefferson had a wide range of interests, from politics and government to agriculture, literature, and inventions — and all were evident in the way he designed his mountaintop estate at Monticello in Virginia. It was part residence, part museum, and part laboratory for his fertile mind.

John Adams (*center*) and Thomas Jefferson (*right*) are shown with Benjamin Franklin signing the Declaration of Independence. Adams and Jefferson are considered fathers of their country, but their lives as private citizens were just as important to them as their public roles as presidents of the United States.

Abraham Lincoln spent many happy hours relaxing at the Soldiers' Home, a convalescent center for Civil War soldiers about three miles from the White House. He also did considerable work there — such as writing a draft of the Emancipation Proclamation.

Lincoln was actually the first presidential commuter. He lived at the Soldiers' Home for much of his time in office and traveled each day to and from his job at the White House. Confederate operatives apparently plotted to capture or kill Lincoln at or near the home, but John Wilkes Booth assassinated the president at Ford's Theater in Washington.

Theodore Roosevelt was a man of means who could afford a lavish home in Oyster Bay on Long Island, New York, which he called Sagamore Hill after a local Native American chief. He traveled there frequently during his presidency and moved much of the executive branch with him to create a "summer White House."

TR led his wife, children, extended family, and friends in pursuit of what he called the "strenuous life" at Sagamore Hill. This included hiking, horseback riding, rowing, boating, hunting, fishing, and camping. "At Sagamore Hill," he wrote, "we love a great many things — birds and trees and books, and all things beautiful, and horses and rifles and children and hard work and the joy of life."

ROOSEVELT WARM SPRINGS INSTITUTE FOR REHABILITATION

Franklin D. Roosevelt enjoyed swimming and other exercises in the naturally heated waters of Warm Springs, Georgia, and spent many days there attempting to rehabilitate his legs, which were paralyzed from polio. He never walked again after he contracted the disease as a young man, but he continued visiting Warm Springs as president because the waters helped him relax.

FDR let down his guard at Warm Springs. Surrounded by trusted family members, friends, physical therapists, and other polio patients, he didn't hide the full extent of his disability, including his withered legs — facts that were kept secret from the outside world.

CORBIS

FDR regularly used Hyde Park, his family home in upstate New York, as an escape from the formal duties of his job, but not his responsibilities. He made many important decisions there. In this 1941 photograph, Roosevelt sits on the porch of Top Cottage, a small building on the estate where he frequently went to unwind.

Roosevelt rarely allowed the media or the public to see him in his wheelchair, but he used it freely at Hyde Park.

Harry Truman, FDR's successor, faced massive challenges when he took over after Roosevelt's death in early 1945. Some of Truman's advisers quickly recommended that he get away from Washington to a warm-weather retreat where he could take vacations, and he settled on Key West, Florida. Occasionally his wife, Bess, and daughter, Margaret, joined him, but it was mainly a place where he could play poker, drink a little bourbon, and enjoy the sun with his male friends and advisers.

Truman became famous for his morning "constitutionals" — brisk walks at the fast pace of 120 steps per minute. He continued this practice even in retirement at his beloved hometown of Independence, Missouri, which he frequently visited during his presidency.

Mamie and Dwight Eisenhower never had a home of their own during their many years as a military couple but finally purchased a farm in Gettysburg, Pennsylvania, in 1950. After he became president in 1953, Ike used it as a retreat and a place to be himself. Mamie discouraged discussions of his work as much as she could, to relieve the pressures on her husband.

Eisenhower occasionally used an office in the town of Gettysburg and became extremely popular with local residents. One reason the former general was drawn to the area was that he identified with the soldiers who fought and died on the Civil War battlefield of Gettysburg, which was adjacent to his farm.

. . .

HIS PRIVATE LIFE, shaped by the values he learned in Independence, was thoroughly normal, which can't be said about many other men who held the presidency. In 1941, he wrote his 17-year-old daughter, Margaret, "You mustn't get agitated when your old dad calls you his baby, because he always will think of you as just that—no matter how old or how big you may get." In 1947, as Margaret tried to launch a singing career with a concert tour, her father, by this time the president, wrote her, "You should call your mamma and dad <u>every time</u> you arrive in a town. . . . Someday maybe (?) you'll understand the torture it is to be worried about the only person in the world that counts. You should know by now that your dad has only three such persons. Your Ma, you and your Aunt Mary."

He let his affection show in public, too. During his famous whistle-stop campaign of 1948, when he traveled across the country in a special railroad car called the Ferdinand Magellan, he introduced his wife to the crowds as "the boss" and Margaret as "the one who bosses the boss."

THE SEVEN-BEDROOM house at 219 North Delaware contained a grand piano, topped with a cluster of family photographs and two candelabra, in the parlor. The Trumans gave the piano to Margaret as a Christmas gift in 1932, when she was 8 years old. She had wanted an electric train, and burst into tears when she saw it. But Margaret dutifully practiced her lessons on it and became an accomplished musician.

Harry also put it to good use. He had loved music since childhood and had taken piano lessons for years when he was a boy. His mother had wanted him to be a concert pianist, and he got up at 5 A.M. to practice. He mastered the instrument (although not well enough to play professionally) and loved to play both in the White House and at Independence. Among his favorites were Chopin's A-Flat Waltz, Opus 42; Mozart's Piano Sonata in A Major; and Beethoven's Piano Concerto No. 4 in G.

He was often asked to play the "Missouri Waltz," both at home and at public events, and he often complied, although it was not one of his favorite compositions.

The kitchen at North Delaware was simple and functional, reflecting the family's Middle-American tastes. Margaret painted the woodwork green in 1948, and Truman chose new wallpaper much later, in 1971. It contained a simple four-burner stove, a linoleum floor, and a simple wooden table and chairs. For breakfast, the president for much of his life preferred toast; bacon; a soft-boiled egg, poached egg, or scrambled eggs; water, milk, or hot tea; and occasionally coffee. Harry often made the toast, but Bess did the rest of the cooking for breakfast and lunch. The longtime family cook, an African American named Vietta Garr, came in to prepare the evening meal.

Harry wasn't a picky eater. "I eat what I like and pass up what I do not," he said. "I never complain." At the start of his presidency in 1945, he gained about 10 pounds, weighing about 185. But he managed to drop down to 175 with a careful regimen of two-mile walks each morning and careful eating. He reduced his intake to only one piece of toast at breakfast, when he declined butter, sugar, and sweets. For lunch, he liked ham or roast-beef sandwiches, and sometimes peanut butter or sardine sandwiches, a glass of buttermilk, and fruit. His main course at supper was frequently steak, well done, with a baked potato, spinach or other vegetable, and a fruit cup, an orange, pineapple, raspberries, or an ice or angel food cake for dessert.

It was in 1949, after tourists repeatedly pilfered items, including shingles from the roof and clippings of shrubbery, that Harry reluctantly agreed to the Secret Service's recommendation that he have a wrought-iron fence built around the property. His wife and mother-in-law didn't like the idea at first but accepted the $5,400 fence when thieves ran off with Bess's prized white tulips. "We are going to leave that fence there, not because we like it, but it's just the American way to take souvenirs," the president observed. "It was said in the First World War that the French fought for their country, the British fought for freedom of the seas, and the Americans fought for souvenirs. . . . Never did like it and never will like it, but it has to be done because of souvenir hunters. They're just people who want to accumulate a lot of stuff and then throw it away. You find most of it in the attic when they die."

In 1950, the back porch was extended and screened to thwart prying eyes.

HARRY LOVED TO walk as a form of relaxation and exercise. He followed this pattern not only at the White House and its surrounding streets but also at his home in Independence and at his winter White House in Key West, Florida, where he took over the commanding officer's residence and made it his own.

He would get up early and set forth at about 6 A.M. He walked at a brisk pace—120 steps per minute, or two steps per second, and covered two miles—and sometimes tired out his Secret Service bodyguards. He kept his famous hat, coat, and an umbrella on hooks at the side entrance to the house at 219 North Delaware so he could easily take them on his jaunts, depending on the weather.

"When a man is over thirty-five, about the only exercise that does him any good is a good walk," Truman said. "The reason why that is so is because it affects every muscle in the body. . . . After you are fifty years old, this is the best exercise you can take. Of course, some aging exhibitionists try to prove that they can play tennis or handball or anything else they did when they were eighteen. And every once in a while one of them falls dead of a heart attack. I say that's not for me."

Truman also loved to read, especially history and biography. (He never went to college but was self-educated and quite erudite.) He perused five newspapers a day. Bess enjoyed mysteries and detective stories. In the evenings, they would often sit side by side in the study, reading. Harry had tremendous powers of concentration. "He has always been able to read a book or a memorandum with the radio or the phonograph playing and my mother and me conducting a first-class family argument," said his daughter, Margaret. "I am convinced that the world would be coming to an end, but he could not look up until he got to the bottom of the page he was reading."

THE HOUSE AT 219 North Delaware Street was home for Harry Truman for 53 years, until he died, in 1972. Bess continued to reside there until her death in 1982, when it was turned over to the federal government according to her will. The National Park Service now operates tours of the property.

TRUMAN WAS NOT wealthy, and like most Americans he could never afford a vacation home of his own. Yet like nearly all other presidents, he felt the need to escape. In the fall of 1946, the year after he succeeded to the presidency, he could not shake a bad cold and an annoying cough. Part of his problem was that he was run down physically because of the enormous pressure involved in his new job—ordering the use of the atomic bomb on Japan, presiding over the end of World War II, coping with the Soviet Union's expansionism, and reconstructing the non-communist world and America's peacetime economy. His doctor urged him to take a vacation.

Admiral Chester Nimitz, the chief of naval operations, told Truman that the perfect site would be Key West, and Truman decided to move into the commanding officer's house at the Navy's submarine base there. The house was vacant at the time. Over the years, Truman began calling it the Little White House. He liked to visit twice each winter and once in the late fall, and would remain there from one to five weeks each time. He found Key West, a three-and-a-half-hour plane ride from Washington, made to order for his needs. In all, he spent a total of 175 days, or nearly six months, on 11 trips to Key West as president, during the period from 1946 to 1952.

The naval base had an added attraction for him—the government didn't have to take dramatic steps to accommodate him there. He rarely used "Shangri-la," which is now known as Camp David, because, as he told an aide, "It takes a whole doggone company of Marines to protect me." Key West was an active naval base with a full-time staff on duty at all times of year.

Truman took a paternal attitude toward the U.S. Navy personnel from the base. Key West was a rowdy navy town, but some things were an affront to Truman's culturally conservative values. Once he read in a newspaper story that homosexuals were "preying" on the sailors, and he told an admiral about it during a briefing and asked if anything could be done. The admiral said he'd take care of it, and that day the shore patrol visited the bars, nightclubs, and gambling parlors, and told the owners to fire all the "queers," or their businesses would be off limits to sailors from the base. Scores of allegedly gay employees were rounded up, placed on a bus, and accompanied by a police escort to Miami, where they were herded off. A month later, many had returned.

Truman brought a large media contingent—up to 30 reporters—on his vacations, and he held press conferences once a week. Everyone involved loved Key West, with its aquamarine waters, warm climate, palm trees, and leisurely lifestyle. Truman quickly got into the spirit. He would enjoy outdoor barbecues, play poker with his pals every night, and take his famous walks through town (with a heavy Secret Service escort and journalists in tow, peppering him with questions). He often wore garish tropical shirts, featuring flowers, birds, or loud colors, and the resulting photographs were widely published in the nation's newspapers, embellishing his Everyman image. Harry could play tourist as well as anyone.

"I believe the outstanding characteristic of the Key West visits was their complete informality," recalled Clark Clifford, who served as White House naval aide and special counsel to the president. "A house had been prepared there for President

Truman. We all lived in the same house. We had our meals together there. . . . The president made it a point to do as little work as possible in Key West, so as not to interfere with the benefit of the rest and relaxation."

Offices were established in one of the buildings on the naval base a few yards from the Little White House, and 12 to 16 staff members, along with about 16 Secret Service agents, would come down from Washington. This group was supplemented by seamen provided by the base commander, and formed the core staff; many other advisers would visit Truman during his stints at Key West, including the secretaries of state, defense, and treasury, and members of Congress. Truman would gather them around him in a semicircle as they had lunch on the lawn, and they would hold discussions in what one participant called "a quiet and unhurried fashion." Some of these senior aides would stay with him in the house, and he would have two dozen bright floral shirts laid out for people to choose from, what he called the "Key West uniform." There was only a military switchboard and teletype—none of the sophisticated communications systems at the disposal of presidents today—and there was no television.

Truman liked to play recordings of classical music, especially Chopin recitals. He occasionally listened to the radio, but more for music or sports than the news. One of his celebrated listening experiences was tuning in to a broadcast of Margaret's recital with the Detroit Symphony in March 1947. The local station owners switched network affiliations briefly, just so the president could hear his daughter sing.

Mail pouches were flown from the White House at least once a day containing important papers, some of which required the president's signature.

Truman mostly went without his wife and daughter, who preferred Independence for their vacations and knew that Key West was something of a discreet stag club. The First Lady saw it, in daughter Margaret's words, "as an all-male setup and thought Dad would have a better time horsing around with [press secretary] Charlie Ross and [chief of staff] Admiral Leahy, playing poker and drinking a little bourbon beyond the range of her critical eye." Even the décor was a turnoff. At first, Bess and Margaret thought the place was dingy and barely livable, and Bess said it looked like a "fishing camp." Truman authorized an upgrade. A firm of decorators from Miami installed fine furniture and repainted it in dark blue and white, and everyone was happy.

When they visited, Bess and Margaret stayed in the same room, in twin beds. Stewards made sure to place floral arrangements in several locations. The president had another room to himself, with a small bed, a simple desk, sofa, and bookshelves.

Truman made clear he wanted to get away from business as much as possible at Key West. On one trip to the submarine base aboard the *Williamsburg*, his presidential yacht, Truman came onto the afterdeck and saw an aide with a table full of papers and books, writing in longhand, hard at work. Truman walked up to the table, picked up the paperwork, and threw it all over the rail into the water, shocking everyone. But he made his point: He was on vacation, and everyone should follow his lead.

But this wasn't really possible. After rising at 5:30 A.M. and reading the morning newspapers on his spacious, shaded porch, Harry would have a shot of bourbon and orange juice and go for a walk before breakfast. He'd stop sometimes and talk to local citizens or tourists.

On one such march, he encountered a woman taking her own walk at 6 A.M. "Gracious sakes, it's Mr. Truman," she exclaimed.

"Morning, ma'am," the president replied.

She had some advice: "You keep after 'em, sir. Keep 'em hopping."

Later that day, he remembered her words and decided to have a press conference to blast Senator Joe McCarthy, who had just made his latest round of outrageous charges about alleged communists in the government.

Over his poker game that evening, Truman was quite pleased with himself. "It was time somebody rebuked that low-down skunk," he said happily. "What I said was—and I meant it—I think Senator McCarthy's the greatest asset the Kremlin has." Shuffling the deck, the president added an observation about Key West: "Where else could you get such good advice from a little lady at six o'clock in the morning?"

After his morning constitutionals, he would hold informal staff meetings to discuss pressing matters over breakfast at 7:30 or 8 A.M., soliciting comments about the news of the day, discussing policy issues, and giving out assignments. At 10 or 10:30 A.M., Harry would signal that the holiday had resumed, and everyone would head for the beach, where they would go swimming. The president would plunge in, still wearing the thick trifocals that magnified his eyes to distorted proportions, and do his doggy paddle or sidestroke in the ocean. Once he lost his glasses in the water, and the Secret Service men and staff made repeated dives to find them, which they did.

The staff and Secret Service occasionally would play volleyball, and the president would watch avidly and joke about the friendly rivalry. At 1 P.M., Truman and his senior aides would have lunch together, and then everyone would spend the afternoon as they wished (although senior staffers were expected to be on call in case of emergency). Truman usually took a nap and did some reading. Occasionally he took a big convertible out for a spin through the streets of Key West or, more rarely, on longer drives across South Florida, wearing a jaunty white cap. Meanwhile, if Bess was there she would spend much of her time reading Agatha Christie murder mysteries on the porch or in the living room.

He enjoyed taking cruises in the presidential yacht, and one of his favorites was an excursion to the Dry Tortugas, near Key West.

In the late afternoon, generally about 4 P.M., Truman's little coterie would gather again for cocktails, and the president would enjoy a drink or two and play a little poker before dinner at about 6:30 P.M. The president would occasionally watch a movie (though his guests saw first-run films nearly every night). He much preferred newsreels sent from Washington. At other times he would treat his guests to a rendition of Chopin on the piano in the living room. But the evenings were mostly reserved for the nightly poker game on the porch from 8 until 11 or later.

This was one of Truman's great relaxations, although it wasn't publicized because gambling was involved and Truman didn't think most voters would approve. He had a poker table installed with a portable mahogany top that would cover up the cards and poker chips from visitors who might be troubled at the president's habit. Truman referred to the games in code. After completing the official business that was required of him, he would announce to aides with a wink: "It must be time for a little paperwork." Or he'd call for "a visit on the south porch." This meant he and his pals would make their way to the big veranda where the poker table with eight chairs awaited them.

He not only enjoyed the game but relished the male companionship with advisers including Charlie Ross, Harry Vaughan, and Clark Clifford. There was constant joshing and needling, and what Clifford called "good fellowship" lubricated with bourbon and water. It was quite a scene, the leader of the free world and his chums, their faces shadowed with several days' growth of beard, sitting around completely at ease.

Since the game wasn't designed to bankrupt anyone, a rule was devised: No one could lose more than either $50 or $100 during any period the president was there, whether it was two days or two weeks. They called it "poverty poker." Everyone who played poker with the president would put up $50 or $100 at the beginning of a vacation. If anyone lost his entire stake, he could draw from the pot without limit.

Clifford said Truman "was too optimistic a poker player. . . . He would stay in too many hands in the hope that he might make a lucky draw. You can get a lot of enjoyment out of it, but you can't win playing that kind of poker. He didn't win too much but as a matter of fact, it was not his basic purpose to win." In fact, Truman told some of his aides that he didn't feel comfortable winning at all, because he had asked his pals to play with him and he didn't want to "take their money."

In November 1946, Truman's curiosity took over when he boarded a captured German submarine, U-2513. The American crew offered to take the president for a ride, and he readily agreed—as Theodore Roosevelt had done in a comparable situation at Sagamore Hill four decades earlier. The U-boat submerged for a time and the crew members delighted in showing off their efficiency and exuberance. When the story made the newspapers, however, there was criticism that the president had been endangered because the sub had taken him underwater. Truman, however, never felt imperiled and loved the experience.

The Navy generally brought the *Williamsburg*, the presidential yacht, to Key West and the president enjoyed taking cruises, as did Bess and Margaret. Their meals were prepared on the yacht, which was anchored nearby, and transported to the Little White House. The yacht eventually contained special communications equipment for the commander in chief's use, and accommodated the overflow of staff and guests who stayed overnight. But Harry never liked fishing and did so only about once a trip, if that, mostly as a favor to his staff. He watched his staff and Navy personnel reel in sailfish and tarpon but only rarely dipped in a line of his own. Once the entourage had a fishing contest, and someone filled a fish with buckshot to win the prize for heaviest catch.

Once, George Elsey, an aide, went to the president's cabin with a radio message and tapped on the door. The president and Mrs. Truman said to come in and he found them playing double solitaire. Elsey apologized for interrupting, but Harry said, "Oh, that's all right, I'm ahead anyway." At that, Mrs. Truman laughed and said teasingly, "Yes, he's ahead and he's ahead because he cheats."

Truman may have been an everyday person, but he had a taste for the perquisites of power. Obviously he had no qualms about flying off to Key West at taxpayer expense, and he liked creature comforts. He felt he worked very hard and getting pampered was not too much to ask. After it became clear that Truman would be a repeat visitor at Key West and wasn't happy with the condition of the coarse beaches available to him, the Navy hauled in tons of sand to create a suitable beach within the naval base, and reserved it for the president and his party. It became known as Truman Beach.

The newspapers knew of it but never made it a big issue. They were more interested in feeding the public appetite for every tidbit of information about Harry. Once some photographers persuaded a Truman aide to allow use of a blimp to take some pictures and, believing that higher-ups had approved, the aide arranged it. But when the blimp showed up and the cameramen started taking photos of the president sunbathing in his shorts, all hell broke loose. Charlie Ross, the White House press secretary, exploded in rage, jumped in a car, and recalled the blimp to the naval air station, where he confiscated the film. Harry also was miffed at the invasion of his privacy.

The house itself was built in 1890 of Dade County pine, which was resistant to termites, and Truman hired a designer after his upset victory in 1948 to renovate the place. After the work was done, he wrote Bess: "Wish you and Margie were here. They have fixed you up a palatial bedroom next to mine. You've never seen a nicer one. I've a notion to move the capital to Key West and just stay."

Actually, the house was spacious but not palatial. No one would know a president vacationed there. There were virtually no political memorabilia anywhere to be seen. It was clear Truman wanted to get away from his responsibilities as much as he could, not reinforce his status with showy artifacts.

Yet as with all presidents, he could never fully get away. It was in the living room at Key West that he decided to fire Douglas MacArthur for insubordination during the Korean War because the general called publicly, as commander of U.S. forces in the region, for a dangerous escalation of the conflict. This was contrary to his commander in chief's wishes. The firing turned out to be one of his most unpopular decisions because MacArthur was a hero to so many Americans. Truman declined to seek another term as the war deteriorated into a bitter stalemate.

FROM THE START, he revealed the depth of his affection for Key West in a letter to Bess, written on White House stationery from Key West on November 18, 1946:

> *Dear Bess: This place is what I hoped it would be and what I was certain it would not be. I am in a house built on the southern plan, with galleries all around upstairs and down. It is the house of the commandant of the Submarine Base. They have no commandant at present, so I'm not "ranking" anyone out of his house.*
>
> *There is a salt water swimming pool a couple of blocks away and a sea beach a half mile away. I've made up a schedule to swim in the pool at eight in the morning, have breakfast at nine, rest a half hour and go to the beach at ten; stay there two hours and come back to the house and rest until one. Take my usual nap and then "work" from four until seven. Have dinner and a "social" evening until eleven, go to bed and do it over the next day. Maybe I'll go fishing a couple of mornings.*
>
> *I'm seeing no outsiders. I don't give a damn how put out they get. I'm doing as I damn please for the next two years and to hell with all of them.*
>
> *I've just now returned from the beach. It is perfect and so is the pool. Went there at eight and swam seven hundred and seventy feet. The pool is one hundred ten feet long so you can figure how many rounds I went. It looks as if my larynx is to clear up quickly.*
>
> *The only regret I have is that you are not here. If you and Margie were with me I'd be sure we were back in Biloxi. You know, I guess I'm a damn fool, but I'm happier when I can see you—even when you give me hell I'd rather have you around than not.*
>
> *Lots of love,*
>
>
> *Harry*

. . .

TRUMAN LIKED TO joke and pull a surprise now and then. Once he walked in on some soldiers in the shower, just to shake them up. He awakened another group before reveille at their barracks. He lined up at an enlisted men's tent for a chow line.

He had cards made up that he distributed to friends and staff. "Don't go away mad," the cards said, ". . . Just go away." When members of his entourage fell asleep on the beach, he had a bucket of ice water dumped on their heads.

His impish quality came through when reporter Robert Nixon was covering the president at Key West. It was about 7 A.M. one day when Nixon was awakened by a knock at his door at the temporary media center in the Bachelor Officers' Quarters. Standing there in his pajamas with a dazed look on his face, the reporter opened the door and found the president smiling broadly, with a couple of members of his staff. He teased Nixon for still being asleep that late in the morning.

In 1949, he made sure his plane arrived before the press corps' and he stood waiting for the reporters as they disembarked. With paper and pencil in hand, he asked them questions, reversing roles for a few minutes. He sometimes invited reporters to go swimming or boating with him.

HARRY TRUMAN'S RETREATS reflected his homespun tastes and lack of pretention. He was Middle American to the core, with a strong commitment to his family, his home state, and his duty as he saw it. His well-publicized trips to Independence and Key West solidified his reputation as the man whom correspondents nicknamed "Truman the Human."

———∞∞∞———

CHAPTER NINE

DWIGHT EISENHOWER AND GETTYSBURG, PENNSYLVANIA

D URING HIS MANY years of hopping from one Army post to another while he was a career soldier, Dwight Eisenhower and his wife, Mamie, never had a home of their own. As the result of her prodding, while he was president of Columbia University in 1950 they spent $40,000 to buy a run-down farm in an almost inaccessible part of Gettysburg, Pennsylvania, about 75 miles from Washington, D.C. They intended to retire there eventually. Not long after the purchase, however, Ike accepted President Truman's plea to take over as supreme Allied commander of NATO and left for Europe, postponing plans to restore the property.

But buying the land made perfect sense. Eisenhower had spent his early years on a farm in Kansas, and he was very familiar with agricultural life. He retained a lifelong interest in what he called soil conservation—ways to make land more productive. He once said, "I wanted to take a piece of ground . . . and try to restore it . . . and when I die I'm going to leave a piece of ground better than I found it."

Just as important, he felt a personal connection to the famous Civil War battlefield next to his farm. He always remembered with great pleasure the visit he and his graduating class at West Point had made to Gettysburg in 1915. He was haunted by the site. In 1918, Eisenhower, a newly married officer, had commanded a tank training unit at Camp Colt, near Gettysburg, as one of his early assignments in the Army, and he was reconnected to the area. In addition, he and Mamie very much liked the Pennsylvania countryside. In 1950, friends George and Mary Allen had bought a small farm in the Gettysburg area, and they recommended it to Ike.

The proximity of the battlefield appealed to Eisenhower as a military history buff and hero of World War II. Like the Civil War generals of Gettysburg, Ike had made life-or-death decisions affecting the outcome of a war when he planned and ordered the Allied landing at Normandy. During the years he owned the farm, he enjoyed taking visitors, including former British prime minister Winston Churchill and former British field marshal Bernard Montgomery, across the battlefield where Confederate general Robert E. Lee's second invasion of the North was stopped in its tracks, at a horrible cost to both sides.

The location had a mystical quality for the old general. "As I drive between farm and office," he once wrote, "as I sit here at my desk overlooking the road where thousands of retreating and pursuing troops poured through on a July afternoon in 1863, all about me are physical reminders that the history made here was an accumulation of little incidents, small contributions, minor braveries, and forgotten heroisms. I am in the path of the disordered Union troops of Howard's XI Corps, driven back by Ewell's Confederates coming in from north and east. In mind's eye, I can see the blue uniforms as they turned again and again in brief stands against the Confederates, many of them making good their escape to Cemetery Hill, a few hundred yards to the south, where two days later the Confederate tide would begin its long, protracted ebb into Lee's surrender at Appomattox and Johnston's at Durham's Station."

For her part, Mamie thought the house was quaint and the setting lovely. "[The farm] had three of the most wonderful trees in front and a great pine kitchen with a rocking chair and geraniums in the window," she observed. "Being a city girl, this all appealed to me. I just loved that place." It helped that her husband, although he was accustomed to the power of military command, deferred to her on virtually everything about the house, from its construction to its décor. He never could muster the energy or will to argue with her about it.

He valued the farm for another reason. Throughout most of his presidency, from 1953 to 1961, Gettysburg gave Ike a place to find the rest and relaxation he needed to escape the pressures of his job. After suffering a heart attack, he made the farm a sort of personal recuperation center, and this further strengthened his attachment to the place.

WHEN HE BOUGHT the 189-acre farm in 1950, two years before he was elected president, it contained several ramshackle buildings dating from the 18th and 19th centuries, along with 25 cows and 600 chickens. At Mamie's insistence, Eisenhower began to rebuild the old farmhouse in early 1953, just after he became president, but it wasn't until 1955 that the structure was ready for occupancy. It cost $250,000 to renovate the place, partly because Mamie often got a project going and changed her mind or hadn't anticipated problems along the way. Ike couldn't deal with her badgering, at one point telling the builder, Charles Tompkins, "For God's sake, just give her what she wants and send me the bill."

"Because he [the builder] had no prepared architectural plans," Ike wrote, "the house had to be built step by step, according to Mamie's ideas. Building this way, work frequently had to be redone. Mamie occasionally forgot a detail or two. For example, when the walls were going up, we discovered that no plans had been made for central air-conditioning. Part of the walls had to be torn down so that air ducts could be installed. We found that electric switches were not in the proper places. Other work had to be done over because of our improvised design. But the work was done well and the house, although not completely convenient, did conform largely to her ideas."

Another reason for the high cost was that Eisenhower agreed to use union labor. He once explained that as president he wanted to show respect for the labor movement and he thought it was only fair to use union workers for his personal projects. That meant bringing skilled tradesmen from Washington, D.C., since there were not many union workers available in the sparsely populated Gettysburg area. It also meant paying them for their travel time, a two-hour drive each way. Using these union workers added about $65,000 to the cost, according to the prime contractor.

When the house was finished, in 1955, the Eisenhowers invited the household staff from the White House to help them celebrate at a combined housewarming and party for their wedding anniversary. The butlers, maids, telephone operators, carpenters, plumbers, and other workers came to the party in two shifts so there was always a staff contingent on duty at the Executive Mansion that afternoon. It was a considerate and classy thing for the Eisenhowers to do, and the staff never forgot it.

EISENHOWER, LIKE WASHINGTON and Jefferson before him, retained a deep interest in his property throughout his presidency, particularly in attempting to improve, through careful breeding, the handful of Angus cattle he owned. He loved to show off his prize bulls. In some cases, he would climb into the corral with a huge bull and poke him in the rump with a shotgun until the animal stood up. Ike wanted visitors to see the bull's rump and he would point out that it would make fine beef for the table. Meanwhile, the president's Secret Service bodyguards would fidget and blanch, hoping the commander in chief would not get himself injured.

Initially, Ike was upset at the huge red barn that dominated the landscape, and he decided to have it repainted. President Eisenhower mixed the new color himself in a big pot and ended up with a light gray green that made the barn blend in with the countryside of rolling hills, pastures, and majestic trees.

Meanwhile, Mamie was busily moving furniture and beloved household items into the new place. She had complained often over the years that since she never had a home of her own during their married life, just about all their possessions had ended up in storage. Now was her chance to realize her dream, and she delighted in furnishing and decorating the new house according to her own eclectic taste, which leaned heavily toward things of sentimental value even if they didn't always fit together.

Her clothes—a vast collection of dresses, formal gowns, nightgowns, hats, gloves, and handbags—filled nearly all the sachet-scented closets of the second floor. Some were from fancy stores in New York and Europe; others were bought off the rack at Penney's. When she was criticized for wearing flowery halter-top dresses that seemed more fitting for a younger woman, she said, "I hate old-lady clothes and I shall never wear them." From all indications, Ike liked his wife's femininity and her old-fashioned ways.

"Despite Mamie's penchant for bargain hunting and visiting five-and-dime stores, she loved quality—fine antiques, rich silks and brocades, and the best china and sterling silver money could buy," recalled Susan Eisenhower, her granddaughter. "Bedsheets had to be linen or satin, never percale; nightgowns had to be silk, never nylon; and carpets had to be wool. . . . Even though my grandparents' home in Gettysburg was a farmhouse, it reflected Mamie's love of beautiful things as well as her appreciation for formality, which was belied by her breezy unpretentiousness. There was only one room that was austere and merely functional: my grandfather's nap and dressing room, just down a short hallway from the bedroom they shared. It was the one spot in the house that had been by-passed by Mamie's touch—a concession to their differences in both outlook and upbringing.

"Since Mamie treasured elegance, I always wondered how this pampered daughter of a wealthy Midwestern businessman had survived the rigors of the old army; how she had managed thirty-five moves in as many years."

IN ALL, IKE spent 365 days of his presidency at his Gettysburg farm over the span of six years, from 1955 to 1961, including a 38-day stretch when he was re-cuperating from the heart attack that he suffered while vacationing in Denver in September 1955. After spending seven weeks in a Colorado hospital, he moved to Gettysburg for an extended convalescence.

His frequent vacations rankled his opponents. In June 1956, Democratic Na-tional Committee chairman Paul M. Butler complained that Ike was a "part-time president" who spent too much time away from Washington: "We say that aside from his health, aside from his illness, the president has been absent from the White House more than any other president in the last 24 years."

But most Americans sympathized with Eisenhower's need to take it easy be-cause of his heart problems and believed the septuagenarian worked hard and de-served lots of time off.

After his near-death experience, he followed his doctors' advice very carefully to reduce stress as much as he could. "He realized how important it was to take time off to relax, for his health," says Carol Hegeman, senior historian at the Eisenhower National Historic Site in Gettysburg. His physicians kept careful watch on his condition; in the months after his first heart attack they took read-ings of his heart rate and blood pressure every few hours; his nutrition and sleep schedule were monitored; and all such information was recorded in medical di-aries. Ike would take walks every morning and use the trees along his driveway as markers of his progress. Each fir tree had been donated by a different state, and he would report back to Mamie how far he had gotten. When he got to Texas, the farthest from the house, "he had it made," Mamie recalled.

From then on, the Eisenhowers began spending most weekends and summer vacations at the farmhouse, often with grandchildren and other family members or friends staying in the main house with their hosts or in a guest cottage. Sometimes they combined trips to the farm with visits to Camp David, the official presidential retreat, which was only 20 miles away. Two members of the household staff at the farm actually lived at Camp David and commuted to Gettysburg each day the Eisenhowers were there. In fact, Ike made Camp David what author W. Dale Nelson called "an annex to Gettysburg."

And he needed the solace he found at both places. There was neither a great war nor an economic calamity, as had occurred during the Roosevelt and Truman eras, but the Cold War with the Soviet Union was a constant preoccupation, and the nation's domestic problems, such as racial frictions and debates on the fate of the New Deal, called for prudent, sound judgment, which the old military man provided. "The Eisenhower presidency was one of the most unusual in modern American history," writes historian David L. Stebenne. "Both Eisenhower himself and many of his top aides had no previous experience in public office. Even more atypical, he and they had spent most of their adult lives rising to the top in other fields of endeavor, most notably the military, business, law, and education. In no other twentieth-century presidential administration did the professional politician enjoy less prestige and influence. Despite, or perhaps because of, those circumstances, Eisenhower's presidency was highly competent, effective, and successful, the most so of any presidency since World War II."

ONE ENTERED IKE'S world at Gettysburg through a small foyer and immediately encountered a large glass-enclosed display case that gave guests a sense of the Eisenhowers' down-to-earth tastes. Inside the case was part of Mamie's vast collection of knickknacks and figurines, including tiny statues of American presidents and First Ladies (including Ike and Mamie) that were available as prizes in boxes of breakfast cereal.

Adjacent to the foyer was a formal living room featuring a piano, the top of which was cluttered with family pictures. Ike would occasionally sit at the keyboard and bang out West Point Army songs. In addition, there was a circular sofa that had captured Mamie's eye, but it wasn't very practical and made for an awkward conversational grouping. Some of the people who sat there found that they had their backs to each other.

Nearby was a low-lying coffee table given to Mamie as a gift from Syngman Rhee, the leader of South Korea, made of black lacquer with inlaid mother-of-pearl. Near the marble fireplace was a costly rug given as gift to President Eisenhower by the Shah of Iran (whom Ike had helped stay in power). Over the mantel of the oval fireplace was a large painting of Prague, a gift from the residents of that city in recognition of Ike's armies liberating Europe from the Nazis. Even more cabinets were filled with still more of Mamie's figurines, many made of porcelain and most given to her as presents.

Family photos were everywhere. Pictures of Ike as a young man in uniform. Pictures of the family together in various spots around the country. Pictures of Mamie as a girl in Denver. Pictures of her children, grandchildren, the children of friends and staff members. She kept a West Point photo of her husband on her dressing table amid the perfume bottles, lipsticks, and other cosmetics. He had written on the photo, "For the dearest and sweetest girl in the world."

The living room, decorated by Mamie, was too formal for Ike, with heavy curtains and plush furniture, so it became an elegant if cluttered repository for her belongings, including even more of her figurines and knickknacks.

The room where Ike (and, eventually, Mamie) spent most of his time was a glass-enclosed porch out back with a gorgeous view of Seminary Ridge to the east. It was behind this ridge, all along the tree line, where, as every student of military history such as Ike knew, the Confederates massed their infantry in 1863 for their ill-fated attack, known as Pickett's Charge, on the Union forces at Cemetery Ridge.

The rectangular room could be protected from the sun with a set of white drapes that could be drawn the length of the room. Around a rectangular table were five plush beige swivel chairs, and a couch stood in the center of the room.

Ike and Mamie would spend much of each morning here after breakfast. Ike would paint portraits and outdoor scenes with an easel and palette he kept in the center of the room near the big picture windows, while Mamie played solitaire, read, or watched television. She loved the soap operas. He loved the light that filled the room from the east each morning, facilitating his painting.

Ike had taken up painting as a hobby in 1948, when he was president of Columbia University in New York. It relaxed him, reduced his stress, and helped him to ruminate, and he kept up the hobby for the rest of his life, during which he completed 300 paintings. He gave nearly all of them to family and friends, although he displayed a number of them at his home.

He once described himself as a messy but enthusiastic painter:

> *My hands are better suited to an ax handle than a tiny brush. I attempt only simple compositions. My frustration is complete when I try for anything delicate. Even yet I refuse to refer to my productions as paintings. They are daubs, born of my love of color and in my pleasure in experimenting, nothing else. I destroy two out of each three I start. One of the real satisfactions is finding out how closely I come to depicting what I have in mind—and many times I want to see what I am going to do and never know what it will be.*
>
> *In spite of this, I have frequently wished for more daylight hours to paint. Its only defect is that it provides no exercise. I've often thought what a wonderful thing it would be to install a compact painting outfit on a golf cart.*
>
> *In the White House, in bad weather, painting was one way to survive away from the desk. In a little room off the elevator on the second floor, hardly more than a closet, the easel, paints, and canvases were easy to use. Often, going to lunch, I'd stop off for ten minutes to paint. In Gettysburg, I've tried many landscapes and still lifes but with magnificent audacity, I have tried more portraits than anything else. I've also burned more portraits than anything else.*

Ike would meet with his advisers on the porch to write speeches, and discuss issues ranging from the budget to East-West relations. And this is where the First Couple would often eat their dinners off tray tables in front of the TV, where they watched hit shows of the fifties, especially the Westerns, such as *Gunsmoke*, that Ike favored.

One of their favorite activities was playing cards. Mamie would sit at a table with her lady friends on the south side of the porch, playing canasta or Bolivia, and Ike would play bridge with his male pals on the north side. The president was so competitive he would regularly complain when a partner made a wrong move.

Ike had a putting green installed a few yards from the house to indulge his passion for golf, and over the years it contained from one to six holes. In addition to playing golf as often as he could at local country clubs, part of Ike's routine was to get out on the putting green in the morning and afternoon to work on his game.

When they had dinner guests, the Eisenhowers would have cocktails on the porch. Ike enjoyed Johnnie Walker scotch; Mamie, a Manhattan. Mamie would strictly limit the time for pre-dinner drinks so no one would have time for more than one. She hated it when people drank too much, so she didn't give them a chance.

At 7 P.M., they had dinner in their formal dining room, which featured a bright red rug and eight red chairs around a long rectangular table under a big chandelier. Ike sat at the head of the table and would take pride in carving the customary roasts himself. It was a skill he had learned at West Point, at a time when the social graces were taught there so future officers would also be gentlemen. After his heart attack, however, he had to limit his portions of red meat to lower his cholesterol. From then on, he would still carve the beef for his guests, but as he piled their plates high, he sometimes looked longingly at their large portions while he had to content himself with only a few modest slices.

He also loved lamb shanks as prepared by his cook, Dolores Moaney (wife of his personal assistant, Army Sgt. John Moaney, both of them African American), but had to limit his consumption of them as well. On some occasions, he ate chicken while his guests had the heartier fare. The Eisenhowers would sometimes serve wine with dinner, but they preferred cocktails, as did many men and women of the World War II generation.

Another of Ike's favorite haunts was a den on the lower level, a dark, wood-paneled room with a huge fireplace and four exposed wooden beams in the ceiling, and a bathroom with shower. After his heart attack, the president would take naps in the den or in a small bedroom on the second floor immediately following lunch.

He had about a thousand books throughout the house, among them *A History of Western Art* by John Ives Sewall; *Gray Fox* by Burke Davis; *Mr. Lincoln's Army* and *A Stillness at Appomattox*, both by Bruce Catton; various Western novels by Zane Grey and Louis L'Amour; *Order of Battle Maps, Operations in Italy, Volume II*; and several copies of the Bible.

Sometimes Ike would go hunting for quail and pheasant that were raised on his property. He honed his skills by shooting skeet on a range he had set up near the main house. (He liked to fish for trout, but preferred Camp David to the Gettysburg area for that activity.)

OTHER PRESIDENTS MAY have talked politics in their free time, but not Ike. Mamie wouldn't hear of it. She told friends that one of her duties was to make sure her husband left work behind as soon as he walked in the front door, whether he was a soldier, a college president, or president of the United States. "He never brought his work home," she once said. "When he came home to me, he came home. So many people say to me, didn't you know thus-and-so, I said why no, because he never discussed his business at home. So when he came home here, we had fun."

Their conversations would center on their family, conditions on the farm, and other mundane topics—not what Mamie called "his business." Ike liked it that way, too.

Unlike other First Couples, the Eisenhowers shared the same bed, although they had separate dressing rooms. Their daily habits were much different from each other. Ike would get up early, about 6 A.M., and start his day. (He would be in bed by 9 each night.) Mamie would remain in bed and write letters or do paperwork while propped up on pillows for much of each morning.

He would tend to meetings with staff, sometimes at an office he kept at the local post office, but he tried to keep his schedule at Gettysburg light.

If the grandchildren were around, he would supervise them riding their horses and ponies (including Tony the Pony, Sporty Miss, and Doodle-e-doo). The president would occasionally take a ride himself but he wasn't an avid horseman, especially after his heart attack, when the doctors advised him against vigorous riding.

Eisenhower also enjoyed cooking. He liked to barbecue foods when he had guests in good weather, and sometimes spent hours preparing a vegetable soup, slicing carrots, chopping up okra, celery, and cabbage, and boiling up chicken stock. He even published the recipe in his 1967 memoir, *At Ease: Stories I Tell to Friends*. He once told Pat Nixon, wife of Richard Nixon, his vice president, that one of the few things he could start and see completed in a short time was the food he cooked—in contrast to his job, in which problems never seemed to get resolved easily.

He relished grilling steak on the barbecue behind the sun porch (he liked his meat rare) and concocting a special sauce made of mustard, pepper, and salt. Ike taught the male members of his family his grilling secrets, and when he considered them ready, he let them wear a cook's hat and apron. David Eisenhower, his grandson, called it a "status symbol" and a "ritual" that certified "male Eisenhowers" in the president's eyes, entitling them to "the choice pieces of beef." Ike was very proud of the quality of beef he raised, and enjoyed showing it off. Once he made the mistake of announcing to his family that they were eating a cow known as Number 9. It turned out that his granddaughter Susan had taken a liking to the animal, and she was shocked and heartbroken.

EISENHOWER HAD SOME important guests. One was Prime Minister Jawaharlal Nehru of India, in December 1956, who stayed in a second-floor guest room just down the hall from the Eisenhowers' bedroom. Other guests included West German chancellor Konrad Adenauer, in May 1957; British prime minister Harold Macmillan, in March 1959; and former British prime minister Winston Churchill, in May 1959. Vice President Richard Nixon visited on several occasions.

When showing Field Marshal Bernard Montgomery around the battlefield on one occasion, Ike said if one of his subordinates ordered the kind of head-on attack known as Pickett's Charge, he would have sacked him. This made the newspapers and caused a fuss in the South, where leaders saw him as criticizing Robert E. Lee.

But the most important guest of all was Soviet premier Nikita Khrushchev. Ike took him on an impromptu visit to the farm from Camp David for 75 minutes on September 29, 1959. The president and the premier sat on the plush swivel chairs on the enclosed porch and talked about East-West relations, especially the status of Germany and the divided city of Berlin. Khruschchev complained about the tremendous costs of national defense, and repeatedly emphasized the importance of disarmament. Eisenhower said Khrushchev must work harder to lower tensions with the West over Berlin.

At one point, Eisenhower had his grandchildren come in to meet the Soviet leader, and Khrushchev dropped all his bluster and struck Ike and his advisers as quite "grandfatherly." He translated the names of the kids into Russian, invited them to the Soviet Union, and seemed to delight in the opportunity to show his humanity.

David Eisenhower, the president's 11-year-old grandson, was so taken that he told his sixth-grade classmates the next day: "If I didn't know better I'd be a communist because Nikita Khrushchev was such a nice guy." The story made the newspapers and caused no small amount of embarrassment for the First Family.

Khrushchev also enjoyed the tour Ike gave him of the president's prize Angus cattle, and Ike even gave him a heifer as a gift.

But this cordiality was short-lived.

On May 7, 1960, Eisenhower took an encrypted call on the black phone in the small office on the ground floor of his farmhouse. It was General Andrew Goodpaster, the White House staff secretary, with word that Khrushchev had the wreckage of a U-2 American spy plane that the Soviets had shot down over their country—and the pilot was in Soviet custody.

This soured East-West relations for the rest of Eisenhower's presidency.

IKE USED HIS retreat as a personal recuperation center. As one of the oldest men to serve as president, his health deteriorated after he took office and he needed frequent breaks to pace himself and get away from the pressures of the White House. Gettysburg, with its proximity to Washington and serene rural setting, gave him the perfect escape. Gettysburg also provided Eisenhower with proximity to one of America's most sacred battlefields, and he never lost his attachment to its symbolism. He was criticized for allegedly lax work habits and for taking too many vacations there, but few Americans seemed concerned by the popular old soldier's frequent absences from the West Wing.

— ∞ —

CHAPTER TEN

JOHN F. KENNEDY AND HYANNISPORT, MASSACHUSETTS

AMERICANS STILL PICTURE John F. Kennedy as the iconic leader of a modern Camelot, the embodiment of power, glamour, hope, and optimism in a dangerous age. The reality of his presidency was less impressive.

"His was an administration short on practical accomplishments," writes historian Michael Kazin. "At the time of his assassination, the president had signed no major piece of domestic legislation and had failed to achieve his main foreign policy objective—turning back the tide of Communist-led revolutions in the developing world. He was still favored to win reelection, but racial tensions that would soon rend the Democratic party were already beginning to cut into his approval rating."

These critiques all but vanished with Kennedy's shocking death on November 22, 1963. The murder elevated JFK to heroic stature in the popular imagination, and he has remained there ever since. "Jack Kennedy subscribed to the 'great man' theory of history," says Sally Bedell Smith, one of his many admiring biographers, "and the White House that he and Jackie [his wife] presided over was a microcosm of that concept, filled with lively, smart, strikingly young, and strong-willed individuals who pushed ideas and policies, rather than being swept along by them. The Kennedys and their circle set out ambitiously, almost grandiosely, to create an America in their own image and according to their own tastes. To a remarkable degree they succeeded, leaving behind a more assertive nation, infused with a vision and an aesthetic that found its inspiration in Jeffersonian ideals. . . . In the process, they cast aside the bland exertions of the 1950s, and set America on a higher path that combined the sophistication of the Old World and the vitality and power of the New. They were special people who intersected at a special time, a time when nothing seemed impossible."

IN PRIVATE, KENNEDY was smart, vigorous, and egotistical, infused with an almost royalist sense of entitlement. All of this was very much in evidence in his behavior at his various retreats. He traveled to the family compound at Hyannisport, Massachusetts, as often as he could during his thousand-day presidency, with an extended stay each summer. He also spent considerable amounts of time at a leased estate at Glen Ora in Middleburg, Virginia, which was later supplanted by Camp David when the lease ran out, and at his father's estate in Palm Beach, Florida.

Jackie and their two children went to Hyannisport full-time for most of each summer while Jack commuted from the White House. This was the same pattern used by Bess Truman more than a decade earlier when she fled Washington for Independence, Missouri, and Harry stayed behind. And like Bess's, Jackie's frequent absences were little remarked upon in the press. Scrutiny of the private lives of public officials was much less rigorous and intrusive than it is today. It turned out that she had a low tolerance for her official duties and felt the need to escape the Washington scene. She was, after all, only 31 when she became First Lady.

Mrs. Kennedy particularly liked the weekdays at Hyannisport when Jack was back in the White House. She used the leisurely atmosphere to read books, mostly light fiction but occasionally a heavier volume such as *Democracy*, Henry Adams's novel about Washington, which she enjoyed. She went sunbathing, did some painting as she listened to chamber music, and of course went to the beach and played with her children. Sometimes she slipped out of Hyannisport to have dinner with friends in Boston or to catch a show there or in nearby Provincetown.

The president made the 90-minute flight to Hyannisport from Washington for a long weekend every month or so in the warmer months, and sometimes more frequently, arriving on Friday afternoon or evening, and returning to Washington Monday morning.

It wasn't the only place Kennedy had roots. His father had bought property in West Palm Beach, Florida, in 1933, and it became customary for the family to gather there at Christmas and New Year's, Easter, and on other occasions. Kennedy observed this tradition during his presidency. In the 1940s, his father got into a routine of going there from Thanksgiving to Memorial Day, then to Cape Cod for the other half of the year.

Kennedy also spent considerable time at Camp David, especially in late March or April (1962 and 1963), when the Catoctin Mountains move beautifully into the lushness of spring, and again in the lovely fall season. His rented property at Glen Ora was where General Robert E. Lee had set up headquarters during one of his Civil War campaigns and which had developed into horse country for the rich. Kennedy built a hilltop retreat there, at a spot called Rattlesnake Mountain, during the winter of 1962. Jackie used it to ride horses, but the president couldn't find the time to visit the property until October 1963, just before he died.

BUT HIS ROOTS in Hyannisport ran deepest of all. Kennedy had spent the summers of his boyhood there, had loved the place all his life, and wanted his children to use it far into the future.

"Hyannisport really is the Kennedy homestead," Senator Edward Kennedy, the late president's brother, told me. "It is the place where all of my brothers and sisters grew up and it's where we formed, really, the family unit but also where we really developed as individuals. And [it's] where we got the great sense of love and support from our parents and the sense of faith that they had, and the sense of fun and joy of life and the sense of competition which was always present in different forms and shapes, and also the sort of challenge of excelling which was an important force in all of our lives. High standards were set. . . .

"I always thought for President Kennedy the attachment was particularly close at Hyannisport. I think as a young person, he was very close to the sea and was a great swimmer, sailed. . . . So the sea was enormously important to him . . . and then he fought on it [in World War II as a PT boat commander in the South Pacific] and I think he returned to it as a way of reattaching himself to his roots as well as having the time to contemplate and to sort of meditate.

"And I think he understood that the sea was almost a metaphor for life," Senator Kennedy continued. "I mean, he saw the sunshine on it and also the storms that came with it. And I think he had a very, very deep attachment. I mean, one of my favorite quotes of President Kennedy . . . which he made up in Newport when he went up to watch the America's Cup race [was when] he pointed out that we have the same amount of salt in our blood and in our sweat and in our tears as there is in the water, and when we go back to the sea, we go back to whence we came."

Discussing the area's broader history, author Theodore White wrote in 1960, "Hyannisport is the name of a hundred-odd cottages and summer homes that sprawl along the edges of Nantucket Sound just west and adjacent to the village of Hyannis (population not quite 6,000), which is part of Barnstable Township, county seat of Barnstable County, and summer center of the most fashionable area of Cape Cod's summer season. The houses are large and roomy, clapboard and shingle, white and brown, separated from one another across well-tended lawns by hedges or New England stone walls. . . . For generations the good families of Boston had built these homes for solid comfort; the Kennedys, thirty-two years ago [in 1928], were the first of the Irish to invade its quiet. A large compound encloses a number of homes at the end of Scudder Avenue where it reaches to the water; there Joseph P. Kennedy had bought a seventeen-room house to shelter his amazing brood of children. As the years passed, his son Jack had bought another house within the same compound, a few hundred feet away; and a few years later another son, Bobby, had acquired a third. Together the three houses form a triangle on a smooth green lawn that runs off into the dune grass before plunging to the sands of the beach."

Many of the Kennedys' neighbors were displeased that their community had been overrun with snarls of reporters, advisers, and curiosity seekers who clogged the once tranquil streets. Gradually, as the president's mystique grew, most of them got used to it.

KENNEDY PLANNED HIS presidential campaign in Hyannisport. On October 28, 1959, he gathered his loyal lieutenants in the living room of Bobby's house (which would be his command center on Election Day, 1960). There, as they sat on the yellow and green lounge chairs and several easy chairs, they reviewed each state individually to set up his political organization, all hidden from the view of the press and the public. It all seemed quite preposterous to outsiders. Kennedy was only 42 years old at the time, had never emerged as a real leader in the Senate, and was a Roman Catholic in a Protestant-majority nation. Just as important, he was aiming to supplant the ruling Republicans in a country that had been at peace and enjoying relative prosperity during Dwight Eisenhower's eight years as president.

Using brilliant political tactics and a natural charisma that radiated from his good looks—he was a telegenic six-footer who weighed a trim 165 pounds and struck many women as a matinee idol—he won the Democratic nomination in Los Angeles in July 1960. He returned to Hyannisport to rejuvenate himself in a pattern he followed after stressful periods throughout his life. He got plenty of rest, went swimming, cruised on his family's yacht, took sunbaths on lawn chairs, sipped cocktails in the sun, and plotted the general-election campaign at his leisure. Jackie needed the rest, too, since she was five months pregnant.

He found that Hyannisport had changed dramatically, even more than he expected. "It looked more like a town under military occupation, or a place where dangerous criminals or wild beasts were at large," recalled Arthur Schlesinger, Jr., an historian and Kennedy adviser. "Everywhere were roadblocks, cordons of policemen, photographers with cameras slung over their shoulders . . . tourists in flashy shirts and shorts waiting expectantly as if for a revelation. The atmosphere of a carnival or a hanging prevailed. . . . A stockade now half surrounded the Kennedy compound, and the approach was like crossing a frontier, with documents demanded every ten feet."

But he put up with the security—which would ease at his insistence when he finally won the White House—and after his period of R & R, threw himself into planning for the campaign. He quickly began a series of meetings with Bobby, his brother and campaign manager, and aides including Larry O'Brien, Ken O'Donnell, Dave Powers, Pierre Salinger, and Ted Sorensen. This was the brain trust that would see him through to victory and enter the White House with him the following January.

AFTER VOTING EARLY on Election Day, November 8, 1960, in the Third Precinct, Sixth Ward of Boston, which included his voting residence at 122 Bowdoin Street, Kennedy entered his motorcade and drove to the airport, then flew to Hyannisport with his family. After the 25-minute flight, accompanied by 100 reporters and 80 staff members in other planes, he made his way to his family compound. He had breakfast at his father's house, across the lawn from his own home, with family members including his wife, Jackie, his parents, brother Robert and sister-in-law Ethel, brother Edward and sister-in-law Joan, and brother-in-law

Peter Lawford. Later that day, other family members would arrive to be with him as he followed the returns.

He walked to his personal cottage to unwind and sat on the porch in the sun, still wearing his overcoat against the cold November air. A newspaper plane buzzed the house, swooping to within 200 feet of the porch, to get his picture. If he won, the Secret Service and the military would never allow such a thing to happen again. Neighbors had a horseshoe of red roses sent to him and it was passed to a guard and then presented to him without inspection, another security lapse.

He was exhausted but filled with nervous energy. At different points that afternoon, as America voted, he chatted privately with his father, threw a football around with his brothers, Bobby and Ted, had lunch alone with his wife, and gave a sack of toys to his three-year-old daughter, Caroline. It included a huge teddy bear almost as big as the girl herself. Finally, he managed a nap.

He got up about 5 P.M. and strolled to the sunroom of Bobby's cottage, where a command center had been set up that included 30 telephones, four wire-service teletype machines, and other facilities to receive and compute the returns from around the country. For the rest of that long night, Kennedy, dressed in a tweed jacket, white shirt, tan trousers, green necktie, and white wool socks—he had expected photographers to take his picture in victory—would walk back and forth across the lawn between his house and his brother's several times to assess one of the closest elections in the nation's history. Jackie mostly stayed away from the male-dominated nerve center and kept track of the results in the cozy white-and-yellow living room of JFK's three-bedroom home, surrounded by watercolors and sketches of family and friends.

At one point, when returns from Philadelphia gave him a huge margin there, he lit up a Havana Royal panatela cigar. It was premature. Things did not go well in many other areas of the country, where Republican Richard Nixon was doing far better than the Kennedy strategists had expected. At 10:30 P.M., Jackie thought the returns looked promising again and she used a pet name in addressing her husband. "Oh, Bunny, you're president now," she cooed. "No," he said tersely. "It's too early yet."

At 4 A.M., Kennedy went to bed, as did most of his staff. (As with most aristocratic couples of the era, the Kennedys had separate bedrooms.) At 9:30 A.M., sitting on his bed in white pajamas, he learned from aide Ted Sorensen that he had indeed been elected the 34th president of the United States.

Later that day, 31-year-old Jackie, eight months pregnant and wearing a rain-coat clutched to her chest to ward off the autumn cold, went for a solitary walk on the beach, pondering her new life. The 43-year-old president-elect, eager to have a family photo taken in victory, set out across the dunes to bring her home. When they returned to the living room of his parents' 17-room white clapboard house, the assembled family members burst into a round of applause.

KENNEDY MADE HIS first trip back to Hyannisport as president on Saturday night, May 27, 1961, four months after his inauguration.

It was raining hard, and the new commander in chief, traveling without the First Lady, was running late as *Air Force One* lifted off from Washington. Joseph Kennedy, his father, was impatient as he waited at the family compound. "He's the President of the United States!" the elder Kennedy complained. "You'd think he could at least order somebody to make a telephone call and tell his family what goddamn time he'll be home!" As a bawdy joke, the president's father "had spread pictures of voluptuous women all over the President's bedroom," reports historian Michael Beschloss.

The next morning, JFK wrapped himself in a gray blanket and shuffled out of his father's house on crutches. His chronic back pain, which he was keeping secret from the country, was growing worse. He sat on a lawn chair in the chilly fog and read briefing papers on his upcoming summit meeting with Soviet leader Nikita Khrushchev. That encounter, scheduled to begin a few days later in Vienna, weighed heavily on his mind.

Before leaving Hyannisport on Monday afternoon, the president told his father he didn't have a cent of money with him, and Joseph Kennedy sent a secretary for a stack of large bills from his private stash upstairs. "I'll get this back to you, Dad," the president said as he took the money. Watching his son walk down the front steps, old Joe said quietly, "That'll be the day."

The summit with Khrushchev went badly, with the Soviet leader taking his youthful adversary's measure and finding him immature and weak. The new president was shocked and demoralized by Khrushchev's intransigence and belligerence. An added problem was that the pressures of the summit aggravated the chronic pain in Kennedy's back, a lifelong affliction. He got some relief from injections of procaine, an anesthetic, two or three times a day from Dr. Janet Travell, his private physician.

On Thursday, June 8, he flew to Palm Beach to unwind at the vacant home of friend Charles Wrightsman. He wanted privacy even from his father. "He slept late and lounged in his pajamas, hobbling on crutches to the heated saltwater pool," says Beschloss. "In the evening, he entertained friends and several of the White House secretaries with daiquiris and Frank Sinatra records on the phonograph." The atmosphere was a bit bizarre because the house had been closed for the hot summer season and much of the furniture was cloaked in dust covers.

Despite the respite, his back condition remained debilitating. When he left for Washington, he had to use crutches again and have himself carried to *Air Force One* on a hydraulic lift. He was unable to walk up the stairs. When he got back to the White House, his doctors ordered him to stay in his bed with a heating pad. He told advisers that the United States might soon be "very close to war" with the U.S.S.R. over Berlin, a city divided between the U.S.S.R. and the West.

THE ISSUE OF West Berlin—which the Soviets were threatening to seize— was a central problem of Kennedy's presidency, and it seemed always to preoccupy him, even at his retreats. In early July 1961, for example, he joined his wife and several key advisers, including Defense Secretary Robert McNamara and Secretary of State Dean Rusk, for lunch on his father's yacht, *Marlin*, for the kind of afternoon maritime expedition he loved. Wearing a beige tweed jacket and chinos, the president took his customary position at the fantail of the boat and talked again about Berlin over fish chowder and hot dogs.

The First Lady slipped into the water to ski, and as McNamara and General Maxwell Taylor took a swim, Kennedy complained to Rusk that the State Department still hadn't given him an adequate response to Khrushchev's hard line a month earlier in Vienna. Rusk said he was trying to clear the text with U.S. allies and he didn't want the Soviets to pounce on any wording to create fissures within the Western alliance. Kennedy pushed harder, and said the United States was responsible for Berlin, not its allies, and he didn't want to be given a choice between what he called "holocaust or humiliation." When McNamara and Taylor came back on board, Kennedy gave Rusk ten more days to submit a plan for negotiations to reduce tensions over Berlin, and gave McNamara ten days to submit a plan for non-nuclear resistance in case a military conflict broke out. He was obviously playing for time.

Kennedy didn't have many qualms about discussing such sensitive matters at his Hyannisport compound. His military advisers and the Secret Service told him it would be nearly impossible for the Soviets to eavesdrop on personal conversations there, and he also had secure communication by telephone from the estate. It was a different story when he was on the water. Talking by phone from the yachts might be overheard, so he rarely did it. He knew that Soviet trawlers outside the 12-mile territorial limit would try to listen in on any conversations between the vessels and the military command post at Hyannisport.

During still another weekend at Hyannisport that August, national security adviser McGeorge Bundy gave the president a "checklist of the actions that you are obligated to take if and when you contemplate a decision on the use of nuclear weapons." If he was at his summer home, the memo said, he was to be taken to the new secret presidential fallout shelter on Nantucket Island built under a submarine surveillance base and disguised by the Navy as a "jet assist takeoff fuel bottle storage area."

ON NOVEMBER 24, 1961, Kennedy met with key advisers, including McNamara and Attorney General Robert Kennedy, his brother and chief troubleshooter, in the living room of his father's house at Hyannisport. Bobby had been outside playing touch football with his sisters and some of his cousins, and was wearing a red jumpsuit. The president was to give an interview the next day to Alexei Adzhubei, Khrushchev's son-in-law, which was to be published in *Izvestia*, a Soviet newspaper, and he wanted a briefing on nuclear deterrence.

McNamara said the ability to destroy 20 to 50 percent of Soviet society would be enough to deter an attack on the United States. He said this would require about 400 one-megaton bombs. But other advisers pointed out that there was a strong feeling on Capitol Hill in favor of a bigger buildup, especially since Kennedy had made the "missile gap" a big campaign issue in 1960. McNamara agreed that the administration would be pilloried as weak if Kennedy proposed a missile force of less than one thousand. Adviser Ted Sorensen argued, however, that a thousand missiles would accelerate the arms race with Moscow. Responding to the congressional dynamic, Kennedy chose the politically safe course and decided on a thousand.

The next day, November 25, Adzhubei and Georgi Bolshakov, a "journalist" and Soviet military intelligence agent with a direct line to Khruschchev, met with Kennedy in the sunny living room of the president's house. Jackie introduced the

Russians to Caroline and John. Adzhubei gave them a doll weighted down at the base, which he described as "like the Russian people—you can keep pushing it down but it will always come up."

Kennedy sat in his rocking chair, sipping coffee, and his guests sat on a sofa across from him. What the Soviets didn't know for sure but certainly suspected was that the president was having the conversation secretly taped. The Secret Service's Protective Research Unit had equipped his living room (as well as the White House library, Cabinet Room, Oval Office, and presidential bedroom) for sound. Kennedy apparently wanted the system to make sure there were no misunderstandings or misquotes of what he said in highly sensitive conversations such as the one with the Soviets, but he also wanted to have ammunition to use against his adversaries in case the substance of such meetings became controversial.

The November 25 session did little except illustrate how far apart the two sides were, and how dangerous the world had become. Despite each side's claim to want peace, Kennedy argued that the "great threat to peace" was the Kremlin's "effort to push outward the Communist system, onto country after country." Adzhubei replied that the capitalist world had opposed the Soviet Union since the Bolsheviks came to power, in effect blaming the West for the confrontational atmosphere.

Afterward, Kennedy took him for a walk to the oceanfront in the frigid air, and both began shivering. The president had more than the weather on his mind. "When Stalin and Churchill and Roosevelt gained their victory, they were already very old men. . . . The world was very mixed up when they found it, and they didn't want to straighten it out. They couldn't. . . . But if there's a chance for us to do it now, we should do it. Otherwise in twenty years it'll be a world that we can't undo."

SUCH PROFOUNDLY SERIOUS conversations were not uncommon at Hyannisport, but Kennedy really went there for escape, and he was, as a rule, a lot looser and more relaxed than he was virtually anywhere else. For one thing, even as president he had considerable freedom to move about the community, a refreshing change in his routine. He left his family compound regularly to go on short drives or to visit a candy store in town with his kids, Caroline and John Jr., sometimes holding hands with them. The Secret Service accompanied him, of course, but they didn't cordon him off from bystanders. Even when he was sailing, his bodyguards and Coast Guardsmen kept a discreet distance in their own vessels. "It wasn't the intensity then that there is now, or the intrusiveness," Edward Kennedy told me.

Kennedy's lifestyle was worthy of the lord of a manor. His family wealth was immense, and he thoroughly enjoyed being a member of the upper class. During his frequent trips aboard the family yacht, he would sit in the stern, reading a newspaper, smoking a cigar, wearing an open-necked shirt, casual pants, and cool shades. Generally a few friends were along to keep him company, often World War II buddy Paul "Red" Fay or journalist Ben Bradlee and their wives, who would sit with Jackie and chitchat while the men lavished their attention on Jack. Stewards prepared and served his meals while he relaxed in the breeze. In the background, Secret Service and Coast Guard boats provided security, but frequently pleasure boats came into view and were allowed within surprising proximity to the First Family.

Home movies filmed at JFK's request by White House photographers present a fascinating video record of life at Hyannisport and the other Kennedy retreats—a life that the public and the media never were privy to. Caroline and John Jr. had all the privileges of the upper class, not a surprise given the lineage of their parents, and that included ponies, nannies, yachts, and mountains of toys.

Kennedy showed abundant affection for Caroline and John Jr., two sweet and loving children, but he rarely showed overt affection for Jacqueline. Almost completely absent were hugs, hand-holding, or even a peck on the cheek. She emerged as a devoted mother and a gorgeous but somewhat aloof wife, he as a doting father but remote husband. Perhaps Kennedy simply shunned public displays of affection, as did many men of his age and upbringing. Perhaps Jackie was quietly simmering at the many rumors of her husband's affairs. Whatever the reason, the Kennedys seemed to take each other's presence for granted and paid far more attention to other members of their family and their friends and guests.

The president would greet his children happily when they ran up to him after his helicopter arrived, and he would cavort with them in the swimming pool or as they splashed in the Atlantic after jumping over the side of his yacht under the supervision of his Secret Service bodyguards. Kennedy apparently didn't roughhouse with the kids; his bad back prevented that, according to family members and friends. But there always seemed to be burly friends, aides, and bodyguards around to toss the kids up in the air, lift them up to mount their ponies, and teach them swimming and other sports.

The president would send word that there would be a softball game for the local children at 3 P.M. when he was there on weekends, and even the toddlers would be included, along with Caroline and John.

He was creative in inventing games he could play with his kids. On some mornings, he would walk down to the beach with his two children carrying a three-foot toy sailboat, which he would allow to float out to sea. Then he and the kids would return to the house, change into their bathing suits, and board a real sailboat, sometimes an hour or two later. The challenge was to find the toy sailboat bobbing somewhere along the coast. Kennedy was an expert on the tides and the winds, and he always could predict where the small vessel would be, but his kids delighted in the adventure. And the president would subtly teach them about sailing and the patterns of the local waters.

He told John and Caroline about a whale that frequented the area which would eat stray socks. While sailing, he would suddenly reach over and pull off the socks of whichever of his children was wearing them, and throw them overboard. The kids would peer into the water looking for the whale. They never saw it, but they would have another story to tell their friends about being on the high seas with their father.

President Kennedy had a knack for skipping stones on the water, and his kids loved to imitate him. When they got frustrated with the stone skipping, he would collect scallop shells, which he called "floaties," and help the children float each shell on the water. The game was to see whose floatie stayed up the longest, and even the smallest children could play. Finally, he would catch blowfish and instruct his kids on how to tickle their tummies so they would puff up.

There is one memorable scene of JFK captured on silent film that shows not only the lax security in those days, but also the casual, private side of the young president and his attention to his children. He is wearing slacks and a gray sweater, and walks toward a candy store in the town of Hyannisport with John Jr. in tow. As they approach, an elderly woman steps up to the president and apparently introduces herself. He shakes her hand amiably and goes into the store. His bodyguards are nowhere to be seen. And although they were probably just out of camera range, the proximity of the elderly woman and other bystanders and the cars moving down the street, only a few feet from the commander in chief, would never be allowed by the Secret Service today.

When Kennedy leaves the store, he is holding the tiny hand of John Jr. with his left hand and a pink teddy bear in his right. At this point, a lone blank-faced bodyguard is visible a few steps behind him—not the sunglasses-wearing, grim-faced, menacing-looking squad of Secret Service agents who surround the president today.

The president and his son walk past a car that has apparently stopped to let the commander in chief pass, and bystanders are visible a few feet away. Kennedy slides behind the wheel of his big pink Lincoln convertible and settles into the red upholstery, with pal Red Fay in the passenger seat and "John-John" [John Jr.'s nickname] standing in the back (seat belts were virtually unknown in those days). Fay blows bubbles from a plastic jar of soapy liquid, to John Jr.'s delight.

The president dutifully halts the car at a stop sign and lets the traffic go by. Meanwhile, a young girl walks along a path two feet from the vehicle, ignores the president, and waves to someone in another car. After a few moments, the intersection clears and Kennedy guns the engine with a grin and turns left, demonstrating that the Secret Service's idea of a motorcade was rather lackadaisical in that era.

Later in his presidency, however, the Secret Service prevailed upon Kennedy to be more careful, and he began to feel a lack of privacy on his family estate, which was viewable to passing motorists and pedestrians. So in 1962, he rented a seven-bedroom home from tenor Morton Downey, a wealthy friend, on Squaw Island, a half mile from the family compound. It was more secluded and easily controlled by the Secret Service because it was separated from the mainland by a short causeway. This eased traffic congestion and helped preserve the privacy of the president and his neighbors.

ALTHOUGH, LIKE ALL modern presidents, Kennedy was never out of touch with Washington, his routine was kept as carefree as possible. An examination of the logs of his weekend activities, as recorded by his staff, reveals an astonishing social life. As author Richard Reeves pointed out in his book *President Kennedy: Profile of Power*, he was "very impatient, addicted to excitement, living his life as if it were a race against boredom." His schedule at Hyannisport, and also at Middleburg, Virginia; Palm Beach, Florida; and Camp David, reflected that.

In the summer of 1961, for example, reports biographer Sally Bedell Smith, "The routine was unvarying—cruises in good weather and bad on Joe Kennedy's fifty-two-foot cabin cruiser, the *Marlin*, often with a water-skiing display by Jackie; an early evening trip to the Hyannis Port candy store by the President in his pale blue golf cart with up to eighteen children hanging on—and sometimes toppling off; tennis matches; swimming in the Ambassador's pool, followed by a baking in the Finnish sauna; dinners with family and friends; movies in the Ambassador's screening room."

He would rise about 8 A.M. and, while reading the newspapers, have his favorite breakfast of four strips of lean bacon, two soft-boiled eggs, fresh-squeezed orange juice, toast with butter and marmalade, and coffee with cream and sugar. Jackie usually had toast and honey, orange juice, and coffee with skim milk.

In addition to his time with the kids or doing his official work, which he would try to confine to 4 to 7 P.M., he spent many happy hours socializing and talking with friends, sailing, taking swims and regular naps in the afternoon, and dining with Jackie and family members and friends. Jack's favorite outfit was khaki pants, a loose sweater, and loafers with no socks. Occasionally he brought his male friends along to shoot skeet. He loved to play five to nine holes of golf with his guy pals, sometimes more than once on weekend afternoons.

He dropped in at the homes of his father and brothers at Hyannisport and the homes of local associates, sometimes for supper or parties. Sometimes the parties included celebrities such as Frank Sinatra and Dominican playboy Porfirio Rubirosa. One of Kennedy's social recruiters was brother-in-law Peter Lawford. These affairs lasted into the wee hours, while Kennedy sipped daiquiris or Heineken beers. Yet JFK made sure to attend mass on Sundays, a requirement for Roman Catholics.

In the evenings, whether at his various retreats or at the White House, he unwound by watching movies. On Friday night, February 3, 1961, a few days after he took office, he left the White House with Red Fay and watched *Spartacus* at the Warner Theater on 13th Street and E Street, NW, a three-minute motorcade ride away. The film, which focused on the rebellion of slaves against the Roman Empire and starred Kirk Douglas, became one of his favorites. His movie-watching tended toward such action-adventure films and lighter fare.

His schedule was just as relaxed at his father's estate in Palm Beach, where he had spent many Christmas and Easter holidays since he was 16. Despite his wealth, Joe Kennedy never showed much of an interest in home decoration, and the linoleum was cracked in spots and the curtains were worn. But the home was spacious, with several patios and courtyards and a manicured lawn that ran to the beach and beyond, to the sea. JFK and his father, brothers, and male friends would lounge on cushioned benches and wicker chairs inside a four-foot-high enclosure near the swimming pool. They often sunbathed in the nude and had massages there.

MUCH HAS BEEN written and said about Kennedy's womanizing, and there is little doubt that he was a philanderer. In this, he was imitating his father, who was brazen about his affairs. When Jack was 12 years old, Joe Kennedy brought movie star Gloria Swanson to their home in Hyannisport to have dinner with his wife, Rose, and their children. Swanson was at the time Joe's mistress. Rose ignored the outrageous conduct, but it must have stayed with Jack for the rest of his life once he realized what had been going on.

JFK's romps with his consorts have become the stuff of legend, and he conducted some of his affairs, it appears, during visits to his father's compound in Palm Beach and during his other travels around the country, when his wife wasn't with him.

During a visit to Palm Springs, California, in March 1962, he received a visit from Marilyn Monroe at the home of singer Bing Crosby. His ostensible reason for the trip was to confer with former president Eisenhower to discuss problems with the Soviets and other issues. But his wife was away at the time visiting Pakistan and India, and Kennedy made the most of her absence.

"Behind the scenes," Kennedy biographer Sally Bedell Smith writes, "Kennedy engaged in private sexual escapades in the White House, Palm Beach, Malibu, Manhattan, and Palm Springs, activities that many in the Kennedy court heard as rumors, others refused to acknowledge, and a select few—primarily trusted White House aides Kenneth O'Donnell and Dave Powers, as well as inner-circle crony Charles 'Chuck' Spalding—witnessed and sometimes abetted."

For her part, Jackie tolerated her husband's infidelities. She apparently loved her husband and tried not to take his philandering personally. She seemed to accept the idea that powerful men would stray—it was the natural course of things in an aristocracy—and wives must make the best of it. But she always made sure to keep herself as attractive as she could. Between her pregnancies, she kept her slim figure—at 5 foot 7 she rarely weighed more than 120 pounds—and maintained a strict beauty and health regimen. She ate sparingly, often only fruit and a bowl of broth for lunch and a similarly light dinner. She sprinkled perfume on her hairbrush and gave her mane 50 to 100 strokes every night, and put a dab of skin cream on her eyelashes to make them shine.

OVER THANKSIVING 1961, as JFK's first year as president was drawing to a close, the family gathered for its traditional Thanksgiving reunion at Hyannisport. It was a particularly joyous and raucous affair.

After dinner, everyone retired to the father's house. Red Fay sang a loud and hilarious version of "Hooray for Hollywood." Teddy danced, prompting mother Rose to observe that with his "big derriere, it is funny to see him throw himself around." Jackie demonstrated the new dance craze called "the Twist" in her pink Schiaparelli pantsuit. Meanwhile, JFK puffed a cigar and enjoyed the show as the new patriarch of the clan.

THROUGHOUT HIS PRESIDENCY, JFK took frequent cruises on the president's yacht, which he renamed the *Honey Fitz*, for his maternal grandfather, former mayor John Fitzgerald of Boston. He loved sitting in the stern in a brown leather chair bolted to the deck, at the center of a party of guests and family. He would puff on a cigar and enjoy the sun and the sea, sometimes reading newspapers as the uniformed crew took care of all the details. This was typical for a man of his standing and background, and he continued the pattern in the presidency, when he really was king of the hill.

The cruises off Hyannisport or Newport, Rhode Island, generally departed in late morning and returned in early afternoon, so Kennedy could enjoy a round of golf, often with Red Fay. On board ship, stewards served lunch, starting with a creamy New England clam chowder, a Kennedy favorite, followed by a salad and meat course, and sometimes hand-dipped ice-cream cones for dessert. The president often had a drink in his hand, and his kids would often come up and ask him to inspect a toy or watch them play. He indulged them happily.

Meanwhile, Jackie sat on the side of the rear deck, talking with her women friends, soaking up the sun, and occasionally sipping a drink and smoking a cigarette—even while obviously pregnant in mid-1963. (The infant, Patrick, would die two days after birth later that year.) Jackie, it turns out, was a heavy smoker of filtered L&M cigarettes, a pack-a-day habit she tried to keep private. This was before the dire government warnings about the harmful effects of smoking.

Sometimes Kennedy would let his mind wander. On one *Honey Fitz* cruise, he saw a jet plane soaring in the distance and speculated on whether he could fly the jet as a passenger if the pilot died at the controls. Friends said it was part of his fascination with death by violence or accident. Senator George Smathers of Florida, a friend, said Kennedy asked him 20 or more times over the years to discuss the best way to die: "What would it be like to drown? Would you rather be in an airplane and crash? Would you rather be shot? Is it the best way to get hit in the head or in your chest somewhere and have time?"

ONE OF THE most tragic moments in Kennedy's life took place at Hyannis-port during the summer of 1963. On August 7, while Jackie and the kids were away at Squaw Island, the president was informed at the White House that his wife was undergoing emergency surgery at Otis Air Base to deliver a baby boy, three weeks before the due date of August 27. She had suffered severe pain that morning as she took Caroline out for riding lessons, and her obstetrician recommended that she go to the nearby base hospital. Kennedy flew to meet her immediately, arriving at 1:30 P.M., and by that time she had delivered by Caesarian section a four-pound, ten-and-a-half-ounce son who was immediately baptized with the name Patrick Bouvier Kennedy.

The boy developed a breathing problem that afternoon and was moved by ambulance to Children's Medical Center in Boston. The president went to Squaw Island to be with Caroline and John, visited Jackie again at the base hospital, then flew to Boston to check on the baby. He stayed the night at the Boston Ritz Carlton.

The infant was moved to Harvard's School of Public Health and placed on a respirator. Kennedy again flew to Cape Cod to see his wife, went back to the Harvard Medical Center, and spent the night there to be near Patrick, lying in a vacant bed, with an aide sleeping beside him. Before dawn that morning, the infant died after 39 hours of life.

"He put up quite a fight," Kennedy told a friend. "He was a beautiful baby."

The president then went to the hospital room where he had been sleeping, sat on the bed, and cried.

Later, the president tried to console his wife, and spent the rest of the day at Squaw Island playing with Caroline and John, taking them to the beach, and going for a swim in an effort to maintain a sense of normalcy in their lives.

He had returned, again, to the sea, to find solace and a sense of peace, as he had done all his life.

IN ADDITION TO his attachment to the sea, the young president experienced a rare tranquility at Hyannisport because he was surrounded by his devoted family and immersed in a lifetime of happy memories. His aristocratic background was very evident in how he behaved there and at his other retreats, where eager staff members and friends took care of his every whim. When he visited his father's estate in Palm Beach and took other trips around the country, philandering was also on the agenda when Jackie was not with him. Of course, his ability to relax and indulge himself was tempered by the communist threat and the dangerous world situation, which, he knew, could erupt at any moment.

CHAPTER ELEVEN

LYNDON B. JOHNSON AND THE LBJ RANCH, TEXAS

A T A BULKY 6 foot 3 with huge ears and a face as creased as a basset hound's, Lyndon Baines Johnson was big and boisterous, flamboyant, demanding, tireless, and often offensive. He was described, variously, as a tidal wave and a tornado in pants, and during his years as a U.S. senator from Texas, as vice president, and as president, he was always a crude self-promoter, a crass opportunist, a friend of the downtrodden, and an inside operator capable of great success and great failure.

"Some men want power simply to strut around the world and to hear the tune of 'Hail to the Chief,'" LBJ said. "Well, I wanted power to give things to people— all sorts of things to all sorts of people, especially the poor and the blacks." He pushed several of John F. Kennedy's domestic programs to fruition and went on to create one of the most prolific legislative records in history, expanding the power of the federal government beyond what his predecessors ever imagined. But he also got the United States bogged down in the Vietnam War, deploying half a million troops and launching a massive bombing campaign in a futile effort to stop a communist takeover in what was essentially a civil war. He was, time and again, wrong in his belief that he could break the will of the North Vietnamese and their Viet Cong allies in South Vietnam. His stubborn commitment to that war, more than anything else, made him deeply unpopular at home and forced him to bow out of the 1968 presidential race.

"Lyndon Johnson is an excellent case study in the limits and possibilities of presidential power," writes biographer Robert Dallek, who termed LBJ a "flawed giant." "As a domestic leader, he seized upon uncommon circumstances to drive a host of major reforms through a receptive Congress. But much of what he did is now in dispute. The war on poverty cut the number of indigent Americans almost in half. However, as critics accurately point out, it did not make most of them productive citizens but dependent members of welfare rolls. . . . Likewise, Great Society programs like Medicare and Medicaid, environmental protections, and federal aid to education retain substantial support, but other reforms such as public housing, urban renewal, affirmative action, and federal aid to the arts and the humanities are now in bad odor. In general, Johnson's unbounded confidence in social engineering by the federal government has lost its hold on the public's imagination, partly because so much of what he believed in did not work all that well in practice."

THE FULL, BREATHTAKING dimensions of Johnson's personality were nowhere more evident than on his ranch in the rolling Hill Country along the Pedernales River in west central Texas.

He returned to his ranch 74 times during his five-year presidency and spent part or all of 484 days there. In 1965, for example, he was there for 118 days; in 1966, for 103 days; in 1968, for another 118 days.

He would board a medium-size Jetstar executive jet in the government fleet on many Friday afternoons and fly from Andrews Air Force Base in three hours. (Nearly 40 years later, President George W. Bush would follow the same pattern, traveling frequently to his own ranch in central Texas.) He had no qualms about running the government from what became known as the Texas White House, a 28-room, two-story white frame structure with a green shingled roof and green trim. There was a wide porch across the front for entertaining, and a swimming pool nearby for relaxing.

Immediately after he succeeded John F. Kennedy on November 22, 1963, he ordered improvements on the 2,800-acre ranch to enable him to conduct more business from his retreat than any of his predecessors had done. He had roads built or improved, had the communications upgraded, added security, and improved the airstrip, lengthening it from 3,570 feet (installed in 1955) to 6,150 feet. This extension allowed the president's Jetstar from Washington to land directly on his property. It also allowed other jets to land and come to a stop only a few yards from his doorstep. A helicopter landing strip was installed near the main house. A full-time staff of Secret Service agents was stationed at the ranch, even when Johnson was not there.

Seventy-two phones were hooked up in the 28-room house so LBJ could make and take calls at any time, from virtually any location. Some of the phones had multiple lines, and one had 24 direct lines so he could reach key aides, Cabinet secretaries, and ranch personnel with the touch of a button. There were phones in the living room, the offices, the bathrooms, at the headboard of his bed, even next to his big chair at the head of the dining-room table. He had radio phones placed in his cars so he was never out of touch on his driving jaunts. The scattering of family cottages and other buildings on the property were updated so his aides, friends, and bodyguards could stay there.

HE WAS BORN less than a mile from the ranch, which belonged to his grandparents at his birth and then was passed along to his aunt Frank Martin and uncle Clarence Martin. When he was a boy, the family used to celebrate major holidays there, such as Christmas and Thanksgiving. He would recite poems for his assembled relatives in the living room, and he always had fond memories of the place.

Johnson bought the ranch from his widowed aunt Frank when he was a senator in 1951, and he and his wife, Lady Bird, expanded the main house over the years.

"From that time on, it was his home," says Harry Middleton, a longtime LBJ aide who accompanied him on trips to the ranch during the last two years of his presidency and advised him after he left the White House. "It certainly was a connection with his roots. It was a place where he could relax, but he also could work. His feeling for it was quite deep. For him it was the best place to be. He had no problem entertaining heads of state there. He had dinner with foreign leaders in the dining room, where his forbears had their meals so long ago." He took considerable satisfaction in the fact that powerful men from around the world would hang on his every word in the same place where, as a boy, he was required to listen silently while his relatives joked about the cows, horses, and the weather.

LBJ once remarked, "I guess every person feels a part of the place where he was born. He wants to go back to the surroundings that he knew as a child. And this is my country, the Hill Country of Texas. I first remember walking along the banks of the Pedernales when I was a boy four or five years of age, walking from the little home where I was born down the river up to my grandfather's house, where he would always give me peppermint stick candy or a big red apple. . . . They're treasured memories. . . . Nowhere have I found the same feeling that I get when I come here. It's always good for what ails you."

He added: "I guess we all search at times for serenity. And it's serene here. There's not the traffic problem that you fight all day long when you're in the city. There are no jet airplanes roaring through the skies. The Hereford cattle are lowing on the river banks and converting the grass into red meat that you harvest and make your living off of. The sheep and the goats are on the hillside, getting their daily food intake. And there's something about this section that brings new life and new hope, and really a balanced and better viewpoint after you've been here a few days."

HIS FATHER, FARMER and businessman Sam Ealy Johnson, Jr., had represented the area in the Texas legislature. But it was Lyndon who became the pride of the region when he served as a Democrat in the U.S. House of Representatives—and helped bring electricity to the rural region—and the Senate, rising to become Senate majority leader, then vice president and, finally, president by succession in 1963. Johnson was elected on his own in a landslide against Republican nominee Barry Goldwater in 1964, but then things deteriorated as Americans grew disenchanted with Johnson's leadership in the Vietnam War and in dealing with the civil rights movement, the counterculture, and rising crime.

But no matter how badly he was doing in the opinion polls or in the elite salons of Georgetown, LBJ always felt that his neighbors in West Texas really cared about him. "It's one place where they know if you're sick and care if you die," he once said.

The ranch was an acquired taste for Washington's movers and shakers. President Kennedy, for one, was never a big fan of the place. He had gone deer hunting with LBJ at the ranch shortly after being elected president in late 1960, and didn't have fond memories of the experience.

Johnson, who was JFK's vice president–elect, met Kennedy at the ranch's airstrip, wearing a cream-colored leather jacket, cowboy boots, and a 10-gallon cowboy hat. He insisted on taking the incoming president on a tour in one of his big white Lincoln Continental convertibles with the top down, even though it was drizzling. With Johnson at the wheel, giving orders periodically on the car's radio-telephone to foremen, ranch hands, and aides, he pointed out the Pedernales River, the graveyard where his grandfather was buried, and other sights. One of them was what Kennedy aides derisively called "the LBJ flag," with white initials on a blue background, which was flown when he was in residence.

After dinner that evening, Johnson announced that everyone had to get up at 5 A.M. for the deer hunt. Kennedy suddenly looked anguished and shocked, and asked if Johnson was joking. "Of course I'm not joking," LBJ said. "You just can't leave this ranch without shooting a deer."

Kennedy went along, knowing how important it was to Johnson and wanting to keep things on a cordial plane. But as he got dressed before dawn, he told an aide, "This is ridiculous. It's still dark outside."

As Kennedy aide Ken O'Donnell recalled it, "We drove around the lonely back roads on the ranch for more than an hour before we spotted a few deer in the distance, rather small and scraggly little creatures. The President got out of Johnson's car reluctantly, having no zest for shooting any kind of wildlife. But at the same time his Kennedy competitive spirit was aroused, and he had no intention of losing face with those Texans watching him critically. He got his deer on his second or third shot."

Three years later, Kennedy was supposed to visit the LBJ Ranch again, and he wasn't looking forward to it. As JFK and his wife flew to Texas on Thursday, November 21, 1963, Kennedy called aides Ken O'Donnell and David Powers to his cabin aboard *Air Force One* and said, "You two guys aren't running out on me and leaving me stranded with poor Jackie at Lyndon's ranch. If I've got to hang around there all day Saturday, wearing one of those big cowboy hats, you've got to be there too."

The visit never came to pass. Kennedy was assassinated in Dallas the following day, November 22.

AFTER HE BECAME the 36th president, Johnson quickly put his stamp on the office, a fact that was never more evident than at his property on the Pedernales River. "The iconography of leadership changed in an instant, from the rough and tumble touch-football games on the lawn at Hyannisport to the more bucolic, more homey, but more geographically distant and culturally remote setting of the LBJ Ranch," writes author Hal K. Rothman in his history of the Johnson property.

The day after his landslide victory over Barry Goldwater in the 1964 election, Johnson was riding particularly high. He had himself photographed on horseback at his show barn as he circled a prize bull, waving his hat to startle the animal into a pen. LBJ wasn't dressed to work cattle, since he was wearing a jacket, dress shirt, and tie—but he couldn't resist the opportunity to show off.

That same day, he humiliated Hubert Humphrey, a former senator from Minnesota who was LBJ's vice presidential running mate, by ordering him to wear an oversized Stetson hat and a Western outfit and to take a horseback ride. Humphrey dealt with it all good-naturedly, but he looked ridiculous. That was LBJ's approach to humor—it was generally at someone else's expense.

Not long after this trip, Johnson took reporters on a tour of the ranch and stopped at the family graveyard. He pointed out the spot where he would be buried and declared, "If Goldwater had won that election, there's where I'd be right now!" Then he proceeded to unzip his fly and urinate on his burial plot—which the reporters interpreted as a sign of both his euphoria and defiance.

His brio extended to his liaisons. A month after he took office, he walked in on several reporters from the White House press corps as they relaxed in the bar of the Driskill Hotel in Austin, on New Year's Eve, 1963. LBJ pulled up a chair and, in the course of the conversation, said brazenly, "Now, boys, let me tell you something. Sometimes you may see me coming out of a room in the White House with a woman. You just remember, that is none of your business." The reporters, in keeping with the standards of privacy of their day and not wishing to offend the commander in chief, agreed.

"The ranch served as a haven for Johnson," Rothman says, "a place where he could relieve the stresses of national political life, where he could control a microworld in a comprehensive manner to which the larger world only rarely responded. . . . On the ranch, Johnson's penchant for managing every detail could be fulfilled; he could establish the peremptory domination of the efforts of his staff for which he was renowned. The ranch was small enough to function in this individualistic and idiosyncratic fashion, returning to the president the sense of control essential to him that seemed to spiral away as U.S. cities erupted in flames [in racially based disturbances], as the war in Vietnam began to consume lives and resources at an ever-greater rate, and as Americans, particularly young ones, expressed their dismay about their society in a range of civil and often extralegal protests."

Adds Liz Carpenter, a frequent ranch visitor as an adviser to Lady Bird Johnson: "It was bred in him, that land; it shaped him, shaped him to be an optimist. You had to be an optimist to live there. As a boy, help the family eke out a living from it. The skies were blue, fleece white clouds. They lift your spirit. They make self-resilient, people who are self-reliant, and they also create people who know the need of good neighbors that you can call on in trouble and that you will help."

Once he arrived, LBJ couldn't wait to inspect his 2,800-acre spread of low hills, cactus, scrub, live oaks, and cedar, with an occasional armadillo and rattlesnake. He also liked to tour the adjacent lands that he leased from neighbors, and would take his speedboat at full throttle on a local lake, with Secret Service agents struggling to keep up in their chase boats.

Moments after his plane landed on his airstrip, he would jump into one of his two big white Lincoln Continental convertibles, get behind the wheel, order aides or guests to climb in with him, and gun the engine. He would race down the tarmac, sometimes at 90 mph, while sipping beer from a can or a paper cup with the radio blaring country music. It was a nerve-wracking experience for his passengers and his Secret Service bodyguards.

If he noticed a friend, ranch hand, or neighbor at the side of the road, he would pick him or her up to join the jaunt. On such occasions, he might ask a staff member to exit the car to make room for the newcomer. LBJ would promise to send a car to bring the staffer to the ranch house, but sometimes he would forget, and the hapless staffer would trudge back on his own.

Johnson would often badly damage the vehicles, driving them into pastures, over gullies, into low streams. Once, his driving destroyed one of the cars' gasoline tanks. He ordered the Secret Service to always have them repaired by the next day at dawn, in case he wanted to go out on another joyride early in the morning.

On another occasion, he drove his Lincoln into a field and insisted that three big buses filled with guests follow his lead. They did, bouncing roughly over the ground and knocking down tree branches in the process, to the shock of the passengers and the bus drivers.

Over the years, Johnson had the military install a large number of towers and other communications facilities so he could talk by car radio to people anywhere in the world, through sophisticated and expensive relay systems. He would try to impress other leaders with America's technology by nonchalantly telling them he was on the phone as he drove around "looking at the cows."

In 1964, it was reported that LBJ was a litterbug because he made a habit of tossing empty beer cans from his car. It made headlines because at the time his wife was trying to beautify the country's roads and highways as her main project as First Lady. Johnson got angry. He thought it was another case of the Eastern-oriented news media trying to embarrass him by portraying him as a crude hick.

On his road trips, Johnson liked to point out his prize cattle. Blaring the car's horn and raising his voice, he would scare the animals into standing up in order to show his guests how impressive they looked and how much profit they would bring when he sold them. On one occasion, he pointed to individual cows and compared them to politicians he knew. If the spirit or the beer moved him, he would pull over and relieve himself noisily at the side of a road or in the brush. The president would invite his passengers to do the same but they were generally too embarrassed to do so. By this time, LBJ knew some of his passengers' bladders were full from the beer he kept pressing on them, and he took perverse pleasure in prolonging the ride over rough roads, cattle guards, and pastures, to make them even more uncomfortable.

Once a visiting reporter from the East was shocked when Johnson stopped the car, hopped out, and started to urinate. The nervous journalist asked Johnson if he was worried about a rattlesnake striking at his private part. "Naw," the president replied over his shoulder as he zipped his pants, "it's too tough."

He was always talkative, by turns earthy and philosophical. He thought nothing of walking with a reporter to an outhouse, getting inside to answer nature's call, and conducting an interview all the while. At one point, he showed off a prize bull to a group of journalists that included a few women, and turned to Associated Press correspondent Frank Cormier and said, "Frank, how would you like to be hung like that?"

WEARING EXPENSIVE LEATHER cowboy boots, a khaki shirt and pants, and a 5-gallon hat, he loved to observe the white-tailed deer leap over fences at dusk. "That's the way he ended just about every day out there," aide Harry Middleton said. "He loved to watch the deer." Sometimes he would feed them cigarettes to encourage them to come close.

At other times he would shoot them. His ranch, like many in the area, had become overpopulated with the animals, and it was legal to hunt them from inside a car, which LBJ did. In addition, he had his men build high fences that the deer couldn't jump, and herd bigger-than-average animals into these confined spaces, in effect trapping them. It was really no contest. The deer had little chance.

Johnson was a good shot, but when he had guests he generally didn't hunt. Instead, his male guests were expected to go on a "hunt" in the company of the president, who was behind the wheel of the Lincoln convertible and who insisted that his passengers do the shooting. At other times, he used a Lincoln Zephyr, which was equipped with a gun rack and a wet bar that was fastened to the back of the front seat.

He enjoyed mocking guests who were repelled by the experience or who weren't very good at it. This was another of his many control mechanisms. "It was easy for LBJ to turn the killing of a whitetail buck into a test of manhood," writes John L. Bullion, a family friend and one of his hunting companions. "Johnson himself did not hunt with guests, so his own prowess at the sport was left implied. . . . Missed shots created a different atmosphere. Once that happened, the contest was joined, and the stakes were one's manhood. Johnson's goal would become humiliation, not hospitality; the underlining of inferiority at men's work, not a relaxed sharing of men's sport. Under these conditions, deer hunting at the LBJ Ranch became the country mouse's revenge over his city cousin's impotent pretensions and posturings."

Johnson also had an amphibian car, made to operate on land and in water. Without telling his passengers about the small blue vehicle's capabilities, he would drive to a spot near the Pedernales or nearby LBJ Lake and head toward the water. Suddenly, he would shout, "The brakes won't hold" or "The brakes don't work." The car would plunge into the river with a huge splash and Johnson would roar with laughter at his frightened passengers. Once, however, a woman passenger who couldn't swim jumped out and badly bruised herself. From then on, Johnson made sure to ask if his passengers could swim before he tried the practical joke.

Another habit that correspondents found strange was the president's evening walks to visit Oriole Bailey, one of his relatives, who lived a quarter mile away from his home in a small house. After supper, LBJ would announce "Let's go see

Cousin Oriole," and he would gather up his guests and occasionally a few reporters and, using a flashlight, march along in the dark to her house. Escorted by Secret Service bodyguards and a ranch hand or two, he would stop to inspect roads, irrigation systems, or cows, as the agents blinked their flashlights to each other to signal Johnson's location. Finally, the president would pass a guardhouse at the east end of his property and walk up to a small building with a screened porch. He would bang the screen a few times, and shout, "Oriole! Oriole!" His cousin, who was partially deaf, would appear, and the president would chat with her or watch the 10 o'clock news in white wicker armchairs in her parlor, then go back home.

A reporter once described such a visit in an article and included the fact that Oriole was barefoot, which Johnson felt was making fun of her, his family, and his roots (although she was indeed barefoot when the reporter saw her). It was part of the growing tension between the Hill Country native and his supposedly more urbane press corps.

In the evenings, LBJ would enjoy playing dominoes with his male guests while Lady Bird would play bridge with her female friends. Sometimes he would watch movies in his aircraft hangar, which could be converted into a theater, but he generally found films boring.

DESPITE HIS TALK about how the ranch brought him serenity, the estate became a frenzied hive of activity when Johnson was there, in contrast to Hyannisport, which had been relatively tranquil under the leisure-minded Kennedy.

Forty or fifty advisers, Cabinet secretaries, clerical staff, and security personnel would usually accompany LBJ on his visits. Officials would fly in, drop off paperwork or have meetings, then shuttle back to Washington. Sometimes, people would complete their assignments, then stand around the grounds with nothing to do and unsure where to go.

The 4,500-square-foot house swarmed with advisers, clerical staffers, military personnel, and Secret Service agents. They weren't allowed into private areas, such as the bedrooms or private offices, unless invited, but there was really little privacy for the First Family. Johnson, a gregarious man who loved being the center of attention, didn't mind, but Lady Bird never quite got used it.

The controlled atmosphere was particularly resented by the press corps, which would follow Johnson to Texas on a chartered jet and then remain sequestered in Austin, about 65 miles away. Reporters were allowed admittance to the ranch only if they traveled on buses provided by the administration. During off hours they felt abandoned in a small city without the amenities they were accustomed to in Washington and New York. Sometimes they were housed even farther away, in San Antonio, which made them feel even more isolated. This intensified the hostility between LBJ and those who covered him, especially after his popularity began to fade amid rising public doubts about the Vietnam War.

The ranch seemed to them and even to LBJ's aides another venue in which an overbearing Johnson could lord his power over everyone else, deciding who got access to him and what his activities would be on the spur of the moment, without regard for other people's feelings or schedules. He always seemed to have people waiting for him. They were in his dining room in front of a big picture window that offered a panoramic view of his lands; in his living room, where they would sit elbow to elbow on couches and chairs and wait for the president to walk in and put his feet up in a green recliner across from a big fireplace. They were outside in the yard, where dignitaries would sit on yellow lawn chairs around a big wooden picnic table. They were in the hangar near his airstrip. They were waiting for the president as they held the line on the phone. Having people wait for him seemed to be another control mechanism, a way for President Johnson to dramatize his power.

In the early years, when he was widely considered the martyred Kennedy's heir and at the height of his popularity, it was difficult for anyone to resist him. It helped that he knew how to manipulate people. "On one occasion," reports Rothman, "[columnist] Stewart Alsop was seated in a floating chair in the ranch's heated swimming pool with a scotch and soda in his hand after a full day of the 'Johnson Treatment,' the incredibly potent blend of badgering, cajolery, promises of favors, [and] implied threats that typified Johnson's efforts to sway an individual." George Reedy, Johnson's spokesman, later said Alsop wrote "one of the finest [pro-LBJ] columns I have read about Lyndon Johnson out of that."

LBJ brought a fevered intensity to everything he did. Among his visitors in the weeks after Christmas in 1963, as he was settling in as president, were West German chancellor Ludwig Erhard, General Maxwell Taylor and the U.S. Joint Chiefs of Staff, Walter Heller, chairman of the Council of Economic Advisers, and Kermit Gordon, director of the Bureau of the Budget. At one point, Johnson conducted a conversation about economic policy with Heller and Gordon as they shot deer from the comfortable seats of one of the president's Lincoln Continentals. The pace rarely eased.

During the 1964 Christmas season, a dozen Cabinet officers shuttled in from Washington, including Interior Secretary Stewart Udall, Labor Secretary W. Willard Wirtz, Defense Secretary Robert McNamara, and Treasury Secretary C. Douglas Dillon. Also visiting the president for meetings were the Joint Chiefs of Staff; Agriculture Secretary Orville Freeman; Postmaster General John Gronouski; and Health, Education, and Welfare Secretary Anthony J. Celebrezze.

He had teletypes brought in so he could check the news on the wire services at any time of day or night. He had three television sets installed in his living room and three more in his bedroom, so he could watch the evening news on all three broadcast networks at once. Arthur B. Krim, a businessman and Johnson friend, recalled, "No matter where we were, in an automobile . . . or in a chopper, on the hour he'd listen to the news. . . . And then he would generally manage to get back to the ranch in time to have those three TV sets on, which he would manipulate, because if he was at a console [he would watch] first one channel, then the other, and then the third. Of course that would lead to conversation. More often than not, we saw him on those programs, and there would be comments about that."

Even the social occasions at the ranch were outsized, theatrical affairs. His barbecues became legendary. To start, Johnson would sometimes take visitors, from congressional pals to United Nations ambassadors, on horseback tours of the ranch before their meal. LBJ liked to ride "Lady B," a blaze-faced black mare and a Tennessee Walker, his favorite breed of horse, while the visitors rode cow ponies. But more often, he showed guests around by car. Then they proceeded to the barbecue in a grove near the river under several magnificent oaks.

Typically, the round tables were covered with red-and-white checkered tablecloths and featured coal-oil lanterns. The servers wore Western clothes and the event was designed to resemble a chuckwagon dinner, with the aroma of chicken, beef, and pork in the air, and plenty of beer to go around. (Johnson preferred steaks cooked through, enjoyed soufflés in more formal settings, and he loved turnip greens and black-eyed peas. For dessert, he favored banana pudding and rice custard.) LBJ made sure that a few cowboys and a couple dozen of his cattle were visible across the river to add to the Western atmosphere. At most events, all guests were expected to wear red-and-white bandanas around their necks. The master of ceremonies often was "Cactus" Pryor, a Johnson employee and Western storyteller.

Sometimes, Johnson would provide country and western music. At other times he would hire actors and actresses, along with ranch hands and neighbors, to depict moments in Texas history as the entertainment. The performances ranged from reenactments of the early Spanish explorers meeting Native Americans to the arrival of settlers from the East. To some, these pageants seemed quaint and reflective of a healthy state pride. To others, they seemed to suggest an arrogance and jingoism about a Texas culture that outsiders thought backward and racist.

Johnson made it a practice to give his special guests big Stetson hats at the end of such evenings. He would gleefully insist that each one try on a hat, which often was too big or too small. His guests frequently felt foolish. It was another way for Johnson to assert control. He also would pluck a forkful of potatoes or a chunk of meat from a guest's plate if he was still hungry. He was the boss, after all.

JOHNSON WAS A micro-manager in running his property, as Washington and Jefferson had been long before him in supervising their own estates. His need to demonstrate mastery made him very difficult to work for, especially at the ranch, where he felt unencumbered by Washington's protocols and rules. "I don't get ulcers," Johnson was fond of saying, "I give 'em."

Johnson often phoned Dale Malechek, his longtime foreman, from the White House for talks that went on for two or three hours, as the president demanded to know what was going on. In Washington, Johnson insisted on receiving daily weather reports for the ranch, and during bad conditions he expected hourly updates, according to author Rothman.

Things got worse for the ranch hands when the president was there. Johnson would literally look over their shoulders as Malechek and the other employees did their work, and he would harangue them if they displeased him. "He was a son of a bitch to work for," Malechek said after LBJ's death. "One son of a bitch. I'll guarantee you. He expected 110 percent 120 percent of the time."

LBJ's badgering ways were clear in a tape recording made of a telephone conversation he had with Malechek on the morning of October 10, 1964. It was typical of the way he treated his "help." Johnson told Malechek he was lying in bed at the ranch and wanted a series of updates. He proceeded to brusquely quiz him on one subject after another.

"Did you lose all your hay that you got out there and got wet?" the commander in chief asked.

Malechek said, "No, sir," and began to explain the status of the hay, when Johnson cut him off with another question. "How are your cattle? Are they doing any better?"

Malechek replied, "They're startin' to pick up now." Again, LBJ cut him off. "Did you sell any of 'em yet?"

Malechek said he had only sold a couple of calves, and the president expressed displeasure. "Nobody wants bulls anymore," Johnson complained. "We're in the wrong business, I think. . . . I don't know why they don't want an LBJ bull. Looks like they would."

After a few minutes, Johnson asked, "What are you gonna be doin' this afternoon?

"Plowin'," the foreman replied.

The president announced, "I'd like to see you plow, and I'll try to come by."

LBJ insisted that his ranch make money from its cattle production—he generally had up to 600 head on his property and nearby rental land—and from raising winter oats, alfalfa, Sudan grass, or Bermuda grass. He would fume when he noticed a lightbulb glowing when no one was around. He felt it wasted money on electricity. He insisted that Styrofoam cups be rinsed out and used more than once. The ranch personnel didn't dare disappoint him, and the operation was generally profitable.

"He was fond of saying that he was 'just a country boy,'" wrote George Reedy, LBJ's former press secretary. "The statement—however inadequate as a description—was true but he never answered the question of whether he enjoyed being a country boy. The ranch was close to him because it gave him a sense of identity. It was his tie to the past and his assurance that there really was a Lyndon B. Johnson. His self-painted portrait of a cattleman tending his herds, however, was difficult to accept with a straight face. He *did* know something about cattle, but he 'tended' them from a Lincoln Continental with a chest full of ice and a case of scotch and soda in the backseat."

JOHNSON EVEN TREATED his Secret Service agents badly, which was surprising since the agents were a key part of his life since Kennedy's assassination. He hated it when their vehicles would follow too closely. Once, he stopped his car abruptly, and when an agent ran up to his door to ask if anything was wrong, the president railed, "Damn it. I don't want you tailgatin' me! Now, you keep that [station] wagon back outta sight or I'm gonna shoot out your tires."

The agents hardly knew what to expect from day to day. New bodyguards were warned to be careful late at night around the main house. Johnson would sometimes slip out his bedroom door to urinate in the bushes or on the grass rather than walk a few extra steps to the bathroom. The veteran agents didn't want the newcomers to shoot first and ask questions later.

Some of those familiar with LBJ and his eye for women suspected that he had trysts on his property. They weren't likely to occur in the main ranch house; there were generally too many Secret Service agents, aides, household staff members, ranch hands, and family members around for that. But it would have been quite easy for LBJ to rendezvous with one of the beautiful women who always seemed to be in his entourage at the cottages and houses in the vicinity of his main house. "Johnson had a 'network' and there were plenty of opportunities for it," one LBJ expert familiar with his activities said.

ON THE OTHER hand, Johnson did have a caring and considerate side, even if he didn't show it often. Friends say he knew just how far he could push people. When he sensed that a staff member needed a boost or was ready to quit, he would give the aide a gift or grant a special favor, such as a trip to Washington with family members and a ride home on *Air Force One*.

He asked his more affluent aides and friends to box up their old clothes so he could distribute them to some of his ranch employees or to needy people in the area. He remembered birthdays and liked to surprise aides and visitors with gifts, which he had stocked in closets, drawers, and storage rooms. Among them were inscribed photographs of himself, medals commemorating his inauguration in January 1965, small busts of his head, pocket knives with his signature on them, cuff links bearing the presidential seal, and buttons for use on a blazer, also with the presidential seal. Occasionally, he would reward someone with a small portable television. He kept scores of them, still boxed, in a storage room near his bedroom.

Sometimes guests at the ranch witnessed moments with Lady Bird that suggested how much she cared for him despite his flaws, and how he relied on her.

John L. Bullion recalls hunting with LBJ and returning to the main house to prepare for dinner and an overnight stay. Lady Bird suggested it was a good time to clean up. "When I came out of the bathroom, I intruded on a touching scene," Bullion recalled. "The two Johnsons were standing in the hall close together. Lady Bird reached up and laid her left hand on his cheek. Then she asked, 'How are you feeling, darling?' Sounding for all the world like a small boy who craved his mother's touch and her sympathy, he said plaintively, 'I'm better, but I still don't feel perfect.' She leaned into him and stroked his cheek. I coughed to reveal my presence." It turned out that Lyndon had been suffering from a cold, with a lingering sore throat and headache, and he hadn't quite gotten over it. For that moment at least, his bluster was gone and he was simply a man relying on his wife for some comfort.

JOHNSON HAD MORE of a penchant for secrecy than most presidents. He once awakened Army Col. Jack Albright, commander of the White House Communications Agency, at 1 A.M. with a request that was more bizarre than usual. "How much money you got?" the commander in chief inquired to the sleepy officer. Albright meekly asked what the money was needed for, and Johnson cut him off. "Never mind," the president said. "How much you got in your funds? How much can you make available to me by tomorrow morning?"

Albright mumbled that he might be able to provide a couple of hundred thousand dollars, but Johnson again interrupted. "I need a million and I need it by tomorrow. It's for a very highly hush-hush project. I'd rather not talk about it. Can you get it?"

"Yes, sir," Albright responded, and Johnson hung up.

The colonel called his superiors, who made arrangements to transfer funds secretly within military accounts, and he told the president so a few minutes later. Albright never knew what happened to the money, although he later learned it was for something LBJ called a "relocation site."

On another occasion, Johnson made a secret—and, in the minds of his military aides and Secret Service agents, dangerous—trip to Mexico to inspect a huge tract of land he was considering buying, apparently with other investors. He told his pilot, James Cross, that he wanted to inspect some property about 900 miles away from his own ranch—deep inside Mexico. Johnson didn't even want to notify the Mexican government, fearing that his trip might be publicly disclosed. This caused his aides considerable heartburn because they were afraid the Mexican government might consider the aircraft hostile or threatening—or mistake it for a drug runner—and shoot it down.

Another potential problem was communications. Without adequate preparations and with all the secrecy, the only way the president's plane could keep in contact with the White House or the ranch was through the radio on board the small Convair turboprop aircraft that would be used. (The larger 707 that Johnson customarily used as *Air Force One* was too big to land at the site and, the president thought, would attract too much attention.) This meant the pilot had to keep one engine running after LBJ got off, to keep the radio working. This in turn raised questions about fuel consumption because the Convair only had enough fuel for about eight hours of operation. It took three hours to fly from the LBJ Ranch to the landing site, and an anticipated three hours to get back, leaving Johnson a maximum of two hours on the ground.

In the end, Johnson and a handful of others, including the First Lady, Albright, a couple of aides, and four or five very nervous Secret Service agents, made the trip. The Convair landed, roughly, on a gravel air strip. People were waiting in three or four vehicles when they arrived—indicating that Johnson had alerted the owner, whom the staff believed was a former president of Mexico. Albright speculated later that the Mexican air traffic controllers must have seen the plane as it crossed the border but nothing came of it because "they had sort of a sloppy system in Mexico" at that time. Johnson spent an hour and 15 minutes on the ground surveying the site. Albright also said the pilot, James Cross, must have alerted the Air Force, "because if something happened they'd have to come after us."

"This was the hairiest trip I ever had," recalled Albright. Why was Johnson so secretive about it? Albright believed the president feared that public disclosure might drive up the price, and he was very frugal about his investments.

The trip was never publicized. But in late 1972, nearly four years after Johnson left office, the Mexican government began an investigation into whether Johnson surreptitiously and illegally held nearly 109,000 acres of ranch land in the border state of Chihuahua. Local farmers said Johnson was using the land, known as *Las Pampas*, in a partnership to raise cattle with former Mexican president Miguel Aleman.

A month later, Johnson died, which apparently ended the investigation. Arthur B. Krim, a close Johnson confidant, later said Aleman did indeed allow Johnson to run cattle at the ranch and that Aleman worked out a deal under which LBJ acquired a lease with an option to buy. The option was never exercised, according to Krim.

But this was only part of the story. Johnson also took an interest in the local families, brought clothing for the children, and started a school. He considered it his private project after he left the presidency, and he never wanted it known publicly.

AS HIS POPULARITY plummeted, Johnson began to ruminate out loud at the ranch and the White House about not running for reelection in 1968. In one of the many talks he had with friends, Johnson drove around the ranch with former Texas governor John Connally and Representative J. J. "Jake" Pickle on September 8, 1967, for eight hours, talking about what he should do. Connally and Lady Bird Johnson have said that they believed LBJ made his decision not to run at this time, and was mainly considering when and how to announce it.

On January 4, 1968, the Johnsons, Connally, and Connally's wife, Nellie, sat in Johnson's bedroom for three hours and talked again about whether Johnson should run. Connally said LBJ should only seek another term if he could look forward to the job for four more years.

A few weeks later, Senator Eugene McCarthy ran a strong second to Johnson in the New Hampshire Democratic primary, and Robert Kennedy, the slain president's brother, entered the race. LBJ's doubts grew about his electability, the political viability of his Great Society social programs, and whether his health would allow him to stay on the job. On March 31, 1968, he announced that he would not run. It stunned the political world.

Republican Richard Nixon won the election that November, and Johnson retired to his ranch with considerable bitterness at how his presidency had ended. He delved into the details of ranch operation more than ever, but remained obsessed with his popularity. He would even drive to his birthplace nearby, a cottage that had become a tourist site, and check the license plates of visitors to see how many states were represented. He required written reports every week on attendance.

Yet being at the ranch full-time seemed to mellow him eventually. Part of the change was due to his physical condition, which was deteriorating as his heart

weakened and his energy level declined. Part was due to his desire to show historians that he was not a vindictive man. And part was due to his wish to argue his
case for the Vietnam War in a more positive light. He told a former aide that he
had come to terms with the young protesters who despised him. His comments
are etched on a wall of the LBJ Library in Austin, Texas, in the middle of an exhibit on Vietnam. He said:

> My heart was with the students, although they would never know that,
> and I don't suppose they would ever believe it. I'd hear those chants—"Hey,
> hey, LBJ, how many kids did you kill today?"—and I knew there was a long
> gulf between them and me which neither one of us could do much about. I
> was doing what I thought was right, right for them, and right for their coun-
> try and their future and their children. But they couldn't see that.
>
> What we were doing was based on decisions that were made and actions
> that were taken before some of them were even born and that's a hard thing
> to understand. I didn't blame them. They didn't want to get killed in a war,
> and that's easy to understand. It would be wonderful if there were a way each
> generation could start off fresh, just wipe the slate clean all around the world
> and say, "O.K., the new world begins today." But nobody's ever found a way
> to do that. There's a continuity in history that's one of our greatest strengths,
> and maybe it's one of our weaknesses, too.
>
> If a young man says, "You're sending me to Vietnam because of the
> SEATO treaty, but I wasn't around when you passed the SEATO treaty, and
> I don't believe in it and I don't think it's right to put my life on the line for
> decisions that were made by men when I was in my cradle"—well, there's
> something there to listen to.
>
> But it's possible for us to say to young men and women: You're free, you
> can vote, you can deny the state the right to enter your house, you can speak
> your mind without fear of prison—and we can say all these things to them
> because of decisions made and actions taken before any of us were born, be-
> fore our parents and grandparents were born.

On January 22, 1973, LBJ suffered his third heart attack while resting in his
bed. This was exactly the scenario he had feared ever since his heart began giving
him trouble many years earlier: suffering a severe attack and having no one there

to help. He tried to reach his chief Secret Service agent, Mike Howard, on the phone, but Howard wasn't in the immediate vicinity and the call went unanswered. No one, it turned out, was nearby, and the former president's pained cries for help went unnoticed. By the time staff members and bodyguards arrived, Johnson had died, alone.

AT HIS RANCH, LBJ showed even more of his famously abusive and egotistical personality than he did elsewhere. He had a strong need to control everyone and everything around him, which was one of his greatest strengths and, because it led him to overreach in exerting presidential power, one of his biggest vulnerabilities.

CHAPTER TWELVE

RICHARD M. NIXON AND SAN CLEMENTE, CALIFORNIA, AND KEY BISCAYNE, FLORIDA

RICHARD NIXON MADE his personal retreats into hideaways from the outside world.

He was a singularly private individual, a brooder who sought to create his own private places to consider the great issues of the day and to plot against his adversaries. He did this many times at Camp David, the official presidential retreat in Maryland's Catoctin Mountains, and in a secret office in the Executive Office Building, which he could reach by walking across a small street from the White House. At both places, no one would bother him; that's the way he wanted it.

But more than anywhere else, he consistently found isolation at two retreats outside the Washington area, one in San Clemente, California, for extended stays, and another in Key Biscayne, Florida, for weekends and short trips.

It was at San Clemente that a photograph was taken of Nixon that became an iconic image of his presidency: a picture of him walking on a sunny beach, wearing black formal shoes and looking quite out of place, stiff and formal despite the leisurely setting. It reinforced the public's perception of Nixon as a workaholic who didn't know how to relax.

This image was an accurate one. Early on, he concluded that only through his own determination and work ethic could he break out of the grueling life experienced by his parents, Frank Nixon and Hannah Milhous Nixon, working-class

Quakers who ran a grocery store in Whittier, California. The family was always teetering on the verge of poverty, a condition that enraged and embittered his father. When Richard was 12, his beloved 7-year-old brother, Arthur, died of meningitis. Eight years later, Harold, the oldest of the four Nixon brothers, died of tuberculosis. Nixon's response to his childhood of hard work, economic setbacks, and personal grief was to throw himself into a life of achievement and to nurture resentments toward the privileged few who had success handed to them.

Nixon had to work for everything he had, but he found a niche in politics. After serving as a Navy supply officer in the Pacific during World War II, he returned home and, by outworking his opposition, harshly attacking his adversaries, and using wealthy patrons to bankroll his campaigns, moved from the House to the Senate to the vice presidency under Dwight Eisenhower. He lost the 1960 presidential race to John F. Kennedy but came back to win the White House in 1968.

NIXON KNEW FROM the start of his presidency that he wanted to get away from Washington as much as possible. He had long planned for it, and a few weeks after taking office, in April 1969, bought a rambling 14-room, five-bath home with white stucco walls and a red-tile roof overlooking the Pacific in San Clemente, 50 miles south of Los Angeles. He gave the estate, set among cypress, palm, and eucalyptus trees on 350 feet of oceanfront, two grand names: *La Casa Pacifica* ("House of Peace") and the Western White House.

Some of his aides tried to dress it up in fancy explanations. Herb Klein, a Nixon media adviser, told reporters it was a workplace and a showplace designed to allow a new geographic segment of the population to see government in action. "Government is not an exclusively Eastern institution," Klein said. "The San Clemente operation gives Westerners a symbolic share in the business of government, pulling West closer to East and unifying the nation."

This explanation, it turned out, was far from reality. San Clemente was Nixon's private haunt, not a place to let anyone share in the business of government. *La Casa Pacifica*, like Key Biscayne and Camp David, was where he could "have private time" to ruminate and reflect, says Ken Khachigian, one of Nixon's speechwriters, who helped him write his memoirs. "He wanted places where he could get out and do things without being confined, where he could relax and not be on stage. For him it was a getaway, and for him the getaway was less to get his batteries recharged than not to be distracted. . . . Nixon also liked to write and to think. He gets short shrift as a profound thinker as president, but he was."

In his memoirs, Nixon wrote that he needed to escape even more than he had expected. "On the personal side, the biggest surprise of the first year for Pat and me was that we had not been prepared for the paradoxical combination of loss of privacy and sense of isolation that we experienced in the White House," he observed. "When I was Vice President we had had many official obligations, but at the end of the day we went home to our family in a residential area of Washington where we did our shopping in the local markets, and had a large circle of friends with whom we could unwind and relax. But the President and First Lady soon discover that everything they do or say is potentially news. They are surrounded by Secret Service agents, staff members, communications teams, medics and doctors, transportation aides, and scores of reporters and photographers whose only job is to try to get a word with them or a picture of them. Any moments of real privacy suddenly seem especially precious, and increasingly Pat and I liked to spend time at Camp David, in Key Biscayne, and at our home in San Clemente, California.

"At the same time," Nixon added, "I discovered how isolated from the reality of American life a President can feel in the White House. For all its cosmopolitan self-confidence, Washington is a parochial city preoccupied by politics and gossip—which at times in Washington are the same thing. Like other Presidents before and after me, I felt a need to get out of the White House and out of Washington in order to keep some sense of perspective."

Strangely enough, he would occasionally leave his California estate, apparently on the spur of the moment, and take a drive along the congested San Diego Freeway in the middle of the afternoon. None of his aides was sure why he liked to ride on freeways, but he directed that traffic not be disrupted too much by his adventures. The Secret Service formed a motorcade behind the president's vehicle but the agents allowed routine traffic to pass the president on each side of his car, which he kept in the center of three lanes.

He wore a coat, tie, and slacks much of the time, even when on vacation. The product of a more formal era, he thought men of power needed to dress formally to uphold their image. His concession to leisure wear came when he slipped into a knit shirt, slacks, and loafers. "He was not a beach strolling kind of guy at all," says Khachigian.

His idea of exercise was jogging in place for five or ten minutes, pumping his arms vigorously. He said it would get his "blood running." Sometimes he took a dip in his swimming pool or the ocean. But Nixon always was careful about his diet. For breakfast he generally had orange juice, wheat germ, and a glass of milk. His favorite morning meal, which he ordered only on special occasions, was corned beef hash and poached eggs. His usual lunch was what his White House stewards called a "Hawaiian hamburger"—two pineapple rings next to a scoop of cottage cheese with a glass of skim milk. Nixon would have the meal brought to him on a tray, wolf it down in three minutes, and then be back at work. For dinner, he enjoyed a grilled or barbecued steak, nothing fancy. On infrequent occasions, especially at the beginning of his administration, he would go out to dinner at local restaurants with his wife, family members, and friends.

He is thought of as a hard-nosed political operator, but he had a sentimental attachment to the areas where he bought homes. Nixon was born and raised not far away from San Clemente in Orange County, and he had courted his wife, Pat Ryan, many years earlier in San Clemente. In fact, she accepted his proposal of marriage while they sat in a parked Oldsmobile on a bluff overlooking one of the local beaches.

From the start, Nixon made *La Casa Pacifica* his own distinctive environment. Pat redecorated the Spanish-style house, installing the French provincial furniture that the family had enjoyed in their previous residence, an apartment in New York. She favored yellow and white, with royal blue accents. The president's bedroom was red and white with a painting of Vietnam over his bed. Every room had a white telephone, and there were some special red ones for the president's exclusive use.

Nixon was frequently criticized over the years by his congressional opponents and the news media for using taxpayers' money to improve the property or to make extravagant changes for his own convenience. Even though the Camp Pendleton Marine Corps Base and a U.S. Coast Guard station were nearby, he had the military add a helicopter pad on his estate to save himself a few minutes' car trip. He also had the government make more than $1 million in additional questionable expenditures on the Spanish-style house and surrounding property, which he had bought for $340,000. Later, Nixon would be the target of considerable criticism from the media and Congress for alleged sweetheart deals in purchasing his San Clemente property, for acquiring his estate in Key Biscayne, and for having the government finance improvements to both sites. Among the changes at *La Casa Pacifica* was a $500,000 renovation and building project for offices and improvements to the 30-acre estate and adjacent government land, including a new heating system for the house, furniture, and bulletproof windows. Nixon aides said it was all done to improve security.

The house had been built in 1926 by oil millionaire and Democratic fund-raiser Hamilton Cotton, and Franklin Roosevelt had once played poker there. Nixon had his wife take charge of renovating the place, which had attracted the Nixons because it had a lovely courtyard on which all 14 rooms, except Nixon's second-floor study, opened. The focal point of the courtyard was a fountain featuring a cupid sitting atop a pyramid, with four green frogs spraying water, and an outdoor fireplace.

The inside was a different story, all dark and depressing to Nixon's two daughters, Tricia and Julie. Assisted by decorators from Los Angeles, the First Lady changed the carpets, drapes, furniture, and wallpaper, and gave the house a new coat of paint to lighten the atmosphere, which delighted everyone.

The Nixons spent three weeks at San Clemente in August 1969, his first summer in office. Julie and her husband, David Eisenhower, even persuaded the president to go swimming and bowling, and to play golf. *Time* magazine, like most of the media, looked favorably on what it called Nixon's "Tranquility Base" and ran a picture of the new president, wearing a suit and tie at the wheel of a fringed-top golf cart that he used to drive the 400 yards between his "villa" and the offices set up for White House staffers. Leisurely pursuits were unusual for Nixon, however. He loved the presidency and didn't feel comfortable unless he was working.

During this August visit, he established a pattern for his "vacations." He would read internal reports and memos, confer with key aides who made the trip with him, and talk on the phone with other advisers in Washington. He would occasionally leave the estate for a dinner of enchiladas and tacos and a margarita at El Adobe, a restaurant he favored in nearby San Juan Capistrano that featured a strolling mariachi band known as the Guadalajara Boys. He even brought the performers, wearing huge blue and silver sombreros, to entertain Lyndon Johnson, his predecessor, for a 61st birthday party that Nixon hosted.

Nixon used the occasion to bring the Johnsons 800 miles up the coast to the new Redwood National Park, where he dedicated a 300-acre redwood grove to Lady Bird Johnson.

For a while at the start of his presidency, Nixon hosted Hollywood stars at San Clemente and seemed able to smooth some of his rough edges. Over Christmas in 1970, he had dinner there with Bob and Dolores Hope, golfer Arnold Palmer, Henry Kissinger, and Gerald Ford and his wife, Betty.

Ford, who was invited spontaneously after he called Nixon to congratulate him on an interview with four TV correspondents, recalled, "The Nixons gave us a tour of *La Casa Pacifica* and the grounds, and our stay was delightful. Seldom in all the years that I'd known the President had I seen him so relaxed."

Nixon also hosted a number of foreign leaders at San Clemente, including Japanese prime minister Eisaku Sató, Mexican president Luis Echeverría Álvarez, South Vietnamese president Nguyen Van Thieu, and Soviet leader Leonid Brezhnev. Throngs of demonstrators sometimes raised a din outside the gates of the compound, protesting Nixon's policies in Vietnam and the Watergate scandal.

Brezhnev caused special problems when he insisted on staying in Nixon's villa during his visit in July 1973, not in the suite reserved for VIP visitors at nearby Camp Pendleton. The Nixons had no guest room, so they put him into daughter Tricia's bedroom, despite its blue and lavender wallpaper and delicate wicker furniture. Soviet security guards slept in daughter Julie's room.

"Sometimes our family was called square and as far as we were concerned, that was just fine," Nixon wrote. "In the environment of Washington, 'square' often means rooted in principles that ignore chic, transitory fashions. . . . Our whole family has always loved theatre, movies, and music. Our favorite relaxation after dinner at Camp David or in Florida or California was to watch a movie. Sometimes we would experiment with films we had never heard of; sometimes we would choose current hits; and sometimes old family favorites."

SPENDING TIME AT San Clemente allowed Nixon time for reflection, which often brought out his natural bitterness toward his adversaries. He frequently left his retreat in a combative mood, ready to confront his opponents or undertake big initiatives.

In the summer of 1969, he decided while in San Clemente on his replacement for Abe Fortas, who had resigned from the Supreme Court amid accusations of conflict of interest and calls for his impeachment. On August 18, Nixon announced that his nominee would be Judge Clement F. Haynsworth of South

Carolina, chief judge of the Fourth Circuit Court of Appeals, who had a segregationist past and his own conflict-of-interest problem. Nixon wanted to ram Haynsworth down the throats of the Senate liberals he hated, but opposition was too strong in the Senate and he was never confirmed.

After a harrowing incident in the mid-term congressional campaign of 1970, Nixon repaired to San Clemente to ponder why some Americans hated him so much. In the final three weeks before the election, Nixon had campaigned in 22 states, and faced angry demonstrators almost everywhere he went. At a rally of 5,000 supporters at California's San Jose Municipal Auditorium, Nixon recalled in his memoirs, a crowd of about 2,000 antiwar protesters began beating on the doors all around the building prior to his arrival. As he emerged from his limousine, he saw the protesters and grew angry when they chanted, "One, two, three, four—we don't want your fucking war." To taunt them, he stood on the hood of his limo vehicle and gave them the V-sign, for victory. Someone threw a rock, which hit the car's roof. All of a sudden, the air seemed filled with flying rocks, eggs, and vegetables, and the Secret Service insisted that the president get back in the limo. One of the other cars in the motorcade stalled and its windows were broken, along with windows in the press bus. Worse, several Secret Service agents and others were hit by rocks and glass. The organizer of the demonstration said later, "After dropping that many bombs on the Vietnamese people how can anyone associated with the government claim to be upset about people throwing some eggs and rocks at Nixon? What's so precious about Nixon that he can't take a few eggs when he can dish out so many bombs?"

Nixon admitted the incident was "very disturbing," and he couldn't take his mind off it when he arrived at San Clemente that night, October 29. He sat in his study for more than an hour and pondered the sad state of affairs. His unsettled mood deepened when he was awakened by the Secret Service just before midnight because smoke was filling the house from a fire in the dining room wall and ceiling. It had started when he left a blaze going in the fireplace of his second-floor den before retiring for the night, and it spread through the metal backing of the fireplace and into the internal walls. There wasn't much damage, but the president was forced to leave the house in his pajamas, robe, and slippers and spend the night in a guest house on the estate.

"As far as I knew this was the first time in our history that a mob had physically attacked the President of the United States," he recalled. "I did not care what these demonstrators or their leaders thought about me personally, but if they did not respect the office of the presidency, I thought that people should be made to recognize that fact and take sides on it."

His brooding led to one of the toughest speeches of his presidency, delivered two days later at Sky Harbor Airport in Phoenix. "Violence in America today is not caused by the war," Nixon declared. "It is not caused by repression. There is no romantic ideal involved. Let's recognize these people for what they are. They are not romantic revolutionaries. They are the same thugs and hoodlums that have always plagued the good people."

In August 1972, he watched on TV from San Clemente as the Democrats nominated liberal senator George McGovern of South Dakota as their presidential candidate. After dinner, Nixon sat in the living room with John Connally, the former Texas governor who had become a Nixon confidant, and assessed the speeches. Things ran so late that McGovern didn't begin his address until nearly 3 A.M. Eastern Time, and Nixon said the proceedings had "the air of a college skit." Just as important, Nixon concluded that McGovern was far too liberal for the country and could easily be caricatured as a somewhat loony, dangerous radical on both domestic issues and national security. This is precisely what Nixon did, and he won a second term in a landslide.

NIXON USED KEY Biscayne, Florida, for shorter stays. It was only a two-and-a-half-hour flight aboard *Air Force One* from Washington, and Nixon liked the mild Florida weather in winter, as so many Northerners do.

Nixon called the estate his "Southern White House" but he had an emotional attachment to the area, like San Clemente, that far predated his presidency. It was where he went to pull himself together after he lost the 1960 election to John F. Kennedy. In the days immediately following his narrow and bitter defeat, he was urged by Republican leaders to challenge the results because they believed there was massive voter fraud in Illinois and a recount might reverse the outcome. On Friday, three days after the election, Nixon ordered Herb Klein, one of his spokesmen, to announce that he would accept the outcome and move on. Later, Nixon said that was the wise course because he had little chance to prevail, and that a fight over the election would divide the country and damage American prestige abroad. Finally, he concluded that such a battle would brand him a sore loser, eliminating any chance of a comeback.

Just after winning the 1968 election, Nixon decided to institutionalize his visits to Key Biscayne when he paid $252,800 for two houses on adjacent properties there. These properties were next to estates owned by wealthy Nixon friends Charles "Bebe" Rebozo and Robert Abplanalp, who allowed the Secret Service to use their property as buffer zones to insure the president's privacy.

Nixon's estate, combined with the adjacent properties, commanded 600 feet of prime beachfront and was landscaped with pine and umbrella trees, sea grape, and hibiscus. Yet following the same pattern he adopted at San Clemente, he had the government spend more than $625,000 for improvements. This caused a furor when congressional investigators and auditors concluded that Nixon was spending too much of the taxpayers' money to upgrade his property and give himself such creature comforts as a $621 ice-making machine because he didn't like ice "with holes in it."

More justifiably, he spent $418,000 for a helicopter pad near his home in Key Biscayne, drawing the money from secret military accounts. And he had a metal fence installed underwater so sharks could not get close.

On average, it cost taxpayers more than $7 million a year to fly staff members and others between Washington and the two houses.

Nixon's routine at Key Biscayne was based on his desire to rejuvenate himself. He occasionally went for a swim or for a boat ride. But he couldn't really let go—a problem he always had when he tried to relax. In June 1972, for example, after a hectic period in Washington, he left for a weekend in Florida "on his own." His wife, Pat, was making appearances on the West Coast, and his two daughters, Julie and Tricia, were with their husbands. In his briefcase he took a campaign strategy memo from speech writer Pat Buchanan, briefing memos on welfare reform, and two books—Irving Kristol's *On the Democratic Idea in America* and Winston Churchill's *Triumph and Tragedy*. Not exactly light reading. But he always sought to keep his mind active and in this case he wanted in particular to reread Churchill's analysis of the Yalta Conference with Franklin Roosevelt and Josef Stalin, in hopes of gaining insight into the future of U.S.-Soviet relations after his recent meetings with Soviet leaders.

He spent Friday afternoon, June 16, and all day Saturday at Grand Cay, a small island in the Bahamas owned by his friend, Robert Abplanalp. He went for a swim and took a walk around the island. "The caretaker's wife gave me two brightly colored shirts she had made for me," the president recalled, "and I talked with her 12-year-old daughter, who showed me some of the turtles she had been raising."

Then his pace began to quicken. On Saturday, June 17, he called H. R. Haldeman, his chief of staff, to check on various issues. He told Haldeman, among other things, to make sure there was a plank in the Republican platform that election year supporting federal aid to parochial schools. In the afternoon he went boating with Abplanalp and Bebe Rebozo.

On Sunday morning, June 18, Nixon and Rebozo left for Key Biscayne. When they reached his house, Nixon went to the kitchen for a cup of coffee. "There was a *Miami Herald* on the counter, and I glanced over the front page," he wrote in his memoirs. "The main headline was about the Vietnam withdrawals: GROUND COMBAT ROLE NEARS END FOR U.S. There was a small story in the middle of the page on the left-hand side, under the headline MIAMIANS HELD IN D.C. TRY TO BUG DEMO HEADQUARTERS."

Nixon claimed that this was the first he knew of the break-in by pro-Nixon political operatives at the Watergate Hotel to tap the phones and steal records of the Democratic National Committee. After reading the story, he recalled, "I dismissed it as some sort of prank."

Later that morning, he reached Haldeman at the Key Biscayne Hotel, where he was staying with the traveling staff, and they discussed whether to have a signing ceremony for a higher education bill, and whether George Meany, head of the AFL-CIO, would endorse liberal Democrat George McGovern if McGovern won the Democratic presidential nomination. Unable to take his mind off his job, he proceeded to make phone calls for the rest of the day, talking to adviser Henry Kissinger, who was on a trip to Beijing, and to aide Chuck Colson, twice, to discuss the possible Meany development and Nixon's concern that the media would be sympathetic to McGovern. He found time for a swim in the ocean that afternoon, had dinner at home with Rebozo, watched a movie, and ended his day by reading the last chapters of *Triumph and Tragedy* in his study before retiring in mid-evening.

On Monday, instead of enjoying the light breeze and sunshine, he went straight to his study and got on the phone again. "The Watergate break-in was still the furthest thing from my mind as I talked with Julie, Tricia, Rose Woods [his personal secretary], Al Haig, and Billy Graham. I also talked with Chuck Colson; the only note that I dictated in my diary about our conversation recounted our detailed analysis of a new set of poll figures covering everything from confidence in presidential leadership to the economy." He talked to Haldeman several times by phone, including one hour-long chat that covered a multitude of topics, including the possibility that George Wallace might become a third-party presidential candidate, the increase in food prices, the appointment of a new chief of protocol, and the coming week's schedule. In the afternoon, he went boating and took a long walk before dinner. He boarded *Air Force One* at 7:48 P.M. for the trip back to Washington.

He wrote in his diary at the end of that day: "I am convinced that it is essential to get more exercise. I think one of the reasons that I feel tonight not only more rested but frankly more sharp and more eager to get work done is because I have had rest, and also have had the fresh air and the exercise. I am going to try a routine of bowling for a half hour at the end of each day before coming over to the Residence. This may have a good effect.

"On the way back, I got the disturbing news from Bob Haldeman that the break-in of the Democratic National Committee involved someone who is on the payroll of the Committee to Re-elect the President." Nixon said this was the first he'd heard of the break-in's link to his committee.

NIXON'S HOUSES AT San Clemente and Key Biscayne became hideaways in the literal sense. Nixon had to be persuaded to leave the buildings under virtually any circumstances, even to play golf or take walks. At Key Biscayne, for example, Nixon stayed at his compound and kept the staff at hotel villas a half mile away across a peninsula. Within that compound, Nixon would sometimes avoid even his wife, sleeping in a bedroom at the converted office two lots away from his residence rather than his regular bedroom next door to hers.

On August 24, 1969, he flew his Urban Affairs Council to San Clemente for a lengthy meeting about his New Federalism initiative to send states and local governments lump sums of money instead of tying such grants to specific programs. He told the group he had just met with Cardinal James Francis McIntyre, Roman Catholic archbishop of Los Angeles, and said, "Speaking of education, I've never assumed that education is the sacred cow some believe it is. It is so goddamn ridiculous to assume everyone should go to college. I'm not suggesting that there be more manual laborers. I am suggesting that in terms of violent frustration, far more than black, white, or potentially Mexican, the frustration of a man or woman with a college degree, having nothing he is prepared for, is the greatest. There is nothing for him or her to do but join the revolution."

At one point, Commerce Secretary Maurice Stans described the problem of cutting government programs. "In eighteen months," during the Eisenhower administration, "we succeeded with only one—a program of fifty thousand dollars a year to eliminate weeds on Indian reservations." Nixon, trying to lighten the mood, said, "What are the poor Indians going to eat?" It apparently was designed as a playful wisecrack, but it also revealed, at minimum, Nixon's insensitive side.

OCCASIONALLY, HE HOSTED a foreign leader in one of his lairs. In December 1971, Nixon met for six hours at Key Biscayne with West German chancellor Willy Brandt over the Christmas holidays.

Nixon probed for information about Soviet president Brezhnev, whom Brandt knew relatively well. Brandt said he thought Moscow was genuinely interested in normalizing relations with the United States and Western Europe. Nixon replied that perhaps this was because the Soviets were worried about threats from China and wanted to calm relations with the West so the Russian leaders could focus on Beijing. Nixon concluded that he should take steps to widen the rift between the two communist countries.

ON THE PERSONAL side, Nixon's clumsiness was evident to his closest aides, as was his lack of everyday practicality. He was very unmechanical, and needed assistance in adjusting his chair and the sound system on *Air Force One*, no matter how many times he tried on his own.

He was generally Spartan in his personal habits, but he indulged himself on occasion. For example, he made sure that his staff stocked several gallons of macadamia-nut ice cream from the Alpha Beta Supermarket near San Clemente when he visited the estate. The store was one of the few in the nation to bring in the dessert from Hawaii, where it was made.

THE DAY AFTER his reelection triumph in November 1972, Nixon met with the White House staff at 11 A.M. To everyone's surprise, he gave them perfunctory thanks, said he would immediately begin to "tear up the pea patch," and walked out of the room. H. R. Haldeman, his chief of staff, then took over the meeting and demanded everyone's resignation. He made the same demand of the

Cabinet at noon. Even Nixon's intimates were appalled at his insensitivity and what Henry Kissinger called "this political butchery." But Nixon was eager for a fast start in his second term, wanted to avoid the "lethargy" he had seen during Dwight Eisenhower's second term, and had many scores to settle with his adversaries. He wanted new subordinates who were full of energy and ready for battle. It was no time for sentimentality.

Later that day, he flew to Key Biscayne, where, without the demands of protocol or the endless stream of interruptions he faced in the West Wing, his paranoia and vindictiveness had full sway.

For several days, his wife; his daughters Julie Eisenhower and Tricia Cox; their husbands, David and Edward; his friend Bebe Rebozo; and a handful of aides, including Kissinger, Haldeman, and domestic adviser John Ehrlichman, joined him. While the others swam and lolled in the sun, Nixon, Haldeman, and Ehrlichman isolated themselves as they plotted a government reorganization and a plan for political revenge.

Nixon wanted as much decision making as possible concentrated at the White House and confined to a small cadre of people who were personally loyal to him, such as Haldeman and Ehrlichman.

On November 10, he ordered Haldeman to send an "action memo" to the staff. "Be sure," the president wrote, "we have established a total embargo on *Time* and *Newsweek* and especially no background material to [Hugh] Sidey [a *Time* columnist who specialized in the presidency]." Nixon also ordered a "complete freeze on the *Washington Post, The New York Times*, and CBS." On November 12, as his anger percolated, he demanded unspecified retribution against Democratic contributors.

On November 15, he told Haldeman to prepare a monograph listing predictions that commentators and columnists had made that turned out to be wrong, such as dire international repercussions and a possible world war from Nixon's sending of troops into Cambodia in 1970. Nixon also directed his staff to prepare a monograph that he called "Dirtiest Campaign in History Against a President," in which attacks on him would be enumerated from the 1972 campaign and earlier. Finally, Nixon wanted a monograph entitled "RN Won It!," in which the argument would be made that he defeated Democratic challenger George McGovern "against overwhelming odds," and that Nixon had stood up for principle in Vietnam and elsewhere despite political adversity.

His anger and resentment intensified in the heat and humidity of Key Biscayne as he let his mind wander over the perceived and real slights of his political career. After a week of this, he flew to Washington briefly and then continued his ruminations at Camp David, where he persisted in plotting his vendettas for several more days.

The year ended on a sad note for him. Peace talks in Paris had bogged down again, with both the North Vietnamese and the U.S.-backed government of South Vietnam stubbornly at odds with Nixon's ideas for ending the fighting. Feeling that one final push might end the Vietnam War, he ordered a massive bombing campaign against Hanoi, which began on December 18, 1972.

The reaction was furious and negative. The stock market suffered its biggest drop in a year and a half. Members of Congress were up in arms. After all, Henry Kissinger had declared "peace is at hand" only a few weeks earlier. Had that been a lie? Senator William Saxbe, an Ohio Republican, said Nixon "appears to have left his senses." Senate Democratic leader Mike Mansfield of Montana called it a "stone-age tactic." Columnist James Reston called it "war by tantrum" and commentator Anthony Lewis said Nixon was acting "like a maddened tyrant."

When the president flew to Key Biscayne for Christmas, he ordered a 24-hour halt to the bombing for the day. Noting that he and his wife were depressed because their daughters were in Europe with their husbands, and the house seemed empty without them, he wrote poignantly in his diary: "It is inevitable that not only the President but the First Lady become more and more lonely individuals in a sense who have to depend on fewer and fewer people who can give them a lift when they need it even though ironically there are millions more who know them and would help if they could just be given the chance to do so. It is a question not of too many friends but really too few—one of the inevitable consequences of this position." Much later, Nixon confided that Christmas of 1972 was also difficult because he had received so few holiday greetings from anyone, even from fellow Republicans in Congress or members of his Cabinet, during his time of tribulation. "It was the loneliest and saddest Christmas I can ever remember," he said.

Still, he stuck to his guns. The day after Christmas, he ordered the biggest bombing raid yet against Hanoi, with 111 gigantic B-52 bombers dropping their deadly payloads from the sky. That afternoon, Hanoi proposed the resumption of peace talks in Paris. After private discussions among the belligerents, Nixon again suspended the bombing of Hanoi and the talks did indeed resume.

But public reaction was mixed. The hawks said the bombing should have continued. Others argued that the bombing had been too costly—15 B-52s had been downed, with 93 American airmen missing and 31 more captured as POWs—and that Nixon had been forced back into the talks by world outrage. As 1972 ended, there was still no sign that the South Vietnamese government in Saigon would accept Nixon's terms for peace—representing no change in its position from before the bombing.

In January 1973, Nixon gave his mind free rein at Key Biscayne as he pondered his agenda for the next four years. He was deeply troubled by many perceived trends in American society, such as the rise of federal power; the government's resistance to change; the liberal bias and anti-Nixon hostility of the media; the alienation of cultural elites in politics, academia, the arts, and the churches to the traditional notion of patriotism; and the increase in self-doubt among these elites about America's enduring values.

On January 11, he summarized his hopes and plans in handwritten notes he made on a large desk blotter in his study at Key Biscayne. "This was to have been the blueprint for my second term as President," he wrote in his memoirs. Under the heading, "Goals for 2nd term," Nixon listed among his objectives of "substance" as "Russia—Salt; China—Exchange. Mideast—Settlement. Europe—Community. Trade." And on domestic issues, he included crime, drugs, education, health, and race. He listed three "personal" goals—"Restore Respect for Office—New idealism, respect for flag-country, Compassion—understanding." They were worthy goals, but all of them would be thwarted by the Watergate scandal.

A WHITE HOUSE aide called the break-in at the Democratic headquarters a "third-rate burglary," and Nixon always maintained that he knew nothing about it in advance.

But Jeb Stuart Magruder, one of Nixon's key aides, told a different story. Years after leaving the White House, he reversed his previous comments and claimed in a PBS interview broadcast on July 30, 2003, that Nixon personally ordered the burglary during a telephone conversation on March 30, 1972. Magruder said Nixon was in Washington and he gave the order to Attorney General John Mitchell, who was staying in Key Biscayne. Magruder was in the same room as Mitchell and Fred LaRue, another Nixon aide, and he says he overheard Nixon through a telephone receiver held by Mitchell. LaRue denies the story and says Nixon never knew of the burglary in advance.

The truth may never be known. But the subsequent cover-up of White House involvement became part of the Watergate scandal, and it led to Nixon's resignation on August 9, 1974—making him the only president in U.S. history to resign, as his impeachment and conviction seemed unstoppable. "Nixon fell," writes author Roger Morris, "because his first instinct, when informed of a burglary in which, as far as we know, he had played no part, was to hide the embarrassing but probably not lethal truth (that high-ranking aides in his campaign and in the White House had been involved), and to make illegal use of government agencies to conceal evidence; and he fell because the extent of his dishonesty ultimately became irrefutably clear when a congressional investigation uncovered the existence of a secret taping system in the White House that had recorded almost all the president's conversations."

On that same day, August 9, he flew to San Clemente and began a new life with his wife, Pat, at their villa. They stayed there for months in seclusion.

But over the years, they felt isolated from their daughters and their grandchildren, who lived on the East Coast, and many of their friends and associates in the Washington area. They eventually moved to New York in a remarkable irony: Nixon at the end of his life no longer wanted the isolation he got from his retreats, which had been so important to him during his turbulent era in the White House.

THE WAY THAT Nixon behaved at his hideaways reinforced the image of him as an intensely private, solitary man. He was heavily criticized for using taxpayers' money for his homes, which intensified perceptions that he was a dishonest politician who was feathering his own nest at public expense. Above all, Nixon was unable to use his retreats to actually get away from his work, and he displayed a penchant for plotting there against his adversaries.

CHAPTER THIRTEEN

GERALD FORD AND VAIL, COLORADO

FOR NEARLY ALL of his life in politics, Gerald Ford didn't expect to be president. He didn't seek the job, didn't dream about it, didn't plot to attain it.

So it came as a surprise to Ford that Richard Nixon plucked him from the House of Representatives, where he was a veteran member from Grand Rapids, Michigan, to make him vice president. This came after the October 10, 1973, resignation of Spiro Agnew, who was under a legal cloud for alleged corruption in his previous life as governor of Maryland. Nixon settled on plain, non-threatening Jerry Ford because he knew the congressman's many friends in the Senate would confirm him easily.

Not long after Ford ascended to the vice presidency, Nixon got into deep trouble with the Watergate scandal and resigned in August 1974. A scant 10 months earlier, Ford's political life had been defined by Rotary Club meetings and road projects in Grand Rapids. Now he was president of the United States and facing a nightmarish challenge: a divided country, serious domestic and international problems, and anger toward his party over Nixon's transgressions.

Ford took the oath of office on August 9, 1974, and declared that "our long national nightmare is over," but he was wrong. Ford's pardon of Nixon on September 8, 1974, absolving him of any crimes he may have committed as president, made matters worse. His popularity sank like a stone. A week later, a Gallup poll found that only 49 percent of Americans approved of his job performance, down from 71 percent.

The pardon was instrumental in causing Ford's defeat at the hands of Democrat Jimmy Carter in 1976, after only 895 days in office. This was one of the shortest terms in U.S. history and the shortest in the 20th century. Many voters suspected that he granted the pardon as part of a corrupt bargain in order to secure power for himself.

As if all that wasn't enough, it was a very difficult time to be president for other reasons. American involvement in the Vietnam War was ending badly, with the North Vietnamese and Viet Cong taking over the country in a humiliating rout of the U.S.-backed government in Saigon. The economy was in trouble, with soaring inflation that rattled the nerves of everyone from home buyers to grocery shoppers. The country fell into recession, and the unemployment rate rose. A generation gap divided young from old, and racial tensions split America's cities and seemed to be poisoning the culture.

In an interview for this book, Ford told me, "We were as full of problems back then as they are today. . . . I would say what we had on our agenda was a darned heavy load."

Try as he might, he was largely unable to lessen that load at the retreats he chose for his vacations, mainly the ski resort at Vail, Colorado. His presidential vacations did something they rarely did to his predecessors—made his image worse, by intensifying the perception that he was a bumbler.

WHAT WAS PARTICULARLY unfortunate about Ford was that he was never able to convey to the country his best qualities—his work ethic, his openness, his integrity, his intelligence, his serenity.

During his first few weeks in office, Ford seemed a refreshing change from the secretive, manipulative, and scandal-plagued Nixon. He came across as unpretentious and approachable. It helped when the White House staff made it known that he fixed his own English muffins for breakfast. He held frequent press conferences, and got off to a good start.

But then, things deteriorated. A graduate of the University of Michigan and Yale Law School with a strong understanding of all the major issues of his time, he was falsely caricatured as a nincompoop. As David Gergen, one of his advisers, said later, "While he was in office, that image of Ford as a bumbler, someone who meant well but, as Lyndon Johnson once said, couldn't walk straight and chew gum at the same time, took deep root in public thinking. . . . Those of us around him in the government knew that he was more intelligent and more physically graceful than the press said (after all, he had been offered a contract to play professional football), and we struggled to help people see the man we worked for each day. But, in retrospect, most of us inside did not take the full measure of the man, either. We should have."

"Until he spared Nixon, Ford enjoyed an outburst of media admiration," Gergen adds. "But after the pardon and the WIN campaign [an ill-conceived effort called Whip Inflation Now, in which consumers and industry were supposed to voluntarily restrain their demands for the good of the nation], the press turned on him with ridicule that was severe and merciless. Now he was the man who played too many football games without his helmet, the president who bumped his head when he turned to wave from his helicopter."

UNFORTUNATELY, HIS VACATIONS at Vail intensified this image. "The Fords had a tradition that they would spend Christmas as a family in Vail," recalls Ron Nessen, Ford's White House press secretary. During Ford's years in Congress, he was either working late hours in Washington or traveling the country to campaign for other Republicans, and Betty, his wife, was left at home to care for the kids. So their time at Vail became one of the few periods when the whole family could be together, skiing, hiking, going out to dinner, and sitting around the fire enjoying one another's company. During his presidency, Ford also managed to visit Vail in warm weather occasionally to play golf and relax.

For years, the Fords had a three-bedroom condominium at Vail overlooking the center of town, and even when he was vice president, some of his advisers were leery about the family outings at the expensive resort. In 1973, the year before he took over from Nixon, some of them raised objections to his upcoming Christmas trip because of widespread energy shortages and lengthening lines at gasoline stations. It just wouldn't look right, they said. Ford lost patience and overruled them. When he started doing knee-strengthening exercises at the office, his staff knew he was serious about his annual ski trip, which he proceeded to take.

Betty Ford remembers that excursion as revelatory, in a negative way, because of the around-the-clock Secret Service protection of the new vice president. "Old habits had to be changed," she says. "We stayed in our condominium in the Lodge at Vail during Christmas vacation of 1973, and it was devilish. For the command post to operate, there had to be a truck parked down below our windows, and there were agents sitting at a table outside our front door, and other people who had apartments in the lodge weren't allowed to come up the outside stairs."

After that experience, the Fords rented a much larger chalet at the foot of the ski lifts from wealthy friend Richard Bass, a Dallas businessman. This gave them more privacy and more room. But the media dwelled on the poshness of the quarters. On January 1, 1975, under the headline IT's NOT EXACTLY A "WINTER WHITE HOUSE," *The New York Times* reported, "The Bass home is a four-story natural cedar chalet with a moss rock foundation and turquoise trim, which sits among tall spruce trees and 18 other private homes in an area called Mill Creek Circle. Another house on the circle is currently being offered for sale at $350,000. The house is at the base of the ski mountain, only about 100 yards from the main gondola lift and about equal distance from the center of Vail . . . The living room fireplace, made out of lichen-covered granite, reaches up and through a 29-foot sloped beam ceiling."

Under the headline PRESIDENT PLAYS TENNIS AND GOLF IN COLORADO, *The New York Times* carried an Associated Press dispatch on August 18, 1975, that gives short shrift to the business part of the trip, a two-day visit to four states, but adds, "Mr. Ford and Secretary of State Kissinger took their wives dancing at a discotheque in Vail last night, and heard the Inkspots. Today Mr. Ford played tennis with Richard Bass, the Dallas businessman who owns the vacation home Mr. Ford is using here, James Brown, a Utah rancher, and Trammell Crowe, another Dallas businessman. The President played golf, for the seventh day, in the afternoon." Such coverage made it seem that Ford was a hopeless elitist.

But privately, he was as down-to-earth and considerate as ever. At one point, his dog, Liberty, answered nature's call on the floor of the Bass house during dinner. As a steward rushed in to dispose of the mess, Ford stopped him. "No man should have to clean up after another man's dog," the president announced, and did the job himself.

But Ford's experiences on the slopes deepened his stumblebum image. Like virtually everyone who skis, he fell once in a while. Yet every time he did, photographers would capture the image and send it around the world: the president taking a spill or looking hapless in the snow.

The media and *Saturday Night Live*, the hit television show that was gaining a huge audience with its irreverent humor, piled on. Comedian Chevy Chase did a hilarious impersonation of Ford as a clueless incompetent that stuck in the nation's consciousness.

Ford didn't get openly upset or angry. Ron Nessen, his press secretary, said he heard his boss complain about his image problem only once during his two and a half years in office. Ford had invited Nessen over for drinks during one Christmas at Vail, and as they watched his latest spill on TV, the president said ruefully, "You know, those reporters get most of their exercise on the bar stool." Then he let the matter drop.

In his autobiography, Ford sums up the situation: "I flew to Vail with the family for a one-week Christmas holiday. I was looking forward to relaxing and skiing with my family and friends. I spent three hours on the slopes on Christmas Day and skied every day of my vacation after that. Some of my aides warned me that I was taking a risk. My public image, they pointed out, was that of an amiable bumbler who was sitting in the White House just waiting until a 'real' president came along. If I fell on the slopes, the press would seize on that and my image problems would intensify.

"I told them their concerns were ridiculous. I had skied for most of my life and I wasn't about to stop doing something I loved to do just because reporters and photographers might be there. *Every* skier falls, I said. Surely, the press would understand that. But I was wrong. One day I took a tumble in the snow and footage of my fall was on the network news that night. Photographs appeared on the front pages of newspapers everywhere, and editorial cartoonists had a field day. I remember one cartoon in the *Denver Post*. There I was skiing, backward, down a hill; a bystander was explaining: 'I understand his ski instructor is also his campaign manager.'

"The photographs and cartoons didn't bother me as much as they upset my family and staff, but that particular cartoon in the *Denver Post* hit uncomfortably close to home. My campaign, in fact, did seem to be sliding downhill."

In an interview for this book, the 90-year-old Ford still was sensitive about his treatment three decades earlier. "I never publicly criticized the press for it but I couldn't help but not like it because I was not a bad skier, and it just happened that all the pictures they showed were my infrequent falling on my fanny. They somehow always got a picture of me on my back and that's what they used. . . . But, you know, that's part of the ball game and I never let it really bother me openly." Privately, he seethed, which he admitted to me.

And he devised a plan to soften his coverage and perhaps embarrass his tormentors at the same time. Ford invited the White House press corps to go skiing with him in 1975, and half the reporters and photographers accepted. So off they went up the chair lifts on the more challenging runs at Vail, with Ford in the lead along with a professional skier who lived at the resort.

What Ford hadn't told the journalists was that he had conspired with the pro skier to lead the press corps on some particularly challenging runs to show them that anyone could take a spill on the slopes. Ford recalled it later as "a real workout" that left several of the news people on their own fannies along the powdery trails.

The problem was that the gambit didn't result in better coverage. The story line of the inept president was just irresistible, even if it wasn't true.

THE FORDS ALSO would spend Easter at Palm Springs, California, where Ford would play golf and tennis, and stay at a house owned by wealthy friend Fred C. Wilson. The president endeared himself to the crew members of *Air Force One* by inviting them over for meals, since they had to be away from their families because of his vacations.

But his Easter trip to Palm Springs in 1975 coincided with the fall of Saigon, and worsened his image. His advisers had warned him against going, arguing that it would make him appear insensitive and aloof, but again he overruled them. He had spent eight previous Easters at the desert resort, he said, and he and his family were looking forward to continuing the tradition. Besides, he added, he was working very hard and needed a break. He proceeded to rent the fancy home of insurance millionaire Wilson for nine days, at $100 a day out of his own pocket.

As with his time at Vail, this arrangement caused him more problems. *The New York Times*, for instance, noted that the Wilson home was worth $355,000—a particularly large sum in 1975—and referred to the "lavishness of the estate," which included one swimming pool and two other pools described by a presidential spokesman as "ornamental." *The Times* also pointed out that Ford's schedule called for regular games of golf with rich businessmen.

He was indeed on the golf course nearly every day—and news photographers were allowed to take his picture in his baseball cap, short-sleeved shirt, and plaid pants, as South Vietnam collapsed under the invasion of the Communists. "In better times, Ford's week in Palm Springs would have raised few eyebrows; the last four Presidents have all vacationed there," reads an article that appeared in *Newsweek*. "But viewed against a background of domestic recession and foreign war, the luxurious spa worried the President's aides. Ford stayed in a posh neighborhood called Thunderbird Heights, a development that adjoins a country club, is patrolled by private police and lists its residents by name beneath street signs. Neighbors include industrialist Leonard K. Firestone, entertainers Alice Faye, Phil Harris, Hoagy Carmichael and Ginger Rogers." The *Newsweek* article goes on to describe in vivid detail the extravagant nature of Ford's rented digs, offering such details as the "enormous glass-walled living room with a 20-foot bar and fireplaces at each end. . . . 50-foot, turquoise-tiled, S-shaped swimming pool . . . a double-jet fountain, inlaid with mosaics and adorned by a bronze nude."

Each night, the network news showed harrowing pictures of South Vietnamese trying desperately to escape from their capital, standing on rooftops as U.S. helicopters airlifted as many out as they could but with many women and children left behind. Those images were juxtaposed with Ford on the links at the playground of the super-rich.

Reporters were allowed to ask the president a few questions as he teed off, and they quizzed him about why he was playing golf when a crisis was occurring with America's ally in Southeast Asia. He had no adequate explanation, except that he worked hard and deserved a vacation with his family. When reporters badgered White House Press Secretary Ron Nessen about why Ford was playing golf while South Vietnam was being humiliated, Nessen replied heatedly, "Would it prevent anything from happening in Vietnam if he did *not* play golf?"

Taken alone, it might not have made much difference in his image. But with millions of Americans suffering because of the faltering economy, it made Ford look aloof and uncaring.

IN OUR INTERVIEW, Ford was magnanimous in retrospect. And he told me that having a regular place to go for R & R and to be with his family isn't mandatory for a president. "It's important but it's not critical," he said. "I had two places that I utilized for that purpose—Camp David being one and Vail, Colorado, another. I looked forward to going to either or both, but I'm kind of a workaholic, so I could still do my job without over-emphasizing a retreat."

He added, "When we would go to Vail at Christmastime, for example, I would have my top people come out. We would schedule a couple of days where I could spend maybe three hours with them. And then the rest of the time I would use for relaxation, family get-togethers, and so forth. At Camp David that was quite different. I didn't have the pressure of the family involving itself. My wife always was along and on occasion we would take one or more of our children, or some other members of my staff, but there was a lot more opportunity to continue work at Camp David than at Vail."

VAIL WAS ALSO associated with an unsettling family development for the Fords. Just before Thanksgiving in 1975, their 18-year-old daughter, Susan, told the First Lady she wanted to move to Vail to live near Brian McCartney, her boyfriend at the time. He was a 27-year-old member of the ski patrol who had met Susan during previous Ford family ski trips. She wanted to decide if they loved each other enough to be married. Against her father's wishes (her mother was more tolerant), Susan took off from her freshman year at Mount Vernon College, moved to Vail, and shared an apartment with another young woman. After several weeks, she and Brian stopped dating, and Susan eventually moved back to Washington and then attended Kansas University. But the Vail interlude caused no small amount of parental angst for the president and First Lady.

FORD SAID ONE of the most important decisions he made at Vail was to convene an annual meeting of what became known as the Group of Seven, the leaders of the world's seven wealthiest industrialized democracies. The United States, Europe, and most nations in Asia were suffering through a period of serious inflation combined with high unemployment and lack of productivity—dubbed "stagflation"—and Ford decided to hold an "economic summit" with three of his counterparts—Prime Minister James Callaghan of Great Britain, President Valéry Giscard d'Estaing of France, and Chancellor Helmut Schmidt of West Germany. Those four then decided to add Canada, Italy, and Japan to the invitation list, and the G-7 was born. The group still meets each year for an international summit in one of the member countries, on a rotating basis, and is considered important in forging personal relationships among the leaders.

On the political front, Ford used a "working vacation" at Vail in August 1976 to devise his campaign strategy against Democrat Jimmy Carter. The challenge was daunting. The Gallup Poll placed Carter ahead of Ford by 56 percent to 33 percent, and Bob Teeter, Ford's campaign pollster, projected that if nothing changed, Ford would lose by nearly 9,500,000 votes.

Ford decided to replace the ailing Rogers Morton with James Baker as his campaign chairman. Stu Spencer would remain as deputy for political affairs. Teeter would be in charge of polling. Dick Cheney, then White House chief of staff, would continue as liaison between the White House and the Ford reelection committee. Bill Greener, assistant secretary of defense for public affairs, would become the campaign spokesman. Doug Bailey and John Deardorff would be brought in to run the television and radio ad campaigns. Ford also decided to begin negotiations with Carter on the number and format of debates.

Then came the hard part. Ford found that he had plenty of talented people to choose from in selecting key personnel to run his campaign. But figuring out the strategy to overtake Carter proved much more difficult.

As Ford sat with his senior advisers, including his vice presidential running mate Bob Dole, around the fireplace in the basement of his rented chalet, the strategy took shape. He would base his campaign on the theme of trust. "The voters, in my opinion, didn't care that much about my position on this specific issue or that," Ford would write later. "What they wanted was someone in the White House who would be honest with them. I had tried to run an open administration for the past two years, and my term had been scandal-free. I hoped this would convince people that I deserved their trust."

Ford also decided that he had to make Carter the central issue. "If we could portray him as untested and untried," Ford concluded, "if we could tie him to the liberal spending policies of urban Democrats and say that he was taking those stands because he didn't know the facts, we might be able to provoke him into a serious mistake."

Unfortunately for Ford, Americans decided that it was Carter who would run a more trustworthy administration, and it was the incumbent rather than the challenger who was forced into a serious mistake.

In his debate with Carter on October 6, 1976, in San Francisco, Ford was asked about the political situation in Eastern Europe, and he said, "There is no Soviet domination of Eastern Europe, and there never will be under a Ford administration." It was a huge gaffe. What he meant to say was that the spirit of the Eastern European people remained independent despite the control exerted over them by Moscow, but it didn't come across that way. Again, the image was revived that Ford was too dumb to be president.

On the night of November 1, on the eve of the balloting, Ford and his wife made a stop in his hometown of Grand Rapids, Michigan, which he had represented in Congress for so many years. His voice was a rasp, and he was exhausted, but he found several thousand people waiting for him in front of the Pantlind Hotel, and this gave him new life.

The next morning, just after he and Betty cast their ballots, they unveiled a large mural at the Kent County Airport. Ford said, "That was the most special moment of the entire campaign." The mural depicted Ford's career, starting with a scene of him as an Eagle Scout with his parents, and proceeding through his presidency.

"I guess the name will be the Gerald R. Ford Mural," he said. "It means so much to me because of the first Gerald R. Ford and his wife, Dorothy, my mother and father. I owe everything to them and to the training, the love, the leadership"— here, he paused as he wept and brushed away the tears—"and whatever has been done by me in any way whatsoever, it is because of Jerry Ford, Senior, and Dorothy Ford. And that is what that mural will always mean to me in the years ahead."

The next day, things came tumbling down. Ford had pulled very close as doubts about Carter grew, but in the end the former governor of Georgia won the election and ousted Ford from the presidency. It was the only election that Ford ever lost.

Jerry and Betty then retired to Palm Springs, the site of their Easter vacations for 15 years. They loved the warm climate; there were plenty of golf courses for the former president to enjoy; and the hot, dry weather was much better for Betty's arthritis than the frigid, damp winters in Grand Rapids. They also wanted a clean break with Washington after their bitter loss, so they decided not to stay in their house in suburban Alexandria, Virginia, which they had used while Ford was a congressman. They also held on to what became their summer residence near Vail.

It was at Palm Springs that Betty Ford finally recognized that she had a drinking problem and was overly reliant on medications for arthritis, a pinched nerve, and muscle spasms in her neck. She publicly admitted she was an alcoholic, entered a treatment program, and became an example for many Americans trying to conquer their addictions.

Because of health problems and advancing age, they no longer skied at Vail but remained active and, by all accounts, content with their place in history. Above all, they were serene in the idea that they had done their best under trying circumstances and had restored a measure of integrity to the presidency.

FORD'S ACTIVITIES AT his retreats reinforced the image of him as too cozy with the rich and powerful, which may have been true. But they also strengthened the perception that he was clumsy, dumb, and aloof, and none of these was accurate. He never took the criticisms personally—further evidence of his basic decency.

CHAPTER FOURTEEN

JIMMY CARTER AND PLAINS, GEORGIA

L IKE FEW CANDIDATES in American history, Jimmy Carter made his home a cornerstone of his presidential campaign. With his trademark grin, rural background, and claims to represent basic virtues such as honesty and common sense, he ran in 1976 as a simple peanut farmer from Plains, Georgia, who promised not to lie. It was an effective anti-Establishment strategy at a time when Americans were disenchanted with their leaders after the Watergate scandal, the resignation of Richard Nixon, Gerald Ford's unpopular pardon of his predecessor, the Vietnam War, and the failure of the Washington establishment to improve the economy.

Carter, a Democrat, had been governor of Georgia for one term, so he wasn't totally lacking in government experience. But he tried to make his outsider status a badge of honor. He used his peanut farm in Plains to present a down-to-earth, non-Washington image as a refreshing contrast to the perceived corruption of the nation's capital. It worked, and he was elected narrowly to succeed Gerald Ford.

Preaching lowered expectations, he started out well. Carter declared in his inauguration speech that "even our great nation has its recognized limits, and that we can neither answer all questions nor solve all problems." He cut the size of the White House staff to demonstrate his commitment to austerity, stopped the playing of "Hail to the Chief" at his public appearances to minimize the imperial trappings of office, and held town meetings with everyday citizens. Carter even wore a cardigan sweater instead of a suit and tie in a televised address to the nation, as he sought to connect with the public as Franklin Roosevelt had done in his fireside chats on the radio. He appointed an unprecedented number of women and African Americans to government jobs, and seemed affable, intelligent, and hardworking. After 100 days in office, 75 percent of voters approved of his job performance.

From then on, Carter ran into trouble. He was unable to control inflation, which soared into the double-digit annual range, and he was unable to end a spike in unemployment. He tried to cut the budget deficit but was deserted by liberal Democrats in Congress, including Senator Edward Kennedy of Massachusetts, who complained that he was trying to slash important social programs. Energy prices soared amid severe gasoline shortages.

WHEN IT CAME to his hometown, it turned out that Carter meant what he said during the campaign. He was indeed rooted in Plains, Georgia, and traveled there often as president, even though the White House press corps didn't like the small town and its lack of fine restaurants, hotels, and other amenities. The town, after all, was really little more than a hamlet with a post office and a few stores surrounded by family farms. But for Carter it was home, and understanding his experiences there was essential to comprehending the man, the basis of his philosophy, and his conviction that the values he learned in this small town could be the basis for a presidency.

"Plains has always been a haven for us," Carter told me in an interview for this book, conducted in the small sitting room of his modest ranch house. "We [his family members] have two farms. One we acquired in 1933 and one in 1904, and that's the land we still own, and we still cultivate it. We're quite familiar with every square acre of it, so our roots are deep here."

After his service in the Navy, where he rose to become an officer on a nuclear submarine, Carter decided in 1953 to return to Plains to run his parents' peanut farm. Rosalynn, his wife, was miserable. She, like Carter, was originally from the area, but she had a difficult time getting re-acclimated to rural life. Wrote Rosalynn Carter in her memoirs: "[W]hen Jimmy and I first came back from the Navy, I was overwhelmed by the awful thought of having to live here forever." Eventually, she got used to it, and settled into the role of a 1950s-era housewife, cooking, sewing, making curtains and clothes for her children. Her husband was immersed in the peanut business, buying and selling seed and fertilizer, helping to load it on farmers' trucks, visiting prospective customers, keeping the books, even cleaning the office.

"But later," Mrs. Carter explained, "as public service and politics claimed more and more of our time, Plains became a refuge—a calm, quiet place in which to regroup my thoughts and renew our ever more exciting plans. It was always the welcome rest stop in months of campaigning, the one place I didn't have to consider every living soul as a potential vote for Jimmy, where there were no speeches I had to give, no hands I had to shake."

Despite Jimmy's work ethic, 1954 was disastrous for the peanut business because of a severe drought, and the Carters' annual income was less than $200. But in 1955, the rains returned and things greatly improved. Rosalynn began helping with administrative duties such as sending out invoices, paying bills, and answering phones, with her children at her side. "From mid-August to mid-October that year," Rosalynn wrote, "peanuts poured into our warehouse by the truckload, ton after ton after ton. We weighed them, determined their quality and value, bought them from the farmers, and stored them in our warehouses or loaded them onto tractor-trailer trucks to be shipped out of Plains; then they would be roasted and made into peanut butter or candy or peanut oil. 'Peanut season' involved hard, hard work. Days stretched into evenings without a break; all of us, including the seasonal workers we hired, often worked around the clock."

Jimmy, drawing on his Navy career as a no-nonsense administrator, always wanted things shipshape and was a stern taskmaster who demanded that everyone perform their tasks efficiently and thoroughly, including his wife and two growing sons, Chip and Jack. Amy, the daughter who would become so well known during Carter's White House years, would be born on October 19, 1967.

As their financial situation improved, Jimmy had a new house built on the property in 1961, and was relieved from the constant burden of keeping the farm afloat. He became interested in politics, first serving on the local school board, then in the state senate. He was elected governor of Georgia in 1970, and led a generally centrist, progressive administration that was scandal-free. He told me in an interview that this job was ideal for him—it brought out his executive skills and was powerful enough that he felt he could make a real difference in the lives of Georgians.

This record of integrity, coupled with the fact that he was free of the taint of official Washington, made him a strong if unexpected contender for the Democratic presidential nomination in 1976. His credentials and background seemed perfect at a time when the nation was eager for a fresh start. Shortly after winning the Democratic nomination, as he prepared his agenda for the fall campaign, he brought in busloads of experts in many fields, from the economy and health care to education and the Middle East, for discussions. He met with a dozen or more of them for hours at a time at a makeshift conference center about two and a half miles from his house. For the guests, many of them self-important and considering themselves very sophisticated, the homespun, isolated nature of Plains was a strange experience.

THE RESULTS WERE unclear for many hours on election night, and when Carter finally arrived in his hometown at dawn on the next day as the 39th president-elect, he was overcome with emotion. He addressed 600 friends, relatives, and supporters in front of the old Plains railroad station; many had waited for him all night. "I came all the way through—through twenty-two months and I didn't get choked up until I . . ." he said, and then couldn't continue as his eyes welled. He bit his lip and turned to hug his wife, Rosalynn, who was weeping openly. Carter recovered quickly and continued, ". . . until I turned the corner and saw you standing here and said, 'People who are that foolish—we can't get beat.'" The crowd erupted in cheers.

But the resulting change in the Carters' lives came as a shock. "I had never had a cook in Plains," Rosalynn Carter recalled, "but during this transition period [between the election and her husband's inauguration] I always had friends and neighbors to help. Usually my mother; my secretary, Madeline; and Sybil, [brother-in-law] Billy's wife; and I made stacks of sandwiches—hamburgers, barbecue sandwiches, and ham, cheese, and tomato—and put them on the breakfast-room table for whoever happened to be there along with gallons of lemonade, iced tea, and coffee. The neighbors sent food in, too—fried chicken, baked hams, cakes, and casseroles—but the Secret Service disapproved of this 'unsecured' food and put a stop to it, or thought they did. My mother had 'clearance,' so our neighbors started delivering the food to her instead, and she would bring it to us. Even though we bypassed the Secret Service, all of the food was from friends, and no danger was involved in eating it. It was a busy time and I tried not to worry about things not being perfect, but can you imagine my chagrin to look up one day and see Henry Kissinger sipping iced tea from a Tweety-Bird jelly glass. Oh, well, I thought, I'll have plenty of time to serve him from crystal."

AS PRESIDENT, CARTER didn't fare well. Without a firm base in the capital, he alienated congressional leaders and was quickly stymied. A frustrated Carter eventually came to regard Washington as an island "isolated from the mainstream of our nation's life." This attitude didn't sit well with the power brokers of the capital, even though Congress was controlled by fellow Democrats.

The economy worsened, with inflation rampant, unemployment soaring, and energy shortages widespread. When Americans were taken hostage in Tehran in November 1979, Carter seemed helpless to free them, and "the hostage crisis" dragged on throughout his final year in office. Carter suffered another blow when the Soviet Union invaded Afghanistan, ending his hopes for an improved superpower relationship. Finally, Carter ordered a mission to rescue the 52 hostages in Iran that April, but it resulted in two U.S. helicopters colliding in the desert and the death of eight U.S. soldiers. Suddenly, he seemed impotent and naïve.

His standing in the Democratic party was so low that Senator Edward Kennedy challenged him for the nomination and almost unseated him. In the end, Carter lost overwhelmingly to Republican Ronald Reagan in the general election of 1980.

THROUGH IT ALL, Carter saw Plains as the anchor to his roots, to his born-again Christianity, and to a sense of normalcy. He visited his home on average every three months and spent three of four Christmases there. In an interview, he told me, "It was a place of kin folks and lifetime friends, fellow church members, high school classmates. It's a tiny town. It only has six hundred and thirty-some people. And I felt that everybody in Plains was my friend and shared my joys and concerns and my victories and defeats. I didn't feel that I needed psychological nurturing, but it was always pleasant to come here and know that we were among unanimous friends."

He added, "My life has been immersed in agriculture. My family has been over here since the 1600s, and all of us down through me have been in effect full-time farmers and so it's, when I walk in my woods and fields now, when I cross the terrace, even if it's got trees in it that are sixty years old, I know that my father built that terrace and I remember having worked in that field with my father. So the land is very important to us, and our hometown is very important to us, and our home community, in more wide, generic terms—all of those things are very important, and that's been an attraction. . . . Plains was a focal point of our life."

After taking office, he would meet with aides in his small sitting room just inside the front door, and they sat on comfortable plush chairs in a small circle as they discussed world problems. For larger meetings, he would take them into his large living room, filled with photos and paintings of his wife and children, and furnished with tables and other woodwork he had constructed since the 1950s, much of it in a shop he had converted from a garage.

He got up about 5 A.M. each day, had a light breakfast and spent a couple of hours by himself. "It's my most productive thinking time and it's when I ordinarily have solitude," Carter said. "We had the advantage of my Cabinet and staff members being more reluctant to bother me when we were down here, and the same thing applied at Camp David. . . . There had to be something urgent or unique on the agenda for them to call me. They knew I needed some rest and some relaxation."

He tried to get his official work done in the morning so he could take personal time in the afternoons and evenings. He sometimes visited friends and neighbors in the community, trailed by a platoon of reporters and photographers. Each of the broadcast networks of ABC, CBS, and NBC set up mobile homes converted into studios and parked them under the town water tower five blocks from Carter's home. "We staked him out every day as he went about Plains," recalled CBS producer Susan Zirinsky. "We followed him—about three feet behind—and he would talk with us as we went along." Carter disliked the tag-along routine, but he accepted it to get positive publicity and help inform the country about what he was thinking.

To minimize confusion on one trip to Plains, his staff promised to give the press corps 30 minutes' notice before the president left his farm. The instant the notice was given, the White House press office would hang a red blanket from the balcony of the Best Western Motel in nearby Americus, where many wire-service and TV reporters and photographers stayed. This triggered a breakneck 10-minute drive to Plains.

During his first few trips there, President Carter showed his intensely competitive side in zealously played softball games between the White House staff and the press corps. Carter would argue umpires' calls and chide his teammates for lapses on the field or for bad hitting. It was clear that he hated to lose.

But Carter preferred to stay on his land, sometimes conducting business over meals of his favorite down-home foods, such as pepper steak and pistachio nut cake. Away from the prying eyes of reporters and their cameras, he and his wife would often ride bicycles and inspect the 160 acres, mostly woodlands of pine and other native growth. He loved playing tennis on his court a few yards from the main house, and the First Couple enjoyed fishing for trout. Carter also would hunt quail on his property with three bird dogs during the winter season, November to February.

The quail hunting caused him some image problems, partly because the animal rights movement was gaining momentum. The traveling press corps got wind of one of his expeditions, and a few reporters showed up on a public access road they figured he might cross while looking for the quail. Carter had the Secret Service block their access and he went about his business. But the correspondents were waiting when he returned to the access road, and he told them he had killed six or seven birds, which was widely reported. The next Sunday morning, several hundred animal rights protesters picketed his Baptist church where he attended services—carrying signs calling him a murderer, Carter recalled ruefully. It was no wonder that he tried to keep the press corps at a distance and shield his private activities from outsiders' eyes.

Similarly, he invited very few foreign leaders to Plains, following the example of Harry Truman at Independence, Missouri. "I really preferred to keep them out of my private life," he says. He did make liberal use of Camp David to host his counterparts from abroad, however, and Carter led a series of grueling negotiations there between Egypt and Israel that led to a historic Middle East peace accord.

Unlike other presidents, such as Washington, Jefferson, Lyndon Johnson, and George W. Bush, Carter didn't take an active part in managing his property. He thought it might be a conflict of interest with his policy making, so he put all his financial and commercial interests in a blind trust and forbade his trustees from informing him about the financial condition of his farm and warehouse business.

CARTER VIVIDLY REMEMBERS his presidential Christmases in Plains. His first, in 1977, was strange all around. "Early the first morning at home, I went downtown to visit Carter's Warehouse, and was pleased to find that everything was in good order in the office, and that the peanut-shelling plant was operating smoothly," he recalls in one of his memoirs. "By the time I finished this visit, the news reporters and television crews were alerted, and they followed me as I spent a couple of hours just wandering down the main street, stopping at all the stores and shops to visit old friends. Most of them enjoyed the prospect of being on the evening news, but we usually talked long enough to forget about the surrounding observers. I was relieved that I was still just 'Jimmy' to all the citizens, or 'Brother Jimmy' to the men who had, at one time or another, been fellow members or deacons at our church. Always, after I became well known as governor and president, the little black children called out, 'Hey, Jimmy Carter.' To tourists, of course, I was 'Mr. President.' "

He and a cousin of his wife's, Nub Chappell, went quail hunting the next day with several Secret Service agents and White House doctor Bill Lukash. That evening they had quail for supper. But, Carter adds, "Things in Plains were not as quiet and pleasant as they used to be. The town's life had been seriously disturbed when I became a presidential candidate the previous year, with a massive influx of tourists and the vendors who moved in to meet the demand for all kinds of souvenirs. It was nice this Christmas to see that eight of the fly-by-night junk shops had closed, letting old-time Plains citizens have an opportunity to regain partial control of the town. But the community had changed in another way, now that I was in office but not secluded in the White House or Camp David. The town was filled with demonstrators and people seeking recognition or special favors."

On Christmas Eve, Carter met with Georgia farmers who had formed tractor caravans and descended on Plains to tell the president that they needed federal help from the effects of a crippling drought and soaring fuel and fertilizer prices. Carter, drawing on his own farming background, sympathized with them and listened attentively to their concerns. On Christmas Day, he and his family were upset when TV crews staked out their house and their every move around town as they made their traditional Christmas rounds to visit neighbors.

At one point, Carter's 9-year-old daughter, Amy, rebelled against the Secret Service agents. She and her cousin Mandy realized one morning that the agent assigned to the president's daughter had stepped into the restroom. The two girls ran from the house, jumped on their bicycles, and pedaled furiously down the road a few hundred yards. They hid the bikes behind some plum bushes and crawled into a corrugated pipe on a construction site. They gleefully discussed how they had found an excellent hideout and made plans to return with dolls and other toys. When they emerged, they found an agent at each end of the pipe. "Are you girls ready to go home?" one asked with a smile.

The president had a getaway technique of his own. He ordered the Secret Service to block all access to a farm road so he and Rosalynn could walk alone in the fields to an ancient Indian village site, where they found several arrowheads.

Carter describes the 1978 holiday season as "one of the worst times of my personal life." He came down with a painful case of hemorrhoids. He had first endured the embarrassing ailment as a young submarine officer but this time he was almost incapacitated. He received emergency treatment after he had to leave a White House Christmas party and subsequently he had to cancel his scheduled events for the next day. All the while he concealed his problem from the public and the news media.

When he got back to Plains, he again found protesters everywhere, including the angry farmers who had returned to get some more publicity, Ku Klux Klansmen protesting Carter's strong civil rights policies, and Taiwanese Americans protesting Carter's normalizing of diplomatic relations with mainland China. Meanwhile, the president tried to ignore his pain and work the phones to finalize his budget for the following year, encourage the Soviets to prepare for talks on reducing nuclear weapons, and do other work.

On Christmas Eve, he was having such trouble walking that he stayed home while his son Chip and daughter, Amy, trudged into the woods to cut down a Christmas tree, a tradition that Carter had enjoyed supervising for many years. Early the next morning, after exchanging gifts, he went into his study and turned on the radio to check the news. He was aghast when he heard that Egyptian president Anwar Sadat had announced to the world that his friend Jimmy Carter had hemorrhoids and made a public appeal for all Egyptians to pray for his cure. The next day, Carter reported later, his pain went away.

IT WAS A difficult and turbulent four years, but Carter says he enjoyed them. "I never looked on my work as a burden," he told me. "I was eager each day to see what was on the agenda and to get a briefing about international affairs and sometimes domestic affairs . . . but it was an exciting and challenging, gratifying experience."

"When Jimmy lost the election in 1980, there was no question about where we would go," Rosalynn writes. "We would go home."

Since then, they have written several books, and set up his presidential library and the Carter Center at Emory University in Atlanta. The center is in some ways the crowning achievement of Carter's public life, serving as both a think tank and an activist organization where programs are devised for fighting poverty and disease around the world. The former president remains very active in such causes, and has played a personal role in supervising elections and in mediating internal conflicts in many countries, including Haiti, Ethiopia, Nicaragua, and Somalia. He won the Nobel Peace Prize for his efforts.

They also travel widely, and host many friends, family members, and guests, including foreign leaders they knew while in office, such as President Sadat of Egypt, Prime Minister Begin of Israel, and former President Giscard d'Estaing of France. In addition, Carter remains active in Plains's 130-member Maranatha Baptist Church, where he has served as finance officer and preaches an average of once a month. Sometimes he mows the church lawn with other parishioners, and Rosalynn vacuums the carpets.

They truly have returned to their pre-political roots. Jimmy has resumed his interest in woodworking, Rosalynn enjoys baking and cooking. They planted a large garden, and can, dry, or freeze the vegetables they harvest themselves. It's a simple life, but one the former First Couple seems to relish. "Walking through the woods and fields for miles without seeing a house," Mrs. Carter writes, "and only rarely meeting a car while bicycling along the back roads around our home, are luxuries we hadn't fully appreciated before."

PLAINS REFLECTED THE down-home, "Washington outsider" values that Carter projected as president and that were responsible for his initial appeal. While he sometimes came across as naïve and was unable to solve the country's pressing problems, he never abandoned the verities he had learned in his hometown as a child—commitment to his faith, his family, and his country, and to fairness and human rights at home and around the world. His work to end age-old hatreds in the Middle East culminated in the peace agreement that he negotiated between Egypt and Israel at Camp David in 1978 (discussed later in this book).

CHAPTER FIFTEEN

RONALD REAGAN AND *RANCHO DEL CIELO*, CALIFORNIA

For most of his adult life, Ronald Reagan was a celebrity. The handsome, athletic actor with the mellifluous voice and ingratiating manner started out as a radio announcer in the Midwest. He moved to California, where he achieved fame as a movie star and popular host of television's *General Electric Theater* and *Death Valley Days*. He became well known as a conservative hard-liner on the speaking circuit, won two terms as governor of California, and achieved the height of fame in his eight years as president from 1981 to 1989. He was one of the most controversial chief executives of the 20th century.

Reagan led a conservative revival: cutting taxes, restraining the growth of government, and standing up to what he called the evil empire of communism. He compromised when he felt it was necessary, and to the utter surprise of his critics, the economy grew rapidly. By the close of his administration, superpower tensions had eased and the cold war was ending. Yet at home, his policies led to historically high deficits and many social inequities.

Perhaps Reagan's greatest achievement was restoring the nation's optimism in the American future. His sunny disposition and even temperament were infectious, and even if many voters disagreed with his policies, they appreciated his strong leadership and his belief that America was a "shining city on a hill," whose best days were still ahead.

Not even the Iran-Contra arms-for-hostages scandal, which broke in November 1986, could dim Reagan's luster for long. Administration operatives sold arms to Iranian "moderates" in order to win the release of American hostages held in Lebanon, and some of the proceeds were diverted to anti-Marxist Contra rebels in Nicaragua. This diversion was illegal and the arms sale itself violated Reagan's pledge never to negotiate with terrorists. Yet, despite several embarrassing investigations, Reagan's popularity rebounded after the public tired of the complicated saga.

"Ronald Reagan . . . seemed to have revitalized the presidency," observes historian Gil Troy. "His celebrity presidency made the experts stop talking about Richard Nixon's imperial presidency, and Jimmy Carter's impotent presidency. Reagan showed how, in the age of television, focusing on the well-dramatized big picture and having a strong vision could balance out many smaller failures."

Through it all, Reagan remained a private individual who, as he said in his memoirs, tried to keep part of himself hidden from the public. The real Ronald Reagan was most evident at his beloved ranch in the hills north of Santa Barbara, California. Few people outside the Reagan family and inner circle ever saw it while he was president, but he was immensely proud of the two-bedroom adobe house at the end of a tortuous dirt road. As I wrote in an article for *U.S. News & World Report,* "It certainly didn't live up to the grand name the proud owner bestowed on it: *Rancho del Cielo.* But it was here, at his 'ranch in the sky' set at 2,239 feet above sea level amid 688 acres of scrub oak and scented pine, that Ronald Reagan spent 345 days of his eight-year presidency. It was here, friends and advisers now say, that the 'real' Ronald Reagan could be found."

In these private moments, the 40th president found his bliss in the simplest parts of life—the company of his wife, Nancy, the pleasures of manual labor outdoors, the isolation of the Santa Ynez Mountains, and liberation from the artificial glamour that dominated his public world for so many years in Washington, Sacramento, and Hollywood. "*Rancho del Cielo* can make you feel as if you are on a cloud," he once said. And he wrote, "Some place along the line, a fella has to have time to sit on a hill and think, or maybe just sit on a hill."

As he admitted in his 1990 autobiography, *An American Life,* Reagan never let down his guard to anyone except Nancy, and as a result his public persona never fully reflected his true self. "I'm sure that the fact our family moved so often left a mark on me," he wrote of his boyhood. "Although I always had lots of playmates, during those first years in Dixon [Illinois], I was a little introverted and probably a little slow in making really close friends. In some ways, I think this reluctance to get close to people never left me completely. I've never had trouble making friends, but I've been inclined to hold back a little of myself, reserving it for myself."

Actually, he held back more than a little. His four children complained for many years of his aloofness, and he always kept aides at an emotional distance. Longtime friends suggest that the painful breakup of his first marriage to actress Jane Wyman contributed to his refusal to reveal himself to people around him; he didn't want to be hurt or disappointed again.

Although Reagan projected a heroic image—which he considered vital to playing the role of president—he always thought of himself as an ordinary man with a few extraordinary skills, just a regular guy with an ability to communicate on television and an instinct for articulating, even embodying, the dreams and desires of America's middle class. On Election Day in 1980, as early returns made it clear he would win the presidency, he was asked what Americans saw in him. "Would you laugh if I told you that I think, maybe, they see themselves and that I'm one of them?" he answered. "I've never been able to detach myself or think that I, somehow, am apart from them."

He never forgot his upbringing in Dixon and his life in the Midwest, even though it was less idyllic than he liked to admit, because of his father's alcoholism. Yet, in his gauzy recollection, his boyhood represented the American ideal of middle-class life, based on family, friends, faith, a strong work ethic, and optimism. "I got the impression he was a very simple man," says Frank Donatelli, Reagan's political director in the White House. "Even though he served two terms as governor and two terms as president, he saw himself as a citizen-politician, in the mold of Jimmy Stewart in *Mr. Smith Goes to Washington*. He never saw himself as a professional politician."

FEW AMERICANS COULD have known how much Reagan craved solitude; that while president he would leave the Oval Office at 6 P.M. on many days, change into his pajamas in the White House residence, and eat dinner on tray tables in front of the TV, alone with Nancy. He needed to get away from the rigors and routines of his public life. And after becoming president at age 69, he needed to pace himself.

But the only time he would truly kick back for extended periods of time, according to friends, was at the ranch in the Santa Ynez Mountains, about 30 miles northwest of Santa Barbara. From the day he bought the property, he tried to re-create the vigorous, independent lifestyle of a 19th-century landman. "I always felt the ranch was an expression of his Midwestern roots," says Marlin Fitzwater, Reagan's White House press secretary. "It was the Spartan life he knew as a child. He insisted on doing things by himself, building something of his own. The ranch represented stability and self-reliance, and a kind of basic dignity."

The Reagans purchased the property, then known as Tip Top Ranch, in Santa Barbara County, California, on November 13, 1974. Previously, he had purchased and sold three much smaller ranches—one near Northridge, in the San Fernando Valley; another in the Santa Monica Mountains east of the Malibu Beach area; and the third in Rancho California, near Temecula in San Diego County. But he was immediately impressed by the beauty and isolation of this property, nestled in chaparral and oak, with lemon and avocado groves, a network of creeks, and riding trails. The ranch house rested at the top of a twisting road that extended up a mountainside. From one spot he came to particularly love, he could see the Pacific Ocean on one side and the Santa Ynez Valley on another.

When he first saw it on a fall day in 1973, then in his seventh year as gover-nor, he was impressed with the extent of the estate, the views, and the possibility for making improvements. Reagan would later write in *An American Life* that the seller, cattleman Ray Cornelius, "put us on horses and we took a ride over the place. Well, after that, I was really sold." He realized that the spread would be per-fect for indulging his passion for riding. Much later, Reagan said, "From the first day we saw it, *Rancho del Cielo* cast a spell over us. No place before or since has ever given Nancy and me the joy and serenity it does."

The main house, made of adobe, was renovated by the Reagans over the years to include an L-shaped living-dining-recreation room, a master bedroom and bath, a maid's room and bath, a kitchen, a bar, and a den—1,500 square feet in all, with plentiful windows in the living room and dining room that offered a view of the property. Next door was a two-bedroom guest cottage built in the early 1980s af-ter he became president; another small guest house was converted from a trailer.

Up a hill from the main house was a barn housing the tack room, a work-shop, Reagan's blue Jeep, and other equipment. There were also a caretaker's cot-tage, a stable, and a prefabricated metal building that housed a Secret Service command center during Reagan's presidency. A helicopter pad, installed after he took office, was removed after he retired from Washington in 1989. The Secret Service not only provided round-the-clock protection of the ranch, even when the president was away; it also developed its own topographic map of the property and set up an electronic protection system around the perimeter. The agents were particularly concerned after the nearly fatal assassination attempt on Reagan in Washington a few weeks after he took office.

The Disney Corporation designed several imitation boulders that contained motion detectors and other electronic sensors. Numbers were placed on rocks along the riding trails so agents could pinpoint Reagan's precise location during his frequent horseback excursions. Of course, secure phone lines were installed to allow the president to be instantly reachable and to contact Washington whenever he wished.

There were occasional intruders, usually solitary hikers or bicycle riders. The Secret Service agents would emerge from their hidden positions in the woods and startle the outsiders, check them for weapons, and ask sternly why they were there. Generally, the intruders didn't realize they were on private property. "We did receive occasional intelligence communiqués that something was going to happen, but it never did," recalls John Barletta, former chief of the Secret Service detail at the ranch. There was at least one case of a mountain lion prowling the property, but nothing came of it. Rattlesnakes were regularly seen, and some were killed by Secret Service agents.

An unusual feature was the pet cemetery, nicknamed "Boot Hill," on a promontory near the main house. At the Reagans' direction, some of their beloved pets were buried there, including Mrs. Reagan's favorite horse, No Strings, interred in 1992. It also contained Little Man, the president's favorite horse; Kelly, another horse; a bull; a cow; and several dogs. Reagan carved nearly all the sandstone headstones himself.

In the mid-1970s, Reagan decided to improve a pond that evaporated every summer; he had it dug deeper, lined with vinyl, and covered with dirt, and he installed a dock. Reagan called it Lake Lucky, and to his delight he found he could use it year-round; it got 12 to 13 feet deep in winter and 7 to 8 feet in summer. He would wade into Lake Lucky from time to time and catch water snakes by hand, place them in a bag, and drop them off at a cooperative neighbor's pond. He eventually built an aerating system so the "lake" would support goldfish. The lake served another purpose. When he got a new pair of jeans, he would take a dip and let the clothes dry on his frame. That way, he got a form-fitting garment without a lot of bother.

Yet he never wanted to fully modernize the residence. When the 1,500-square-foot house got cold, the household staff had to stoke fireplaces in the living room and family room (mostly to satisfy the First Lady, who would curl up in a plush chair in front of the flames and chat on the phone with pals like Betsy Bloomingdale and Nancy Reynolds). He laid the stone patio in front of the ranch house himself by uprooting stones from around the property, hauling them back to the residence, and fitting them into the ground.

There was a hat rack to the right of the front door; on it hung a blue baseball cap bearing the "seal" of the "United States Mounted Secret Service"; this is the sweat-stained cap he wore when clearing brush and cutting firewood. On the rack also hung a Stetson, a purse made from an armadillo shell, an Indian canteen covered with rawhide, an Irish shillelagh, and a leather bag used to carry firewood. The Reagans hung Native-American rugs on the walls and placed others on the floors. At the center of the living room was a Kenneth Wyatt oil painting, "The Lame Horse," depicting a cowboy leading his horse in a downpour.

In many ways it was the 1950s or 1960s, frozen in time. The master bathroom, painted bright yellow, contained the most basic of fixtures, including a small commode tucked behind a shower stall, and no bathtub. The kitchen featured a modest, brown four-burner electric range and refrigerator, and no dishwasher. The instructions for using a roof antenna for the console TV were scrawled by Nancy on a scrap of paper kept on a table.

Aides were reluctant to bother the septuagenarian Reagan with official business when he was "up on the mountain," as they called it. (One exception: He issued orders to notify him immediately, day or night, if any American soldiers were killed overseas.) Like Harry Truman's winter retreat in Key West, the house contained virtually no sign that a president lived there, except for the white phone in the master bedroom with a direct line to the Secret Service. Nor were there many reminders of his Hollywood days. As president he had a sign hung above the patio depicting a black horse standing above the words "The Reagan's [sic] 1600 Pennsylvania Avenue," but that was one of the few reminders of his life in Washington.

In fact, he kept his public life out of the ranch as much as he could; he rarely invited senior advisers or even his children to stay there. It was his private refuge, to be enjoyed mainly with his soul mate, Nancy—a place where, says a confidant, "he didn't have to answer questions about anything."

Sometimes he was *too* laid back. Doing a routine microphone check before a Saturday radio address from the ranch, he got into trouble when he joked, "My fellow Americans, I am pleased to tell you I have signed legislation to outlaw Russia forever. We begin bombing in five minutes." Reporters broadcast the remark around the world, embarrassing the president for his foolishness.

Still, no president can ever escape the requirements of office for very long, and world events sometimes intruded. On September 8, 1983, a Soviet missile destroyed a Korean airliner, Flight KAL 007, while the Reagans were at the ranch. National Security Adviser William Clark immediately phoned the president—it was late afternoon in California—and Reagan replied, "Well, Bill, let's pray that it didn't happen. If it's confirmed that it did occur, with all that we have going on with arms negotiations, let's not overreact." He advised Clark to go out to dinner and "not sit around waiting for the phone to ring."

Even after the shootdown was confirmed, Reagan refused to leave the ranch, arguing that he could handle the crisis from there. But his aides persuaded him that he would look isolated and lazy if he didn't return to Washington. At one point, network TV cameras with telephoto lenses captured Reagan working around the ranch and riding around on his horse, which conveyed the image that he was disengaged. His aides said that in a crisis such as this, he needed to be back at the White House, showing himself to be in charge. He reluctantly cut his vacation short. His issued a condemnation of the attack, but his overall reaction was restrained.

Reagan allowed the ranch to be used as a backdrop—a rarity—during his first year as president after he won congressional passage of a massive tax-cut bill. On August 13, 1981, he signed the Economy Recovery Act of 1981 at a patio table outside the front door, while about 20 reporters and photographers watched in the fog. They were bused in for the occasion, one of the few times that journalists were allowed on the property.

THE HOUSE WAS filled with sketches and paintings of cowboys and Indians on horseback, often lone figures on the prairie. Some acquaintances speculate that this was the way Reagan saw himself during the many years when his conservative philosophy was out of favor, as a solitary rider wandering the vast political plain. His bookcases reflected his down-to-earth tastes and lack of intellectual curiosity about things outside his normal ken of the West and the outdoors. Among the titles in his 200-book collection: *The Fence Jumper* by Otis Carney; *The Shootist* by Glendon Swarthout; *Lonesome Dove* by Larry McMurtry; *Spanish Colonial or Adobe Architecture of California, 1800–1850*, and, in a change of pace, *African Game Trails* by Theodore Roosevelt.

Opposite the bar in the dining room was a mounted pair of "jackalopes," a whimsical creation popular among tourists in Western souvenir shops—a fanciful combination of a jackrabbit's head and, on the male of the species, antlers. The Reagans thought it was funny.

The Reagans spent much of their time in the den, which was next to the living room and featured a high ceiling. It had a bright and airy feel and was decorated in red, yellow, brown, and orange. The floor was covered with sheepskin and cowhide rugs, and there was another big fireplace in a corner. The furniture consisted of two sofas, three armchairs, one hassock, and a cabinet containing a television set.

REAGAN WOULD GET up about 8 A.M. and receive his daily national security briefing, which summarized overnight developments around the world. This was most often accomplished via a secure telephone call from aides in Santa Barbara or Washington but occasionally with national-security advisers in person at the ranch. Sometimes he would tape his brief weekly radio commentaries—he did so from the ranch 35 times during his presidency, mostly on Saturday mornings from the patio table outside the front door. Then he did what he called his "Washington homework" for an hour or two, reading memos and signing papers. "[You] could forget the world for a few hours," Nancy Reagan recalled, "but every day a government car would drive up the mountain with a big envelope of mail, security documents, and newspapers."

After all this, he would go up the hill to the tack barn and prepare for his daily horseback ride. When everything was ready, he rang a bell outside the barn to summon his wife, and she would walk quickly to meet him.

Then they would go for a leisurely horseback ride, the president on his white Arabian named El Alamein, a gift from the president of Mexico, and Mrs. Reagan on her less flashy brown quarterhorse, No Strings. Several Secret Service agents always followed, also on horseback. His code name was Rawhide; hers, Rainbow.

But the rides were not as spontaneous as White House image makers made them appear in the photos released to the media. To protect him, the Secret Service insisted that he go over his riding route on a map in advance so his bodyguards would always know his whereabouts. And while official photos of the rides focused on the mounted president, the First Lady, a bodyguard, and a friend or two, there was actually quite an entourage tagging along. Several agents would ride at a discreet distance, and behind the small column of horses, out of camera range, was a special four-wheel-drive vehicle containing even more armed agents, sophisticated communications gear, medical kits, and the "football," a briefcase containing nuclear-missile launch codes—just in case.

When they returned from their ride, Nancy would allow only her husband to help her dismount. Once a new Secret Service agent tried to lend a hand, but she wouldn't budge. Moments later, the agent was startled by a familiar voice behind him. "That's *my* wife, and *I'll* be the one to help her," the president said as he brushed past the bodyguard and gently eased the diminutive First Lady from the saddle to the ground, his hands firmly grasping her slender waist. They would end each ride with a hug and a kiss.

Afterward, Nancy would return to the house and the president would remove the saddles, clean the horses' hooves, and occasionally groom them.

On the rare occasions when he had visitors there, the president was a gracious host. "One year," recalls Elaine Crispen Sawyer, former press secretary for Nancy Reagan, "the Reagans invited my daughter Cheryl and me to their ranch for Thanksgiving dinner. Although Cheryl had met the Reagans many times at receptions and other events, she was excited and a bit apprehensive. 'Mom, we'll be there for four or five hours. What am I going to talk with the President about for that long?' she said. I told her she needn't worry about it, and it turned out that it was like being with a favorite uncle.

"The President took us on a tour of the tack room; he showed us his saddles, and his famous woodpile where he did so much chopping. At the table, he said grace and carved the turkey, then regaled us with stories about Hollywood days, summits with Gorbachev, even world economics. Cheryl was so enchanted that, to this day, she can't remember if she said much of anything at all!"

Sometimes he would drive one of the two Jeeps he kept at the ranch. This was one of the very few places where his bodyguards allowed him to get behind the wheel as president, and he relished the opportunity.

He spent several hours each day building fences with ranch hands, clearing brush from trails, and cutting wood for the two fireplaces. Willard "Barney" Barnett, his longtime driver and ranch employee, says, "We spent quite a lot of time at the ranch building fences. We used telephone poles and the president participated in putting just about every one of them in the ground. It was quite an experience. The poles were his idea because he had seen a fence built like this before. He, [Reagan aide] Dennis LeBlanc, and I got them all in the ground. I don't know how many miles we covered, but we put the fence completely around the ranch. We also worked together to fence the orchard and a little pasture of four or five acres for the horses in the summer. . . . President Reagan would never ask us to do anything he wouldn't do himself."

He found the outdoor activity bracing and a way to divert his attention from the pressures of office. "He attributed his physical well-being, his longevity, to being able to go to the ranch, both for the physical nature of the work and for riding his horses," says Dennis LeBlanc, who regularly worked alongside Reagan. "He liked that adage, 'The best thing for the inside of a man is the outside of a horse.' He rode on an English saddle and everyone else up there rode Western. When you look at pictures of the group, he is always sitting straight as an arrow, while the others are slouching."

WHEN HIS PUBLIC-relations advisers initially raised concerns that he was spending too much time at the ranch and might look lazy, Reagan scoffed. He would live a lot longer, he said, if he went to his hideaway at regular intervals, and he wasn't going to stop. He had a point. "There were times when the president would look like an old man when he arrived, and would appear twenty years younger after a week or two at the ranch," wrote Larry Speakes, his White House spokesman.

Nancy said, "Ronnie is so happy there! He loves to be outside, building fences, cutting down trees and brush, and chopping wood for the two fireplaces, which are our only source of heat. The ranch is on top of a mountain and when you get up there, the rest of the world disappears."

.   .   .

FOR JOURNALISTS COVERING Reagan's ranch vacations, life was grand. Since he left the property so seldom and made so little news, the reporters and photographers contented themselves with exploring the beautiful environs of Santa Barbara, 30 miles to the south, competing with each other for dinner guests from the official entourage, and attending a daily briefing at a Santa Barbara hotel.

That briefing quickly became a joke within the press corps because it was so useless. Often as not, it came in a written statement from the press secretary reporting that the Reagans had breakfast together, after which the president tended to "routine paperwork," went for a horseback ride, cleared brush, and chopped wood.

Desperate for visuals and some news, the network TV crews set up camera positions on a mountainside in Los Padres National Forest, near the Reagan ranch, used very powerful telephoto lenses, strong enough to view the space shuttle, and sometimes got images of the president leaving and entering his house and riding his horses. Reagan knew the cameras were trained on his front door and joked with aides that some day he would fake a heart attack on his porch—just to teach the networks a lesson about invading his privacy. For a while the networks could monitor Secret Service conversations—until the agents started using scrambling devices to thwart the eavesdroppers.

During a long stretch without any news, ABC reporter Sam Donaldson groused to Barbara Walters on the television show *20/20*. When Walters asked what was going on, Donaldson replied, "Nothing much. We have the ranch report here and, once again, he chopped wood and cleared brush. I suspect that just before he gets there, they haul up truckloads of brush and wood for him to chop because, if he chopped as much as they say he does, there wouldn't be any trees left on the ranch."

Reagan was watching the show and the next day he told his ranch foreman to pile up all the brush he had cleared over the previous week or ten days. After it was placed near the house he had a photographer take pictures of it and sent one to Donaldson with the inscription: "Dear Sam, Here's the proof I chopped it all with my own little hatchet."

HIS RELATIONSHIP WITH Nancy was clearly the most important in his life; even the presidency took second place. "They were a team—it was the Reagans against the world," says political consultant Stuart Spencer, who worked closely with Reagan throughout his political career. Testaments to the depth of their love affair were everywhere at *Rancho del Cielo*. At the foot of their bed was an embroidered pillow depicting two sets of bare feet emerging from under the bed covers with the words, "Roommates 1952 forever." Behind the house was a canoe, named Tru Luv, that Reagan gave his wife in 1977 on the 25th anniversary of their March 4, 1952, wedding. To celebrate, he paddled her out on their small lake and proposed again.

Mrs. Reagan was utterly devoted to him. "At the top of my list of duties as first lady . . . was taking care of Ronnie," she writes. "I still considered that to be my most important job, as it had always been. For that matter, I do believe taking care of the president is the most important thing a first lady can do—the essential thing, in fact, that she *must* do—because she is the person in the White House who knows him best."

He returned her devotion in kind. This was clear in their obvious affection for each other, their holding hands, hugging, and kissing in public. It also was evident in the hundreds of letters he wrote to her over the years, compendiums of which were published after they left the White House. "I'm . . . crazy about the girl who goes to the ranch with me," the president wrote Nancy on December 25, 1981, Christmas Day. "If we're tidying up the woods she's a peewee power house at pushing over dead trees. She's a wonderful person to sit by the fire with or to ride with or just to be with when the sun goes down or the stars come out. If she ever stopped going to the ranch I'd stop too because I'd see her in every beauty spot there is and I couldn't stand that."

Some Reagan friends say spending so much time at *Rancho del Cielo* was Nancy's huge concession to her husband, that she disliked the rustic nature of the place but kept him company there because of her devotion to him.

To the president, "Mommy," as he called her, was his rock, much as his adoring mother, Nelle, had been the source of strength and security in his childhood. As an adult, Reagan had no close friendships. "He seems to need only one other person—me," wrote Nancy. In fact, he so adored his wife that when she was away, he couldn't sleep. "It's so lonely here," he once wrote in his diary when Nancy was gone from the White House. "I feel desolate. I can't wait until Mommy comes back."

And why not? Nancy monitored his every move, from his schedule to his travels and his diet. After their rides, for instance, he would unsaddle the horses and do a few chores in the barn until Nancy rang a dinner bell summoning him to lunch (as he had summoned her to ride by ringing the bell at the tack barn). Reagan loved macaroni and cheese, but his wife only let the cooks at the ranch prepare the fatty fare for him occasionally. Otherwise, it was chicken, fish, salads, and fruit.

AFTER HE LEFT office in January 1989, Reagan noticed his mental capacities were slipping away. On November 5, 1994, he released a two-page, handwritten letter to the American people that contained a startling and eloquent admission. "I have recently been told that I am one of the millions of Americans who will be afflicted with Alzheimer's disease," he wrote. "I intend to live the remainder of the years God gives me on this earth doing the things I have always done. I will continue to share life's journey with my beloved Nancy and my family. I plan to enjoy the great outdoors and stay in touch with my friends and supporters. Unfortunately, as Alzheimer's disease progresses, the family often bears a heavy burden. I only wish there was some way I could spare Nancy from this painful experience. When the time comes, I am confident that with your help she will face it with faith and courage."

He concluded, "I now begin the journey that will lead me into the sunset of my life. I know that for America there will always be a bright dawn ahead. Thank you, my friends. May God always bless you."

As his Alzheimer's disease intensified, the increasingly frail former president could no longer ride horses, and eventually his doctors wouldn't allow him to leave his home in Belair to visit his ranch at all. In April 1998, Nancy sold the property to the Young America's Foundation, a group of conservative activists and Reagan supporters, who have kept it intact as a memorial to him.

For many months during his final decline, Nancy still climbed into bed next to him every night and slept by his side. She feared he might wake up and panic if she wasn't there, as she had been throughout their long marriage. She was deeply saddened when, in his last days, he could no longer recognize her. He died on June 5, 2004, and was buried on a hillside at the Ronald Reagan Presidential Library in Simi Valley, California.

Some day, Nancy will be at his side in death, too, in that crypt overlooking the Pacific. As Reagan explained to his biographer, Edmund Morris, "They'll seal the door . . . temporarily, until she joins me. Then we'll lie there, just the two of us, and look at the sea together."

REAGAN'S RANCH REVEALS his solitary nature, his love of the outdoors, and his view that the presidency was a 9 to 5 job. It was where he made his infamous comment about bombing the Soviet Union, and heard about the shootdown of a Korean airliner and gave his initial, cautious response, counter to his image as a reckless cowboy. More than anything else, the ranch illustrated Reagan's love for and partnership with Nancy, who was the most important person in his life.

CHAPTER SIXTEEN

GEORGE HERBERT WALKER BUSH AND KENNEBUNKPORT, MAINE

Georgia Herbert Walker Bush, the 41st president, spent part of every summer of his life at his family estate in Kennebunkport, Maine, except for 1944, when he was flying combat missions for the Navy during World War II.

The property had been held by his family since the turn of the 20th century. His grandfather, George Herbert Walker, built a house on the promontory around 1902, and it quickly became known as Walker's Point. Bush bought it from Mary Walker, his aunt, for $800,000 in the mid-1980s. He had to sell his home in Houston (and buy a small lot in Houston for use in his retirement), and sell another house in Kennebunkport where he had summered for a decade, in order to afford the purchase. But he thought it was essential. "Walker's Point always had been an important part of George's life," Barbara Bush writes in her memoirs. "For the next twelve years, it would be the perfect refuge from our high-profile lives and is now our summer home."

But not without some emotional cost. It was "clobbered," George Bush says, by two 100-year storms over the years, including the one popularized by the movie *The Perfect Storm*, in October 1991, while he was president. The house sits exposed on a rocky promontory, and the backyard deck was ripped up, stone walls were destroyed, the porch was washed away, and the whole downstairs was demolished. Chairs, tables, china, many treasured photographs, and other family mementos were ruined or taken out to sea.

The family quickly had it all reconstructed, but Bush still gets misty-eyed when he discusses the wreckage. "It was devastating and very hurtful to our family," he told me in an interview for this book. "I just could hardly control my emotions when I saw what had happened. . . . It affected our family deeply, and certainly Barbara and me. It was horrible."

Marlin Fitzwater, his press secretary, recalls the president's emotionally wrenching inspection tour: "By the time we arrived in Maine a few days later to inspect the damage, some of the major debris had been removed, but the aftermath was painful. It was muddy, and large pools of water had collected in all the low areas. . . . I felt sick. I watched the president to be sure he was all right. Actually, I think he was in shock, at least in some emotional sanctum where I didn't want to intrude. He prowled the area, looking for lost items. . . . When the president went into the house to walk through rooms, nothing was left but the mint green carpet in the living room. It was soaked with mud, weeds, and brine. He tugged at it and asked for help. Together, he and several of his staff dragged it out to the yard, draped it over a fence, and he began to squeeze it and beat it to get the water out. It was hopeless. It could never be saved. But he worked at it for hours because that's all there was."

BUSH ALWAYS DEFENDED his stays at Walker's Point, even when he was attacked for goofing off while the nation was mired in a recession. In August 1991, for example, he stubbornly announced that he would not alter his customary routine of vacationing at Kennebunkport: He planned to play "a good deal of golf . . . a good deal of tennis, a good deal of horseshoes, a good deal of fishing, a good deal of running—and some reading. I have to throw that in for the intellectuals out there."

Why was he so stubborn? "Kennebunkport gave him a sense of freedom," says Roman Popadiuk, a former White House aide who accompanied Bush to Kennebunkport many times. "He could get on his boat and the whole world was gone. . . . Bush was a very physical president, and at Walker's Point he could play tennis, swim in the pool, go boating, play 'speed golf.' . . . But most important, it's on a peninsula isolated from the rest of the world."

Most of all, he loved to pilot his 19-foot cigarette boat, *Fidelity*, and feel the exhilaration of bouncing across the Gulf of Maine and the challenge of bringing the sleek vessel into his dock in rough weather. He also liked to scare his passengers by going at breakneck speeds. While he was vice president, he took NBC correspondent Tom Petit out on *Fidelity*, raced over huge swells, and sent Petit sprawling. The newsman later learned that he had fractured a vertebra.

Marlin Fitzwater describes a typical ride: "He kept it full-throttle all the way, water spraying over the bow, taking every wave with a thud and burst of speed. It was great fun for the first hour, than my back started hurting, my legs began to tire from flexing with the waves, and my fanny ached from bouncing on the back bench. But his face was glued to the wind, hair plastered back so he looked like the hood ornament of a 1956 Oldsmobile, and his windbreaker had long since failed to do its job. As we neared Walker's Point, close enough to see the lights of the house, he found a bit more power in the twin engines and we raced into the cove at full speed. I asked why. He said it was the closest he could come to duplicating the race of the wind from an open-cockpit airplane, the TBM Avenger he flew during World War II."

Bush took his fishing seriously, too—at a much slower pace. His pattern was to troll the ocean and use the leisurely moments to chat about world affairs and other issues with trusted aides. "Throw a line in," he would say. "Let's see what's out there." Fitzwater recalls trolling for bluefish in August 1991, four months after the end of the Persian Gulf War. At one point along the coast, *Fidelity* passed a white house in an inlet with dozens of young people on a deck, drinking and playing music. They spotted Bush and began doing "the wave," standing side by side and raising their arms one person at a time, in salute. "Let's return it," the president said, and Bush and his four companions did their own wave in return.

"Suddenly we got into a school of fish," Fitzwater notes, "and from then on it was all fishing. The president drove and we pulled out about ten apiece. When we got back to the house, he carried the buckets of fish up on the rocks, pulled a long, thin knife out of the tackle box, and cleaned them for dinner. We just stood and watched."

THE HOUSE ON Walker's Point was spacious and airy, with marvelous water views from the windows on three sides and a spectacular panorama visible from a sun room overlooking the sea.

After his many years in public life—from his days as a Republican U.S. representative from Texas, U.S. envoy to the United Nations, and vice president—Bush had grown accustomed to a loss of privacy, and he didn't mind the gawkers who tried to glimpse him from every vantage point in the area. But others in his family weren't so happy about it, including his son, George W. Bush. The younger Bush, who was to become president in January 2001, told me he could never get used to the prying eyes of tourists using binoculars and photographers using telescopic lenses to see the Bushes whenever they came out of the oceanfront house. He also didn't like the feeling of being watched when he was out with his dad on *Fidelity*. George W. fixed that problem when he bought a 1,600-acre ranch in east central Texas, a property so large that he can have the privacy he craves.

During an hour-long interview with me in February 2004 for this book, George and Barbara Bush made clear their devotion to their home, in some cases finishing each other's sentences as they reminisced. Asked why the home meant so much to them, they talked about how relaxing it was to be there, how even during George's presidency they could sit together in a secluded nook at the side of the house and look at the sea in all its moods. Barbara said, "We also had a hundred years of . . ." and her husband interjected, "memories."

The former president added, "Hard to describe it, but the air, the pounding of the sea at night, the joy I get from being out on the ocean. I mean, all of this stuff came together to make it a good place to think, you know, without a lot of phones ringing around you. And it was conducive to making decisions."

Both of them expressed pride that their five children still came home every summer for a big reunion. Kennebunkport was where they all learned their competitiveness, a family trait. Going back two generations, to George's parents, everyone played games there, such as football, golf, softball, tennis, swimming races, Ping-Pong, cards, even tiddlywinks. His mother, Dorothy "Dottie" Walker Bush, fostered their drive and ambition but wouldn't stand for any bragging. She encouraged her brood to always work harder and to resist the impulse to call attention to themselves, even in victory, avoiding what she called The Great I Am. To her, the team, the family, were most important, and the future president maintained those standards for the rest of his life.

In our interview, Barbara said she would bet that her eldest, President George W. Bush, would continue that tradition of returning "home" after he left office. Her face brightened when she raised the prospect that he might make an extended stay every August for the rest of his life.

"I hope he will," agreed the ex-president softly.

. . .

BUSH NEEDED ALL the solace and comfort that his home place could provide during his one term as the 41st president.

Elected as Ronald Reagan's vice president and heir, he tried to smooth some of his predecessor's hard ideological edges and promised a "kinder, gentler" brand of leadership. He started off well, adopting an accessible and open style, and seemed to be more of a centrist than Reagan. In early 1991, he led the United States and a large international coalition in the Persian Gulf War to force Iraq out of Kuwait, which Saddam Hussein had invaded. The allies won a smashing victory and Bush's popularity soared. His prudent handling of the unraveling of the Soviet Union also won him plaudits.

But Bush ran into deep trouble when the economy slipped into recession and he seemed aloof and out of touch. When he agreed to tax increases in order to reduce historic deficits, his critics blasted him for breaking his word. He had, after all, made a very dramatic promise in his 1988 campaign: "Read my lips. No new taxes." Now his word was suspect.

He lost his bid for reelection in 1992, gaining only 38 percent of the vote, with independent Ross Perot taking 19 percent, and Bill Clinton, 43.5 percent. Bush was humiliated and he returned to Texas, where he kept his distance from public life and left politics to two of his sons, Jeb Bush, who became governor of Florida, and George W. Bush, who became governor of Texas and president of the United States.

UNLIKE RONALD REAGAN'S ranch, which was a private love nest for him and Nancy, Kennebunkport was a hive of activity for the whole Bush clan. Bush "41" once told me that the thing he was most proud of in life was that his children still came home—and he was talking about Walker's Point. His four sons—George W., Neil, Jeb, and Marvin—and daughter, Dorothy, continued the tradition by visiting Kennebunkport for at least a few days every summer with their spouses and kids.

Reflecting his priorities, Bush cherished a photo of him and Barbara in their bed on a weekend morning, surrounded by a passel of rambunctious grandchildren. "For the Reagans, the ranch was a place where they could go and stroll and hold hands," Popadiuk says. "But for President Bush, it was family." And he was constantly entertaining friends, often on the spur of the moment. He sometimes would call Barbara during the afternoon and tell her to expect a dozen or more folks for dinner. Luckily, they had a staff that could handle such last-minute arrangements.

And Bush, ever the gentleman, kept on good terms with his neighbors. He overruled the Secret Service and allowed the local people to leave lobster traps just offshore from Walker's Point, which they had done for generations. The Secret Service had felt it was too dangerous because one could never know who was plying those waters. But Bush had confidence in his neighbors, and he knew there were military frogmen on duty when he was there, so he didn't worry about his safety. He made a habit of going out for dinner with guests and local friends. A favorite was Mabel's Lobster Claw in the middle of Kennebunkport. The First Couple's regular table was in a corner near the front windows. Bush enjoyed the stuffed lobster and Mrs. Bush preferred the eggplant parmesan. The Bushes also liked to take their speedboat to nearby Ogunquit to dine at Barnacle Billy's, a dockside restaurant featuring lobster and beer.

Sometimes, it wasn't easy to strike a balance between security and common sense. Several weeks after Bush took office, in January 1989, the Secret Service added a large number of security measures at Walker's Point, including a chain-link fence, a helicopter pad, and a small house for a doctor and military aide; and they cut down a number of trees to make room. "Suddenly we looked like a prison instead of a beautiful summer home," Mrs. Bush wrote later. "It all made me cry. I'm not too proud of that, but it hurt to see a ten-foot-high fence when we rounded the drive instead of the ocean." Eventually, part of the fencing was taken down, at Barbara's insistence.

Entertaining wasn't always easy. Their first year in office, in 1989, they planned to host French President François Mitterrand and his wife, Danielle, at the 70-year-old bungalow of Bush's mother. But during an official walk-through with French officials, the advance team from Paris remarked that the small, ancient bed seemed shabby and uncomfortable, and complained about a "riser" on the toilet to facilitate the elderly woman's use of the facilities. The bed was replaced and the riser was removed. The visit apparently went well overall, but Bush wasn't pleased—and was maybe a little hurt—when the French leader declined to take a ride on his speedboat, apparently considering it a bit déclassé.

It was one of many visits of foreign dignitaries. As with other presidents and

First Ladies, the Bushes realized that other leaders were eager to be invited to the president's retreat; it gave them special status back home and an unusual connection to their American counterparts. "They got to know the personal side, that you were a personal friend," said Barbara.

THE POINT, AS the Bushes called it, was frequently filled with their children and grandchildren, especially in the summers. "We can sleep thirty-four people and that is a lot of sheets and towels," Mrs. Bush noted. In her role as taskmaster (in contrast to her more lenient husband), Mrs. Bush posted a note on the back of the bedroom doors, addressed to "Bush Children and Grandchildren." It set forth these house rules:

1. Please hang up damp towels and use twice if possible.
2. Try to make beds and keep room picked up . . . makes dusting and vacuuming easier.
3. Please collect your gear from around the house and keep it in your room.
4. If possible let the kitchen know your meal plans:
   —picnics.
   —specific requests for you or your children.
   —missing a meal.
5. Breakfast served from 8 to 9 A.M.—coffee beginning at 6:30 A.M. [It's really more like 5:30 A.M.!]
6. Please put dirty clothes outside your door every night.
7. Ask Paula if you can help her.
8. Above all—have a great time! This is our happiest time of the year!

BUT THERE WERE serious times, too.

Early on the morning of June 3, 1989, Bush was sleeping in his big king-size bed at Walker's Point, where he had gone after attending a NATO summit in Brussels. Aides awakened him with news that Chinese authorities had ordered an attack on a huge crowd of student demonstrators in Beijing's Tiananmen Square. Hundreds of people had apparently been killed, and thousands wounded.

Bush's response was very restrained. He issued a written statement deploring the use of force but proclaiming how much he valued "a constructive relationship beneficial to both countries." This was his position throughout the crisis, in which China's democracy movement was crushed and Communist leaders Deng Xiao-ping and Li Peng retained power.

A former U.S. envoy to China, Bush told aides the worst thing he could do was appear to be pressuring the Beijing regime; that would only harden its position and make matters worse, he felt. He was, as in most things, keenly interested in stability and gradual change and fearful of upheaval that could get out of control. He was widely criticized by the Democrats for being too tolerant of China's hard-line regime.

IN EARLY AUGUST 1990, Saddam Hussein's Iraq invaded Kuwait, setting off the worst crisis of Bush's presidency. Even after sending troops into the Middle East region to deter Iraq from taking over other countries, Bush insisted that he could proceed with his long-planned vacation in Kennebunkport. After all, he had all the communications he needed to stay in touch, and his senior advisers would be close by. Besides, he told aides, he didn't want to be imprisoned at the White House as Jimmy Carter had been, by refusing to travel during most of the Iranian hostage crisis in 1980. To cancel his vacation, he said, would be "show biz."

His aides weren't pleased. They said he would look disengaged and isolated, but the president told Fitzwater, his press secretary, "Look, I need the rest. This is going to be a long and arduous task. I know that this is the best place for me to go to get my mind off of this and be with my family, and I don't give a damn what people think about it. I'm going."

Fitzwater suggested gently that perhaps Bush might forgo riding in his cigarette boat, *Fidelity*, which made him look like a rich preppy. "No," Bush responded tartly. "I'm not staying out of the boat. That's how I relax. That's where I want to be and I'm going out on the water." But he conceded, "I'll take the cell phone with me."

In our interview more than a decade later, Bush told me, "I didn't want to panic the country. . . . Why change what you're doing and kind of throw a panic out across the country when you can do it just as well from where you were? And it wasn't a selfish thing. I did not want to send a signal that this was crisis time. I mean, it was a long way between that August day of August 2 'til we went to war. And we didn't think we were gonna go right then, we knew damn well that we weren't, so, you know, it's better to project a certain calmness and a certain normalcy, even though times weren't totally normal."

But at the time, Bush's image was a constant worry. Fitzwater even asked him to stay off the golf course because Fitzwater, a farm boy from Kansas, considered golf a pastime of the country-club set. "No," came the president's reply. "I'm not staying off the golf course. That's part of what I do up there. It's why it is so relaxing, and we're going to do it and that's where we'll make these decisions."

There was another benefit to getting away from Washington—an opportunity to think about the long-term consequences of the crisis. White House National Security Adviser Brent Scowcroft accompanied Bush to Kennebunkport for some R & R, but he had another mission in mind. The retired Air Force general had been waiting for the right moment to draw Bush into a broader discussion of what the crisis meant to America and the world.

At dawn on August 23, the president called Scowcroft at his hotel and asked if he wanted to go trolling for bluefish. Scowcroft saw his chance and immediately accepted.

For much of the day, as the two men fished lazily in the Gulf of Maine under cloudy skies and amid the drone of *Fidelity*'s powerful engines, they talked in detail about a "new world order" that the Iraq crisis could create. It was during this fishing expedition that Bush's strategy for Iraq and the wider Middle East took shape. Bush aides later said they weren't sure such a relaxed, sustained discussion could have happened in quite the same way anywhere else.

First, they agreed that Bush was perfectly positioned to lead an anti-Iraq coalition because of his expertise in personal diplomacy and his friendship with many foreign leaders. Bush decided he could construct a coalition that would outlast the immediate conflict and serve as a permanent structure for discouraging the "thugs of the world." With the cold war over and the Russians seeking Western aid, Moscow was being extraordinarily cooperative with the president in confronting Saddam Hussein, even though Iraq had long been a Soviet client state. Bush and Scowcroft concluded that multilateralism, particularly through the United Nations, with the United States aggressively taking the lead and firmly in charge, could be the way of the future in resolving global disputes and containing the world's brigands.

Scowcroft pushed the idea that it would be wrong for the United States to go too far. He said that pursuing a war beyond the liberation of Kuwait by occupying Iraq and deposing Saddam Hussein would be a mistake. It could cause anti-

American anger in the Arab nations, and lead to vast instability in Iraq that the United States would be ill prepared to deal with, Scowcroft argued. Bush agreed.

This was the multilateral thinking that governed Bush's handling of the Persian Gulf War and his entire foreign policy. By the end of the morning on *Fidelity*, there was a promising omen: The president landed three 14-pound bluefish.

Strangely enough, it would be Bush's son, President George W. Bush, who would reverse this approach a decade later and construct a policy based on American unilateralism to invade and occupy Iraq in 2003. And in large measure, he would design his own policy of preemptive war—so alien to his father's values—at the presidential retreat of Camp David, where he could escape the routines and protocols of the West Wing to ruminate and consult with his advisers, just as his father had done at Walker's Point.

As the crisis deepened, George Herbert Walker Bush grew impatient with the criticism by his Democratic opponents and media pundits that he was still on vacation. On August 22, 1990, reporters asked him why he wasn't asking Americans to make sacrifices, especially to conserve fuel at a time when Middle East oil supplies might be in jeopardy. "I call upon Americans to conserve," Bush said halfheartedly. But he turned snappish when a reporter asked if he would cut down on use of his fuel-guzzling speedboat, to set an example. "I'm going to keep using my boat," he snapped. "And I hope the rest of America will prudently recreate. I don't think we've reached the point where I want to call on everybody in the recreation industry to shut it down or everybody that's taking a vacation in America to shut it down."

Clearly, his cavorting on *Fidelity* meant a great deal to him. Years later, the episode still raised his hackles. "It was all like, 'You don't get it,'" he told me in a 2004 interview. "I mean, 'Our gas prices are going to be fifty dollars a gallon or something, and you're out there running around in your boat.' It used less gas than a Chevrolet, for God's sake. It was just the doldrums of the summer, everybody got on it. The press got all over me. . . . But I was determined to do it my way, as they say. And maybe I made a mistake, maybe I didn't, but I can tell you that I had more peace of mind."

AFTER THE GULF War, the second biggest foreign-policy crisis of the Bush era was the attempted coup that almost toppled Mikhail Gorbachev from power in the Soviet Union during the summer of 1991, almost exactly a year later. Again, the crisis happened while Bush was at Kennebunkport.

At 11:30 P.M. on August 18, National Security Adviser Scowcroft, clad in powder blue pajamas, was sitting on his bed in his hotel room in Kennebunkport.

Scowcroft was trying to catch a final tidbit of news before he went to sleep and he sat back and flipped on Cable News Network. What he saw startled him. It was a report that Gorbachev had been removed as Soviet president. Not wanting to leap to conclusions, the retired Air Force general thought it must be a simple change of title or a garbled story, but two minutes later CNN reported that an emergency committee had been created to take power.

This sounded ominous. It reflected private U.S. intelligence that Bush had secretly passed on to Gorbachev three months earlier that a coup was possible. Gorbachev's reply at the time was that only paranoiac madmen would make such an attempt.

Scowcroft dialed the Situation Room in the White House basement for a quick intelligence assessment, but the duty officer, surrounded by computer terminals linked to the CIA and the State and Defense Departments, had no more information than what Scowcroft had picked up from TV.

The national security adviser decided to alert the president, whom he called at Walker's Point on a secure phone line at 11:45 P.M. He told Bush it looked like a coup might be under way in the Kremlin, and Bush told him to call back when he heard more. It was the classic Bush response—an unwillingness to act until he had as many facts as possible. This prudent caution was left over from his days as director of Central Intelligence in the 1970s, when he learned that the initial reports about an unfolding crisis were almost always wrong. His reaction was, in one of his favorite phrases, to "let things sort themselves out."

This proved wise. Bush handled the Soviet crisis deftly, organizing international support for Gorbachev and Boris Yeltsin, the advocates of reform, and speaking out against the hard-line coup leaders. In the end, Gorbachev kept his job after his citizens demonstrated en masse against the return of a communist dictatorship.

But during his time in Kennebunkport, Bush again demonstrated how much he was tethered to Walker's Point and his summer routine. On the morning of August 19, as news of the coup spread around the world, Bush was intent on playing golf. Some of his aides were aghast. He could easily look like he was more interested in improving his putt than in salvaging Gorbachev's reformist regime. This would have been unfair, because Bush was up before dawn diligently making phone calls that day to other world leaders, including British prime minister John Major and French prime minister Mitterrand.

The public-relations problem was solved when a severe rainstorm forced Bush to cancel his golf game. He held a press conference at a Secret Service office near his seaside mansion, making a cautious statement that the coup was "disturbing," but not ruling out the possibility that the plotters might continue Gorbachev's reforms. "It's not a time for flamboyance or show business or posturing," he said.

A few hours later, he reluctantly decided to return to Washington. Some of his aides just could not bear the image of him playing golf and fishing while the Soviet Union was imploding. But what persuaded Bush was, again, the weather. Hurricane Bob was bearing down on the region, and White House advisers warned that it could flood Walker's Point and possibly disrupt communications. He resented it, but agreed to return to Washington.

ON AUGUST 11, 1992, came one of Bush's low points at Kennebunkport. He held a press conference with Israeli prime minister Yitzhak Rabin on the lawn of Walker's Point as his family, including his mother and some of his grandchildren, looked on happily. They expected a routine series of questions and answers, and then a return to the activities of the day. What actually happened startled everyone.

After a discussion of the Middle East, Cable News Network reporter Mary Tillotson changed the subject to a recently published book that claimed Bush had an affair with Jennifer Fitzgerald, a personal assistant for many years, in 1984. Tillotson dropped a bombshell by asking point-blank if Bush had had an affair with Fitzgerald.

The president was shocked. Noelle, his granddaughter, began to cry, and Barbara, also stunned, took her away from the scene. Finally, Bush said he was deeply disappointed with CNN for raising the issue and snapped, "I'm not going to take any sleazy questions like that from CNN." But he answered, "No, it's a lie."

MY OWN EXPERIENCE at Kennebunkport began in 1987. I was among the reporters covering Bush's fledgling presidential campaign, and I started making pilgrimages to Maine hoping to get to know him and his staff. He was vice president at the time, and began inviting reporters and their families to Walker's Point for burgers, hot dogs, beer, and soft drinks.

Bush was unfailingly gracious and polite. He would think nothing of fetching a brew or a burger for a visitor he had invited over. He would shake every hand and hold every baby, and he loved to show off his home to guests.

But his wife, Barbara, had a prickly side that was not in keeping with her self-effacing, grandmotherly image, and it emerged in particular when she felt her privacy was being invaded. At the media parties, I noticed how "Bar," as her husband called her, would be friendly for about an hour, and then retreat to the periphery of the main house and stay away from the media pack. She was always worried (with considerable justification) that we would trample her flower beds.

Once, during a summer cookout for the press corps, a chill wind came up and Bush graciously appeared on his backyard deck with an armful of warmup jackets that he had been given by colleges and sports teams around the country. I took one and offered one at random to Mrs. Bush. She looked at me with disdain after noticing that the garment was an extra-large. "Do you think I'm fat?" she said loudly. Chagrined, I said of course not, but she had made her point: She knew how to keep interlopers off balance when it suited her.

Bush's playful side often came out at Kennebunkport. He would place golf balls made of chalk on the tee for guests at the local golf course, and laugh with delight when his victim took a mighty swing and left a white puff behind.

When he made public statements or gave press conferences at Walker's Point, he sometimes would wear chinos or worn khakis and sneakers. He knew this was below camera range, because the TV networks showed him above the waist in his tweed jacket, white shirt, and red tie.

He loved to play horseshoes in the backyard. As a reporter covering him in 1988, I once attended a backyard barbecue at the estate and asked Bush if there was any special terminology in his version of the game. Yes, he replied, when someone tosses a ringer or makes a good throw, that's a "good shoe" and when a player misses the mark and his throw lands in the sand pit, the phrase is "ugly pit." Summing up, I innocently said, "So those are the two main terms?"

"Yeah," Bush replied matter-of-factly. "Good poo and ugly shit." He immediately realized his mistake and turned red, but shrugged his shoulders to signal that he couldn't help himself.

Americans eventually realized that such bizarre transpositions and malapropisms were the way he expressed himself sometimes. In the press corps, we called them "Bush-isms."

· · ·

AFTER THEY LEFT the White House in January 1993 to make way for Bill Clinton, the Bushes set up residence in Houston. But Kennebunkport remained their true home and they visited in the spring and summer, often to host family members.

This included their son, George W., who became president in January 2001. He came back in the summers to fish, spend time with his parents and siblings, and relax. On one morning, the new commander in chief returned from a run and plopped down on the couch in his parents' bedroom, wanting to chat.

But the new president made the mistake of casually putting his feet up on a table. Barbara ordered him to remove them, and her husband was shocked. "Bar," he protested, "he is THE President of the United States." But she was unmoved. "I don't care who he is," the former First Lady announced as she turned to her son. "Get your feet off the table!"

The chastened commander in chief quickly complied.

Yet there was no doubt that relationships in the family were changing. In July 2001, George W. and Laura went to Walker's Point for a long Independence Day weekend, along with other members of the clan. After an early-morning golf game involving the new president, his father, and brother Jeb, followed by an afternoon of fishing, the family gathered for dinner to celebrate W.'s 55th birthday, which was on July 6.

As the commander in chief walked in, his father did something unusual: He gestured to the seat at the head of the table and suggested that his son take it. In this symbolic way, Bush the elder relinquished leadership of the family to his ascendant son. Power had shifted to the new generation, and George Herbert Walker Bush would never take much of a role in America's public life again.

WHILE AT KENNEBUNKPORT, George H. W. Bush was unmoved by criticism, or advice from his aides that he was spending too much time at Walker's Point, especially during crises. It was where he heard about the killings at Tiananmen Square, Iraq's invasion of Kuwait, and the attempted coup against Mikhail Gorbachev. And it was where his theories about creating a "new world order" first emerged, during a bluefishing expedition across the Gulf of Maine on his speedboat.

—∞∞∞—

CHAPTER SEVENTEEN

BILL CLINTON AND MARTHA'S VINEYARD, MASSACHUSETTS

WHEN HE TOOK office in January 1993 as America's 42nd president, Bill Clinton did not own a home of his own, and not being a man of means, he had no retreat to use as an escape.

Yet he was desperately in need of one. After a grueling campaign and a nonstop transition to power, the new president was already in trouble. "When he reached Washington," writes former Clinton adviser David Gergen, "I am convinced, his physical exhaustion caught up with him. It is stressful for anyone to accept the responsibilities of the presidency but Clinton's reaction seemed extreme. Those who saw him in his first weeks at the White House often found him out of sorts, easily distracted, and impatient. I was watching from afar, and the harried man I saw on television bore little resemblance to the confident, relaxed leader I had known. Coming to the White House early that summer, I concluded that he was almost too tired to think straight. . . . Not until August of his first year did Clinton get away for a proper rest. Escaping to a low-key vacation in Martha's Vineyard, where he could sleep, play golf, read, and spend time with family, he returned almost restored to full vigor." This became his pattern.

Over time, he and his wife also made liberal use of Camp David, and for more extended getaways they borrowed a succession of homes from wealthy friends around the country. "The world was his vacation place," says Clinton confidant Terry McAuliffe, who joined the president on many vacations and served as Democratic National Committee chairman.

On two occasions, in 1995 and 1996, he chose Jackson Hole, Wyoming. On others, it was Florida, or ski country in Utah. Once, it was the Virgin Islands, where Bill and Hillary Rodham Clinton, his wife, were photographed slow dancing on the beach in their swimsuits, a picture that was published around the world. Clinton also enjoyed "Renaissance Weekends" over the New Year's holiday in South Carolina—gatherings organized by Clinton friends to combine seminars and speeches with receptions designed to bring the elites of America together to mix and mingle. He frequently stopped over in Hawaii during Asia trips for what he called "extended mini-vacations."

Intellectually curious, Clinton liked to tack a few personal days or even a few personal hours onto his international trips so he could do some sightseeing. He liked to show off his knowledge of the famous sites he was about to visit, such as the historic pyramids near Mexico City and the Rembrandt collections at the Hermitage museum in St. Petersburg. On a visit to Australia, he spent a day snorkeling on the Great Barrier Reef. On a trip to Paris, he took a private tour of the Louvre. He made time to see the the Sistine Chapel in the Vatican, the glorious lake country of Argentina, the notorious Robben Island prison in South Africa. He loved to experience the local culture wherever he went.

"He was a man defined by no routine," says Joe Lockhart, Clinton's press secretary in the White House. "This was a guy for whom every day was an adventure and he didn't get adventure by going to the same place again and again." Lockhart says every president needs a place where there are clear boundaries beyond which his staff will not go—where there is a zone of privacy and he can have time to himself. At the start, the gregarious Clinton needed quiet time more than he knew.

CLINTON'S RESTLESSNESS IN his choice of vacation spots was perhaps a result of his upbringing. He was born as Billy Blythe in Hope, Arkansas. His father had died in a car crash three months prior to his birth, in 1946. His mother remarried in 1950 and her son eventually took the name of his stepfather, Roger Clinton. But their family life was harsh and unsettling. Roger Clinton, it turned out, was an alcoholic who abused his wife. Bill Clinton followed a familiar pattern in the children of alcoholics: He avoided confrontation and became an expert at smoothing over problems.

John F. Kennedy found comfort at the family estate in Hyannisport, Massachusetts. He sometimes drove himself and his son, John Jr., to a candy store in town or took the boy on a stroll, carrying young John's stuffed animal in one hand.

JFK was drawn to the sea from boyhood. The perfect recreational outing for him was to cruise on the presidential yacht, or on his father's boat, off the coast of New England.

Kennedy was a talented golfer, despite the chronic back pain that bedeviled him all his adult life. He played as often as he could on the links around Hyannisport.

Lyndon B. Johnson was the king of the cowboys at his ranch — dominating everyone and everything around him. Whenever he visited his land on the Pedernales River in central Texas, he was constantly barking orders to his presidential staff and to his ranch hands. He also enjoyed the natural splendor, including the lush meadows of spring and summer, where he sometimes walked with his wife, Lady Bird.

A tour of the ranch given by LBJ was always an adventure. He took enormous pride in the place, and often drove a big Lincoln convertible over the rough roads and even into pastures and over ravines, eager to show off his Texas roots.

Richard Nixon was a workaholic who had a difficult time relaxing. His aides and family found it a challenge even to persuade him to stroll along the lovely beaches at his retreats in San Clemente, California, and Key Biscayne, Florida. When he did so, his clothes — and his formal black shoes — sometimes didn't seem quite appropriate.

San Clemente was the estate that Nixon used for extended stays. His expenditure of federal funds for refurbishing — which he defended as security-related — caused a furor among his adversaries.

The president's house in Key Biscayne was used for weekends and short "vacations," although Nixon worked there far more than he played. He also used government money to improve the property, which caused another brouhaha.

Gerald Ford, who succeeded to the presidency when Nixon resigned, was a smart and athletic man who developed the unfortunate image of a bumbler. Whenever he played golf or skied in Vail, Colorado, where he owned a home, he would be pursued by photographers on the lookout for errant golf shots or presidential spills on the slopes. Ford provided plenty of material.

Jimmy Carter used his tiny hometown of Plains, Georgia, to embellish his image as a Washington outsider who would restore simple American values to the White House. Here he helps himself to fried chicken and brownies at a family reunion in Plains just after he was nominated by the Democratic party as its presidential candidate in 1976.

Ronald and Nancy Reagan spent countless hours riding horses on their California ranch. Photographers with long-distance lenses tried to capture their images from nearby mountaintops, and the Reagans occasionally used the moment to promote larger goals, such as when Nancy held up a "Just Say No" sign. It called attention to her anti-drug campaign slogan.

The Reagans were content to spend their time alone together at *Rancho del Cielo*. They rarely entertained or hosted overnight guests.

George Herbert Walker Bush was an avid fisherman who enjoyed trolling for bluefish in his cigarette boat, *Fidelity*, off the coast of his family home in Kennebunkport, Maine. Walker's Point, as the estate is called, gave him a place to entertain family members and friends. Bush made a number of important decisions in Kennebunkport and conferred with aides to devise the American response to Saddam Hussein's invasion of Kuwait.

When he became president in 1993, Bill Clinton didn't have a home of his own, so he vacationed at the homes of rich friends and supporters. He particularly savored Martha's Vineyard, Massachusetts, where he could go boating and attend many social events with celebrities, such as former television anchor Walter Cronkite. He always wanted to be the center of attention.

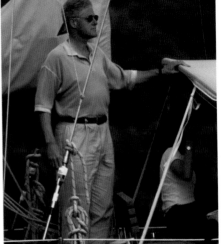

Bill and Hillary Rodham Clinton weren't camera shy, and they did things that other First Couples had resisted, such as letting themselves be photographed in their swimsuits. Photos such as this were widely used around the world.

George W. Bush uses his Prairie Chapel Ranch in Crawford, Texas, to find privacy, to enjoy the company of friends and family, and to get exercise. He spends much of his time there cutting and burning cedar and brush.

Bush's ranch has many scenic charms, and he and First Lady Laura Bush have begun a project to restore as much of the natural vegetation as they can.

Bush considers an invitation to his ranch one of the highest compliments he can pay to foreign leaders, such as Russia's Vladimir Putin. Bush sometimes takes his counterparts on tours of his 1,600-acre property — with the president at the wheel of a white pickup.

Camp David has become an important part of American history. John F. Kennedy hosted his predecessor, Dwight Eisenhower, at the permanent presidential retreat in Maryland's Catoctin Mountains in April 1961. Despite the informal surroundings, it was hardly a social call. They discussed relations with the Soviet Union shortly after the disastrous U.S.-sponsored invasion of Cuba.

One of the most historic achievements ever to occur at Camp David was Jimmy Carter's brokering a peace agreement between Israeli Prime Minister Menachem Begin and Egyptian President Anwar Sadat in 1978. Carter considered Camp David essential to the talks' success because of its privacy and isolation from the news media.

"Those who make war against the United States have chosen their own destruction," President Bush declared in a radio address to the nation from Camp David on September 15, 2001. It was four days after the terrorist attacks of 9/11, and by this time Bush had already spent many hours cloistered at Camp David with his war cabinet considering possible responses. He concluded that the United States needed to wage an all-out, global struggle against the "evildoers."

Bill Clinton graduated from high school in Hot Springs, Arkansas, and demonstrated that he was a high achiever with a deep need to please. He graduated from Georgetown University in Washington, D.C., became a Rhodes Scholar, received his law degree from Yale, returned home, and served one term as Arkansas attorney general and then five terms as governor in Little Rock.

Clinton was an imposing man at 6 foot 2 and a weight that fluctuated between 200 and 225 pounds. He had a paunch and dark pouches under his eyes, but exuded considerable charisma and exhibited a larger-than-life appetite for food (Big Macs with fries from McDonald's were special favorites), attention, and the adulation of female admirers, which, it turned out, almost ended his career. These traits, along with his empathetic quality and raspy, vulnerable-sounding voice, became his trademarks, widely popularized and caricatured on television and in other media.

But he could never discipline himself in his personal life, and in the end, his self-indulgence got the best of him and nearly cost him his presidency.

He handed his enemies a potent weapon to use against him when he began an affair with a White House intern named Monica Lewinsky. She described the relationship to the staff of Independent Counsel Kenneth Starr, who was investigating Clinton on other matters. Starr had enormous latitude and he pursued what became a sex-and-lies investigation into the president's private life. He forced Clinton to testify under oath; the president made misleading statements and, the counsel said, committed the impeachable offense of perjury.

The scandal absorbed the nation for many months as sordid details of Clinton's sexual exploits with Lewinsky were widely reported in the media. This nearly paralyzed the White House for most of 1998 and early 1999, resulting in a squandered year for Clinton and a terrible blemish on his reputation. The furor led to Clinton's impeachment by the House of Representatives in late 1998 for perjury and other charges, but the Senate refused to remove him from office in early 1999. He had survived the biggest crisis of his life, but at a huge cost. By the end of his presidency, most voters approved of his policies but felt that his character was weak.

Throughout the maelstrom, Bill Clinton emerged as a likable rogue who outraged his enemies, disappointed his friends, and frustrated his supporters. But he always managed to stay at the epicenter of public attention, even when he tried to escape from the White House on his many vacations.

During all his years as a public servant in Arkansas, he and his wife, Hillary, never purchased their own home. After he left the White House in January 2001, they maintained houses in Washington, D.C., and Chappaqua, New York, which they listed as their legal residence. Mrs. Clinton was elected a Democratic senator from New York in 2000.

BUT IT WAS Martha's Vineyard—a posh island resort for the rich and famous not far from Boston—to which the Clintons were irresistibly drawn during his administration. It became their perfect getaway. Summering at the Vineyard for six of Clinton's eight years as president gave the couple several things they relished: time to relax, a lovely beach setting, the opportunity to spend time with their daughter, Chelsea, and the chance to socialize as much as they wanted with friends and social climbers who made them the center of attention.

In fact, Clinton always detested the feeling of being what he called cooped up. People energized him, as they did for Theodore Roosevelt nearly a century earlier at Sagamore Hill. While Richard Nixon and Jimmy Carter sought time alone or quiet moments with their family and confidants, Clinton hated isolation. If he could have a dinner party or a big, noisy bash every night, that's what he would do. His friends said he had a kind of isolation meter. He knew when he needed to get out of Washington for a change of pace, and he would plunge into an informal but frenetic series of social engagements that he couldn't fit into the formal, highly structured environment of the White House.

All this concerned some of Clinton's Democratic allies, who feared he would look like a hypocrite for campaigning in 1992 as a man of the people, only to surround himself with the rich and famous at an elite resort frequented by celebrities. "He spent his time cavorting with the people we tried to kick out of the leadership of the party," recalls Al From, founder of the centrist Democratic Leadership Council. Dick Morris, Clinton's pollster, told the president that his associations at the Vineyard would "offend the social populists." Still, Clinton couldn't stay away.

"One of the nicest things about Martha's Vineyard was also one of the most difficult things, frankly," Clinton told me in an interview for this book. "I'd go up there and we would be so tired . . . and because there are so many people who were up there in the summertime and so many of them who had been friends and supporters of ours, it took longer to unwind than it might have otherwise taken because, you know, everybody was having dinners every night, and a bunch of them we had to attend. So part of the joy of being there was seeing all these people, but it made it a little harder to unwind."

THE ROUTE THAT Clinton took to making Martha's Vineyard his main vacation destination was typical of his zigzag style of decision making. In the middle of his first presidential summer, in 1993, Clinton's staff was eager for him to get out of town. A workaholic, he had exhausted his advisers with endless planning and strategy meetings on health-care reform, budget priorities, trade policy, government reorganization, and other topics. Nothing ever seemed to reach a decision point, and tempers were fraying.

In late August, the new president announced to his staff that there was too much work to do and he wasn't going to take a vacation after all. Many members of his staff were deeply upset. They needed the time off, even if the president thought he could soldier on. Some had already made plans in anticipation of Clinton's R & R. Others argued that Clinton needed to take a break, even if he didn't realize it himself. He just wasn't as sharp as he needed to be and he was getting short-tempered.

His wife, Hillary Rodham Clinton, who was exhausted by her own participation in the endless policy debates, also urged her husband to leave town. So did many of his senior advisers. The president reconsidered, but he couldn't make up his mind on where to go. At one point, he considered adviser Roger Altman's ranch near Jackson Hole, Wyoming. But he decided it was too out of the way. Telluride, Colorado, a lovely resort town nestled in the San Juan Mountains, was also considered and rejected for similar reasons. Clinton gave thought to vacationing at the Patuxent River Naval Base, about 60 miles from the White House, but it didn't have an ocean setting, which the president said he craved.

In the end, pal Vernon Jordan persuaded former defense secretary Robert McNamara to lend the Clintons his estate in the Oyster Pond section of Martha's Vineyard. Jordan also vacationed on the island, and Clinton loved to play golf with the gregarious Washington power broker. Finally, the First Family left Washington for the Vineyard on August 19, the president's 47th birthday.

"Clinton loved his vacation," writes author Elizabeth Drew. "The Clintons were the toast of the Vineyard; they went out every night but one during their ten days there. The place was stocked with celebrities. There was dinner at Carly Simon's. Jacqueline Onassis and her family, including Edward Kennedy and his new wife, took the Clintons for a luncheon cruise. Hillary Clinton and Chelsea water-skied with Caroline Kennedy Schlossberg. Later, Mrs. Onassis took the Clintons to dinner. For Kennedy worshiper Bill Clinton, this was sheer heaven. Massachusetts' other senator, John Kerry, took the Clintons for a cruise on his motorboat. The Clintons hit the bookshop and the ice cream parlor and went clamming outside their house, and Clinton played golf nearly every day. He was having such a good time that he extended his vacation by two days."

Bill and Hillary also had the chance to talk about the state of his presidency and what his message to the country should be when he returned. They also talked about his place in history, and how he should shape it. They decided he wasn't communicating his vision and his positive personal qualities to the country and they resolved to do better.

The president got back refreshed and ready for new battles, and the nature of his ruminations over the previous weeks quickly became clear. He told an interfaith breakfast at the White House on August 30 that he finally had the time during his vacation to ponder the problems facing the country and to read *The Culture of Disbelief*, an analysis of how spiritual life was becoming trivialized in American culture, by Yale law professor Stephen Carter. "I am convinced that we are in a period of historic significance, profound change here in this country and throughout the world," Clinton told the religious leaders, "and that no one is wise enough to see to the end of all of it, that we have to be guided by a few basic principles and an absolute conviction that we can re-create a common good for America."

But the salutary effects of the vacation didn't last long. Clinton immediately resumed his furious pace and was exhausted again by the end of September.

The following summer, in 1994, the Clintons stayed at the sprawling Martha's Vineyard estate of Massachusetts real-estate developer Richard Friedman in Oyster Pond. The Friedman complex contained a 19th-century farmhouse and a handful of relatively modest shore homes, each with two or three bedrooms, and a larger central house that the president used. This gave him a measure of both luxury and privacy that he couldn't have at the White House.

His vacation pace was peripatetic. In the mornings, the Clintons slept late, until 9 or 10 A.M., and lounged around the house with Chelsea. While their daughter hung out with her friends, the president and First Lady would nap in the sun, play Scrabble and other word games, and talk policy with advisers and associates in an informal setting. The president also enjoyed playing golf on a nearby course, jogging, and riding horses and walking on the beach.

In the afternoons, Bill and Hillary sat in the sun or on their porch and read books, with the president generally immersed in a mystery novel, a biography, or a philosophical or political science tome. Among the volumes he took with him to the Vineyard or purchased while he was there were thrillers such as Adam Hall's *Quiller Salamander* and Eric Lustbader's *Floating City*, novels like Anna Quindlen's *One True Thing*, mysteries such as Walter Mosley's *Black Betty*, histories such as David McCullough's Civil War book, *Brave Companions*, Jennifer Roberson's science-fiction fantasy, *Shapechangers*, and Alison Shaw's book of photographs, *Vineyard Summer*. He enjoyed the company of writers and dined at the house of author William Styron, where the guests included Colombian author Gabriel García Márquez and Mexican author Carlos Fuentes.

In the evenings, there were the parties with liberal contributors and activists such as actors Ted Danson and Mary Steenburgen, singer-songwriter Carly Simon, and film producer Harvey Weinstein. He mingled with media and entertainment luminaries including Walter Cronkite, Katharine Graham, Mike Wallace, Dick Ebersol, and Susan St. James—always the center of attention as he charmed women and men alike. During his August vacation on the Vineyard in 1997, he went to nine parties in 13 nights.

He would make his way around a crowded room, as he did when he was campaigning, trying to say hello to everyone and impress them with his erudition, his sensitivity, and his ability to connect with any individual. He liked to stand at the center of a crowd with a beer in his hand as he held the group spellbound with his ability to discuss any subject. A tall, slightly overweight man with a full head of silvery black hair, a bulbous nose, and piercing eyes, he didn't have movie-star good looks, but he seemed to find something in common with everyone. He was a notorious flirt.

Clinton once told me in an interview that one of the joys of being president was associating with the stars and entertainment industry leaders he had long admired from afar, from singer Barbra Streisand to movie maker Steven Spielberg. He got the chance to do that at the Vineyard. It was all very bracing for the son of an alcoholic from small-town Arkansas.

"It goes to the psychology of Bill Clinton," says a friend. "He didn't have a home. He was always at loose ends, rootless. And he always had to do something to ingratiate himself to whatever crowd he was with."

Adds Joe Lockhart, Clinton's White House press secretary: "He liked the Vineyard partly because Chelsea and Hillary liked the Vineyard. They had a nice setup there. . . . It was secluded, and he liked the system they have up there of a rotating evening social schedule, going from one home to another."

It was the same pattern the Clintons had enjoyed at the annual Renaissance Weekends, in which they and scores of their friends and associates from around the country would gather to socialize and attend highfalutin seminars and lectures. "The whole idea was smart people talking about interesting and bizarre subjects," says a participant. "It was what Clinton liked to do—intellectual gab."

At many social occasions on the Vineyard or in other places, he would stay up to the wee hours, enjoying the crowds that hung on his every word. If his glass was partly empty, there was always someone nearby to fill it. If the president dropped his spoon at the table, his dinner companions would immediately offer their utensils to the commander in chief. If he felt like sampling more of an appetizer after devouring his own, he would reach over to the plate of his neighbor and pick up a few morsels with his fingers.

At Martha's Vineyard, there were no formalized lectures or seminars, but there was plenty of policy talk and mingling. Clinton particularly enjoyed the parties thrown by Vernon Jordan, the Washington power broker and one of his closest confidants outside government. "Vernon rented a place every summer and threw a clambake," says a mutual friend. "Now, how many times in a year can the president attend a clambake? He loved it."

Jordan served as an informal social director for the Clintons, suggesting which parties to attend and organizing some receptions and dinners just for Bill and Hillary. Some were fancy; others called for jeans.

At one of Jordan's clambakes, Clinton got a phone call and came back to the larger group in a somber mood. He had just learned that Princess Diana of England had been killed in a car crash in Paris. It hadn't been reported by the TV newscasts yet, and it cast a pall on the party, particularly on Hillary, who considered Diana a close friend.

Clinton's staffers back at the White House did all they could to let him get away from his official duties. "Things I might have bothered him with in Washington, at least by memo, I wouldn't bother him with because he was on vacation," recalls former Clinton adviser Bill Galston. "I'd suck it up and make decisions myself."

Adds Galston: "A lot is revealed not just by where they [presidents] go but why they go there. . . . And our presidents have had different capacities to actually relax. Some found it easier than others. It's very revealing to see how much work they did, how much work they took with them. When Reagan was away, he was really away." Clinton, however, was a workaholic. He would always return from "vacations" with a stack of ideas and memos for dealing with policy questions—and it would be up to the staff to follow up. Galston says, "Senior staff would regard his vacations with a certain amount of dread. He'd come back filled with ideas. He had a chance to ruminate, and he'd write notes to himself. His mind never stopped working."

Staffers came to understand why Clinton's mood would frequently sour during his time away from the West Wing. "These [bad] moods were inevitable on his vacations, for despite the press photos of Clinton happily golfing, the president hated vacations," Morris writes. "He loves his work and dislikes being exiled from it. But he doesn't know this about himself; he thinks he likes them—until he is on one. Then he becomes cranky, anxious, nervous, overwrought, and desperate for contact with the real world. . . . He broods, turns nasty, and starts lacing into people."

And politics were in the forefront. Morris even tested public opinion on where the First Family should spend their summer vacations. In 1995, the year before Clinton's successful reelection campaign, Morris told the president and his other strategists that key swing voters, especially middle-class married people with kids, liked camping and they would be most accepting of a presidential camping trip, rather than Martha's Vineyard, where he had happily vacationed in 1993 and 1994. Morris recommended "a mountain vacation, that he hike and camp out in a tent."

"This advice was the ultimate in carrying polling to a mindless extreme," Morris admitted later. "Nevertheless, on his vacation he did camp in a tent."

It happened in August on the Clintons' trip to the Grand Tetons in northwestern Wyoming, as their vacation was drawing to a close. Everything had gone well when they stayed at the home of Senator Jay Rockefeller and his wife, Sharon. Hillary had relaxed around the residence and worked on a book outlining her policy views. Bill and Chelsea went hiking and horseback riding, with the majestic mountains as a backdrop. Then they actually made the camping trip that Morris had recommended.

"I hadn't camped out since college," Hillary recalls, "and Bill never had, unless you count the one night we spent sleeping in his car in Yosemite Park while driving across the country. We were game but clueless. When we told the Secret Service we wanted to hike and camp in a secluded spot in the Grand Teton National Park, they went into overdrive. By the time we arrived at our campsite, they had staked out the perimeter and had agents patrolling with night-vision goggles. Chelsea laughed at our idea of 'roughing it'—a tent with a wooden floor and air mattresses."

Actually, Hillary put a more positive face on it than was deserved. Other White House insiders remember it differently. "We wanted to put out a White House photo of the happy camping trip but we needed rolls and rolls of film to get one shot of them together looking happy," recalls a former White House aide. "The Clintons are not outdoor people. They don't like camping. And the bugs were bad."

In the summer of 1996, his reelection year, Clinton again consulted the polls about his vacation and he returned to the Grand Tetons. Clinton even phoned Morris during the trip for consultation. "I want to take Chelsea rafting," the president said. "She really likes it. Do you think it's okay?"

"Is it dangerous?" Morris asked.

"No, there's no danger," the president replied, "but do you think they'll make a joke of it?"

Morris finally caught on. "You mean about *white-water* rafting?" He suddenly realized that Clinton was talking about the Whitewater investigations that were causing a stir in Washington, involving a failed land deal by the Clintons in Arkansas.

"Yeah."

"No sir, go rafting," Morris advised. "Even if they joke about it, they'll have to write that you went rafting, and that will be good for you politically."

Clinton went on to win reelection against Bob Dole, the longtime Republican senator from Kansas. He had presided over a period of economic prosperity, which would continue through his second term. He adopted centrist social policies, steering between the extremes of liberals and conservatives. He was politically astute, tireless, and eager to establish a legacy the historians would admire.

But he fell victim to his penchant for distorting the truth, and his belief that he could talk his way out of every jam.

AT THE START of his presidency, Clinton seemed to have vast potential. He had a brilliant mind, an intuitive sense of what was popular, and excellent skills as a public communicator. When he took office at age 46, he was one of the three youngest presidents in American history after Theodore Roosevelt (42) and John Kennedy (43). Born just after World War II, he was, like so many other baby boomers, the product of an affluent society, the civil rights movement, the sexual revolution, the anti-Vietnam War movement, the postwar meritocracy, and the television age. His supporters predicted grandly that he would prove himself a transformational leader who would combine the best of John Kennedy, Franklin Roosevelt, Harry Truman, and Thomas Jefferson.

"At the outset of his first term, Clinton seemed well positioned to craft an enduring political realignment," writes historian Matthew Dickinson. "He was likable, well-educated, and articulate. Elected four [consecutive] times as governor of Arkansas, he was an experienced public executive (albeit of a small state). As a politician, he possessed an uncanny knack for overcoming adversity and escaping crises. He was also ambitious, setting his sights on the White House as a young man and becoming an avid student of presidential biography."

The problem was that, despite his familiarity with history, Clinton repeated some of his predecessors' biggest mistakes, especially by attempting to do too much, as Jimmy Carter, Lyndon Johnson, and Woodrow Wilson had done. He narrowly won congressional approval for a deficit-reduction package that raised taxes, but it alienated many conservative voters in the process and raised concern among moderates that he was really a tax-and-spend liberal. His biggest error was attempting to overhaul the nation's health-care system and putting his wife in charge of the project. She proved to be an abrasive figure but, more important, the legislation came across as a radical shift from the status quo, and the proposal failed, even though Congress was controlled by fellow Democrats. These and other setbacks were magnified by the news media and his adversaries, and led to the 1994 Republican takeover of the House and Senate for the first time in a generation. It was a humiliating defeat for the new chief executive.

But Clinton learned his lessons. He turned toward the political center, and tilted his policies toward the prevailing views of the voters as revealed in public-opinion polls. He worked with the Republicans to balance the budget, pass tough crime legislation, promote free trade, and end the federal welfare system. Riding a wave of prosperity, he was reelected in 1996 and his policies remained popular through his second term.

His character was another story.

THE AFTERNOON OF Monday, August 17, 1998, turned out to be one of the worst of Clinton's life, to be followed by what was probably the worst week of his life. This was the day he gave sworn testimony to lawyers from Independent Counsel Kenneth Starr's office about his sexual relationship with former White House intern Monica Lewinsky. Starr's investigation at first had delved into other matters, but his jurisdiction was open-ended, and he had begun pursuing a case against Clinton for perjuring himself in an earlier civil case.

As a result, the president was required by law to submit to an embarrassing and damaging interrogation, which occurred in the Map Room of the West Wing. His testimony was sent live via closed-circuit television across town to a federal grand jury, and it was videotaped for posterity. The president was asked about the details of his relationship with Lewinsky and about his attempts to hide it during previous testimony in a sexual-harassment lawsuit brought against him by former Arkansas state employee Paula Jones.

Later that evening, he made a four-minute nationally televised address in which he confessed to a relationship that was "not appropriate. In fact, it was wrong." He added, "It constituted a critical lapse in judgment and a personal failure on my part for which I am solely and completely responsible. But I told the grand jury today and I say to you now that at no time did I ask anyone to lie, to hide or destroy evidence, or to take any other unlawful action. I know that my public comments and my silence about this matter gave a false impression. I misled people, including even my wife. I deeply regret that."

Clinton then turned angry and blasted the investigation into his affairs as "politically inspired." "I intend to reclaim my family life for my family," he insisted. "It's nobody's business but ours. Even presidents have private lives. It is time to stop the pursuit of personal destruction and the prying into private lives and get on with our national life."

Media and congressional reaction was highly negative, partly because of

Clinton's shift from remorse to resentment. By the next morning, Tuesday, August 18, it was clear that the speech had done nothing to strengthen the president's position. The demoralized White House staff got together to put the best face on things, and to figure out the most graceful way for the president, the First Lady, and their daughter, Chelsea, to make their way out of the White House to a long-scheduled visit to Martha's Vineyard, where they were to stay for two weeks at Friedman's estate.

For many weeks, the Clintons had been looking forward to getting out of Washington, but no one had anticipated the conditions under which the trip would actually begin. The president's political future and his marriage were in jeopardy, and no one in his inner circle was looking forward to it. But at least the First Family could find some privacy and isolation, so they decided to proceed.

The plane trip from Andrews Air Force Base to Martha's Vineyard aboard an executive-style, twin-engine government DC-9 was tense and extremely awkward for everyone on board. There was an excruciating silence between the president and the First Lady that no one could—or tried to—penetrate, and that gave his traveling staff the impression that there would be some serious reckoning ahead.

Air Force One touched down on the island at 5:15 P.M., to a small crowd of well-wishers. What followed was a pleasure trip in name only—in fact, it was one of the most grueling and publicly scrutinized "vacations" of any president in history.

Chelsea met some college friends from Stanford University who were also vacationing there, and she spent lots of time with them rather than with her estranged parents. This was understandable, considering the tension in the air. Bill and Hillary scarcely talked. The president spent considerable time walking alone on the beach with his chocolate-colored Labrador retriever, Buddy. He felt that he couldn't play golf or attend the usual round of island parties because that might suggest—to Hillary and the country—that he was taking his predicament too lightly. He was sleeping on a couch.

To lessen the strain and relieve his loneliness, he called aides to the estate after midnight at least twice to play hearts, his favorite card game. He phoned close friends to vent his anger at Starr, to admit his mistakes, to complain about a "witch hunt" against him, and to express fear that his wife would not forgive him.

The aggrieved First Lady stayed alone with her thoughts and her resentments. She later admitted that she didn't want to even raise the issue of adultery until after her husband dealt with what she knew would be imminent air strikes against Osama bin Laden and his network of terrorists, who were being blamed for recent attacks on U.S. embassies in Africa. Revealing a steely discipline, she didn't want to distract the president at such a sensitive time.

Yet in her book, *Living History*, Mrs. Clinton acknowledges that her pain was intense and the time at Martha's Vineyard had turned into an extraordinary soap opera. "The last thing in the world I wanted to do was go away on vacation," she writes, "but I was desperate to get out of Washington. Chelsea had wanted to go back to Martha's Vineyard, where good friends were waiting. So Bill, Chelsea and I left for the island. . . . Buddy, the dog, came along to keep Bill company. He was the only member of our family who was still willing to."

Mrs. Clinton adds, "By the time we settled into our borrowed house, the adrenaline of the crisis had worn off, and I was left with nothing but profound sadness, disappointment and unresolved anger. I could barely speak to Bill, and when I did, it was a tirade. I read. I walked on the beach. He slept downstairs. I slept upstairs. Days were easier than nights. Where do you turn when your best friend, the one who always helps you through hard times, is the one who wounded you? I felt unbearably lonely and I could tell Bill did too. He kept trying to explain and apologize. But I wasn't ready to be in the same room with him, let alone forgive him."

On Wednesday, August 19, their second day on the island, the president celebrated his 52nd birthday with a dinner of barbecued chicken and corn on the cob at a neighbor's house. But the air strikes were on his mind. After returning to their compound at about 11:30 P.M., the president talked on the secure phone until 3 A.M. with advisers in Washington about the upcoming attacks against suspected terrorist camps in Afghanistan and Sudan run by Osama bin Laden.

Clinton recalls: "I remember one night in particular, the night before the final 'go.' I think it was three in the morning when we finally took one target off the list, decided to leave a chemical company on, based on the CIA's best intelligence. And I thought, you know, it was just amazing I was up there in Martha's Vineyard doing all this just as if I had been in the White House."

The strikes took place the next day, Thursday, August 20. Even though he could have managed the situation from Martha's Vineyard, with secure communications installed especially for his use, Clinton took a respite from his marital strife and flew back to Washington to oversee the operation. Some critics saw the bombing as a crass attempt to divert attention from the president's lies and deceptions.

Returning to Martha's Vineyard the next day, August 21, he got back to nearly full-time monitoring of the efforts to impeach him in the House of Representatives for perjury and other transgressions. Things looked bleak. At one point, he read a newspaper report of remarks by House Democratic Leader Dick Gephardt seemingly raising the prospect of his impeachment. Clinton phoned his lead fund-raiser, Terry McAuliffe (later Democratic national chairman), who was also a friend of Gephardt's, and complained bitterly that the congressman was stirring the pot and keeping alive the possibility of removing him from office.

As his standing deteriorated and more members of Congress of both parties voiced their animosity toward him, Clinton began another round of direct-dial diplomacy, making phone calls to key Democrats from Martha's Vineyard. Clinton's staff urged him to use these calls to apologize for his conduct and for embarrassing his allies; but he couldn't keep his temper in check. In call after call, he condemned Starr and again seemed more interested in expressing his resentment than his regrets.

"By the middle of his second week of 'vacation,' Clinton was growing stir-crazy and decided to get out for a while," writes author Peter Baker. His wife recalls the atmosphere in their summer house as "thick with silence." She adds: "It was excruciating for Bill and me to be locked up together, but it was hard to get out. The media had staked out the island and were ready to descend as soon as we appeared in public."

His staff "looked around for a short day trip he could make," Baker says, "and settled on Worcester, Massachusetts, a short hop away, where he could announce a scholarship program for would-be police officers and a new teacher's guide for detecting troubled youth. No mention would be made of Lewinsky, no new apologies issued." That trip, on August 27, went well, and his hand-picked audience greeted him warmly. Clinton was buoyed.

At the urging of his staff in Washington, where he was being berated by the media punditocracy hour after hour, day after day, Clinton decided to make a more dramatic act of contrition. On Friday, August 28, while attending a church service on Martha's Vineyard scheduled to mark the 35th anniversary of Martin Luther King's "I Have a Dream" speech, Clinton remarked on his ordeal. "All of you know, I'm having to become quite an expert in this business of asking for forgiveness," Clinton said. "It gets a little easier the more you do it. . . . But I have to tell you that in these last days, it has come home to me, again something I first learned as president, but it wasn't burned in my bones, and that is that in order to get it, you have to be willing to give it. And all of us—the anger, the resentment, the bitterness, the desire for recrimination against people you believe have wronged you, they harden the heart and deaden the spirit and lead to self-inflicted wounds. And so it is important that we are able to forgive those we believe have wronged us, even as we ask for forgiveness from people we have wronged."

This still wasn't enough to satisfy his critics. Even many Democrats were still waiting for him to say, simply, "I'm sorry." His being cloistered at Martha's Vineyard probably clouded his judgment, because he couldn't fully understand the firestorm of criticism he was getting back in Washington. The atmosphere in the capital was emotional and angry, and the media were in full feeding frenzy. And it was official Washington that mattered most, because the members of the House and Senate would be deciding his fate.

For her part, Hillary finally found a measure of solace at Martha's Vineyard. "By the end of August," she writes, "there was détente, if not peace, in our household. Although I was heartbroken and disappointed with Bill, my long hours alone made me admit to myself that I loved him. . . . As his wife, I wanted to wring Bill's neck. But he was not only my husband, he was also my president, and I thought that, in spite of everything, Bill led America and the world in a way that I continued to support."

President Clinton finally understood what he had to do on September 4. At a joint appearance with the Irish prime minister in Dublin, Clinton addressed the scandal yet again and told reporters, "I'm very sorry about it." This didn't make the controversy go away, but it did take the edge off the sense among his fellow Democrats that he wouldn't fully apologize.

In December 1998, the Republican-controlled House of Representatives approved two articles of impeachment against him, but the GOP-controlled Senate, with nearly all Democrats holding firm for their president, narrowly voted in February 1999 against removing him from office. He had survived, but the scandal had irreparably damaged his reputation and his influence, and the final phase of his administration was largely one of wasted opportunities.

WHEN THE CLINTONS returned to Martha's Vineyard in August 1999, nearly a year later, for their fifth summer there, the personal storm had passed.

The president and the First Lady had made peace, and Clinton made a lengthy speech urging New Yorkers to vote for her in the 2000 Senate race, in which she was a candidate. At a joint fund-raiser for her in Nantucket, he called her the "most gifted person" he had ever known and, signaling that their marriage was intact, said that when they had entered the White House in 1993, he told her, "I want you to decide where you want to go and what you want to do when we get out of here. For twenty years we've gone where I wanted to go and done what I wanted to do, and I'll give you the next twenty years and if I'm still alive after that, we'll fight over the rest."

They again stayed at Richard Friedman's estate, and resumed their rounds of parties and dinners. There was a 53rd-birthday celebration at Vernon Jordan's place that included William Styron, investment banker Steven Rattner, and television journalist Charlayne Hunter-Gault, and a buffet that featured seafood paella, roast beef, and birthday cake.

It seemed like old times, pre-impeachment, but the blemish on Clinton's record from the impeachment ordeal would be permanent.

CLINTON'S ACTIVITIES AT his retreats illustrated his intellectual curiosity, his rootlessness, and his need for approval and constant socializing. They also showed his workaholic nature. He loved being president, and whatever his mistakes, he got up every morning eager to do his job, even when he was "on vacation." All this was reflected at Martha's Vineyard, his favorite relaxation spot. This was where he endured what was probably the worst experience of his presidency, the ordeal of starting to heal his marriage after he admitted an illicit relationship with Monica Lewinsky.

CHAPTER EIGHTEEN

GEORGE W. BUSH AND
PRAIRIE CHAPEL RANCH, TEXAS

G EORGE W. BUSH's attitude toward his 1,600-acre Prairie Chapel Ranch in Crawford, Texas, has always been blunt. He told friends he would do whatever he pleased with his property, and visit it whenever he wanted—and damn the critics who complained that he was there too much, even in times of crisis. This was similar to his father's feeling about Kennebunkport, though conveyed more sharply.

"There's nothing like having your own property," he told me in an interview for this book. ". . . If you own your land, every day is Earth Day. Well, that's how I feel about it. This is a precious piece of property, which we treat very tenderly. And being on it just kind of changes your attitude.

"It doesn't make you not president. You're always president. You're just president with a different feel."

What he meant was that it is home, a place where he can be himself and do the things he likes most, such as chopping cedar and clearing brush (as Ronald Reagan did on *his* ranch). He goes mountain biking, listens in the morning for the whistling calls of the bobwhite quail, and takes walks with his wife, Laura, amid the ash, walnut, sycamore, oak, and pecan trees. He entertains small groups of friends over dinners of broiled fish caught in his stocked lake and pitchers of iced tea or diet cola (he is a teetotaler and reformed heavy drinker). On a public relations level, being at the ranch conveys an image that Bush has carefully cultivated, that of a Washington outsider who enjoys the simple pleasures of life and isn't really at home in the capital.

Bush started his administration with a constitutional crisis brought on by the disputed and extremely close presidential election of 2000. A controversial 5–4 decision by the Supreme Court gave the State of Florida—and the White House—to Bush. This outcome infuriated Democratic leaders, who from then on raised questions about Bush's legitimacy as president.

He steered a conservative course, winning congressional approval for massive tax cuts and increases in military spending and rolling back some key health and safety regulations, and these policies further divided the country. Those who expected him to govern as a centrist were especially outraged. Then came the September 11, 2001, terrorist attacks on the World Trade Center in New York and the Pentagon in Washington. Bush reacted well at the start of the crisis, uniting the country for what he called a war on terror. But he later ordered an invasion of Iraq, arguing that Saddam Hussein's brutal regime in Baghdad posed a threat to the United States. This in turn caused another angry debate about Bush's doctrine of preemptive war—the concept that his administration would strike at "evildoers" around the world before they attacked America.

The bitter battles of the times encouraged Bush to escape from the capital as often as possible, as so many of his predecessors had done. By August 2004, he had made 38 visits to his ranch, spending all or part of 254 days there.

Eager for a change of pace from Washington, Bush would throw himself into his outdoor activities so feverishly that he would sometimes come back to his main house with scratches on his face and arms from tangling with underbrush as he wielded a chain saw. He didn't bother to put on makeup when he made his next public appearances, and news photographers transmitted pictures of his battered visage around the world.

On May 22, 2004, he suffered cuts and bruises on his chin, upper lip, nose, right hand, and both knees from taking a spill while mountain biking. He was on the 16th mile of a 17-mile ride when he fell. Dr. Richard Tubb, his personal physician, who accompanied him on the jaunt, quickly cleaned the injuries and the president finished his ride. But, again, pictures of the commander in chief looking like he had been in a bar fight were used widely on TV and in newspapers. Bush didn't seem to mind.

·   ·   ·

THE TIP-OFF TO Bush's attitude about his ranch came during the grueling weeks after Election Day in 2000. With the outcome hinging on the results in Florida, where his brother, Jeb, was governor, and with only a few hundred votes separating Bush and Vice President Al Gore, each side used a series of legal maneuvers and court challenges to gain the upper hand. Thousands of votes appeared to have been uncounted or tallied improperly, and for week after week the election hung in the balance.

During the court fight, Gore directed his legal and political team from the vice president's residence in Washington. Bush, however, refused to micromanage. He holed up at Prairie Chapel Ranch, made sporadic public appearances, and while he was updated daily and occasionally watched the news on TV, he left the process largely in the hands of his advisers—a process of delegation he would follow in his overall approach to the presidency. To occupy his time, he cleared cedar, jogged, took walks with his wife, inspected his property in a pickup truck, and went about considering his choices for the White House staff and the Cabinet in case he indeed was declared the winner. "He wasn't flustered or angry or obsessed about things," says a confidant. "He was relaxed. He said the results were out of his hands, so why worry about it? Being at his ranch helped him keep things in perspective."

In an interview for this book, conducted in the glassed-in breezeway of the main house, Bush said, "Amidst all the fury, we were here, feeling just great about life, feeling very comfortable." He recalled that it was here that he had selected Dick Cheney as his running mate in the summer of 2000, so he was comfortable making decisions at the ranch. At one point during the recount furor, he told a friend at Crawford, "If they steal it, they steal it." He would happily remain at home.

In the end, the Supreme Court's 5–4 ruling on December 12 ended the matter as conservative justices held sway and stopped a partial recount in Florida that had been demanded by Democrats. It was the first time since Rutherford B. Hayes's election, in 1876, that a president had won an election despite losing the popular tally, which Gore won by more than 500,000 votes nationwide.

After he took office, whenever he had a free few days, Bush would make the three-hour flight to the ranch—which is 90 miles north of Austin—like a bee to honey. It gave him the privacy he craved and enabled him to do what he wanted outside, whether it was jogging in 100-degree heat, fishing in his man-made lake, gunning his pickup truck over ravines and dirt roads, chopping cedar, or cooling off by jumping into a creek, where Secret Service agents, to their horror, once found a poisonous water moccasin. From then on, his protective detail made sure to regularly inspect the area for the snakes and remove any that turned up.

The president says the ranch gives him a permanent link to his roots in Texas, where he was raised as a boy and attended public schools (in addition, of course, to Andover, Yale, and Harvard Business School). He became a Midland oilman when he started his business career, served as managing partner of the Texas Rangers baseball team, and later was governor of the state for six years. "Obviously, I love Texas," he once said. "It's very important for a president to know who he is before you take this job. A lot of pressure here, a lot of decision making. If you try to figure out who you are on the job, you're not doing a very good job." He keeps in the Oval Office several paintings of Texas scenes that resemble the landscape of his ranch.

None of this hurt his image, of course. As historian Doug Brinkley points out, Bush from the start wanted to convey an impression of "cowboy populism." His handlers made sure that he was shown in countless TV images sauntering around his property in jeans and a short-sleeved work shirt, leaning his wiry 5-foot-10 frame on a fence rail as he talked to reporters, or driving foreign leaders around in a pickup or a Chevy Suburban. Sometimes television journalists would do their standup reports in front of carefully positioned bales of hay or barns and tractors, reinforcing Bush's rural Texas background. Actually, he came from a family of wealth and privilege with roots in New England.

First Lady Laura Bush told me that she and her husband take comfort from the support of their neighbors in Crawford, although actually they have met with the neighbors only rarely. Still, Mrs. Bush listed among their sources of support "the people we go eat hamburgers with at the Coffee Station, the people that we work with on the ranch, our friends who come stay with us or come for dinner that live around there—and of course a lot of our Austin and Dallas friends come as well, and Midland friends, when we're there."

Mrs. Bush added that their associates in Texas give them a different perspective from what they get in official Washington—and from what the media convey. "I think we get a more balanced view," she said. "I think there's a certain—I hesitate to say this to you—but I think there's a certain herd mentality in the press. . . . We see that maybe because [of] being with other people who aren't in the press and see what they think."

She added, "We do love to go to our ranch. We love to go to our own home, which of course that's what our ranch is, and both there and at Camp David we have the opportunity to go outside, which both of us really like. . . . There's a certain groundedness that we are able to get from getting out of the White House and going around the country and certainly back to our own state, in Texas. Those people that we know, that we're with when we're in Crawford, are people who there's no pretention about them. . . . They're very American really in a really good way, and both of us like that and we draw strength from that."

"EVERYONE NEEDS SOMEPLACE to go where they can hear their own thoughts," says Reed Dickens, a young aide who has accompanied Bush to the ranch and has done chores with him on many occasions. "It's amazing to see his countenance change when he's at the ranch. He can clear his mind."

"First and foremost, it belongs to him and Mrs. Bush and not to the government," says Ari Fleischer, who served as Bush's first White House press secretary. "If he breaks a dish, it's his dish and not a famous dish." Fleischer adds, "It's Texas and that's very important to him. One thing about Texans—they all want to return home. It's real America. It's outside the Beltway."

The Bushes paid an estimated $1.3 million for the property, which they purchased in 1999 from B. F. and Earlene Engelbrecht, an elderly couple whose families had lived there for more than a century.

George W. and Laura Bush completely remodeled the house, with the future president leaving the interior design mostly to his wife. They chose David Heymann, associate dean of the School of Architecture at the University of Texas at Austin, to redo the home: "The Bushes told me they had this beautiful piece of land and they wanted the house to add to the land, not disrupt it. Given the complexity of their lives, they wanted a place where they could feel grounded. They wanted to be in the land and related to it." Heymann came up with a clean, unimposing design: a long, single-story, eight-room, 4,000-square-foot house featuring scores of big windows, a wide porch, and marvelous views of a stand of magnificent live oak trees on the west and a man-made lake on the east. There are no stairs, so the First Couple's parents could walk around easily and the Bushes themselves would be able to navigate from room to room in their dotage. There is a small outdoor pool, installed mainly at the request of the president's two daughters. Bush dubbed it "the whining pool" to reflect the fact that his daughters whined for a long time to get it built.

There is a cistern to collect rainwater for flowers and shrubs, a border of gravel to absorb water and prevent flooding, and heat pumps for heating and cooling. The president made two requests, Heymann says: "All he really asked for was a shower and a king-size bed, but he had other concerns as well. He wanted it to be very relaxed. The way he described it, he wanted a house for people to come over, sit on the couch, and eat hamburgers and beans with their shoes off."

Laura decorated the main house in a style that an aide called "simple yet elegant, like Laura Bush herself." It includes an outsized fireplace, lots of bookshelves (Laura is a former librarian and teacher), an open kitchen, an office for the president, and three bedrooms. The guest house has two bedrooms, each with two double beds. On extended visits when dignitaries and family are expected, senior staff members will stay in a double-wide trailer parked not far from the main compound.

Dan Bartlett, Bush's director of communications at the White House, says, "He can be a normal person there, totally relaxed, at ease and comfortable. He gets to climb behind the wheel of his truck, and they can escape the glare of the media. It's therapeutic." The president and First Lady also enjoy entertaining close friends, as long as they don't have to do it too frequently. What they prize most about the ranch is the privacy. "It harkens back for both of them to the days before the [White House] bubble," Bartlett adds.

Yet the privacy is not complete. Secret Service agents accompany the president wherever he goes, even in jaunts around his property. Agents live in a compound on the ranch that is partially hidden in a stand of trees near a helicopter pad, and their security huts are interspersed throughout the area. Sharpshooters keep vigil in the cliffs, and the trails and roads on the ranch are numbered and color coded so the agents can more easily keep track of the commander in chief's meanderings.

Like George Washington more than 200 years earlier, Bush monitors the goings-on at his ranch from the capital (although not in as much detail as the nation's first president). At the White House, he is frequently on the phone with his ranch foreman, Robert Blossman, a former Secret Service agent who worked at the Reagan ranch in California and whose father, Ben Blossman, also an agent, was assigned to the LBJ Ranch. They chat about the weather and rain level and how they are affecting 200 head of cattle and the native grasses, trees, and other vegetation, such as the bluebonnets and other wildflowers that his wife adores; the local birds, such as the cooing quail that the First Lady enjoys; and the fish in his lake. He is also keenly interested in the potential for damaging fires in the isolated scrub country, and will check the weather using an Internet hookup from the Oval Office to see how things are going in Crawford.

Blossman sends the president periodic "ranch messages" providing updates on the property and summarizing the work schedule and what needs to be done—things like whether a supply of wood has arrived on time for building a dock on Bush's lake. Bush in turn gives his assessment orally either directly to Blossman or through White House aides. On more than one occasion, Blossman has been chatting with a presidential assistant on the phone during a Bush motorcade somewhere in the world, and Bush has grabbed the phone and talked to his foreman directly.

When he is returning to the ranch, he sometimes cuts events on his official schedule short so he can get to Crawford as early as possible. He often asks his helicopter pilot to fly over the ranch along different routes from the Waco, Texas, airport, where *Air Force One* lands, so he can see different perspectives from the air. Once he arrives, he prides himself on how well he knows his neighbors in the tiny town of Crawford. He reads the local paper, the *Waco Tribune*, and remembers the names of local youngsters who play on the high school sports teams, so he can mention their exploits to their parents when he sees them.

BUSH AIDES SAY he has a problem focusing on policy when he is away from the White House. When his advisers want him to take up a serious, complex issue or decision, they prefer to do it in the West Wing, not at his Texas ranch or at Camp David. He has a mindset that Prairie Chapel Ranch and Camp David (where he goes nearly every weekend that he is in Washington) are mostly for fun and leisure, not work.

He will bend his own rules and force himself to make decisions at these retreats if need be. He did this in Crawford in August 2001, when he waded through the complexities of embryonic stem-cell research. His conclusion was to restrict federal funding to only the limited number of stem-cell lines that were available for research at that time.

He also reversed course in late March 2004 and decided to allow Condoleezza Rice, his national security adviser, to give sworn public testimony before a commission investigating the September 11, 2001, terrorist attacks. Bush had until that time asserted a claim of executive privilege, arguing that letting Rice testify before the congressionally created panel would undermine presidential powers because the president needs to make policy in private. Under considerable pressure from Democrats and Republicans, he changed his mind after giving the issue a fresh look between bouts of clearing cedar with a chain saw and long walks in the woods. "The president began to think that the public wasn't getting the right impression about our cooperation with the commission," says Dan Bartlett, the White House communications director. "It was a debate all about process, and he wanted to shift it back to the substance."

At both the ranch and at Camp David, he made many key decisions on the war on terrorism. That crisis was an extraordinary moment in history that consumed virtually all of Bush's time and energy for months after the attacks of September 11. "We met on the Iraq War here a lot," Bush told me in our interview. "Transformation issues have come up here as a result of annually the Joint Chiefs coming down, or [Joint Chiefs chairman] Dick Myers coming down with [Defense Secretary] Rumsfeld and others to go over different aspects of military planning. [Former Secretary of State] Colin Powell and [his deputy Richard] Armitage were here. . . . I spend more time particularly when senior members of my administration come, thinking big-picture items—relationship between the United States and Europe, for example. We had a long discussion about that."

And there were some nerve-wracking moments. One came, at least for his family, when Bush secretly flew off to Baghdad from the ranch to meet with victorious U.S. troops on Thanksgiving Day 2003. He told only Laura and a handful of trusted advisers, military officers, and Secret Service officials in advance.

When he departed from Crawford under a thick cloak of secrecy, he left his family at his ranch to mark Thanksgiving without him—a group that included his wife, his twin daughters, and his parents. The tension was unavoidable all day, as the group went through the motions of carving the turkey, having a big dinner, taking naps, walking the trails, and eating the traditional turkey sandwiches in the evening—all while sharing an unspoken fear for the president's safety. By this point, the family knew he was heading into a war zone where terrorists wanted nothing better than to shoot *Air Force One* from the sky or bomb the mess hall where the commander in chief was to eat with the troops. Finally, the tension was broken when word came by secure phone to Laura that *Air Force One* was wheels up and heading home.

Bush arrived back at the ranch to the delight of his family and shared a belated turkey dinner with them as he explained how humbled and thrilled he was at the cheers of the troops.

At 5:30 A.M. the next day, there was a knock on the door of the elder Bushes' guest house. It was the president, wearing jeans and a scruffy coat. "C'mon, Dad," he said. "Let's go fishing." That's what they did, after sharing a cup of coffee and some more reminiscences about his visit to Baghdad—one commander in chief to another.

BUSH'S ROUTINE AT the ranch is considerably less structured than his days at the White House. The president still gets up early, about 5:15 or 5:30 A.M., but the pace is more relaxed. "I will get Laura coffee," he told me. "Nothing like having a nice strong cup of coffee on your own ranch. In the summer the sun's comin' up; in winter, it's dark as heck. A paper shows up about 6. I'll read that. I'll read intelligence briefs, overnight intelligence briefs, homeland security briefs."

About 8 A.M., he has a light breakfast with his wife, and sometimes with overnight guests. About this time, he and the First Lady often go for a walk. After that, he rides, often driving himself, to a secure building on a parcel called "the eleven acres," where he has a briefing in person or in a secure video conference with senior national security officials, including Vice President Dick Cheney, White House Chief of Staff Andrew Card, and FBI and CIA representatives.

He spends an hour or two working the land, mostly clearing cedar. Then he returns to the ranch house to work out on an elliptical trainer in a home gym. He'll have lunch, often checking in on the phone with staffers, take a nap, go fishing on his private lake from 3 to 5:30 P.M., then come back to the house, get cleaned up, and have an early dinner with family or friends.

Bush told me that he and Laura generally spend their evenings reading until they fall asleep. White House officials were reluctant to provide a list of books the president had read at Crawford, but at one point in August 2001, press spokesman Scott McClellan revealed that Bush had enjoyed *In the Heart of the Sea*, about a whaling disaster that inspired *Moby Dick*, and was perusing *John Adams* by David McCullough but hadn't finished it. The First Lady hastened to add in our interview that the president will often watch sports on TV, especially teams from Texas.

Time and again, Bush told me that he enjoys outdoor labor, clearing brush, chopping new-growth cedar (which be believes soaks up too much water and damages other vegetation), and doing other ranch work around the property such as creating or improving trails. He has been known to suddenly stop his work routine on a hot day and jump into his two-acre lake or a nearby stream to cool off.

Improving the property is important to him. But he doesn't require everyone to do outdoor chores. First-term National Security Adviser Condoleezza Rice, who often accompanied the Bushes to the ranch, had no interest in participating. Early on, she told the president, "Nice Southern girls don't do cedar."

But Bush is obsessed with clearing brush. It gives him something he can control. "Cutting brush is a metaphor for what you would like to do in the presidency, but can't," says Steven J. Wayne, a history professor at Georgetown. "Problems that reach the president, by definition, are not simple, nor are most presidential actions and decisions cost-free. . . . You can take out your aggressions on the hapless brush with minimal resistance. And when you finish, you can admire your work."

BUSH TAKES GREAT care about who he invites to the ranch. It's at the very top of his ziggurat in dispensing special treatment, ranking higher than even an overnight visit to the White House. Foreign leaders are well aware of this, and consider an invitation to Crawford a great honor, either because Bush wants something special from them or simply enjoys their company.

It was at Crawford that Bush hosted Chinese president Jiang Zemin in October 2002, and where he pressed his argument that Chinese interests were linked to resolving a confrontation with North Korea even more than the United States' interests, because Korea is in China's backyard. If the Beijing regime wanted a non-nuclear Korean Peninsula, it would be best for the Chinese leaders to "get working together," Bush said. His arguments met with only limited success, but he told me that personal diplomacy has a special resonance in the relaxed, leisurely atmosphere of the ranch.

Bush met at poolside with Japanese prime minister Junichiro Koizumi for three hours and discussed world affairs. He believes he bonded with British prime minister Tony Blair, his strongest ally in the war against Iraq. He recalled seeing Italian prime minister Silvio Berlusconi beginning an early-morning walk in the red-and-black sweatsuit of the AC Milan soccer team, which he owned, and the president asked if he could come along. "I mean, he loved it," Bush said with a grin.

Bush loves to play what aides call "windshield rancher" by taking visitors on tours in his pickup truck. Bush is proud of the variety of the land—the canyons, caves, and stretches of prairie—and he likes to point out the huge patches of cedar that he intends to cut with his chain saw.

Noam Neusner, spokesman for the Office of Management and Budget, says, "Fundamentally he likes to be outside. He likes to break a sweat, and the White House is very confining. This White House in particular has a very strong sense of order and precision, and at the ranch he can look at a four- or five-hour span of time as something under his control. He has a lot more control over his schedule."

When he knows he will be at the ranch for more than a couple of days, he will come armed with a detailed work plan to continue making improvements. During his first year in office, for example, he was focused on building a nature trail through the canyons. In August 2003, he began to clear an area for a new office separate from the main house.

Secret Service agents can listen to a Secret Service radio monitor, which broadcasts periodic updates of his whereabouts. Agents will notify each other on that radio system when the president passes various checkpoints, so his location is always known in case of a crisis or if the president suddenly falls ill.

He will visit a "secure trailer," equipped with sophisticated communications systems enabling him to talk to advisers in Washington or around the world on secure lines, for his daily national security briefing. Bush also has the capability to conduct secure video teleconferences—SVTC, in White House jargon—with his National Security Council and others.

At a prearranged time set by the president, often 9 A.M., a small entourage will gather: The cedar patrol will form up outside the group's trailers and pile into one or more pickup trucks or vans. The president will get into his own pickup, accompanied by a platoon of Secret Service agents, military aides, policy advisers, a doctor, ranch hands, and friends. Those who have helped him in his outdoor work say he is a serious task master. "He works longest and hardest of all of us," says Reed Dickens, a frequent member of what Bush and his aides call "the cedar squad" or "guest pullers," those who help the president clear the invasive cedar and cut brush. They are all volunteers, and Bush doesn't insist that anyone labor with him, although he appreciates those who participate.

He will push everyone to keep at it even when they tire, and will tease anyone who takes a break or who stands around, even momentarily, to observe. The work sessions generally last about three hours, and turn into a frenzy of three or four buzzing chain saws, chopping wood, and whirring weed-cutting machines. In the hot weather, he wears jeans, a tee shirt, work boots, a Crawford, Texas, baseball cap, sunglasses, and earplugs. He will often keep up a running commentary, shouted over the sound of the equipment, about sports, especially baseball, his family, and the ranch—but almost never about policy or politics.

After the work detail, everyone will break for lunch and to relax a while. After this point in the day, the staff will rarely see the president again. Everyone knows that he wants to be left alone. He will go fishing, sometimes take a nap, take a walk with Laura, or drive guests around the ranch.

THERE IS A certain macho quality to Bush's approach to the ranch that explains a lot about his personality. For one thing, he loves what he calls the deep heat, which can go up to 110 degrees in the summer. This may seem curious, even bizarre, to most Americans in their air-conditioned society. But, until he suffered a knee injury that limited his mobility, Bush delighted in showing his visitors his stamina, even to the point of inventing a "100-degree Club" for those who could keep up with him and finish a 3-mile run in the sweltering weather. (He maintained a 7- to 8-minute-per-mile pace throughout—impressive for a man in his fifties.)

"He likes sweating people out, especially people in the media who aren't as fit as he is," Neusner says. "He wants to see who can last. . . . He figures Texans are tough. . . . He has a view that this may be scrub land, but anyone who comes out of West Texas has to be tough. . . . He has a manly gusto that he carries with him all the time."

Says Anne Lewis, a Democratic activist and Bill Clinton's former White House communications director: "It's natural for people to believe their home environment is the model for all others. . . . George W. Bush doesn't like the White House particularly. He doesn't often invite people over. . . . He likes to do what's comfortable for him and Crawford is his creation. He's comfortable there."

"Clinton liked to show the White House off—where Grant used to sit, etc. The presidency was the center of his life," Lewis adds. "But Bush does what CEOs do—you manage your company and take your vacation."

Says Ari Fleischer, Bush's first White House press secretary: "There are only three places he can relax—*Air Force One*, Camp David, and he's got home, Crawford. He can unwind. Crawford is private. Nobody else is on his ranch. . . . On a good day, there are no interruptions."

Yet not everyone in Bush's orbit likes the ranch. One of his senior advisers, brought up in a big city, considers the staff trailer a step away from camping, which is not to her taste, and was distressed at one point to find a large daddy longlegs in the middle of her bed. Other senior officials, such as Chief of Staff Andy Card and Fleischer, were less enamored of the ranch and spent little time there.

Heads of state or government stay in a three-bedroom guest house adjacent to the three-bedroom main house. There is also, about a half mile away from the main house, the "governor's house," a two-bedroom unit where Bush and his wife stayed just before moving to the White House. He was governor of Texas at the time.

It displeases Bush that the media not only don't like the isolated location of Crawford, but much prefer the amenities and weather at Kennebunkport, his father's retreat in Maine. At one point, to needle the traveling journalists, Bush had his staff order special tee shirts bearing the slogan I SURVIVED AND LOVED CRAWFORD 2001—and the items were distributed to them.

Bush has established a pecking order to reward his friends with presidential time. Lowest on the list are people whom he allows to drop by and see him briefly at the White House. Then there are those he sees for longer periods of time in the Oval Office or other parts of the West Wing. An invitation for dinner at the White House is special; more so is an invitation to Camp David. But the biggest honor and flattery Bush can bestow, he tells aides, is to invite someone to Prairie Chapel Ranch. He has done that with only a handful of foreign leaders—people he wanted to bond with or reward. He likes to meet his counterpart in his main living room, with the two of them on overstuffed chairs and their staffs on couches, sipping water, soda, and coffee. But he also has met with them in a breezeway that doubles as an informal living room, and occasionally poolside.

BUSH HAS A master plan for the ranch. He wants to not only construct a building to house a full office for himself (he started out with a small study in the main house) but also build houses for his twin daughters, so they can visit and have some privacy well into the future.

But Bush feels no need to share this with the public. Since the ranch is his home, he tries to keep these plans secret, considering them a private matter. Nor does he share the list of people he has over as guests. "He doesn't feel like he owes anyone an explanation," a friend told me. "It's his sanctuary."

At one point in 2004, as he contemplated the possibility of losing his bid for reelection, he turned philosophical. "If they send me back to my ranch, they send me back to my ranch," he told a friend. If that happened, he said, he would get along just fine. Of course it wasn't necessary, as he defeated Democratic challenger John Kerry by more than 3 million votes.

I WAS GIVEN a special tour by the president on December 30, 2003. By prearrangement, I showed up at the media filing center at nearby Crawford Elementary School that morning at 10:30, and Deputy Press Secretary Trent Duffy, press aide Georgia Godfrey, and a White House stenographer accompanied me onto the heavily guarded grounds about 10 minutes away. With Godfrey at the wheel, we drove through several Secret Service checkpoints to the double-wide trailer where senior staff members stay when Bush is on the property. No one was there, so we waited a few minutes in the living room until Godfrey got a bit uncomfortable sitting in the senior staff residence without their presence. Using her cell phone, she was unable to contact Joe Hagin, the deputy White House chief of staff who was to be our final escort. We went outside in the chill but bracing air and cooled our heels on the porch. This gave me the chance to look around. Clearly visible in a nearby field were two black military helicopters, presumably there to evacuate the president and First Lady if there were an attack.

Duffy's cell phone rang. It was Hagin, who said to head over to the main ranch house. We piled into the car and drove through a final Secret Service checkpoint at a guard's shack. An agent appeared and checked our credentials, then rolled back a heavy metal barrier three feet tall and we drove through.

We proceeded down a gravel road to the main house, passing a large field filled with row upon row of dessicated-looking sticks. I was told it was a tree nursery the Bushes were trying to get started in the parched pasture. It didn't look promising, but Mrs. Bush later told me she had high hopes for it and they planned to sell the trees for a profit later as part of the ongoing ranch business operations.

As we neared the main house, a low-lying single-story building featuring large windows in virtually every room, a small motorcade arrived, kicking up dust in every direction. Bush sat in the passenger seat of the lead pickup, followed by another pickup containing staff members and ranch hands, and two Secret Service vans. Bush rolled down his window and looked at me, raising his voice a bit to sternly advise, "Walk." Apparently he didn't want the vehicles too close to the house.

He got out, shook hands with me, and we headed for the front door. "Thanks for coming," he said with a smile. He was wearing scuffed brown work boots, grimy black work pants torn in several places at the knee and calf, a tee shirt, and denim work jacket. He had obviously been hard at work; his forehead was sweaty, his close-cropped graying black hair mussed, and he seemed a bit fatigued, as did his work crew. He said they had been clearing brush and chopping cedar. Of course.

As we trudged up the driveway, it became clear why Bush hadn't wanted the vehicles to drive any closer. Some heavy equipment was in the front yard, and several workmen were in the final stages of planting a 20-foot live oak just outside the breezeway, a glassed-in room facing east and west, which Texans call a "dog trot." Bush shook hands with each workman and posed for photographs taken by a White House cameraman. (Later, noticing that the foreman was leaving, Bush called out to him with a question: Any cracks? He was asking whether the concrete at the front of the house had been damaged. The foreman said everything was fine.)

We went inside and Bush disappeared to get cleaned up and change his shirt. Laura entered the room, smiled, and said welcome. She offered me a cup of coffee, and as an aide went to get it, she sat in one of the cushioned rattan chairs at a low table across from me. The First Lady explained that in the summertime, the floor-to-ceiling glass in the windows is replaced with screens so the "dog trot" can benefit from afternoon and evening breezes. She added that the sunrises and sunsets are glorious.

When Bush reappeared in a fresh white tee shirt, he sat next to me so I could more easily tape-record our interview. I could see just how vigorous his battle with the brush had been that morning. He had a few scratches on the right side of his face and deeper scrapes on his right arm. The tee shirt said in big red letters, WARNING! followed by, in black letters, THIS RANCH PROTECTED BY HANK THE COW DOG.

"Laura and I get up and go for walks first thing in the morning, and to take off across the prairie, it's pretty dramatic," Bush told me. "And just to see, as they say, where the deer and the antelope play. I don't have any antelope but we have plenty of deer, and turkey. And we're able to just enjoy nature. And one of the things that's happening here is not only are we enjoying nature, we're restoring nature. Laura is very much into wild grasses and wildflowers. . . . We're fixing to start a little blue-stem prairie in order to be able to harvest the seeds so that others can restore their properties to native grasses."

He expressed particular pride in the project he and his wife had undertaken to restore as much native vegetation to the ranch as they could. From his living room, he pointed out his man-made lake in the distance, noting that he had it built and which he said is "full of fantastic fish." The First Lady added that they were having fish caught from the lake for dinner that night. Bush recalled with delight that the previous day he and some friends had caught scores of crappie and bass.

I asked how much he kept up with ranch activities from the White House, and he said his ranch manager, Robert Blossman, calls him with regular reports of rainfall and whether "the creeks are running." Bush also checks in by computer with Weatherbug.com, where he can get the current weather and follow the local radar. "I'm checking on it all the time. I get on the computer," he told me. Blossman also sends Bush a written report and a block calendar with rain totals and inches per day.

Bush also talks regularly with John Taylor, who runs the tree farm. "This is a significant holding, for starters," he said. "We pay a lot of attention to it." Laura added: "And it's our home—you know, our only home." The president emphasized that he wanted the tree farm to eventually become a "commercial venture" that would make money.

After about 20 minutes, the president offered to take me on a tour, and of course I readily agreed. He put on a denim work jacket bearing the embroidered words PRESIDENT GEORGE W. BUSH, and we walked out of the house. He told a waiting Secret Service agent, a bit brusquely, that we were going for a drive. The agent snapped, "Yes, sir," and several aides and agents, including a SWAT team, immediately appeared wearing black jumpsuits and carrying automatic weapons slung over their shoulders. They piled into three other vehicles and waited for the commander in chief's next move. (I learned later that the Secret Service and the military had identified all the possible sniper's roosts on his property, and they always keep watch to make sure no "evildoer" takes up a position.) Bush hopped in the driver's seat of his big white pickup truck, had his black Scottie, Barney, jump in after him, and I took the passenger seat in the front. Two press aides sat in the back. Bush gunned the engine and off we went.

He proved to be an enthusiastic tour guide. With his left hand on the steering wheel, he waved his right arm so vigorously to point out cliffs, streams, and stands of cedar that he almost swiped me in the face several times. He obviously loves the place, and it animates him as few other things do.

He got particularly enthused when he showed me one of the seven big canyons he has on the ranch; they are his favorite part of the property. "Now you can just envision coming out here in the evening, with the sun glowing off those rocks," he said excitedly. "Those rocks are literally gold-looking. And you know what it reminded me of? It reminded me of seeing Jerusalem, the Old City, which is gold. And it settles in, and particularly in the spring or fall, when it's just pure green in here, after some rain. And a lot of game in here." He emphasized that while he shoots dove occasionally, he isn't much of a hunter.

Looking up at some impressive cliffs, he said, "Look at those things. I may carve Laura's face on one of them."

He added: "It's exciting to see the game move around here. Condi [Rice] and Laura and I were driving, just to relax one evening, and ran into a big flock of turkey, which was pretty neat. They roost right in this area here."

Bush drove past several spots where the cedar trees had been cut down and were burning in the open, with the pleasant scent of cedar smoke permeating the air. No one appeared to be at the sites to keep watch, but Bush aides later told me that wasn't necessary, because the fires were slow burning and someone checked on them every few hours.

Bush summed up: "It's the change of pace that's important to keep perspective and your common sense—and not get so wrapped up in the Washington scene that you're not able to see reality. . . . We love it here."

BUSH'S RANCH IS a symbol of the cowboy populism that he likes to convey. It gives him the chance to show his macho side, and he uses his retreat mostly for leisure, not work. Still, he has made many important decisions there, planning parts of the war on terrorism and working out his views about embryonic stem-cell research. Despite all the crises and world-changing events that have occurred on his watch, he is on track to become one of the most frequent vacationers in presidential history.

—⊗∞⊗—

CHAPTER NINETEEN

CAMP DAVID

No place has been as beloved to presidents over the past half century as Camp David.

The retreat in Maryland's Catoctin Mountains, 60 miles north of Washington, was created by Franklin Delano Roosevelt as an institutional haven where presidents could escape from the White House and be on their own. FDR called it Shangri-la, but Dwight Eisenhower renamed it after his grandson, and the less exalted name, Camp David, has remained in use ever since.

The retreat is only a half hour away from the White House by helicopter, but it is a world apart. Known for its solitude and seclusion, and the discretion of the Navy staff that lives there year-round, the 143-acre government estate is centered on Aspen Lodge, the presidential cabin. This lodge features beamed ceilings, oak-paneled walls, large windows, a spacious living room built around a massive stone fireplace, a dining room, a bedroom suite, guest room, kitchen, and study. The picture window in the living room looks out at a gorgeous swath of wooded valley.

Also within the compound are several other lodges, named after native American trees, such as Dogwood, Birch, Witch Hazel, and Walnut; a staff barracks; a chapel; a movie theater; a driving range; a bowling alley; tennis courts; a skeet range; a helicopter pad; and a swimming pool. Laurel Lodge is the conference center and dining facility. The entire property is surrounded by electrically charged chain-link fences topped with barbed wire, floodlights, video cameras, and motion sensors at key locations, all patrolled by Marines and guard dogs. The lush grounds are populated with white-tailed deer, chipmunks, squirrels, and cardinals, orioles, mourning doves, and myriad other varieties of birds.

At a cost of about $2 million a year to operate, it serves a function similar to Chequers, the country home of British prime ministers, the dachas of Russian leaders, and the Pope's summer estate in the hills near Rome. "It is a beautiful place, well maintained," says President George W. Bush. "It's like the ranch. You can actually walk right out of the house and go do something, without motorcades and all the folderol that goes with being the president. So there's a sense of freedom there that you don't have in Washington."

President Reagan once said he got "a little stir-crazy" after several days at the White House, and added: "Just as we did at *Rancho del Cielo*, Nancy and I experienced a sense of liberation at Camp David that we never found in Washington. Because the perimeter was guarded, we could just open a door and take a walk. That's a freedom, incidentally, that you don't fully appreciate until you've lost it."

Nancy Reagan observed, "Thank God for Camp David! I never expected that we would use it practically every weekend, but it became a regular and welcome part of our routine. . . . It was so important to us, in keeping our perspective on things, to be able to be there alone, to have quiet time together to think and reflect and get our thoughts in order."

Virtually every other president and First Lady since FDR have shared those feelings, and each First Couple has made a distinctive mark on the compound and created their own habitat there.

ON THE AFTERNOON of April 22, 1942, Franklin Roosevelt was secretly taken from the White House into the Catoctin woods of Maryland to select the location for a presidential retreat. The drive took two hours, but the area he inspected seemed a world away from Washington, just as he wished.

Roosevelt had his family home in Hyde Park, New York, and his residence in Warm Springs, Georgia, but he wanted someplace closer to the White House as his personal hideaway. He also had available to him about 164 acres that Herbert Hoover had purchased with his own money less than 100 miles from Washington in Virginia's Shendandoah Valley, which Hoover called Rapidan. Before leaving office, Hoover donated the land to the National Park Service as a presidential retreat. But FDR and his successors had little use for the place because of its damp, humid climate.

Roosevelt asked Newton B. Drury, director of the National Park Service, to recommend a site within a 100-mile radius of Washington at an elevation high enough to be cooler and less humid than the capital. The Park Service suggested three sites: Comer's Deadening, in Shenandoah National Park, about a three-hour drive from the White House; Camp #4 in Maryland's Catoctin Recreational Demonstration Area, a two-hour drive; and Camp #3, also known as Camp Hi-Catoctin, not far from Camp #4 but at a bit higher elevation and also a two-hour drive away.

Camp #3 made the most sense from the start. It contained a large swath of land and six ready-to-use, four-cot cabins. The camp also featured a swimming pool, office, central showers, and a recreation hall. It had been planned as a boys' camp but was then being used as a getaway for poor urban families The Park Service estimated that it could be renovated in about a month for $18,650—far less costly than the other sites. And at 1,800 feet, it was 5 to 10 degrees cooler than Washington in the summer.

When FDR arrived, he got out of his car, looked around, and said, "This is Shangri-la." He was referring to the land of mythical beauty and serenity from the 1933 novel by James Hilton, *Lost Horizon*. Later known as Naval Support Facility or NAVSUPPFAC, Thurmont, Md. 21788, the Secret Service would give it a code name: Cactus.

Roosevelt immediately set about designing the renovations. On April 30, he returned to Camp #3 with aides and drew a sketch to enlarge and screen the porch of a lodge he wanted for his own use, also adding a paved terrace, a bedroom corridor, four bedrooms, two baths, an indoor kitchen, and pantry. Roosevelt called it the "Bear's Den," but this would later be renamed Aspen Lodge, the presidential quarters still in use today. Roosevelt ordered trees cut down to improve the view of a valley southeast of the lodge, but he kept dogwoods and shrubs in the foreground. He even had a dog house installed outside the main lodge for his Scottish terrier, Fala.

Roosevelt, whose legs were paralyzed from polio, always harbored a fear of getting trapped in a fire, and to ease his concerns, workmen hinged a section of wall at floor level and designed it to be lowered to the ground as a ramp for the president's wheelchair in case of emergency. Security was greatly increased. The site was surrounded by a 9-foot-high fence topped with barbed wire. Sentry shacks and floodlights were installed at frequent intervals; alarms would sound if intruders breached the obstacles, and Marines were stationed at the perimeter. In all, 100 guards were posted on-site whenever the president stayed there.

For the remainder of his presidency, Shangri-la was an important part of FDR's routine, even though the administration tried to minimize any public references to the compound. The president's aides were very concerned about protecting his life from spies during the war and they often kept his whereabouts secret. "Reporters who covered the White House knew about it, but followed a wartime code of voluntary censorship," writes author W. Dale Nelson.

FDR set the standard for his successors by establishing a casual dress code. He favored slacks, simple shirts, and sweaters. Roosevelt would relax with a dry martini, read military dispatches and mystery novels, play gin rummy, and work on his stamp collection. He had aides bring a square wooden box containing his magnifying glass, *Scott's Stamp Catalogue*, and other items, and the envelopes containing unusual stamps from around the world that the State Department would send to him regularly.

He routinely stayed in bed until noon, working on his schedule with his appointments secretary, William Hassett. He would confer frequently with aides, go over telegrams, hold meetings under the huge wagon-wheel chandelier in the living room, talk with associates on the telephone, and peruse maps of ongoing or future military operations. Sometimes he would take a break by having an aide take him and his guests for a leisurely drive in the area.

On some of his visits to the camp, 100 people would be in his entourage, including Secret Service men, a doctor and medical assistant, radio and telegraph operators, secretaries, chauffeurs, a valet, and a movie projectionist. They used unheated cabins and cleaned up in long water troughs outside. Few of the 20 buildings had running water, and hot water was rare.

The president's accommodations were comfortable but nothing fancy. He had a wash basin in his bedroom with hot water. And his furnishings were spare, very different from his sumptuous home in Hyde Park—a green carpet in his bedroom, an iron-framed bed, a white dresser and chair, and clothes locker. But FDR enjoyed the change to a simple life, even if it was only for a few days at a time. In all, he made more than 20 visits to Shangri-la, sometimes for long week-ends, through 1944. His wife, Eleanor, was busy with her own schedule and was never enamored of the place; she rarely accompanied him.

Another reason FDR was drawn to Shangri-la, strangely enough, was the food. He never liked the plain meals prepared at the White House by house-keeper and cook Henrietta Nesbitt. Roosevelt said her cooking "would do justice to the Automat." But Eleanor refused to alter Henrietta's menus because her meals, which featured broiled chicken and fish and boiled vegetables, were low in calories and fat.

Shangri-la was run by the Navy outside Eleanor's supervision. The military cooks wanted to please their commander in chief, and they prepared rich, tasty meals similar to those his mother used to have served at Hyde Park, including crabs and oysters from the nearby Chesapeake Bay, and peach cobbler with cream.

AFTER MANY EARLY setbacks, the Allies finally turned the tide in World War II, and by the spring of 1943, Roosevelt was ready to meet with Winston Churchill in Washington to plan the Normandy invasion and discuss the new world order that was developing. They took a break from their formal discussions at the White House and moved to Shangri-la, departing by motorcade on May 15.

Once they settled in, Churchill watched in fascination as FDR, his cares melting away, put stamps into his album for a half hour at a time. They enjoyed drinks, cigarettes, and cigars on the veranda of the Bear's Den, and went fishing for brook trout in a mountain stream two miles west of the camp's main entrance. As Secret Service agents stood discreetly to the side, the two leaders sat in portable canvas chairs on the dappled stream bank, casting their lines absent-mindedly into the water as they chatted about the most profound of topics, such as the future of the postwar world under the aegis of the United States, Great Britain, and the Soviet Union.

BUT IN THE final year of FDR's life, new concerns about security arose. The Secret Service and military officials were increasingly worried that Shangri-la was vulnerable to an attack from the air. After all, fighters and bombers were getting more sophisticated, and the Nazis were developing missiles that could travel vast distances. There was also the possibility that enemy agents could steal an American plane and bomb the president in his rural hideaway.

It also turned out that the property wasn't as isolated as everyone thought. Early one Sunday morning, Roosevelt was driving a car around the back roads with a Secret Service agent when he pulled onto private property. A woman suddenly emerged from a cabin with a shotgun slung over one arm. "What are you doing up here?" she asked. "Don't you know this place is posted [with signs indicating no trespassing]?"

FDR said he was president of the United States, and the Secret Service man identified himself as a presidential bodyguard, but the woman was having none of it. "I don't care who you are!" she said. "If you don't have something in writing from Mr. Payne you'd better get out of here." At that, she lifted her shotgun threateningly, and the president backed up the car, turned around, and drove away. The next morning, Charles Payne, owner of the property, was called to the White House. When the incident was described to him, he apologized and gave the president a written permit to use the private road on his estate. The woman with a shotgun had been a caretaker who took her role very seriously. But the Secret Service never forgot the incident and wanted to make sure nothing like that ever happened again.

At one point, at the suggestion of his security officers, Roosevelt considered shifting his retreat to the heavily fortified U.S. naval base at Guantanamo Bay, Cuba. It would take at least three hours to reach the base by air, however, so it would not be very convenient. On one occasion he secretly used the Georgetown, South Carolina, plantation of financier Bernard Baruch. But FDR's death from a stroke on April 12, 1945, at his home in Warm Springs, Georgia, ended the search for a new presidential hideaway.

HARRY TRUMAN, FDR'S successor, had never been to Shangri-la when he took office in early 1945 upon Roosevelt's death. As vice president for only several weeks, Truman was not part of the White House inner circle.

Truman didn't visit the camp until May 1946—more than a year after taking over—and was not pleased. He said the place seemed "hastily slapped together in an emergency." At his direction, work crews cleared the brush that had been allowed to grow close to the presidential cabin now known as Aspen Lodge, improving the view and giving the area a cleaner look.

Bess Truman, the First Lady, was similarly critical. She had visited the place on a rainy day in October 1945, and found it dull. Daughter Margaret thought it was damp and cold. "I thought it was a terrible place and went there as little as possible," she wrote.

Truman visited the camp only nine times during his nearly eight years as president, for a total of 27 days. He took his customary long walks, swam in the pool, and took rides in a jeep. But he preferred to relax with his cronies in the sunny climate of Key West, Florida, to visit family and friends in his hometown of Independence, Missouri, or spend time on the presidential yacht, the *Williamsburg*.

Rather than let the place go to waste, Truman often let his aides and their families use the property, as long as they paid for their food and other expenses.

Still, Truman thought the Catoctin retreat might be used more regularly by his successors, and he ordered many upgrades. He had the buildings winterized and had steam heat installed in the presidential lodge and a few guest cabins. With the war won, he relaxed security, and by the end of 1947 the 100-member Marine contingent of Roosevelt's time had been reduced to 29 Navy personnel. A lone sentry guarded the main gate while another patrolled the perimeter.

This minimalism would soon change.

WHEN HE TOOK office in January 1953, Dwight Eisenhower wanted to close Shangri-la as part of his campaign to reduce presidential perks. But George Allen, a Washington businessman and friend of the president who had also been a confidant of Roosevelt, prevailed on the former soldier to reconsider. On May 12, less than four months after his inauguration, Eisenhower drove to the site with a few aides and friends and spent an evening there. Ike liked what he saw— the mountains, the woods, the privacy, the proximity to Washington all appealed to him, as they had to FDR. He decided not to close it after all.

Many years later, David Eisenhower, Ike's grandson for whom the president renamed the camp, described his impressions of the retreat in 1950s: "Like the fictional setting of James Hilton's *Lost Horizon*, the camp was locked away, remote, a place of 'peace and contentment,' an ideal setting for relaxation or concentration . . . The cabins were drafty and sparsely furnished. Deer freely wandered around the grounds, especially at first light. On my earliest visits, mornings were spent hiking through the hills or practicing chip shots to a green Granddad had installed. Midday was spent poolside deep in the forest. Evenings, there were often a dozen or more guests. Often, Granddad, an excellent cook, would spend the afternoon in the Aspen kitchen preparing the steaks for a cookout. After dinner, the grandchildren staged skits and sang songs on the porch behind the presidential cabin, then were packed off while the grown-ups watched movies."

To erase his wife's disappointment with the camp's rustic design, Eisenhower got the Navy to finance a major redecoration. FDR's monstrous wagon-wheel chandelier was removed, and most of the east wall of the Bear's Den was replaced with glass to provide a better view. A motion-picture projection booth was added in the living room, and the oak paneling in the presidential bedroom was painted pale pink. The other cabins were also repainted and the furniture replaced.

It was Mamie Eisehnower who directed that the buildings be named for native trees. The Bear's Den was dubbed Aspen Lodge, named for the state tree of Colorado, the First Lady's home state (even though the staff for years called it the "Big House"). The conference lodge was called Laurel, and other buildings were assigned the names Dogwood, Hickory, Maple, Sycamore, and Witch Hazel.

Eisenhower used the retreat frequently during his eight-year presidency, mostly in the summer months, when the mountain property offered a respite from Washington's steamy weather, just as FDR had intended. He didn't visit as often in winter because of the difficulty traversing the tortuous roads.

Ike used the camp more than ever after his heart attack in September 1955, and by 1959, the president was routinely hosting foreign visitors there, including Soviet premier Nikita Khrushchev, in September of that year.

Eisenhower did some oil painting at Camp David, which relaxed him, but he complained that there was no place on site to play golf, his favorite pastime. Cliff Roberts, a New York investment banker who played golf frequently with Ike, brought in New York golf course designer Robert Jones, who had laid out the greens at Washington's famous Burning Tree Club, to design a course at Camp David. After the bulldozers and landscapers were finished, a three-hole course had been installed, designed as a combination of Burning Tree and the Augusta National Golf Course in Georgia, one of Ike's favorites. Local merchants provided funds for the project.

Eisenhower also authorized construction of a new bomb shelter, completed in July 1957. It was claustrophobic and had few amenities, but it served the purpose of providing a refuge for the commander in chief during a nuclear attack.

On July 12, 1957, Ike permanently changed the presidential routine surrounding Camp David when he took a Bell Ranger helicopter from the White

House to the retreat rather than ride in a motorcade. This shortened the trip from two hours to 30 minutes.

Some of his aides warned that such helicopter travel wasn't safe, but others said it was perfectly acceptable. Ike liked the reduced commute so much that he became a regular rider on the chopper to and from the Catoctins, and to and from his farm at nearby Gettysburg, Pennsylvania. Presidents have traveled by helicopter to the retreat ever since, unless the weather forces the commander in chief back into a motorcade.

Ike's activities were homey and unsophisticated. The men played bridge and golf. The wives played their own card game of bolivia, popular at the time. Eisenhower often took guests on a drive, especially during weekend visits, following FDR's custom. The First Lady ordered that no liquor be served before 6 P.M., and dinner began at 7. The president enjoyed hosting film screenings, and he was partial to Westerns. Among the movies shown at Camp David in those days was *The Big Country*—starring Charlton Heston, Gregory Peck, and Jean Simmons—which British Prime Minister Harold Macmillan, a guest, panned in his diary as "inconceivably banal."

Mamie Eisenhower used the camp to entertain friends, and both White House aides and Cabinet members were authorized to use it. By 1958, the naval personnel at the camp had expanded to 94—close to the level during the Roosevelt years.

ONE OF THE most dramatic events of the Eisenhower years was his summit meeting with Khrushchev at Camp David in September 1960. At first, the bombastic Soviet leader was confused. In his memoirs, Khrushchev said, "I couldn't for the life of me find out what this Camp David was." He suspected it was a place "where people who were mistrusted would be kept in quarantine." The camp was so little discussed in public that even the officials at his embassy in Washington couldn't enlighten him. Eventually, he concluded that "far from an insult or act of discrimination . . . it was a great honor for me to be invited to spend a few days at Camp David with Eisenhower."

The Camp David talks got off to a good start, with the two leaders meeting in the sun room of Aspen Lodge. There was little substantive discussion, but Eisenhower showed his guest two of his favorite Western movies, *High Noon*, and, again, *The Big Country*. Unlike Macmillan, the rotund, earthy Kremlin leader apparently enjoyed them.

Over breakfast the next morning, which was foggy and humid, Khrushchev wore a white embroidered shirt without a collar and, planting both elbows on the table, regaled his host with stories of his recollections of Stalingrad and Odessa during World War II. But after repeated discussions during the weekend, including one chat during a mile-and-a-half walk over the wooded pathways and a discussion over a lunch of hot dogs, baked beans, and brown bread, the two men were unable to reach agreement on how to deal with the divided city of Berlin. This was one of the main points of contention between the superpowers, since each side was claiming the city was within its sphere of influence.

At lunch, Khrushchev turned belligerent. First, he attacked the recent U.S. trade exposition in Moscow for unfairly portraying America's consumer goods as superior to the U.S.S.R.'s. Ike tried to smooth things over by changing the subject. He asked his counterpart whether he could ever take a vacation that was free of work and telephones. This provoked another Khrushchev rant about how phones were even set up on the beach when he went for a swim—and added that in short order the Soviet Union would develop phones that were better than any made in America. Eisenhower sat in silence.

The president later that day took the premier on a brief tour of his farm at Gettysburg, traveling via helicopter. When they returned to Camp David, Khrushchev was in a better mood and agreed not to set a deadline for negotiations to determine the final status of Berlin. Ike agreed this was the best outcome they could expect for the moment.

Then, unexpectedly, they shared a poignant moment. At the end of the visit, each man agreed that it should be possible to reduce nuclear arms but admitted that his military advisers were making it very difficult. "Tell me, Mr. Khrushchev," Ike said, "how do you decide on funds for military expenditures? Perhaps I should tell you how it is with us. . . . It's like this: My military leaders come to me and say, 'Mr. President, we need such and such a sum for such and such a program. If we don't get the funds we need, we'll fall behind the Soviet Union.' So I invariably give in. That's how they wring money out of me. . . . Now tell me, how is it with you?"

Khrushchev replied, "It's just the same."

Still, Eisenhower was unhappy with the overall results. On November 4, he told a press conference, "I have heard this expression, 'The Spirit of Camp David,' and I don't know what it means. I think the 'Spirit of Camp David' as they [the media] used it, and I must say I have never used it, must simply mean that it looks like we can talk together without being mutually abusive."

He had good reason for concern. Amid preparations for another superpower summit in Paris, Ike visited his Gettysburg farm in May 1960. His relaxation was interrupted by a call from Gen. Andrew Goodpaster, the White House staff secretary. American pilot Francis Gary Powers, Goodpaster said, apparently had been shot down over the Soviet Union in a U-2 spy plane. It turned out that Powers had parachuted out of the crippled aircraft, but had been captured by the Soviets.

That was the end of the Spirit of Camp David during Dwight Eisenhower's presidency. From then on, tensions between the superpowers were on the rise.

LIKE HARRY TRUMAN, John F. Kennedy didn't like Camp David— at first. Just prior to his inauguration, the president-elect and his glamorous wife, Jacqueline, had rented Glen Ora, a French-style villa in Virginia's horse country, and he said in February 1961 that he didn't intend to use Camp David very often. It wasn't exciting enough, and it was too isolated and far from the sea.

But he found himself at the retreat sooner than he expected, and under very unpleasant conditions. On April 17, 1961, less than three months after he took office, a U.S.-sponsored force of Cuban refugees landed at the Bay of Pigs in Cuba, hoping to lead a rebellion. But without air support or reinforcements from the United States, they were immediately cut down or captured by troops loyal to the Marxist regime of Fidel Castro.

It was a debacle, and the new president asked Eisenhower to join him at Camp David, near the former commander in chief's Gettysburg farm, to discuss what to do next.

Ike flew by helicopter to the retreat on April 22, and Kennedy met him at the helipad. Kennedy had never seen Camp David before, but sightseeing was the last thing on his mind. As they strolled the grounds on the cool, overcast day, the youngest man ever elected president sought counsel from the oldest man elected president up to that time. At one point, Kennedy said, "No one knows how tough this job is until after he has been in it for a few months."

The old soldier replied, "Mr. President, if you will forgive me, I think I mentioned that to you three months ago."

Kennedy answered, "I certainly have learned a lot since then."

Given the difficulty of those circumstances, one can understand why JFK was in no hurry to return to Camp David, and he visited only two more times during the first two years of his administration.

But in the spring of 1963, a few months before his assassination, Kennedy lost his lease on the Glen Ora estate because the owner was concerned about the Secret Service altering her property. The Kennedys began to build their own house near Middleburg, also in Virginia horse country, on an estate they planned to call Wexford, after Kennedy's ancestral home county in Ireland. During construction, they began visiting Camp David regularly and discovered that they enjoyed it.

The First Lady had her horses transported there in a van; the president used Ike's three-hole golf course, and they had the Navy build a pony ring for Caroline, their young daughter.

Kennedy made the trip to Camp David 16 times during his last year in office. His routine was to sleep late, have a drink before lunch, chat with friends and advisers, perhaps take a walk in the afternoon, nap, and have dinner. Sometimes he would tour local Civil War battlefields in the company of a historian. After sending his two children to bed on Friday or Saturday evenings, he would relax by watching films, as Ike had done.

He added a new twist: home movies. The Navy was ordered to take films of Caroline riding her pony, Macaroni, of John Jr. chasing a soccer ball, and of the First Lady trying her hand awkwardly at skeet shooting. And he ordered that Secret Service agents in civilian clothes replace the armed, uniformed Marine bodyguards at the presidential cabin so his kids would have a more normal experience. His murder on November 22, of course, made that impossible.

LYNDON JOHNSON'S FIRST trip to Camp David was on a snowy weekend in January 1964, less than two months after he succeeded Kennedy. His goal was to look around the property and sample life at the retreat. At one point, he bowled for the first time in his life on the presidential lanes, knocking down 7 pins on his first throw, then bowling a 10-pin strike. But he was less than impressed with the place overall—preferring his Texas ranch. He didn't visit Camp David again for more than a year.

Perhaps the most dramatic episode at Camp David during LBJ's presidency came on July 25, 1965, in the form of a debate over continuation of the Vietnam War. As Johnson listened quietly, a rarity for him, Clark Clifford, a renowned Washington lawyer and informal counselor to several presidents, argued against further escalation in an emotional confrontation with Defense Secretary Robert McNamara, the inveterate hawk (whom Clifford would later succeed at the Pentagon).

Clifford repeated his earlier arguments against a big buildup but was more passionate this time. He said escalation could lead America into "a quagmire . . . without a realistic hope of ultimate victory."

"It will ruin us," Clifford said in a warning that would prove prescient. "I can't see anything but catastrophe for my country."

McNamara, in his characteristically forceful way, said Clifford was overstating his case and posited that the communists could not keep the war going for very long in the face of the massive military and technological superiority of the United States. Besides, withdrawal would make America look spineless, he said.

The next morning, Johnson asked his advisers to summarize their views again in a debate format. With the president sipping Fresca, they sat at a rectangular table in the living room of Aspen Lodge. Others present included Arthur Goldberg, who was about to leave the Supreme Court to become U.S. ambassador to the United Nations, and LBJ advisers Jack Valenti and Horace Busby. Johnson said he was concerned and acknowledged that Clifford's arguments had some merit, but added, "The basic issue is not to get thrown out under fire."

After the debate, he drove around Camp David for an hour, then walked the grounds by himself. He returned to Washington that night, and in the end sided with McNamara, in one of the most controversial decisions of his presidency. He escalated the war, which resulted in the quagmire that Clifford had warned against and made him one of the most unpopular presidents in history.

ON THE LIGHTER side, Johnson's monumental ego and lack of consideration for those around him were on full display at Camp David. He let his beagles, Blanco and Him, run amok, and they chased down chipmunks and squirrels and barked annoyingly at military guards, Secret Service agents, and guests. On June 20, 1965, Blanco was on the prowl and a Marine guard was startled by rustling in the woods. "Halt, who goes there?" the soldier shouted, causing the dog to yelp as the soldier raised his weapon to fire. It was a close call for the dog, but Johnson ignored the problem. A year later, on June 15, 1966, a driver for Luci, the president's daughter, ran over Him as the beagle was chasing a squirrel near the Southwest Gate of the White House. The dog died.

RICHARD NIXON, TYPICALLY, saw Camp David as a place where he could find solitude rather than social life. Even his wardrobe reflected his workaholic nature. Nixon generally wore a suit and tie, and he showed little interest in the recreational facilities other than the pool.

As Nixon biographer Richard Reeves observes, "In the mountains, Nixon was forever plotting, planning revolutions great and small, sometimes to build a better world, more often just coups against his own staff and Cabinet. He saw himself as a man of ideas, and of surprise moves, his real work done alone with his yellow pads, or with [H.R.] Haldeman and [John] Ehrlichman, his agents of control and organization whom he saw as his two arms."

He was obsessed with creature comforts. Early on, White House Chief of Staff Haldeman complained to his aides that the camp wasn't "presidential enough," and he set about ordering a series of major renovations under Nixon's supervision. During his first six months in office alone, Nixon spent nearly $2 million to change the landscape and add a bowling alley and a new heated swimming pool in front of the main terrace of his lodge, which replaced the smaller FDR-era pool a bit farther away. It turned out that his aides placed the new pool exactly where Nixon had suggested, even though it was over a presidential bomb shelter, code-named Orange One. This required the bomb shelter to be reinforced, at a cost of $261,000. Nixon was unaware of the complication. He was commander in chief, and wanted the pool relocated, so his staff just did it his way, regardless of cost. The money came from secret military accounts.

A study was added to the four-bedroom suite of Nixon's cabin and a screened porch was converted into a glassed-in dining room. A 35-millimeter projection booth was installed for movies, and a special stereo system brought in. Even the bomb shelter, reached via an elevator just outside the front door, was redecorated with new beds and furnishings at a cost of $250,000.

Haldeman said the movie-projection system in the main lodge also needed to be upgraded. The projectors were not aligned properly and the picture was off center, with part of it running on a curtain and the rest bobbing on a screen. It was quickly fixed.

In August 1970, Haldeman told camp commander J. L. Dettbarn to continue the practice of having long cords on the poolside telephones because it was more convenient for officials who wanted to do business while sunning themselves.

Over time, a small lounge in Laurel was converted into a presidential office and bedrooms were added to several cabins. A new tennis court was donated by Donald Kendall, a Nixon supporter and chairman of the board of Pepsi-Cola. Many of these expenditures were kept secret so voters wouldn't think Nixon was profligate.

There was good reason for the sensitivity. Nixon was changing the nature of Camp David from a country retreat to what a Nixon aide described as "Catoctin Hilton." Tricia Nixon Cox, Nixon's daughter, said, "It's like a resort hotel where you are the only guests." Years later, Ron Reagan, the president's irreverent son, would say, "It's rustic compared to the White House, but you're not exactly living in log cabins and peeing in the woods." There were not only comfortable quarters but all the amenities and activities one could want, ranging from the three-hole golf course installed by Eisenhower to horseback riding, skeet shooting, tennis courts, swimming pools, bowling alleys, bicycles, golf carts, a movie theater with a projectionist available at a guest's whim, and fine dining at candlelit tables adorned with fresh flowers.

Nixon even got into the culinary details of camp. He told Haldeman the steaks were too big and there were too many leftovers. As a result, the portions were trimmed.

NIXON FOUND THE solitude of Camp David very helpful as he dealt with the crises of the day. He was at Camp David so often that it was inevitable that he would make many decisions there. Within six months of taking office, he was using Camp David at the rate of three or four times a month. For example, along with key aides Haldeman and Ehrlichman, Nixon spent a long weekend in the mountains starting Thursday, July 17, to develop a plan reorganizing the White House. In an effort to centralize the operation, he assigned Ehrlichman to run a new Domestic Council, which gave him control over the entire domestic policy-making system.

On August 6, 1969, he met with his Cabinet at Camp David and listened to their arguments about a plan to overhaul the welfare system. This was a pivotal meeting in which the president decided to proceed with the idea, which he announced to the nation on August 8. Dubbed the Family Assistance Plan, it was based on a negative income tax guaranteeing every welfare family of four $1,600 annually in income from the federal government. Nixon coupled it with a big revenue-sharing initiative in which Washington would send state and local governments all-purpose cash instead of money tied to specific projects such as road building.

In late October 1969, at Aspen Lodge, Nixon labored over a major address on Vietnam that he was scheduled to deliver November 3. At 4 A.M. on a Saturday, he woke up and, over the course of four hours, wrote a draft of the speech that included the now-famous line asking for support from "the great silent majority of Americans"—his phrase for the middle class that he considered his core constituency. That afternoon, he telephoned Haldeman and said, the "baby's been born."

On a weekend in August 1971, he gathered his economic advisers, including Treasury Secretary John Connally and Budget Director George Shultz, to map out a strategy for dealing with the sagging economy. They were ordered not even to tell their wives or secretaries where they were going. When they arrived, Nixon gathered them in the Aspen living room and announced, "One of the reasons we are holding this meeting at Camp David is for security. There are to be made no calls out of here. . . . Between now and Monday night, when we announce our decisions, everyone here is to button his lip." What the president decided that weekend was to impose a 90-day freeze on wages and prices, remove the excise tax on automobiles, reinstate an investment tax credit, and let the dollar float against world currencies.

There also were important personal moments. One weekend in November 1970, Ed Cox, a beau of his daughter's, came into the president's study and said formally, "Mr. President, as I'm sure you know, I am very much in love with Tricia. I would like your permission to ask her to marry me." Nixon agreed but added that the important thing was to do what Tricia wanted and he was sure she would say yes. The family announced the engagement on March 16, and the wedding was held in the Rose Garden of the White House on June 12, 1971.

NIXON LOVED POLITICAL machinations, and often dissected the other political leaders of his day in private talks at Camp David with a handful of aides. In August 1972, as he was mounting a reelection campaign that would culminate in his victory that November, he gave Haldeman his assessment of two Republican governors, Ronald Reagan of California and Nelson Rockefeller of New York, each of whom had presidential ambitions.

"Reagan is not one that wears well," Nixon said.

"I know," Haldeman replied.

"On a personal basis, Rockefeller is a pretty nice guy," Nixon continued. "Reagan on a personal basis, is terrible. He just isn't pleasant to be around."

Nixon was showing a blind spot. Virtually everyone who dealt with Reagan said he was an engaging and pleasant person, although many found him shallow. Nixon, who wasn't very likable at all but had a deep understanding of the issues, didn't grasp these distinctions.

At about the time of the Reagan conversation, in late August 1972, Nixon was walking with Henry Kissinger on a trail one night when he stumbled and splintered a bone in his foot. This caused him to limp for the next few months. But Nixon, ever the Spartan, rarely complained about the pain.

ONCE HIS REELECTION was safely behind him that November, he had no reluctance about spending even more time at Camp David. In his first year in office, he went 25 times for a total of 61 days. By October 1973, he had made 149 visits, three times more than Eisenhower had made in eight years in office.

Camp David became almost an Oval Office in self-imposed exile. Immediately after his smashing reelection victory in November 1972, following a trip to his estate at Key Biscayne for a few days, he returned to Washington briefly and then holed up in Camp David starting on November 13 to preside over a remarkable series of meetings at Aspen Lodge's rustic living room. Some members of his staff were taken by the gorgeous views of the wintry landscape, but Nixon paid little attention to the scenery.

He took Haldeman, Ehrlichman, and a few other aides aside and told them to prepare to stay for several weeks of uninterrupted hard work to get ready for his second term. It turned out that Nixon wanted to come up with a total reorganization of the executive branch in order to gain more personal power over the bureaucracy, which he felt was not sufficiently responsive to his wishes. He confided to one adviser that the Internal Revenue Service and its agents were "biased against our friends. They hate those with money." In addition, Nixon said, there were "too many Jews" at the IRS and he told Secretary of the Treasury George

Shultz to "clean the house." He also wanted Shultz to figure out a way to punish the Ford Foundation, the Brookings Institution, and other foundations because, he said, they had been used "for partisan, left-wing purposes."

He called in White House National Security Adviser Henry Kissinger and Alexander Haig, Kissinger's deputy, to talk about Vietnam. He wanted to lay down a hard line not only to Hanoi, which was being recalcitrant about ending the Vietnam War, but also to the leaders of the Saigon government, whom Nixon felt were not bending to his will as he tried to arrange an American withdrawal on honorable terms. In a series of secret messages, he did both.

On the afternoon of November 27, he told reporters, who were keeping vigil outside the gates, what he had been doing up there for two weeks. "I find that up here on top of a mountain it is easier for me to get on top of the job, to think in a more relaxed way at times," he said. "My study of elections in this country, and of second terms particularly, is that second terms almost inevitably are down-hill. . . . What I am trying to do is change that historical pattern. The only way that historical pattern can be changed is to change not only some of the players but also some of the plays."

What followed was a stream of announcements for the next few weeks. Melvin Laird would be leaving as defense secretary. George Romney was out at the Department of Housing and Urban Development. Elliot Richardson would shift from Health, Education, and Welfare to Defense. Caspar Weinberger would leave as director of the Office of Management and Budget and take over Health, Education, and Welfare. The changes were dizzying. In all, Nixon accepted 57 resignations and retirements and made 30 new appointments, all designed to streamline the executive branch and shift power to the White House.

During this time, Nixon injured his foot again when he stumbled on the edge of the pool at Camp David, and he began to walk with a noticeable limp. Nixon didn't see a doctor, and just worked through the pain. On December 20, he went to Bethesda Naval Hospital for his yearly checkup, and was told that he had sustained another splinter fracture in his foot.

Camp David was also where he decided to select Michigan Representative Gerald Ford as his new vice president, in October 1973, shortly after Spiro Agnew resigned that post after pleading no contest to charges of income tax evasion. Camp David become a diplomatic annex of the White House, with Nixon hosting many foreign leaders there, including President and Mrs. Georges Pompidou of France, Yugoslavia's Tito and his wife, British prime minister Edward Heath, and, in June 1973, Soviet premier Leonid Brezhnev.

During the Brezhnev visit, Nixon gave his Soviet counterpart a blue Lincoln Continental donated by the manufacturer, and Brezhnev immediately took the wheel and subjected Nixon to a harrowing ride at unsafe speeds around the grounds. At one point, they approached a sharp curve going 50 mph, and Nixon urged him to "slow down, slow down." Brezhnev hit the brakes at the last moment and made the turn. "This is a very fine automobile," the Kremlin leader said happily. "It holds the road very well."

Brezhnev also had at least one young woman "visitor" at his cottage, Dogwood. A Soviet aide identified her as the premier's "masseuse." Others said she was a stewardess. She was escorted to the premier's cabin late at night by KGB agents, then escorted back to her own cabin at daybreak. Dogwood, ironically, was the cottage where Nixon's daughter Tricia and Edward Cox had spent their honeymoon in 1971.

During May 1972, Nixon had microphones hidden in his Aspen Lodge study and two others installed on telephones in his desk and table, in order to record conversations secretly. The previous year, he'd had similar taping systems installed at the White House and Old Executive Office Building next door. Staff supposedly removed the devices whenever a foreign visitor stayed at the lodge. The microphone hidden in the study was permanently disconnected by Nixon's aides on March 18, 1973, and the other two, on the phones, were taken out July 18, 1973, two days after Nixon aide Alexander Butterfield caused a furor when he revealed they existed, in testimony before the Senate Watergate Committee.

ON JUNE 16, 1972, Nixon operatives broke into the Democratic National Committee offices in Washington's Watergate building. From then on, a cover-up was launched by the White House, and Nixon was implicated.

As the Watergate scandal deepened, Nixon cloistered himself at Camp David more than ever. By the spring of 1973, amid one revelation after another of complicity by Nixon's operatives, Nixon was increasingly preoccupied with damage control. He flew to Camp David April 27 for another long weekend. On the evening of Saturday, April 28, Nixon talked with his daughter, Tricia, in the living room of Aspen Lodge in front of a blazing fire, and she tearfully told him that she, her mother, her sister, Julie, and Julie's husband, David Eisenhower, all had agreed that Haldeman and Ehrlichman must resign as the ones most responsible for his plight. "Whatever you do, just remember we will support you, and we love you very much," Tricia said.

That Sunday, April 29, 1973, Nixon met Haldeman and Ehrlichman separately at Aspen Lodge. Haldeman was first. "When I got to Aspen," Haldeman wrote in his diary, "the P was in terrible shape. Shook hands with me, which is the first time he's ever done that. Told me to come look at the view out the window, then stepped to the door and said let's go outside and look at the flowers and all."

They walked onto the porch and, as Nixon admired the freshly open tulips and the new leaves on the trees in the valley, he said, "I have to enjoy it because I may not be alive much longer." Nixon went on to confide that he had prayed on his knees the night before, as he did every night, and hoped he would not wake up in the morning. Then the two men agreed that Haldeman would step down.

Next it was Ehrlichman's turn. Nixon repeated his startling remark about hoping he died in the night, and his loyal lieutenant replied, "Don't talk like that. Don't think like that." Nixon began to weep.

"This is like cutting off my arms," a tearful Nixon continued. "You and Bob [Haldeman], you'll need money; I have some—Bebe [Rebozo, a close Nixon friend] has it—and you can have it." But Ehrlichman said that would only make things worse, and added, "You can do one thing for me, though, sometime. Just explain all this to my kids, will you?"

When White House Press Secretary Ron Ziegler walked into the lodge after Ehrlichman left, Nixon was standing with the lights out looking out the window at the hills. Nixon turned and said, "It's all over, Ron, do you know that?" Again, Nixon began to cry in the dark.

Haldeman and Ehrlichman stayed at Camp David to complete their resignation letters. And Nixon showed up at their helicopter as they departed. "I wish I were as strong as you. God bless you both," he said.

Despite raising the possibility of resigning that weekend, Nixon would stay in office for more than a year, fighting the Watergate scandal. He spent much of his time shuttling between Camp David, Key Biscayne, and San Clemente. He found Washington, where congressional and media investigations brought nothing but bad news, almost insufferable.

On Saturday, August 3, 1974, Nixon flew by helicopter to Camp David with Mrs. Nixon, Ed and Tricia Cox, David and Julie Eisenhower, and friend Bebe

Rebozo. They went for a swim, then sat on the terrace of Aspen Lodge and looked over the peaceful valley. Nixon later said they shared "a sense of the mystery and the beauty as well as the history and the tragedy that lay behind our weekend together in this setting."

On Monday, August 5, Nixon flew back to Washington. He announced on August 8 that he would resign, and left office the next day.

GERALD FORD BROUGHT a new breeze of openness to Camp David, as he did with so much else at the White House. As Nixon's successor, Ford recognized that the political system had been poisoned by Nixon's conduct, and he was determined to do things differently. He decided the public should have a look at the presidential retreat and on October 26, 1974, allowed ABC's Harry Reasoner to stroll with him along a trail. Reasoner then did a formal interview with Ford as they sat on plaid couches in Laurel Lodge.

Ford allowed other interviews and even news conferences at Camp David, but this was unusual. Presidents generally try to keep the place off limits to all but a select few.

Ford did not favor Camp David as his predecessor had. He visited the camp 17 times in 30 months in office, mostly for a night or two on weekends. He enjoyed sleeping late and having a Sunday breakfast of waffles, strawberries, and sour cream. But Ford also allowed his senior staff to use the compound for meetings, and permitted Cabinet officers and White House staff and their families to use the camp for personal getaways when he was not there. (The informal rule had been that staff could use it, but only when the president was completely out of Washington.) Still, no personal photographs were allowed.

He took a personal interest in those around him. When he noticed Secret Service agents shivering in the cold as they stood guard outside his door, he would slip them sandwiches and hot coffee.

But Ford couldn't convey these appealing qualities to the country. This became apparent one day in August 1976, when he was filming a biography of his life, to be shown at the Republican National Convention in Kansas City later that month. As he sat in the Laurel conference room, his media managers urged him to talk directly into the camera and reveal his "human side." But he seemed tongue-tied, stiff, and ill at ease, and the video biography did little to enhance his image.

·　·　·

JIMMY CARTER EXPERIENCED both the high points and the low points of his presidency at Camp David.

He reached the apex there when he negotiated a peace accord between Egyptian president Anwar Sadat and Israeli prime minister Menachem Begin in 1978, reprising the mediator's role that Theodore Roosevelt had played nearly a century earlier in ending the war between Japan and Russia.

The process started in November 1977, when Sadat made a dramatic journey to Jerusalem as a gesture of conciliation. A breakthrough in the Middle East seemed possible, but soon Israel and the Arab nations descended into their traditional enmities and regional tension intensified. Yet Carter sensed an opportunity to make historic progress toward Mideast peace. One afternoon in July 1978, he took a stroll through the woods at Camp David with his wife, Rosalynn, and made a bold suggestion. "It's so beautiful here," he said. "I don't believe anybody could stay in this place, close to nature, peaceful and isolated from the world, and still carry a grudge. I believe if I could get Sadat and Begin both here together, we could work out some of the problems between them, or at least we could learn to understand each other better and maybe make some progress. Everything's going backward now."

As a result, he invited delegations led by Sadat and Begin to hammer out a peace agreement that September at Camp David in near isolation from the outside world. In a 2004 interview for this book, Carter told me, "I don't think it could ever have been successful as it was if Begin or Sadat had had daily access to the news media and could have shared their intense frustrations and disappointments and hopelessness on occasion with the outside world. I think it would have been a devastating factor. And since we came out with success at Camp David with such a very narrow margin, any one or two factors, very small factors, I think, could have been fatal."

Jody Powell, Carter's press secretary, added, "If one is looking for a place to lock up a group of distinguished officials for an extended period of time and deny them easy access to anyone on the outside, it would be hard to find a better one than Camp David." Later, Sadat said he had felt he was "under house detention" at Dogwood Lodge, where he stayed. Begin referred to the compound as "a concentration camp de luxe."

But it worked as Carter had planned. The leaders of both sides got to know each other as individuals. Carter set the style of dress as informal, with a preference for blue jeans and short-sleeved cotton shirts. Sadat wore sports clothes. Begin, however, wore a jacket and tie, arguing that he was not a head of state, as were the two presidents, and he preferred to be more formal in keeping with his view of propriety.

Carter followed his normal routine of jogging, swimming, riding a bike, or playing tennis, often with Rosalynn. Sadat took three- or four-mile walks each morning. Begin, in poor health, traveled around the camp in a golf cart.

Sadat brought his own chef because he was on a special diet of boiled meat, vegetables, and mint tea with honey. Meanwhile, a portion of the kitchen at Aspen was set aside for the pots, pans, and dishes used in preparing kosher food for the Israelis. Carter thought the principals would prefer to dine in their own cabins and staff members would eat together in the staff dining hall at Laurel. But as it happened, Begin often ate with his staff at Laurel, suggesting to Carter that the Israeli leader was more approachable than he had thought.

Sadat asked for a private place to say his prayers. The movie theater at Camp David, which sometimes doubled as a chapel on weekends, was converted to a temporary mosque.

For a while, nothing broke the impasse. The atmosphere got so tense that at one point Carter thought someone might have tried to assassinate Sadat. Early on the morning of September 14, Carter awakened Zbigniew Brzezinski, his national security adviser, and summoned him to his cabin. "Zbig," the president said to Brzezinski, still wearing pajamas, "I am very much concerned for Sadat's life." Carter had been told by Brzezinski earlier that some hard-liners in the Egyptian delegation thought Sadat was on the way to "betraying" his country. Carter told me in our interview that Sadat indeed seemed to be "on the cutting edge of making concessions and seeking peace," and so he took the potential threat seriously. He had gone to see the Egyptian leader at about 10 P.M. the previous evening and was told he was asleep, even though the light was on in his cabin and he normally was a nightowl. Carter feared Sadat might have been harmed by the hard-liners in his delegation. Fortunately, the president's hunch was wrong, Sadat was fine. But Carter placed armed guards around Sadat's cabin after that.

After nearly 13 days of grueling negotiations, with the talks sometimes on the brink of collapse, Carter pushed both sides to reach an accord, partly through his sheer doggedness and the desire of both Begin and Sadat to avoid the blame for ending the extraordinary session. At one point, Carter had publicly described it as the best chance for peace between the Jews and the Egyptians since the time of Jeremiah. It led to a peace treaty between Israel and Egypt on March 26, 1979, and eventually the Nobel Peace Prize for Begin and Sadat. (Carter was awarded the Peace Prize twenty years later for his lifetime commitment to international peace and fighting poverty.)

THIS SUCCESS OF the Camp David negotiations was particularly ironic because Carter initially thought the facilities cost too much and questioned their usefulness. He ordered a study of exactly how much the taxpayers were paying for the retreat, as part of his overall austerity program. A Carter aide asked Stephen Hess, a former Nixon adviser who had become a scholar at Washington's Brookings Institution, for advice. In one of a series of memos to Carter about how to organize the executive branch in early 1977, Hess wrote, "A president should be able to walk in the woods on a weekend if it helps him restore his spirit or rethink his concerns. Herbert Hoover and John Kennedy were able to buy themselves rustic retreats, but should we have to count on a president being rich? I have never been inside Camp David; judge for yourself whether it is too opulent. Do not dismantle it until you have determined that it does not serve a legitimate need." After inspecting the compound, Carter not only kept it in service but authorized various upgrades, including a project to repair structural damage from moisture, termites, and other problems. When Bert Lance, his Office of Management and Budget director, came in with the cost figures, he said, "I'd rather not tell you." Carter replied, "Okay, don't tell me." The former president recalled later that, by then, "I had seen how much Camp David meant to me. It was just 35 minutes from the South Lawn [of the White House]. And it was a great place. Rosalynn and I both loved Camp David. . . . It's completely isolated. . . . We looked upon it as a prime attraction in our lives."

In all, Carter would make 99 visits to the camp for a total of more than nine months during his four years in office. He enjoyed watching movies, reading, fishing, woodworking at the camp's carpentry shop, and dining casually with his wife and daughter, Amy. This was the kind of normalcy that his predecessors had also found in the Catoctins. A devoted Baptist and lay preacher, Carter attended Sunday services in local communities around the camp and also had an Army chaplain conduct services on site. Sometimes, Jimmy and Rosalynn would take moonlight walks and hold hands. The president and the First Lady would also jog along the pathways—Carter would jog on average 40 miles per week—and go cross-country skiing after it snowed. On one skiing jaunt just before he left office, he fell and broke his left collarbone.

CARTER ALSO MADE secret escapes *from* Camp David. He confessed to me that on a few occasions he left his media contingent behind and, without their knowledge, went fishing off the coast of Norfolk, Virginia. More often, he secretly left the retreat to fish on private streams near Gettysburg, Pennsylvania, not far from Eisenhower's farm.

To keep his peregrinations secret, he developed a ruse. He would leave the White House on Friday afternoons and take his *Marine One* helicopter to Camp David, where members of the White House press corps would watch him land safely. Then the reporters and photographers would depart the landing strip, assuming the president would spend the weekend there. He didn't. He and his family or friends would go to their cabins, change clothes, get back on the helicopter, and secretly fly another 35 minutes to a dairy farm in Pennsylvania about 25 miles south of Penn State University. He would stay there for the weekend. Carter would go fly-fishing late Friday afternoon, much of Saturday, and Sunday morning or early afternoon. Then he would fly back to Camp David, change clothes, and let the media see him boarding *Marine One* for the flight back to the White House. "We did that, I would say, with impunity," Carter told me proudly.

CARTER ENDURED A few political disasters at the retreat.

One of the most serious was preceded by an economic summit meeting in Tokyo in late June 1979. The discussions were dominated by the spiraling costs of energy and the oil price increases imposed by an Arab oil cartel. Meanwhile, back at home, lines were growing at the nation's gasoline stations amid widespread petroleum shortages. Consumers' tempers were fraying. Adding to the atmosphere of failure, Congress had failed to pass Carter's energy legislation designed to promote conservation and reduce reliance on foreign oil. In a sour mood, Carter cancelled a brief stop in Hawaii and traveled from Tokyo directly to Camp David on July 3.

He was scheduled to finalize his fifth national address on the energy crisis, to be given the following week. Unable to sleep, he pored over a new public opinion poll by adviser Patrick Caddell describing a deep feeling of unhappiness and insecurity among the American people. Concluding that things were worse than he had imagined, and that his fifth address on energy would be ignored because it contained nothing really new, he cancelled the speech and began summoning advisers to Camp David. They included governors, political strategists, local officials, members of Congress, business and labor leaders, oil industry executives, economists and energy specialists, philosophers, religious leaders and journalists. Carter also made unannounced trips to homes in Pennsylvania and West Virginia to talk with everyday Americans.

As his soul-searching on the mountaintop continued, suspense was building. What would be the result of all this introspection?

In a much-anticipated televised speech on July 15, Carter said, "We were sure that ours was a nation of the ballot, not the bullet, until the murders of John Kennedy, Robert Kennedy, and Martin Luther King, Jr. We were taught that our armies were always invincible and our causes always just, only to suffer the agony of Vietnam. We respected the presidency as a place of honor until the shock of Watergate. . . . These wounds are still very deep. They have never been healed."

The address became known, derisively, as the "malaise speech," even though Carter didn't actually use those words. But Senator Edward Kennedy, who was challenging Carter for the Democratic nomination, in addition to Republican contender Ronald Reagan and many commentators, argued that Carter was blaming the country for his own leadership failures. When he also announced a reshuffling of his Cabinet and senior advisers a short time later, it appeared that the wheels were coming off his administration.

The isolation of Camp David, it turned out, had in this case deepened the president's isolation from public opinion.

Another embarrassment came two months later, on September 15, 1979. Carter was participating in a 6.2-mile run called the Catoctin Mountain Race just outside the compound. After about four miles, about 200 yards from the entrance to the camp, he staggered and nearly collapsed. Secret Service agents grabbed hold of his arms and kept him from falling. He was taken to an electric cart and given oxygen, then put to bed while he was given fluids intravenously, and apparently suffered no permanent injury. But the picture of an exhausted president unable to continue the race became a lasting image.

It was also at Camp David that Carter made one of the most fateful decisions of his presidency. Fifty Americans were taken hostage at the U.S. Embassy in Tehran on November 4, 1979, and Carter spent the next few months trying to win their release. Nothing worked. At Camp David on March 22, 1980, a frustrated Carter authorized the U.S. military to send a small plane to a swath of desert about 200 miles south of Tehran, to determine if that area could be used as a staging ground for a rescue mission. This reconnaissance led to the failed rescue attempt that cost eight Americans their lives in the desert and became a symbol of the futility of Carter's leadership.

RONALD REAGAN, CARTER'S successor, used the retreat mostly as a private sanctuary. Overnight visitors were rare, as was entertaining foreign leaders and members of Congress. Even his daughter, Maureen, who lived nearby in Washington, got to the camp only once, in 1985. Nor did Reagan let his staff use the camp when he wasn't there.

Usually he and Nancy arrived on a Friday afternoon by helicopter and returned to the White House Sunday afternoon or Monday. The Reagans preferred casual clothes such as jeans and a lumberjack shirt for him and a Western shirt for her. He would go for a swim with the First Lady, take walks, and lift weights for exercise. Frequently, the Reagans would ride horses brought in by the National Park Service from nearby stables. They enjoyed watching deer walk gingerly to a salt lick, which the camp staff placed just below Aspen Lodge.

He even left some of his vanity outside the gates. Reagan would wear eyeglasses—which he had needed since high school—instead of contact lenses when he was out of public view at the camp.

In the evenings, they would watch movies and eat popcorn. Mostly they preferred films of the 1930s, 1940s, and 1950s—Reagan's era in Hollywood—including some in which he starred, such as *Santa Fe Trail,* in which Reagan played George Armstrong Custer, and *Bedtime for Bonzo,* in which the future president co-starred with a chimpanzee. On Sunday mornings, they regularly watched the TV public affairs shows, especially *This Week with David Brinkley.*

"Ronnie enjoyed himself in his own usual ways—being outside and riding, in particular," Mrs. Reagan writes. "The Secret Service didn't want him going too far at first, but as time went by, he'd suggest adding a little more to the trail and then a bit more and a bit more, until by the end, he had the kind of substantial ride he was used to.

"Sometimes," she continues, "just the two of us went to Camp David (that is to say, the two of us plus the Secret Service, the White House doctor, someone from the press office, and other White House staff—that's solitude during the presidency). Sometimes [son] Ron and his new wife, Doria, would come, or a couple of close friends, like Charles and Mary Jane Wick and their children. But we never made a big social event out of it. What we really enjoyed doing there was relaxing, wearing blue jeans, reading, riding horses, watching movies—just generally doing the kinds of things that we'd always done on the ranch back home. I think that's largely why we didn't find Washington strange or lonely the way many people who move there from other places say they do. We were still together all the time, and we were still us."

Reagan visited Camp David more than any of his predecessors—187 times for a total of 571 days over eight years. This was especially remarkable since he vacationed at his Santa Barbara ranch for an additional 345 days—meaning he was away from the White House on R & R for more than 900 days!

In July 1981, six months after taking office, Transportation Secretary Drew Lewis paid him a visit at Camp David with news that the union representing air traffic controllers was about to strike. Reagan's reaction was strong and clear: If they did so, he would fire them because no president could tolerate an illegal strike by federal employes. That's exactly what he did, and even though he was criticized for jeopardizing air safety, he stuck to his guns and showed that he was a strong leader.

He also would tape weekly five-minute radio addresses at Laurel Lodge—150 of them during his presidency—and they would be broadcast around the country. His mellifluous voice, cultivated during his many years as an announcer and actor in radio, television, and film, helped him bond with the nation.

Nancy redecorated extensively with the help of interior decorator Ted Graber of Los Angeles, changing the bright colors inside Aspen and the other cabins and replacing them with earth tones, lowering the windows of Aspen to improve the view, and enlarging the kitchen. "For me, one of the best parts about Camp David was that there wasn't a whisper of controversy about the renovations I made there," she wrote. "Because the entire place is off limits to the press, nobody ever knew what I did."

President Reagan also showed a homey side. He made a habit of collecting acorns every fall at Camp David and bringing them in a plastic bag to the White House, where he would scatter them outside the Oval Office each morning for the squirrels.

Just before his State of the Union address in January 1987, Reagan invited Ken Khachigian, one of his longtime speech writers, to visit the camp and help him put the finishing touches on the speech. Reagan had recently undergone surgery for prostate cancer, and Khachigian and his wife, Meredith, didn't know what to expect.

After they arrived, the visitors were told the Reagans wanted them to come over for dinner, and at the appointed hour they ambled across the grounds from their guest cabin to Aspen Lodge, the presidential quarters. Khachigian knocked on the door and the president greeted them with a big smile. As they enjoyed a few cocktails in the living room, Nancy put logs on the fire to keep the blaze going and Reagan felt the need to apologize. "I would never let her do this normally," he said in explaining his momentary lack of gallantry, "but the doctors told me not to do any lifting."

The president dug into the corned beef and cabbage dinner with great relish, explaining that he loved the dish but it was considered too ordinary to serve him at other places. The conversation started out a bit awkwardly for the Khachigians, who couldn't help but feel that they were intruding on the Reagans' privacy. But once the president got warmed up, he began telling the stories he liked best—not tales of politics and government but stories from his days as an actor in Hollywood.

GEORGE HERBERT WALKER BUSH used Camp David as more of a work place than Reagan did. It was there that he made a number of key decisions in the Persian Gulf War, including his final decision to launch the conflict. Aides say he found it ideal for thinking and writing speeches.

On Saturday morning, August 4, 1990, Bush convened his senior advisers around a 25-foot-long conference table in Laurel Lodge to plan how to force Iraq out of Kuwait, which Saddam Hussein had invaded two days earlier. A few days later, Bush would send U.S. forces to Saudi Arabia to ward off any Iraqi threat and set the nation on the course for the eventual war with Iraq, including the assembling of an international coalition to confront the dictator.

Bush met the Joint Chiefs of Staff on December 1 at Camp David and discussed the details of what the war might be like. He was moving inexorably toward hostilities.

On December 31, 1991, New Year's Eve, Bush wrote a moving letter from Camp David to his five children—George W., Jeb, Neil, Marvin, and Doro—about his thoughts and emotions on the eve of war, after spending a few days with the family at the compound over Christmas.

"When I came into this job I vowed that I would never ring [sic] my hands and talk about 'the loneliest job in the world' or ring [sic] my hands about the 'pressures or the trials,' " the letter reads.

"Having said that I *have* been concerned about what lies ahead. There is no 'loneliness' though because I am backed by a first rate team of knowledgeable and committed people. No President has been more blessed in this regard.

". . . I guess what I want you to know as a father is this: Every Human life is precious. When the question is asked, 'How many lives are you willing to sacrifice'—it tears at my heart. The answer, of course is none—none at all.

". . . My mind goes back to history: How many lives might have been saved if appeasement had given way to force earlier on in the late '30's or earliest '40's? How many Jews might have been spared the gas chambers, or how many Polish patriots might be alive today? I look at today's crisis as 'good' vs. 'evil'—Yes, it is that clear.

"And so I shall say a few more prayers, mainly for our kids in the Gulf. And I shall do what must be done, and I shall be strengthened every day by our family love which lifts me up every single day of my life."

Bush gave Saddam Hussein every chance to leave Kuwait, but the Iraqi dictator refused. Bush concluded that nothing short of war would drive him out. On Friday, February 22, Bush traveled back to Camp David, but it was a ruse to suggest that nothing special was about to happen. The next morning, he flew back to Washington to announce that the ground war designed to push Iraq out of Kuwait had begun. He called it Desert Storm, and it was a triumph for American arms, even though the invasion was unable to topple Saddam Hussein from power.

IN GENERAL, BUSH preferred his home in Kennebunkport to Camp David, but he did find many ways to enjoy the Maryland retreat, and spent an average of every other weekend there—24 weekends annually and a week over Christmas—during his four years in office. He particularly enjoyed walking his dog, Ranger, on the endless trails, and allowed the English springer spaniel to run through the brush to catch rabbits.

Bush had a horseshoe pit installed, and organized highly competitive matches with his guests. He even played a game with Soviet leader Mikhail Gorbachev on the Kremlin leader's visit in the spring of 1990. Gorbachev didn't understand the game. Bush later told me the Soviet leader "had never seen horseshoes." But he gamely participated in the president's pastime and threw a ringer on his first toss. At another point, Bush let Gorbachev drive his presidential golf cart "and he almost tipped me over," Bush recalled.

Bush would take a helicopter to the retreat on Friday afternoons, as Reagan had, but he was more scrupulous than his predecessor about keeping in touch. He would call his personal secretary back at the Oval Office as soon as he landed, to find out if anything important had happened during the brief chopper flight. He would check in every morning, even on weekends, for his national security briefing and a domestic policy update starting at 7 A.M.

After that, Bush told me, it was "total relaxation," with games of tennis, skeet shooting, "walleyball" (a form of volleyball played on a racquetball court), jogging on the trails, bowling tournaments, and walks around the grounds with Barbara and their grandchildren.

Bush's routine was based on socializing with family and friends, whom he would invite to the retreat nearly every weekend he spent there. White House staff members, Cabinet members, and their spouses and children were frequent guests.

He was often accompanied by Paula Rondoon, a family cook, who prepared fajitas and tamales the way the president liked them. Again, movies were common in the evenings. At Christmas, Bush organized sleigh rides for the kids.

Bush used an office at Laurel, which houses a conference center, while the First Lady took over the one in Aspen, the president's cabin. They would get up before dawn, work all morning, and dine with their guests at lunch.

The president liked to keep the names of some guests secret, especially entertainers and sports figures who didn't want their political associations known. Another reason was that the Bushes didn't want their visitors to think they were being exploited politically by their hosts. Among the guests were tennis pro Andre

Agassi, actors Bruce Willis and Demi Moore, and country singers George Strait and Lee Greenwood.

Bush's office featured a wraparound desk of blond wood, a lovely view from the windows, and several crammed bookcases. On the desk were a computer, photographs of his family, and a blue coffee mug atop an electric warming disk. On the walls and in cubbyholes around the room were an oil painting of his estate at Walker's Point in Kennebunkport, Maine; a picture of the type of torpedo bomber he piloted during World War II; and a model of the submarine that rescued him when his torpedo bomber was shot down in the South Pacific.

Another distinctive touch could be seen on the floor in one corner. It looked like an old-fashioned gumball machine, but the contraption actually dispensed multicolored dog biscuits to the family canines. A handle in the shape of a bone would release the treats into a slot. Bush later said the dogs never got the knack of pushing it, so they would stand forlornly near the contraption until the president of the United States took pity on them and pushed the handle himself.

Despite his efforts to rest and relax, Bush did push himself very hard, even at Camp David. In May 1991, not long after the Gulf War victory, he experienced shortness of breath while jogging, which forced him to stop abruptly. His doctor took him to the Eucalyptus cabin, where a dispensary was located, and connected him to a cardiac monitor and put an IV in his arm. It turned out that the upper chamber of his heart was pumping at a different rate than the lower chamber—in medical terms, a fibrillation. He was taken by helicopter on a 20-minute flight to the National Naval Medical Center in Bethesda, Maryland, for more tests. A few days later, he was diagnosed with Graves' disease, an autoimmune illness which had weakened his heart.

His consideration of those around him and his enjoyment of his family and friends made Bush very popular with the Camp David staff. But he could never convey his best qualities to the American public, troubled by a painful recession and feeling that Bush was too isolated from everyday life. He lost his bid for reelection in 1992 to the hard-charging baby boomer, Bill Clinton.

AT FIRST, BILL and Hillary Clinton didn't think they would use Camp David very much, just like the Kennedys and the Carters. Clinton initially saw Camp David as simply a conference center. On his second weekend in office, he called his advisers to what he billed as a corporate-style retreat, helped along by a professional "facilitator" recommended by Vice President Al Gore. The conversation, designed to be deeply personal to enable the new policy makers to bond with each other, was apparently unique in the annals of the presidential hideaway. Clinton, for example, admitted that he was teased for being a fat boy in elementary school. It wasn't the kind of thing heard around JFK's Camelot.

His aides were eager to portray Clinton as different from his older predecessors. "He wants to be out with people . . . not isolated," said a senior White House official at the end of 1993, Clinton's first year in office. "He's not a recluse. . . . It doesn't surprise me that he probably feels like Camp David may be a little boring." This of course was a backhanded slap at his predecessors.

One reason for this attitude was that, when the Clintons first moved into the White House, Chelsea, their adolescent daughter, didn't like the Catoctin retreat very much. She preferred to entertain her friends at glamorous 1600 Pennsylvania Avenue. After she went off to Stanford for the fall semester in 1997, however, her parents were free to do what they wanted on weekends, and Camp David grew more appealing to them as an escape. "Camp David has the same sense of barrier that the third floor of the [White House] Residence has," recalls Joe Lockhart, Clinton's White House press secretary. "You'd better have a damn good reason [for intruding]."

Hillary enjoyed her secret passion of bowling, where she easily outshined her husband in late-night excursions to the Camp David lanes with friends. Sometimes, President Clinton would go to Camp David without her and without any senior aides, so he could ruminate, read, and relax on his own terms. Late at night, he would channel surf on his television, flipping from one sports show to another and watching movies. In the morning or afternoon he would jog, shoot skeet, or ride horses. Once, his 87-year-old stepfather, Dick Kelley, slid off his horse in the woods, throwing a scare into the president and startling the elderly rider. But Kelley was uninjured.

More often, Clinton brought an entourage to keep him company. He loved to be the center of attention. On such stays, Clinton would get up late and enjoy a game of golf at a nearby course with his pals. Camp David's three-hole layout wasn't challenging enough for him. He would have a big dinner with his guests, then sit and watch movies for hours on end in Laurel Lodge and play cards or word games such as Boggle and Upwords until 1 or 2 A.M. Terry McAuliffe, a

Democratic fund-raiser, recalls one occasion when he and the president played Upwords until about 6:30 A.M., when the sun came up.

On such occasions, Clinton would hold forth on countless topics, ranging from prospects for peace in the Middle East or Ireland to the U.S. relationship with Russia to domestic politics and whatever was in the news that day. "I don't care what the topic was," McAuliffe says, "he'd give you an hour and a half dissertation on it— sometimes while he was doing *The New York Times* crossword puzzle."

Unknown to most of his staff, the gregarious Clinton got to know Camp David's permanent military residents very well, just as Lincoln had gotten to know the military residents at the Soldiers' Home more than a century earlier. "There are not a lot of real people at the White House," Lockhart says. "A president may get to know the ushers a little, but at Camp David there is a community, a culture up there. The Clintons had a lot of good relationships with the staff and the people who work and live there."

LIKE JIMMY CARTER, Clinton used Camp David as a venue to bring together warring parties from the Middle East—or at least he tried. "You could go a little stir-crazy up there in the mountains, and he used that to force them to negotiate," says Lockhart. "While it's a beautiful and pleasant place, on the third or fourth day the mountains and the trails start to lose their charm. And the layout forces people to interact."

Clinton knew all this, having read accounts of Jimmy Carter's Middle East negotiations at Camp David two decades earlier. But he started out with little reason to expect success, telling an aide he was attempting a "Hail Mary pass"—a touchdown very late in the game with the odds heavily stacked against him.

He invited Palestinian leader Yasser Arafat and Israeli prime minister Ehud Barak to the retreat in July 2000, largely hoping that the force of his personality would bring them together to sign a peace accord. The meetings lasted for two weeks, with Clinton leaving the sessions for a few days to attend an economic summit meeting in Okinawa and returning for round-the-clock final bargaining.

At one point, Clinton met privately with Arafat in Aspen cabin, urging the Palestinian leader to be flexible regarding his claims to the Old City of Jerusalem, which was a sticking point. He stood a few inches from the bearded, much shorter leader's face, a hand on his shoulder, looking into his eyes, pleading one moment, arguing the next. At another point in the talks, Clinton lost his temper at what he considered Palestinian intransigence when Arafat refused to look at a map Barak presented on new boundaries. "This is ridiculous," Clinton shouted. "This is not the way to negotiate. If you insist on stonewalling, this is going to go nowhere."

Clinton felt that Barak was much more accommodating than Arafat, but when his meetings with the two leaders failed to break the stalemate, Clinton met with lower-ranking officials in each delegation, trying to work out wording that their bosses could live with. Presidents usually leave such details to their own negotiators.

At meals, he made sure that there was no "Palestinian table" or "Israeli table" in the common dining room at Laurel Lodge. This encouraged participants to get to know each other as individuals, not as stereotypical enemies across a conference table. Negotiators actually got along well as individuals, sometimes carrying their talks from the formal sessions to relaxed chats over pinball games at Hickory Lodge. To the president, the important thing was for both sides to continue talking.

Clinton even phoned the leaders of Egypt, Jordan, and Saudi Arabia and urged them to pressure Arafat to compromise. But the tactic backfired; they urged the Palestinian leader not to cave in.

Arafat and Barak played their own psychological games. At different points, they ordered aides to pack up their belongings and put the luggage outside their doors, signaling an immediate departure. But such walkouts never materialized, and at the very end, Clinton's painstaking intervention appeared to be making progress. With the president scribbling notes on yellow legal pads, the Israelis and Palestinians first agreed on some issues regarding security, then on the return of refugees, and finally on borders for a Palestinian state. But in the end, Clinton could not lead them to an agreement on the status of Jerusalem and who would have sovereignty over the city's holy sites, and the talks fell apart. It was one of the biggest disappointments of Clinton's presidency.

GEORGE W. BUSH never had any doubts about Camp David. He loved it from the start. He knew how valuable the retreat had been to his father and had spent a number of happy days there while his dad was in office.

As the 43rd president, Bush quickly established his own routine for using the property. As of August 2004, he had made 83 visits there for a total of 262 full or partial days. He would leave the White House at mid-afternoon nearly every Friday and take the half-hour helicopter ride north to the retreat. Once there, he enjoyed watching sports on TV, working on jigsaw puzzles, jogging or riding a bicycle in the countryside, tooling around in a motorized vehicle called Golf Cart One, and taking strolls with Laura.

"He can stretch his legs a little," says Dan Bartlett, Bush's White House communications director and a longtime aide. "He likes all the activities, the trails, the swimming, the basketball courts, a place where he could play 'walleyball' [which his father had played at this same place during his own administration nine years earlier]." He had various new equipment installed without telling the news media, including a rock-climbing wall, new indoor tennis courts, and a batting cage. He also had the two-lane bowling alley renovated.

Mike Gerson, Bush's chief speechwriter, went to the retreat to help the president prepare his State of the Union address in January 2002. At one point, Bush got pulled away by a phone call while they were working in Laurel Lodge, and Gerson realized his boss was talking to generals in the field about imminent military operations to strike at terrorists thought responsible for the 9/11 attacks. Bush looked over at his speechwriter and inquired, "Are you cleared for all this?" Gerson replied sheepishly, "I have no idea." And the president responded, "You are now."

Gerson was invited up to the retreat again, this time with his wife and two small children, the weekend before the State of the Union address in January 2004. Gerson spent Saturday afternoon working on the speech, then he and his family joined the Bushes and other advisers for dinner in the Laurel Lodge dining room. It was served family style—platters of chicken-fried steak, big bowls of mashed potatoes and vegetables, and a side table offering cakes and Blue Bell ice cream in vanilla, chocolate, and strawberry.

Bush invited everyone to go bowling at Camp David's two lanes. There would be two teams with six on a side, he said, and they included then-National Security Adviser Condoleezza Rice, White House Chief of Staff Andy Card and his wife, Rev. Kathleene Card, Bush adviser Karen Hughes, and White House Communications Director Bartlett and his wife. Gerson describes Bush as an "animated, fun, competitive" teammate who dispenses high-fives when a player on his squad throws a strike. At that point, Bush would cross his forearms marking an x, for the strike. He is a vigorous, flamboyant bowler, throwing the ball halfway down the alley, with a huge amount of spin.

And Bush made some big decisions at Camp David, notably his plan for waging the early part of the war on terrorism after the attacks of September 11, 2001.

The first weekend after the terrorist attacks, Bush was exhausted and needed to find a place outside his normal beehive of activity where he could meet with his advisers and ruminate in private. As had so many of his predecessors, he realized that Camp David was the perfect venue.

On the morning of Saturday, September 15, the day after he made an emotional visit to "Ground Zero," where the destroyed World Trade Center in New York had stood only four days earlier, he gathered two dozen aides—what he called his war council—at Laurel Lodge's wood-paneled conference room, the same place his father had met so often to plan and execute the Persian Gulf War. Among those attending were Vice President Dick Cheney, who had been his father's defense secretary; Secretary of State Colin Powell; Defense Secretary Donald Rumsfeld and his deputy, Paul Wolfowitz; Treasury Secretary Paul O'Neill; National Security Adviser Rice; and Director of Central Intelligence George Tenet. Everyone was dressed informally; Bush wore a blue shirt and green bomber jacket. The first session that morning began with a prayer.

At one point, Powell warned that while a large international coalition was ready to hunt down and destroy the al Qaeda terrorists thought responsible for the 9/11 attacks, expanding the war could cause an erosion of support. "At some point," Bush responded, "we may be the only ones left. That's okay with me. We are America." He didn't want lack of international unity to slow him down; it was an early manifestation of the unilateral mindset that has become so familiar since then.

After a break for lunch and rest or exercise, the group convened again at 4 P.M., and there was another wide-ranging discussion of options. But Bush made it clear he was not ready to decide the nation's course on the spot. "I'm going to go think about it, and I'll let you know what I've decided," he said.

On Saturday night, Powell, Rumsfeld, and a few other principals had left, but most of the others and their spouses remained for dinner. One participant remembers Rice, a classical musician, singing familiar tunes including "America the Beautiful," and "Nobody Knows the Trouble I've Seen," while Attorney General John Ashcroft provided accompaniment on the piano, and others joined in. "But the president was very much with his own thoughts," the participant recalls. At one point, he made a halfhearted effort to help put together a jigsaw puzzle, but left early for bed. On Sunday, Bush attended services at the Camp chapel, but spent most of the day ruminating by himself.

On Monday, back in Washington, he called Rice into his second-floor office at the White House Residence and said he had made up his mind. "I know what I want to do," the president announced. He went on to say he wanted to put "boots on the ground" by invading Afghanistan and destroying the Taliban regime, which he felt was harboring terrorists, and not just launching air strikes as Bill Clinton had done. He ordered the CIA to launch a new series of covert operations globally and at home to prevent further attacks. He ordered the Justice Department and the FBI to go all out in protecting America in the future rather than simply focusing on prosecuting those guilty for the September 11 horrors.

In an interview for this book, Bush recalled, "At that point in time, I had made up my mind. I knew we were at war, and I knew we were going to win. And there wasn't any hesitancy about the use of our military to achieve victory over these people. But that meeting was one in which people reported to me their ideas about how we would achieve victory. And it was there that I said I'll let you know what the response is back in Washington—I'll tell you what our plan is going to be, and sat on it and thought about it that night and then on Sunday and then went and told them."

Added a senior Bush adviser: "I think he very often comes to conclusions, decisions about big steps, at Camp David. You can make the decision in the Oval Office about 'check that box,' 'do you want to do this,' or 'do you want to do that.' But it seems to me that Crawford and Camp David provide a different kind of opportunity for thought and decision."

All this was facilitated because the communications system at Camp David had been updated so dramatically that it could now allow live, secure briefings between the president and his advisers around the world. For example, when British prime minister Tony Blair visited to help plan the post-9/11 response, Bush and Blair sat in Laurel Lodge and held a live video conference with Defense Secretary Rumsfeld at the Pentagon and U.S. commanders in the Middle East.

ON THE PERSONAL side, Bush is a committed Christian, and he enjoys attending Sunday services at the Camp David chapel with the Marines who are stationed there and their families. Laura Bush told me this is one of their favorite parts of the weekend routine.

And it turns out that Mrs. Bush has been quietly redecorating. She brought in interior designer Ken Blasingame of Fort Worth, Texas, to give her advice, and has made some purchases on her own. In Mobile, Alabama, for example, she was impressed with the floor lamps at a furniture shop and bought two of them for the camp. Mrs. Bush also has brought in an updated player piano that grinds out a variety of tunes at the touch of a button.

Bush is a gracious and considerate host, as his father was. Noelia Rodriguez, who served for nearly three years as First Lady Laura Bush's press secretary, recalled how the president invited her and her mother for Thanksgiving in November 2001. This was only a few weeks after the September 11 terrorist attacks, and the mood was somber. The president, his wife, and twin daughters, Barbara and Jenna, attended a chapel service that morning along with senior aides including Karl Rove, his wife, and son; Karen Hughes, her husband, and son; and Rodriguez and her mother, Grace Carrejo, who both sat in the back. But the president, after taking his place in the front pew with his family, beckoned the two women to the seats right behind them.

After the service, Bush drove Rodriguez and her mother in a golf cart to Laurel Lodge and gave them a personal tour of the conference center.

The group assembled a few hours later for Thanksgiving dinner at Laurel. They had soft drinks, then walked down a flight of stairs to a buffet line that featured a traditional feast of roast turkey, gravy, mashed potatoes, and green beans. Then everyone went back upstairs and took seats at the big oval table. Looking at Rodriguez's mother, Bush said, "Grace, you're going to sit here next to me." And for the next hour and a half, the president shared his thoughts with her about life in Texas and raising children.

After the main meal, the president leaned back and announced, "Okay, time for dessert." But when Ms. Carrejo started to rise with everyone else, he put his hand gently on her shoulder and said, "No, Grace, you stay here." He asked her if she wanted apple or pumpkin pie, and she asked for pumpkin. The president fetched the dessert himself.

MOST PRESIDENTS FIND these personal moments invaluable as a way of grounding themselves in everyday life. In this way, Camp David under George W. Bush has played the same role it has played for so many other chief executives over the years: providing a respite from the burdens of the job. It has enabled him to reconnect with his family in a cloistered setting where he can let down his guard, and to interact with friends and other guests outside the formalities of the West Wing.

"It's where a president can be a human being again," says Ken Khachigian, former aide to Nixon and Reagan. "It's a place where he can be normal."

And, whether it is at Camp David or other presidential hideaways, retreats, and homes, this is no small achievement.

ENDNOTES

⸺◈◈◈⸺

Chapter One: The Importance of Presidential Retreats

1 George Washington fretted: Lonnie G. Bunch III, Spencer R. Crew, Mark G. Hirsch, and Harry R. Rubenstein, *The American Presidency: A Glorious Burden.* Washington and London: Smithsonian Institution Press, 2000, p. xi.

1 "a place of splendid misery": Bunch, Crew, et al., p. xii.

1 "It's Hell!": Bunch, Crew, et al., p. xii.

1 Ike readily agreed.: W. Dale Nelson, *The President Is at Camp David.* Syracuse University Press, 1995, p. 53.

1 "The presidency has made every man": Bunch, Crew, et al., p. iv.

1 George W. Bush remarked: Transcript of Bush speech of Sept. 2, 2004, *The New York Times*, Sept. 3, 2004, p. P4.

2 "I loved": Author's interview with Bill Clinton, Oct. 29, 2004.

2 Franklin Roosevelt made: These figures were provided by the Roosevelt National Historic Site, Hyde Park, N.Y. Other estimates vary.

3 "In Washington": Author's interview with George W. Bush, Dec. 30, 2003.

4 "Washington is not": Author's interview with Stan Greenberg, July 31, 2002.

4 "It tells you about": Author's interview with Robert Dallek, July 23, 2003.

4 Each president tends: Author's interview with Doug Brinkley, Sept. 14, 2003.

4 "You can learn a lot": Author's interview with Geoff Garin, July 15, 2003.

5 While he was in office: Hedrick Smith, *The Power Game: How Washington Works.* New York: Ballantine Books, 1988, p. 89.

5 "It was open space": Author's interview with Ken Khachigian, March 29, 2004.

5 "Think, for a moment": Cindy S. Aron, *Working at Play: A History of Vacations in the United States.* New York: Oxford University Press, 1999, pp. 2–3.

5 And it was only during the Depression: Aron, p. 4.

6 "People feel that": Author's interview with Bill McInturff, Jan. 12, 2004.

6 "Americans believe": Author's interview with Geoff Garin, Jan. 16, 2004.

6 In the summer of 1811: Author's interview with John Stagg, historian and editor of the papers of James Madison, University of Virginia, Charlottesville, Va., April 6, 2004.

6 When he took: Stanley F. Horn, *The Hermitage: Home of Old Hickory.* New York: Greenberg, 1950, p. 216. See also Robert V. Remini, *The Life of Andrew Jackson.* New York: Penguin Books USA, Inc., 1990, pp. 279–281, and The Ladies' Hermitage Association, *Andrew Jackson's Hermitage.* Hermitage, Tenn., 1986, p. 40.

7 A special spur: William G. Clotworthy, *Homes and Libraries of the Presidents: An Interpretive Guide.* Blacksburg, Va.: McDonald & Woodward, 1995, p. 163.

7 He suffered from: Zachary Karabell, *Chester Alan Arthur.* New York: Times Books, 2004, pp. 93–94.

7 Several newspapers: Karabell, p. 124.

8 "Oak View or": H. Paul Jeffers, *An Honest President: The Life and Presidencies of Grover Cleveland.* New York: William Morrow, 2000, pp. 184–185.

8 In other years: Peter Hannaford, *Ronald Reagan and His Ranch: The Western White House, 1981–1989.* Bennington, Vermont: Images from the Past, 2002, p. 6. See also Special Supplement to *The New York Times,* "Wilson Accepts; Stands on Record of Administration," *The New York Times,* Sept. 3, 1916, p. 1.

8 Harding's companions: Hannaford, p. 6.

8 "In the pre-air-conditioning": Doug Brinkley interview, Sept. 14, 2003.

9 He liked to fish: George Sullivan, *Presidents at Play.* New York: Walker and Company, 1995, pp. 82–85.

9 It is now part: Sullivan, p. 85. See also Hannaford, p. 8.

Chapter Two: George Washington and Mount Vernon, Virginia

10 On the ceiling: Henry Wiencek, *An Imperfect God: George Washington, His Slaves, and the Creation of America.* New York: Farrar, Straus and Giroux, 2003, p. 92.

10 "Washington designed": Wiencek, p. 92.

11 "Having alighted": *The Papers of Benjamin Henry Latrobe.* Yale University, 1977, p. 166.

11 His answers to: Latrobe, p. 172.

11 Latrobe concluded: Latrobe, p. 168.

12 "As food for the": Latrobe, p. 170.

13 "You will meet, sir": Recollections and Private Memoirs of Washington by George Washington Parke Custis, Archives at Mount Vernon.

13 Washington expected his guests: Robert F. Dalzell, Jr., and Lee Baldwin Dalzell, *George Washington's Mount Vernon: At Home in Revolutionary America.* New York: Oxford University Press, 1998, p. 194.

14 "She has something": Dalzell, p. 199.

15 "In the darkest": Dalzell, p. 204.

16 When he ran for: Alan Brinkley and Davis Dyer, eds., *The American Presidency.* Boston: Houghton Mifflin Company, 2004, p. 13.

16 Despite the burdens: Author's interview with Donna Boulter, senior historical interpreter at Mount Vernon, Aug. 19, 2003.

16 In the fall of 1792: Dalzell, p. 208.

17 "I can truly say I had": Letter to David Stuart from New York, June 15, 1790, Archives of Mount Vernon.

18 As historian Henry Wiencek observes: Wiencek, p. 94.

18 Washington, operating from: Donna Boulter interview, Aug. 19, 2003.

18 "Experiments must be": Archives of Mount Vernon.

19 Ever meticulous: Archives of Mount Vernon.

20 He sent orders to: Archives of Mount Vernon.

20 "If anything can": Gordon S. Wood, "Slaves in the Family," *The New York Times Book Review*, Dec. 14, 2003, p. 10.

20 "Washington was": Wood, p. 10.

20 He made some efforts: Dalzell, p. 211.

21 "There is a particular": Wiencek, p. 112.

21 In the summer: Wiencek, p. 96.

21 "I wish to": Wiencek, pp. 314–316. See also Garry Wills, *"Negro President": Jefferson and the Slave Power.* Boston: Houghton Mifflin Company, 2003, p. 210.

22 In 1796, he ordered: For a detailed recounting of Ona Judge's story, see Wiencek, Chapter Nine, pp. 311–334.

22 Historians still debate: For a detailed examination of the evidence, see Wiencek, Chapter Eight, pp. 279–310.

22 This caused him: John Ferling, "Master and Commander," *Washington Post Book World*, Nov. 16, 2003, p. 4.

Chapter Three: John Adams and John Quincy Adams and Quincy, Massachusetts

24 "Popularity was": David McCullough, *John Adams.* New York: Simon & Schuster, 2001, p. 373.

24 He stubbornly declared: Alan Brinkley and Davis Dyer, eds., *The American Presidency*. Boston: Houghton Mifflin Company, 2004, p. 22.

25 As president, he was attacked: McCullough, p. 462.

25 "As president, Adams": Brinkley and Dyer, p. 23.

26 "The hot weather": McCullough, p. 490.

26 "The task of the": McCullough, p. 487.

26 "The President really": McCullough, p. 490.

26 He remained in Quincy: Peter Hannaford, *Ronald Reagan and His Ranch: The Western White House, 1981–1989*. Bennington, Vermont: Images from the Past, 2002, p. 4.

26 The *Aurora*, an anti-Federalist: Hannaford, p. 4.

27 "For Adams the pleasures": McCullough, p. 491.

27 "I have however": Lynne Withey, *Dearest Friend: A Life of Abigail Adams*. New York: A Touchstone Book, 2001, p. 245.

27 His goal, he said: McCullough, p. 383.

28 Adams paid 600 pounds: McCullough, p. 381.

28 This modest farmhouse: Paul C. Nagel, *John Quincy Adams: A Public Life, a Private Life*. Cambridge, Mass.: Harvard University Press, 1997, pp. 6–7.

28 Abigail brought: Wilhelmina S. Harris, *Adams National Historical Park: A Family's Legacy to America*. Washington, D.C.: National Park Service, U.S. Department of the Interior, 1983, pp. 47–49.

29 "The year 1798": McCullough, p. 508.

29 The president described it: McCullough, pp. 509, 514.

30 By September: McCullough, p. 513.

30 If true: McCullough, p. 515.

30 "Because it was a": Brinkley and Dyer, p. 28.

31 "The public sentiment": McCullough, p. 526.

31 His health: McCullough, p. 527.

31 In 1800, his final: Hannaford, p. 4.

32 "His mother worried": Nagel, p. 7.

32 "His four years in the": Nagel, p. 296.

32 To escape: Nagel, p. 293.

33 JQA paid the debts off quietly: Nagel, p. 311.

33 His doctor, according to Adams: Nagel, p. 315.

33 He woke up: Nagel, p. 305.

33 He got to know: Nagel, p. 315.

Chapter Four: Thomas Jefferson and Monticello, Virginia

35 "Many of the Founding Fathers": Donald Jackson, *A Year at Monticello, 1795.* Golden, Colo.: Fulcrum, Inc., 1989, pp. 18–19.

35 "Those who labour": Quoted in Jackson, p. 80.

36 His visits took place: Author's interview with Susan Stein, curator at Monticello, Feb. 17, 2004.

37 He liked to bring: Jackson, p. 87.

37 "Jefferson did the designing": R. B. Bernstein, *Thomas Jefferson.* New York: Oxford University Press, 2003, pp. 109–110.

37 After explorers Meriwether Lewis: Bernstein, p. 159.

37 He also displayed: Joseph Judge, "Mr. Jefferson's Monticello," *National Geographic,* September 1966, p. 437.

37 And while it isn't clear: Bernstein, p. 171.

38 "He did not use": Hamilton W. Pierson, *Jefferson at Monticello.* North Stratford, N.H.: Ayer Company, 2000 (first published 1862), p. 72.

38 "He was never a great": Pierson, pp. 72–73.

39 Bacon reported that: Pierson, pp. 75–76.

39 He considered them: Jackson, pp. 29, 32.

39 Similarly, Monticello's covered walkways: Bernstein, p. 110.

39 "Not only would": Sean Wilentz, "The Details of Greatness," *The New Republic,* March 29, 2004, p. 34.

40 Jefferson also wrote: Henry Wiencek, *An Imperfect God: George Washington, His Slaves, and the Creation of America.* New York: Farrar, Straus and Giroux, 2003, pp. 219–220.

40 "Slaves were everywhere": Jackson, pp. 29–30.

40 Sally spent much of her: Bernstein, p. 110.

41 Finally, when accusations: Bernstein, p. 111.

41 Bacon reported that he would: Pierson, p. 103.

41 He feared that the bondsmen: Author's interview with Sharon Lugar, historical guide at Monticello, Feb. 17, 2004.

41 Donald Jackson reports: Jackson, p. 32.

41 "He was always a good": Pierson, p. 105.

42 "Jefferson, who had begun": Garry Wills, *"Negro President": Jefferson and the Slave Power,* Boston: Houghton Mifflin Company, 2003, p. 210.

42 "Mr. Jefferson was": Pierson, pp. 79–80.

42 He was aghast: Bernstein, p. 105.

43 During his presidency: Bernstein, p. 80.

43 He also insisted on written: Pierson, p. 81.

43 "He always knew all": Pierson, pp. 38–39.

43 "He knew the name": Pierson, pp. 38–39.

43 "If the weather is not": Pierson, pp. 41–42.

43 He was even concerned: Pierson, p. 43.

44 "Quarantine corn, which": Pierson, p. 45.

44 He was an avid collector: Jackson, pp. 48–49.

45 He thought the best: Jackson, pp. 52–53.

46 Four of their: Jackson, p. 19.

46 In one account of: Merrill D. Peterson, *Visitors to Monticello*. Charlottesville, Va.: University Press of Virginia, 1989, p. 53.

47 In another game: Pierson, p. 90.

47 This frustrated: Jackson, p. 33.

47 When she was 11: Jackson, p. 35.

47 She died in 1804: Jackson, p. 36.

47 "Those that expect": Pierson, p. 89.

48 Bacon said, "they": Pierson, p. 124.

48 "There was no tavern": Pierson, p. 125.

48 This was one reason why: Jackson, p. 65.

48 The former tobacco plantation: Pierson, p. 125.

48 "At Poplar Forest": Peter Hannaford, *Ronald Reagan and His Ranch: The Western White House, 1981–1989*. Bennington, Vermont: Images from the Past, 2002, p. 3.

49 his heirs were forced: Brinkley and Dyer, essay by Joyce Appleby, pp. 33–47.

Chapter Five: Abraham Lincoln and the Soldiers' Home, Washington, D.C.

50 "Lincoln believed that": Alan Brinkley and Davis Dyer, eds., *The American Presidency*. Boston: Houghton Mifflin Company, 2004, essay by Jean H. Baker, p. 186.

51 In 1842, banker George W. Riggs, Jr.: Some of the information in this chapter derives from a tour of the Lincoln cottage conducted by Angela Brown on Aug. 2, 2003, and information provided by Sophia Lynn, project manager of the site for the National Trust for Historic Preservation.

51 He endured the death: Michael Burlingame, *The Inner World of Abraham Lincoln*. Urbana and Chicago: University of Illinois Press, 1994, pp. 93–94.

52 "This is the hardest": Burlingame, p. 103.

52 And she apparently held eight séances: Matthew Pinsker, *Lincoln's Sanctuary: Abraham Lincoln and the Soldiers' Home*. New York: Oxford University Press, 2003, pp. 30–32.

52 "Except for the family": David Herbert Donald, *Lincoln at Home: Two Glimpses of Abraham Lincoln's Family Life*. New York: Simon & Schuster, 1999, pp. 230–24.

53 Lincoln had a partition built: Donald, p. 25.

53 President Buchanan, a bachelor: Pinsker, p. 4.

53 In effect, he was a commuter who made the unpainted stucco home his: Author's interview with Sophia Lynn, Aug. 2, 2003.

54 "My thoughts, my solicitude": Pinsker, p. 160.

54 "The president and his": Pinsker, p. 50.

54 "I cannot be shut up": Pinsker, p. 51.

54 No one was sure: Donald, p. 44.

54 After some initial confusion: Pinsker, pp. 56–57.

55 Lincoln replaced the New Yorkers: Pinsker, pp. 114–115.

55 On August 22, 1862, he: Pinsker, p. 115.

55 On September 13, 1862, Lincoln: Pinsker, p. 61.

56 "I see the President": Pinsker, p. 1.

56 He was escorted: Pinsker, p. 5.

56 Lincoln sometimes: Pinsker, p. vii.

56 "Take all of this book upon reason": Pinsker, p. 151.

57 He also enjoyed the work: Pinsker, p. 10.

57 He once helped to rescue: Pinsker, p. 151.

57 "Rode home in the dark amid a party": Pinsker, p. 12.

57 The president would sometimes: Pinsker, p. 68.

58 Hoping to retain: Pinsker, pp. 26–27.

58 Pushed by abolitionists: Pinsker, p. 27.

58 "There were probably hundreds": Pinsker, pp. 11–12.

59 The *New York Tribune* reported: Pinsker, p. 37.

59 "Occasionally, Mr. Lincoln would": Pinsker, pp. 152–153.

60 One game was called: Pinsker, p. 82.

60 In the summer of 1864, as he was: Pinsker, p. 153.

60 Men routinely: Pinsker, p. 84.

60 But she preferred to spend many weeks: Donald, p. 48.

61 Mrs. Lincoln suffered: Pinsker, pp. 102–104.

61 In the spring of 1864, she hired: Pinsker, p. 127.

61 On July 10: Pinsker, p. 136.

62 Johnson said he gave up his plan: Pinsker, p. 134.

62 Union general Horatio Wright: Pinsker, p. 140.

62 One night at: Pinsker, p. 163.

62 All this was: Pinsker, p. 179.

Chapter Six: Theodore Roosevelt and Sagamore Hill, New York

65 A special rail spur was built: Author's interview with Amy Verone, park curator at Sagamore Hill National Historic Site, Oyster Bay, N.Y., Jan. 27, 2004.

65 Starting in May 1903: Sherwin Gluck, *TR's Summer White House: Oyster Bay.* Oyster Bay, N.Y.: Sherwin Gluck, 1997, 1999, p. 1.

65 Special telegraph wires and telephone: Gluck, p. 56.

66 "One summer was like another": Hermann Hagedorn: *The Roosevelt Family of Sagamore Hill.* New York: The Macmillan Company, 1954, p. 173.

66 "At Sagamore Hill we love": Natalie A. Naylor, *Sagamore Hill, 1880–1948, the Roosevelt Country Estate, Oyster Bay, and the North Shore of Long Island: From Farms to Country Houses and Estates to Suburbs.* Research paper made available to the author by the Sagamore Hill National Historic Site, Oyster Bay, N.Y.

66 On a typical day: Edmund Morris, *Theodore Rex.* New York: Random House, 2001, p. 125.

67 He would put ice in his glass: Amy Verone interview, Jan. 27, 2004.

67 On Sundays, TR would take: Hagedorn, p. 136.

67 He had the wound bandaged: Naylor, p. 22.

68 His range of interests was immense: Hagedorn, p. 160.

68 "He stood at the divide": Alan Brinkley and Davis Dyer, eds., *The American Presidency.* Boston: Houghton Mifflin Company, 2004, essay by Michael McGerr, p. 268.

69 Mrs. Roosevelt chastised her husband: Hagedorn, pp. 181–182.

69 The next morning: Hagedorn, p. 154.

69 It might have made a difference: Morris, p. 123.

69 In still another situation, a stranger made: Amy Verone interview.

69 On September 3, 1902: Hagedorn, p. 166.

70 Young Theodore liked to ride: Hermann Hagedorn and Gary G. Roth, *Sagamore Hill: An Historical Guide.* Oyster Bay, N.Y.: Theodore Roosevelt Association, 1977, 1993, p. 11.

70 While he was in college: Naylor, p. 14.

70 "I love all these children": Lewis L. Gould, *The Presidency of Theodore Roosevelt.* Lawrence, Kan.: University Press of Kansas, 1991, p. 5.

70 He named: Hagedorn and Roth, p. 12.

70 At first: Regina M. Bellavia and George W. Curry, *Cultural Landscape Report for Sagamore Hill National Historic Site.* Brookline, Mass.: Olmsted Center for Landscape Preservation, 2003, pp. 1, 17. See also Naylor, pp. 15–20.

70 But it was never a profitable: Bellavia and Curry, p. 17.

70 The 23-room Victorian house: Gluck, p. 9.

71 TR usually had a full-time staff: Naylor, p. 20.

71 TR left his books, his papers: Amy Verone interview.

71 "Every morning Edie": Amy Verone interview.

71 His finances: Amy Verone interview.

72 During haying, he would: Naylor, p. 20.

72 "He had a habit of": Naylor, pp. 30–31.

72 "Quentin and his schoolmates": Gould, p. 103.

73 "The children do have an ideal time": Hagedorn, pp. 174–175.

73 Roosevelt jumped: Kathleen Dalton, *Theodore Roosevelt: A Strenuous Life.* New York: Alfred A. Knopf, 2002, p. 219.

73 He watched their theatrical: Hagedorn, p. 175.

73 Secretary of State John Hay: George Sullivan, *The Presidents at Play.* New York: Walker and Company, 1995, p. 103.

74 "I want you to know all the facts": Morris, p. 123.

74 If a reporter's coverage displeased him: Morris, p. 124.

75 A cartoon depicted the incident: Gould, p. 104.

75 In fact, McKinley's: Hagedorn, pp. 169–170. Also Gluck, p. 19.

75 To protect TR: Gluck, p. 19.

75 And the president's 14-year-old son: Hagedorn, p. 169.

76 She would scan: Dalton, p. 218.

76 She lived at a time when: Dalton, p. 251.

76 She worked hard to keep: Dalton, p. 253.

77 Edith also was worried about: Dalton, p. 327.

77 Whenever the couple tried to relax: Dalton, p. 329.

78 Kaneko never forgot the experience: Hagedorn, pp. 215–216.

78 He felt that Portsmouth would be an excellent venue: Morris, pp. 402–403.

79 During the most delicate phase: Morris, p. 413.

79 "I've had many a splendid day's": Hagedorn and Roth, p. 26.

80 "Theodore Roosevelt, the peacemaker": Quotes in Gluck, p. 232.

80 A treaty was signed: Gould, pp. 186–188.

81 "It's queer. I never appreciated": Hagedorn, p. 242.

81 "Sagamore is our own home": Hagedorn, p. 279.

Chapter Seven: Franklin D. Roosevelt and Hyde Park, New York, and Warm Springs, Georgia

83 "Franklin Delano Roosevelt's": Eleanor Roosevelt, *Franklin D. Roosevelt and Hyde Park: Personal Recollections of Eleanor Roosevelt.* National Park Service, U.S. Department of the Interior, 1977, p. 1.

83 "From the time he was": Eleanor Roosevelt, pp. 7–8.

84 FDR described himself as: Bill Harris, *Homes of the Presidents*. Wayne, N.J.: CLB, 1997, p. 143.

84 He had a substantial: Elliott Roosevelt and James Brough, *An Untold Story: The Roosevelts of Hyde Park*. New York: G. P. Putnam's Sons, 1973, p. 31. See also Jon Meacham, *Franklin and Winston: An Intimate Portrait of an Epic Friendship*. New York: Random House, 2003, p. 297.

84 "It is the government's first duty to keep people from starving," he said: Harris, p. 145.

85 FDR's frequent trips: These figures were provided by the Roosevelt National Historic Site, Hyde Park, N.Y. Other estimates vary.

85 Once he boarded the train: Doris Kearns Goodwin, *No Ordinary Time: Franklin and Eleanor Roosevelt: The Home Front in World War II*. New York: Simon & Schuster, 1994, pp. 112, 72. Also author's interview with park historian Diane Boyce, Jan. 24, 2004.

85 "This was the place": Goodwin, pp. 73, 74.

85 "I think I picked up": Goodwin, p. 419.

86 In the evenings: Meacham, p. 229.

86 Even though the property: Moses Smith, oral history, Jan. 15, 1948, available at FDR Library, Hyde Park, N.Y.

86 The highlight was his annual reading: Goodwin, p. 568.

86 "As we sit quietly": Conrad Black, *Franklin Delano Roosevelt: Champion of Freedom*. New York: Public Affairs, 2003, pp. 1020–1021.

87 He was worried about the outcome: Meacham, p. 76.

87 One summer, he took a drive: Moses Smith, oral history, Jan. 15, 1948, available at FDR Library, Hyde Park, N.Y.

87 On June 19, 1942: Meacham, p. 181.

88 Both FDR and Churchill: Meacham, pp. 182–183.

88 Churchill wanted: Meacham, pp. 232–233.

89 When their conference: Goodwin, p. 546.

89 "The suggestion that the world": Meacham, p. 303.

89 President Theodore Roosevelt gave the bride away at the wedding: Elliott Roosevelt and James Brough, pp. 27–28.

90 She believed fully: Elliott Roosevelt and James Brough, p. 7.

90 She once punished: Eleanor Roosevelt, p. 7.

90 "Nothing is more": Goodwin, p. 150.

90 They developed a strong mutual attraction: Meacham, p. 23.

90 "He had become": Elliott Roosevelt, p. 89.

91 "This, she told him": Elliott Roosevelt, pp. 92–93.

91 "At one level, the marriage": Alan Brinkley and Davis Dyer, eds., *The American Presidency*. Boston: Houghton Mifflin Company, 2004, essay by Mark H. Leff, p. 347.

91 "Sara meant to dominate": Meacham, pp. 22–23.

92 "For good reason, Mother": Elliott Roosevelt and James Brough, p. 97.

92 FDR and his mother: Elliott Roosevelt, pp. 99–100.

92 "If any of us had": Elliott Roosevelt and James Brough, pp. 99–100.

92 They added two wings: Harris p. 147.

92 Sara made sure: Elliott Roosevelt, p. 7.

93 He associated the estate: Meacham, pp. 180–181.

93 Eleanor admitted the furniture looked: Eleanor Roosevelt, p. 17.

94 "I found that on my trips": John G. Waite, Associates, Architects, *The President as Architect: Franklin D. Roosevelt's Top Cottage*. Albany, N.Y.: Mount Ida Press, 2001, p. 17.

94 He designed the place: Waite, p. 7.

94 He had a servant set up: Waite, p. 8.

95 She made him promise: Waite, p. 7.

95 The king asked: Waite, p. 7.

95 "Roosevelt never denied": Hugh Gregory Gallagher, *FDR's Splendid Deception: The moving story of Roosevelt's massive disability—and the intense efforts to conceal it from the public*. Arlington, Va.: Vandamere Press, 1994, p. 145.

95 Until he contracted the disease: Gallagher, p. 2.

96 A chauffeur drove him: Turnley Walker, *Roosevelt and the Warm Springs Story*. New York: A. A. Wyn, 1953, pp. 5–9.

96 In October 1924: Doris Kearns Goodwin, p. 116.

97 FDR spent most Thanksgivings there: Theo Lippman, Jr., *The Squire of Warm Springs: FDR in Georgia 1924–1945*. Chicago: Playboy Press, 1977, pp. 12–13.

97 He didn't get there: Lippman, pp. 243–244. Figures on FDR's visits were also provided by the Roosevelt Warm Springs Institute for Rehabilitation.

97 It became even more: Robert F. Cross, *Sailor in the White House: The Seafaring Life of FDR*. Annapolis, Md.: Naval Institute Press, 2003, p. 110.

98 "If you had spent": Harris, p. 145.

99 He recognized that: Lippman, pp. 232–233.

99 Eleanor said her husband: Lippman, pp. 80–81.

99 "Roosevelt's paralysis": Gallagher, p. 214.

100 "Down here at Warm Springs": Lippman, p. 140.

100 "Fourteen years ago,": Cross, p. 111. See also Lippman, p. 143.

100 The agent and his: Lippman, p. 97.

101 He had firebreaks cut: Lippman, pp. 123–124.

101 But throughout FDR's: Lippman pp. 114–115.

101 "And even at Warm Springs": Walker, pp. 266–267.

101 "As soon as": Kati Marton, *Hidden Power: Presidential Marriages That Shaped Our Recent History*. New York: Pantheon Books, 2001, p. 80.

102 "Lucy was the woman he turned to": Elliott Roosevelt and James Brough, p. 325.

102 Eleanor, for whom the day was: Marton, p. 83.

102 When aide Grace Tully: Goodwin p. 598.

103 He went to Easter services: Theo Lippman, *The Squire of Warm Springs: FDR in Georgia 1924–1945*. Chicago: Playboy Press, 1977, p. 238.

103 He was reading a new: Meacham, p. 337.

103 He also relished: Meacham, pp. 337–338.

103 "I get the gruel &": Suckley, p. 408.

103 The president "relapsed": Geoffrey C. Ward, ed., *Closest Companion: The Unknown Story of the Intimate Friendship between Franklin Roosevelt and Margaret Suckley*. Boston: Houghton Mifflin Company, 1995, pp. 410–412.

104 "We have fifteen minutes more": Ward, p. 418. See also Meacham, pp. 342–343.

104 He died at 3:35 P.M.: Ward, p. 418. Lippman, pp. 239–240.

Chapter Eight: Harry Truman and Independence, Missouri, and Key West, Florida

106 In 1887, they moved: Harry S. Truman, *Memoirs by Harry S. Truman, Volume One: Year of Decisions*. Garden City, N.Y., Doubleday & Company, 1955, p. 115.

106 "Usually there were goats": *Truman Memoirs, Volume One*, pp. 117–118.

106 "Independence was southern": David McCullough, *Truman*. New York: A Touchstone Book, 1992, p. 50.

106 Everyone attended church: McCullough, p. 51.

106 Blacks were clustered: McCullough, p. 53.

107 More broadly, Harry learned: McCullough, p. 54.

107 "It was Martha Truman": Alan Brinkley and Davis Dyer, eds., *The American Presidency*, essay by David M. Oshinsky. Boston: Houghton Mifflin Company, 2004, pp. 365–366.

107 "I sit here in this": McCullough, pp. 397–398.

107 "I'm always so lonesome": McCullough, p. 398.

108 "I have nothing": Kati Marton, *Hidden Power: Presidential Marriages That Shaped Our Recent History*. New York: Pantheon Books, 2001, p. 90.

108 "A woman's place": Marton, p. 90.

108 The Trumans' daughter: Laura Vernon, ed., *Harry Truman Slept Here: A glimpse*

at the Trumans' private life in Independence, Missouri. Independence, Mo.: Posy Publications, 1985, p. 5.

108 "I had learned": Harry S. Truman, *Memoirs by Harry S. Truman, Volume Two: Years of Trial and Hope, 1946–1952,* p. 361.

109 "I guess you couldn't": Marton, p. 93.

109 "You can never appreciate": Marton, pp. 93–94.

109 Bess did serve as: Marton, pp. 99, 100–101.

109 One of Bess's and Madge's few concessions: Author's interview with Dave Schafer, former park ranger and historian at the Harry Truman Historic Site, Independence, Mo., Feb. 18, 2004.

110 "In my generation": Truman, *Memoirs, Volume Two,* pp. 331–333.

111 "You mustn't get": Vernon, p. 44.

111 "You should call": p. 45.

111 During his famous: Vernon, p. 45.

111 She had wanted: Vernon, p. 9.

111 He was often asked: Vernon, p. 10.

112 "I eat what I like": Vernon, p. 39.

112 His main course: Vernon, p. 40. Also, author's interview with Dave Schafer, Feb. 18, 2004.

112 "We are going to leave that fence": Vernon, p. 7.

113 "When a man": Vernon, pp. 13, 14.

113 "He has always": Vernon, p. 18.

114 In all, he spent a total: Author's interview with Bob Wolz, executive director of the Harry Truman Little White House Museum, Key West, Fla., Feb. 27, 2004.

114 He rarely used: Robert B. Landry, Air Force aide to President Truman, oral history, Feb. 28, 1974, available at Truman Library and Museum, Independence, Mo.

114 Once he read in a newspaper story: Frank Holeman, former reporter for *The New York Daily News,* oral history, June 9, 1987, available at Truman Library and Museum, Independence, Mo.

114 "I believe the outstanding": Clark Clifford, special counsel to the president, oral history, Feb. 14, 1973, available at Truman Library and Museum, Independence, Mo.

115 Offices were established: Margaret Truman, *Harry S. Truman.* New York: Pocket Books, 1974, p. 352.

115 One of his celebrated: Mary Lou Nolan, "Harry's other house worn by burdens of office, Truman went to Key West to restore body and spirit," *Kansas City Star,* May 24, 1992, T p. 1.

115 Mail pouches were flown: George M. Elsey, former administrative assistant to

the president, oral history, July 9, 1970, available at Truman Library and Museum, Independence, Mo.

115 The First Lady saw it: Michael A. Schuman, "Little White House, Truman's Hideaway," *The Record*, Northern New Jersey, Dec. 5, 1999, p. TO1.

115 Bess said it looked like: Bob Wolz interview.

115 A firm of decorators from Miami: Admiral Robert L. Dennison, oral history, Sept. 10, 1971, available at Truman Library.

116 On one trip: Admiral Robert L. Dennison, naval aide to President Truman, oral history, Oct. 6, 1971, available at Truman Library.

116 "It was time somebody rebuked": John Hersey, *Key West Tales*. New York: Vintage Books, 1993, pp. 223–227.

117 Once he lost his glasses: Charles S. Murphy, administrative assistant and special counsel to President Truman, oral history, available at Truman Library.

117 Meanwhile, if Bess was there: Wolz interview.

117 He enjoyed taking cruises: Wolz interview.

117 After completing: Hersey, pp. 224–225.

118 Since the game: Robert B. Landry, Air Force aide to President Truman, oral history, Feb. 28, 1974, available at Truman Library and Museum, Independence, Mo. The higher figure of $100 comes from Robert G. Nixon, former news correspondent with International News Service, oral history available at Truman Library.

118 Clifford said Truman: Clark Clifford, special counsel to the president, oral history, Feb. 14, 1973, available at Truman Library and Museum, Independence, Mo.

118 In fact, Truman told: Admiral Robert L. Dennison, Truman's naval aide, oral history, Sept. 10, 1971, and Oct. 6, 1971, available at Truman Library.

118 In November 1946: Clifford, Feb. 14, 1973.

118 The Navy generally brought: Robert G. Nixon, oral history, Truman Library.

119 "Oh, that's all right": George M. Elsey, oral history, July 9, 1970, available at Truman Library and Museum, Independence, Mo.

119 After it became clear: William M. Rigdon, assistant naval aide at the White House, oral history, July 16, 1970, available at the Truman Library and Museum, Independence, Mo.

119 Once some photographers: Rigdon, oral history.

119 "Wish you and Margie": Stuart McIver, "Florida's State Visits," *The Sun-Sentinel*: Fort Lauderdale, Fla., Jan. 19, 1997.

120 "Dear Bess: This place": Letter available at Truman Library, Independence, Mo.

121 When members of his: Margaret Truman, *Harry S. Truman*. New York: Pocket Books, 1974, pp. 353–354.

121 His well-publicized trips: Ted Gregory, "Truman's Florida Key West Home Reveals President's Less Serious Side," *Chicago Tribune*, Feb. 8, 1998, p. C9.

Chapter Nine: Dwight Eisenhower and Gettysburg, Pennsylvania

122 "I wanted to take": Videotape exhibit at Eisenhower Farm.

123 The proximity of the battlefield: Author's interview with Carol Hegeman, senior historian at the Eisenhower National Historic Site at Gettysburg, Pa., Dec. 17, 2003.

123 "As I drive between": Dwight D. Eisenhower, *At Ease: Stories I Tell to Friends*. Eastern National, 1967, pp. 43–44.

123 "had three of the most": Susan Eisenhower, *Mrs. Ike: Memories and Reflections on the Life of Mamie Eisenhower*. New York: Farrar, Straus and Giroux, 1996, p. 257.

124 "Because he had no prepared": Dwight D. Eisenhower, p. 358.

124 Using these union workers: Author's interview with Carol Hegeman, Dec. 17, 2003.

124 When the house was finished: Susan Eisenhower, p. 287.

125 "I hate old-lady clothes": Susan Eisenhower, p. 4.

125 "Despite Mamie's penchant": Susan Eisenhower, p. 4.

126 "We say that aside": Special to *The New York Times*, "Butler Deplores President's Trips," *The New York Times*, June 4, 1956.

127 "he had it made": Interview of Mamie Eisenhower with Edwin C. Bearss, recorded Aug. 15, 1973, oral history archive at the Eisenhower National Historic Site, Gettysburg, Pa.

127 "an annex to Gettysburg.": W. Dale Nelson, *The President Is at Camp David*. Syracuse University Press, 1995, p. 36.

127 "Both Eisenhower himself": Alan Brinkley and Davis Dyer, eds., *The American Presidency*, essay by David L. Stebenne. Boston: Houghton Mifflin Company, 2004, p. 380.

128 "For the dearest": Susan Eisenhower, p. 5.

129 "My hands are better": Dwight D. Eisenhower, p. 340.

131 "He never brought": Interview of Mamie Eisenhower with Edwin C. Bearss, recorded Aug. 15, 1973, oral history archive at the Eisenhower National Historic Site, Gettysburg, Pa.

131 Eisenhower also enjoyed cooking: Author's interview with Carol Hegeman, Dec. 17, 2003.

132 Once he made the mistake: Interview with David Eisenhower recorded March 10, 1981, oral history archive at the Eisenhower National Historic Site, Gettysburg, Pa.

133 "If I didn't know": Interview with David Eisenhower recorded March 10, 1981, oral history archive at the Eisenhower National Historic site, Gettysburg, Pa.

Chapter Ten: John F. Kennedy and Hyannisport, Massachusetts

134 "His was an administration": Alan Brinkley and Davis Dyer, *The American Presidency*. Boston: Houghton Mifflin Company, 2004, essay by Michael Kazin, p. 397.

134 "Jack Kennedy subscribed": Sally Bedell Smith, *Grace and Power: The Private World of the Kennedy White House*. New York: Random House, 2004. p. xxix.

135 Mrs. Kennedy particularly liked: Bedell Smith, p. 220.

135 The president made: Author's interview with Allan B. Goodrich, chief archivist at the John F. Kennedy Library and Museum, July 29, 2003.

136 "Hyannisport really is": Author's interview with Senator Edward Kennedy, April 29, 2004.

136 "And I think he": Senator Edward Kennedy interview.

137 "Hyannisport is the name": Theodore H. White, *The Making of the President, 1960*. New York: Atheneum House, Inc., 1961, pp. 6–7.

138 "It looked more like": Arthur Schlesinger, Jr., *A Thousand Days*. Boston: Houghton Mifflin, 1965, p. 62.

138 He quickly began a series: Robert Dallek, *An Unfinished Life: John F. Kennedy, 1917–1963*. Boston: Little, Brown and Company, 2003, p. 277.

139 He walked to his: White, p. 7.

139 Neighbors had a: White, p. 7.

139 He got up about 5 P.M.: White, p. 8.

139 Jackie mostly stayed: Bedell Smith, pp. 4–5.

139 At 10:30 P.M.: Bedell Smith, p. 4.

139 As with most: Bedell Smith, p. 109.

139 At 9:30 A.M.: Bedell Smith, pp. 4–5.

140 "had spread pictures": Michael Beschloss, *The Crisis Years: Kennedy and Khrushchev, 1960–1963*. New York: Edward Burlingame Books, 1991, p. 178.

140 Before leaving Hyannisport: Beschloss, pp. 178–179.

141 "He slept late": Beschloss, p. 235.

141 He told advisers: Beschloss, p. 235.

141 The First Lady slipped into: Beschloss, p. 246.

142 During still another weekend: Beschloss, p. 271.

142 Responding to the congressional: Beschloss, p. 344.

143 Kennedy apparently wanted: Beschloss, p. 346.

143 Despite each side's claim: Beschloss, p. 345.

143 "When Stalin and Churchill": Beschloss, p. 346.

144 "It wasn't the intensity": Senator Edward Kennedy interview, April 29, 2004.

145 There is one memorable scene: These descriptions come from the author's view-

ing of videotapes of home movies saved from the Kennedy era at the John F. Kennedy Museum and Library in Boston. I viewed them during a visit to the complex Sept. 19, 2003.

146 So in 1962: Author's interview with Allan B. Goodrich, chief archivist at the John F. Kennedy Library and Museum, July 29, 2003.

146 "very impatient,": Quoted in George F. Will, "A Man in a Hurry—1963," *The Washington Post*, p. A41, Nov. 20, 2003.

147 "The routine was unvarying": Bedell Smith, p. 219.

147 He would rise: Thurston Clarke, *Ask Not: The Inauguration of John F. Kennedy and the Speech That Changed America*. New York: Henry Holt and Company, 2004, p. 158.

147 One of Kennedy's: Beschloss, p. 312.

148 Despite his wealth, Clarke, p. 37.

148 They often sunbathed: Clarke, pp. 39, 41.

148 When Jack was 12: Beschloss, p. 139.

148 JFK's romps with: Wesley O. Hagood, *Presidential Sex: From the Founding Fathers to Bill Clinton*. New York: A Birch Lane Press Book, 1995, p. 158.

148 During a visit to Palm Springs: Bedell Smith, p. 265.

148 "Behind the scenes": Bedell Smith, p. xxiii.

149 Between her pregnancies: Bedell Smith, p. 110.

149 After dinner: Bedell Smith, p. 248.

150 Jackie, it turns out: Bedell Smith, pp. 110–111.

150 "What would it be": Beschloss, p. 10.

151 Later, the president tried: Kenneth P. O'Donnell and David F. Powers with Joe McCarthy, *"Johnny, We Hardly Knew Ye": Memories of John Fitzgerald Kennedy*. Boston: Little, Brown and Company, 1970, pp. 427–429.

Chapter Eleven: Lyndon B. Johnson and the LBJ Ranch, Texas

152 "Some men want power": Quoted in Alan Brinkley and Davis Dyer, eds., *The American Presidency*. Boston: Houghton Mifflin Company, 2004, essay by Robert Dallek, p. 410.

153 "Lyndon Johnson is an excellent": Brinkley and Dyer, p. 423.

153 He returned to his ranch: Figures provided by Claudia Anderson, senior archivist, LBJ Ranch.

153 This extension allowed: Hal K. Rothman, *LBJ's Texas White House: "Our Heart's Home."* College Station, Tex.: Texas A & M University Press, 2001, pp. 131, 137.

154 one had 24 direct lines: Jack Albright, former commander, White House Communications Agency, oral history, Dec. 11, 1980, p. 40, available at the LBJ Library.

154 Johnson bought the: Author's interview with Dave Schafer, National Park Service ranger and a historian of the LBJ Ranch, Lyndon B. Johnson National Historical Park,

Johnson City, Tex. Dec. 29, 2003. See also Hal K. Rothman, *LBJ's Texas White House: "Our Heart's Home."* College Station, Tex.: Texas A&M University Press, 2001, p. 5.

154 "From that time on": Author's telephone interview with Harry Middleton, Dec. 22, 2003.

154 "I guess every person": Tape recording made available to the author by the LBJ Historic Site, Johnson City, Tex.

155 "It's one place": Frank Cormier, *LBJ: The Way He Was.* Garden City, N.Y.: Doubleday & Company, Inc., 1977, p. 16.

156 "We drove around": Kenneth P. O'Donnell and David F. Powers with Joe McCarthy, *"Johnny, We Hardly Knew Ye": Memories of John Fitzgerald Kennedy.* Boston: Little, Brown and Company, 1970, pp. 259–261.

156 "You two guys": Michael R. Beschloss, *The Crisis Years: Kennedy and Khrushchev, 1960–1963.* New York: Edward Burlingame Books, 1991, p. 669.

156 "The iconography of leadership": Rothman, p. 124.

157 That same day, he: Author's interview with Dave Schafer, Dec. 29, 2003.

157 "If Goldwater had won": Cormier, p. 133.

157 A month after he took office, he: Kati Marton, *Hidden Power: Presidential Marriages That Shaped Our Recent History.* New York: Pantheon Books, 2001, p. 147.

157 "The ranch served as a": Rothman, p. 214.

158 "It was bred in him": Liz Carpenter, oral history, Tape 316, 2, June 7, 1978, available at the LBJ Library.

158 would take his speedboat: Arthur B. Krim, oral history, June 29, 1982, pp. 7–8, available at the LBJ Library.

158 Moments after his plane: Robert Martin, "LBJ's Texas-size monument; Eight-story library-museum was his own memorial," *The Globe and Mail,* Feb. 6, 1982, p. T1.

158 he drove his Lincoln: Mike Howard, a former Secret Service agent at the ranch, oral history, recorded June 6, 1977, available at Lyndon B. Johnson National Historical Park, Johnson City, Tex.

159 He would try to impress: Jack Albright, former commander of the White House Communications Agency, oral history, Dec. 11, 1980, p. 87, available at the LBJ Library.

159 On one occasion, he: Rothman, p. 160.

159 he took perverse pleasure: John L. Bullion, *In the Boat with LBJ.* Plano, Tex.: Republic of Texas Press, 2001, p. 224.

159 "Naw," the president replied: Bullion, p. 224.

159 "Frank, how would you": Cormier, p. 144.

160 The deer had little chance: Bullion, p. 106.

160 At other times, he used: Mike Howard, former Secret Service agent at the ranch,

oral history, recorded June 6, 1977, available at Lyndon B. Johnson Historical Park, Johnson City, Tex.

160 "It was easy for LBJ to": Bullion, p. 105.

160 Without telling his passengers: Jerry Haines, "LBJ's Texas 101," *The Washington Post*, March 30, 2003, p. E02. See also Rothman, pp. 159–160.

160 From then on, Johnson: Mike Howard, former Secret Service agent at the ranch, oral history, recorded June 6, 1977, available at Lyndon B. Johnson Historical Park, Johnson City, Tex.

160 Another habit that: Rothman, p. 205.

161 Sometimes, people would: Rothman, p. 147.

162 "On one occasion": Rothman, p. 163.

162 "one of the finest": Rothman, p. 163.

162 At one point, Johnson conducted: Rothman, p. 157.

163 During the 1964 Christmas season: Rothman, p. 158.

163 "No matter where we were": Arthur B. Krim, oral history, June 29, 1982, pp. 6–7, available at the LBJ Library.

163 (Johnson preferred steaks): Dale Malechek, oral history, tapes 120: 1 and 120: 2, Texas White House.

164 Johnson made it a practice: Bullion, p. 225.

164 "I don't get ulcers": Cormier, p. 138.

164 In Washington, Johnson insisted: Rothman, p. 154.

164 "He was a son of a bitch": Rothman, p. 154.

165 LBJ insisted that his ranch: Rothman, pp. 151–152.

165 The ranch personnel didn't dare: Dale Malechek, ranch foreman, oral history, tapes 120: 1 and 120: 2, Texas White House.

165 "He was fond of": George Reedy, *Lyndon B. Johnson: A Memoir*. New York: Andrews and McMeel, Inc., 1982, p. 154.

166 "Damn it. I don't": Cormier, p. 20.

166 Johnson would sometimes slip: Cormier, p. 136.

166 He asked his more affluent: Liz Carpenter, former aide to Lady Bird Johnson, oral history, tape 316: 1, 2, 3, June 7, 1978.

166 Occasionally, he would: Bullion, pp. 276–278.

167 John L. Bullion recalls: Bullion, p. 199.

167 He once awakened: Jack Albright, oral history, Dec. 11, 1980, pp. 42–45, available at the LBJ Library.

167 Johnson made a secret: Albright, oral history, pp. 80–83.

168 Local farmers said: Richard Severo, "Mexican Farmers Say Johnson Holds a Ranch There Illegally," *The New York Times*, Dec. 31, 1972, p. 66.

169 Johnson also took an interest: Arthur B. Krim, oral history, Oct. 13, 1983, pp. 28–29, available at the LBJ Library.

169 On January 4, 1968: Rothman, pp. 226–227.

169 He would even drive: Roberto Suro, "LBJ Legacy shows trap behind Hill Country's scenic beauty," *The Houston Chronicle; The New York Times* (News Service), June 7, 1992, p. 5.

Chapter Twelve: Richard M. Nixon and San Clemente, California, and Key Biscayne, Florida

173 "Government is not": Stephen E. Ambrose, *Nixon, Volume Two: The Triumph of a Politician 1962–1972*. New York: Simon and Schuster, 1989, p. 371.

173 *La Casa Pacifica*, like: Author's interview with Ken Khachigian, March 29, 2004.

174 "On the personal side": Richard Nixon, *RN: The Memoirs of Richard Nixon*. New York, Grosset & Dunlap 1978, p. 434.

174 The Secret Service formed: John Herbers, "With Nixon on the Coast: The Lighter Side," *The New York Times*, Sept. 3, 1973.

174 "He was not a beach strolling": Author's interview with Ken Khachigian, March 29, 2004.

175 His favorite morning meal: Nixon, p. 1085.

175 In fact, she accepted his: Lael Morgan, "Quiet Days for Casa Pacifica," *The Los Angeles Times*, Orange County Edition, Oct. 16, 1988, p. 84.

175 Every room had: Unbylined Associated Press dispatch, Aug. 15, 1969.

175 Nixon was frequently criticized: Richard Reeves, *President Nixon: Alone in the White House*. New York: Simon & Schuster, 2001, p. 113.

175 He also had the government: Ambrose, p. 294.

176 The house had been built: Ambrose, pp. 294–295.

176 *Time* magazine, like most: "Nixon's Tranquility Base," *Time*, Aug. 29, 1969, p. 11.

176 He would occasionally: Dana Parsons, "The Prodigal President: Nixon's Lasting Hurrah," *The Los Angeles Times*, May 20, 1990, p. 1.

176 Nixon used the occasion: "The Politics of Reconciliation," *Time*, Sept. 5, 1969, pp. 14, 16.

177 "The Nixons gave us": Gerald R. Ford, *A Time to Heal: The Autobiography of Gerald R. Ford*. New York: Harper & Row, 1979, p. 94.

177 Soviet security guards: Lael Morgan, "Quiet Days for Casa Pacifica," *The Los Angeles Times*, Orange County Edition, Oct. 16, 1988, p. 84.

177 "Sometimes our family": Nixon, pp. 538–539.

177 He frequently left: Ambrose, p. 296.

178 "After dropping that": Nixon, pp. 492–493.

178 It had started: Unbylined, "President Roused from Bed as Minor Fire Breaks Out," *The Washington Star*, Oct. 30, 1970.

178 "As far as I knew": Nixon, p. 493.

179 "Violence in America": Nixon, p. 493.

179 In August 1972: Nixon, pp. 653–657.

180 Just after winning: Reeves, p. 58.

180 These properties were: Jeff Kunerth, "Embattled Nixon Found Haven in Central Florida," *The Orlando Sentinel*, April 23, 1994, p. A16.

180 he had the government: Reeves, p. 113.

180 This caused a furor: Reeves, p. 113. See also Bob Woodward and Carl Bernstein, *The Final Days*. New York: A Touchstone Book, 1976, p. 23.

180 he spent $418,000: Reeves, p. 96.

180 And he had a metal fence: Author's interview with Ken Duberstein, Aug. 28, 2003.

180 On average, it cost: Reeves, p. 113.

180 "The caretaker's wife" Nixon, p. 625.

181 "I dismissed it": Nixon, pp. 625–626.

181 He found time: Nixon, pp. 625–626.

181 "The Watergate": Nixon, pp. 626–627.

182 "I am convinced": Nixon, p. 627.

182 Within that compound: Woodward and Bernstein, pp. 29, 32.

182 "Speaking of education": Reeves, p. 122.

183 Commerce Secretary Maurice Stans: Reeves, p. 122.

183 Nixon probed for information: Reeves, pp. 417–418.

183 For example, he made sure: Wallace Turner, "Nixon Presence Felt, Not Seen, at San Clemente," *The New York Times*, July 11, 1972.

183 The day after his reelection: Stephen E. Ambrose, *Nixon, Volume Three: Ruin and Recovery 1973–1990*. New York : Simon & Schuster, 1991, pp. 14–15.

184 On November 10, he ordered: Ambrose, *Nixon, Volume Three*, p. 17.

184 On November 15, he told: Ambrose, *Nixon, Volume Three*, pp. 17–18.

185 Senator William Saxbe: Ambrose, *Nixon, Volume Three*, p. 41.

185 Anthony Lewis said Nixon: Nixon, p. 738.

185 "It is inevitable that": Nixon, p. 740.

186 As 1972 ended: Ambrose, *Nixon, Volume Three,* pp. 44–46.

186 On January 11: Nixon, pp. 764–765.

187 "Nixon fell," writes author Roger Morris: Alan Brinkley and Davis Dyer, eds., *The American Presidency*. Boston: Houghton Mifflin Company, 2004, essay by Roger Morris, p. 439.

Chapter Thirteen: Gerald Ford and Vail, Colorado

189 "We were as full of": Author's telephone interview with Gerald Ford, Jan. 21, 2004.

190 "While he was in": David Gergen, *Eyewitness to Power: The Essence of Leadership, Nixon to Clinton*. New York: Simon & Schuster, 2000, p. 109.

190 "Until he spared Nixon": Gergen, pp. 126–127.

190 "The Fords had a tradition": Author's interview with Ron Nessen, Jan. 20, 2004.

190 In 1973: Robert T. Hartmann, *Palace Politics: An Inside Account of the Ford Years*. New York: McGraw Hill, 1980, pp. 98–99.

191 "Old habits had to be": Betty Ford, *The Times of My Life*. New York: Ballantine Books, 1979, p. 169.

191 "The Bass home is a": James P. Sterba, "It's Not Exactly a 'Winter White House' . . ." *The New York Times*, Jan. 1, 1975, p. 28.

191 "Mr. Ford and": Associated Press dispatch, "President Plays Tennis and Golf in Colorado," *The New York Times*, Aug. 18, 1975, p. 23.

192 "I flew to Vail" : Gerald R. Ford, *A Time to Heal: The Autobiography of Gerald R. Ford*. New York: Harper & Row, 1979, pp. 343–344.

192 "I never publicly": Author's telephone interview with Gerald Ford, Jan. 21, 2004.

193 And he devised: Author's interview with Gerald Ford, Jan. 21, 2004.

193 the Wilson home was: John Herbers, "Ford Plays Golf; Sees Oil Facility," *The New York Times*, April 1, 1975.

194 "In better times, Ford's week": Sandra Salmans with Thomas M. DeFrank, *Newsweek*, April 14, 1975, p. 37.

194 "Would it prevent anything?": Sandra Salmans with Thomas M. DeFrank, *Newsweek*, April 14, 1975, p. 38.

194 "It's important": Author's telephone interview with Gerald Ford, Jan. 21, 2004.

195 Vail was also associated: Betty Ford, pp. 232–236.

196 "The voters, in my opinion": Ford, *A Time to Heal*, p. 410.

196 "If we could": Ford, *A Time to Heal*, pp. 412–413.

197 "That was the most special moment": Ford, *A Time to Heal*, pp. 432–433.

197 They also wanted: Betty Ford, p. 297.

Chapter Fourteen: Jimmy Carter and Plains, Georgia

200 "Plains has always": Author's interview with Jimmy Carter, March 7, 2004.

200 "[W]hen Jimmy and I": Rosalynn Carter, *First Lady from Plains*. Fayetteville, Ark.: University of Arkansas Press, 1994, p. 33.

201 "From mid-August": Rosalynn Carter, p. 34.

201 Jimmy, drawing on his: Rosalynn Carter, p. 42.

201 He told me in an interview: Author's interview with Jimmy Carter, March 7, 2004.

202 He addressed 600: Helen Dewar, "Carter Weeps at Plains Homecoming," *The Washington Post*, Nov. 4, 1976, p. A1.

202 "I had never had": Rosalynn Carter, pp. 160–161.

203 A frustrated Carter: Hedrick Smith, *The Power Game: How Washington Works*. New York: Ballantine Books, 1988, p. 89.

203 "It was a place of": Author's interview with Jimmy Carter, March 7, 2004.

204 "It's my most productive": Author's interview with Jimmy Carter, March 7, 2004.

204 "We staked him out": Peter Hannaford, *Ronald Reagan and His Ranch: The Western White House, 1981–1989*. Bennington, Vt.: Images from the Past, 2002, p. 86.

204 During his first: Edward Walsh, "Carter at Home—Nostalgia and Softball," *The Washington Post*, Aug. 10, 1977.

205 But Carter preferred: Unbylined, Associated Press dispatch, Sept. 30, 1977.

205 "I went downtown": Jimmy Carter, *Christmas in Plains*. New York: Simon & Schuster, 2001, pp. 110–111.

206 "Things in Plains": Jimmy Carter, pp. 111–112.

206 On Christmas Eve: Jimmy Carter, p. 119.

206 At one point, Carter's 9-year-old: Jimmy Carter, pp. 113–114.

207 Carter describes: Jimmy Carter, p. 115.

207 "I never looked on my work": Author's interview with Jimmy Carter, March 7, 2004.

208 "When Jimmy lost": Rosalynn Carter, p. 379.

208 They also travel widely: Rosalynn Carter, p. 380.

Chapter Fifteen: Ronald Reagan and *Rancho del Cielo*, California

210 "Ronald Reagan . . . seemed": Alan Brinkley and Davis Dyer, eds., *The American Presidency*, essay by Gil Troy. Boston: Houghton Mifflin Company, 2004, p. 476.

210 "It certainly didn't live": Kenneth T. Walsh and Lynn Rosellini, "Home on the Range," *U.S. News & World Report*, June 5, 2004, p. 71.

210 "*Rancho del Cielo* can make": Peter Hannaford, *Ronald Reagan and His Ranch: The Western White House, 1981–1989*. Bennington, Vt.: Images from the Past, Inc., 2002, p. ix.

210 "Some place along": Kiron K. Skinner, Annelise Anderson, and Martin Anderson, eds., *Reagan: A Life in Letters*. New York: Free Press, 2003, p. 68.

212 Reagan would later write: Hannaford, pp. 30–31

213 The Secret Service: Hannaford, p. 59.

213 "We did receive": Hannaford, p. 62.

213 An unusual feature: Hannaford, p. 43.

215 On September 8, 1983: Hannaford, p. 74.

216 "[You] could forget the world": Hannaford, p. 73.

217 "One year," recalls: Peter Hannaford, ed., *Recollections of Reagan: A Portrait of Ronald Reagan.* New York: William Morrow and Company, Inc., 1997, p. 157.

218 "We spent quite a lot": Hannaford, *Recollections*, pp. 19–20.

218 "He attributed his": Hannaford, *Recollections*, p. 45.

218 "There were times when the president": Larry Speakes with Robert Pack, *Speaking Out: Inside the Reagan White House.* New York: Charles Scribner's Sons, 1988, p. 110.

218 "Ronnie is so happy there!": Ronald Reagan Presidential Foundation and Tehabi Books, New York: Dorling Kindersley Publishing, Inc., *Ronald Reagan: An American Hero.* Tehabi Books, 2001, p. 218.

219 Desperate for visuals: Larry Speakes with Robert Pack, *Speaking Out: The Reagan Presidency from Inside the White House.* New York: Charles Scribner's Sons, 1988, pp. 110–111.

219 "Dear Sam, Here's": Peter Hannaford, *Recollections*, p. 43.

220 "At the top of my list": Nancy Reagan, *I Love You, Ronnie: The Letters of Ronald Reagan to Nancy Reagan.* New York: Random House, 2000, p. 145.

220 "I'm . . . crazy about the girl": Nancy Reagan, *I Love You, Ronnie*, p. 157.

Chapter Sixteen: George Herbert Walker Bush and Kennebunkport, Maine

223 "Walker's Point always": Barbara Bush, *Barbara Bush: A Memoir.* New York: Charles Scribner's Sons, 1994, p. 170.

224 The family quickly: Barbara Bush, pp. 438–440.

224 "It was devastating": Author's interview with George H. W. Bush, Feb. 20, 2004.

224 "By the time we": Marlin Fitzwater, *Call the Briefing!* New York: Times Books, 1995, pp. 371–372.

224 In August 1991: Michael Duffy and Dan Goodgame, *Marching in Place: The Status Quo Presidency of George Bush.* New York: Simon & Schuster, 1992, p. 42.

224 "Kennebunkport gave him a sense": Author's interview with Roman Popadiuk, July 30, 2003.

225 While he was vice president: Kenneth T. Walsh, *Feeding the Beast: The White House Versus the Press.* Philadelphia, Pa.: Xlibris Corp., 2002, p. 80.

225 "He kept it full-throttle": Fitzwater, *Call the Briefing!*, p. 373.

225 Fitzwater recalls trolling: Fitzwater, pp. 373–374.

226 The younger Bush, who: Author's interview with President George W. Bush, Dec. 30, 2003.

226 Kennebunkport was where: Many friends of the Bush family made these points over the years as I was covering George Bush's presidency and the presidency of his son, George W. Bush. Also see Richard Ben Cramer, *What It Takes*. New York, Vintage Books, 1993, pp. 22–23.

226 In our interview, Barbara said: Author's interview with George H. W. Bush and Barbara Bush, Feb. 20, 2004.

228 He made a habit: Barbara Bush, *Reflections: Life After the White House*. New York: A Lisa Drew Book/Scribner, 2003, p. 121.

228 "Suddenly we looked": Barbara Bush, *Barbara Bush: A Memoir*, p. 293.

228 Entertaining: Barbara Bush, *Barbara Bush: A Memoir*, p. 294.

229 "They got to know": George H. W. Bush and Barbara Bush interview, Feb. 20, 2004.

229 "We can sleep": Barbara Bush, *Reflections*, p. 122.

229 In her role as taskmaster: Barbara Bush, *Reflections*, p. 122.

230 Bush told aides: Duffy and Goodgame, pp. 182–184.

230 "I didn't want to panic": George H. W. Bush interview, Feb. 20, 2004.

231 Fitzwater even asked him: Marlin Fitzwater, oral history, May 15, 2001, transcript of Miller Center of Public Affairs, Charlottesville, Va., p. 140.

231 At dawn on August 23: This account is drawn from my own reporting at the time. For a fuller summary, see Walsh, *Feeding the Beast*, pp. 102–103. Also see Duffy and Goodgame, pp. 150–152.

234 On August 11, 1992: Peter Schweizer and Rochelle Schweizer, *The Bushes: Portrait of a Dynasty*. New York: Doubleday, 2004, pp. 242–243, 403.

234 "I'm not going to take": Schweizer and Schweizer, p. 403.

235 "Yeah," Bush replied: Walsh, *Feeding the Beast*, p. 80.

236 On one morning, the new: Barbara Bush, *Reflections*, p. 240.

236 As the commander in chief: Schweizer and Schweizer, p. 510.

Chapter Seventeen: Bill Clinton and Martha's Vineyard, Massachusetts

237 "When he reached": David Gergen, *Eyewitness to Power: The Essence of Leadership, Nixon to Clinton*. New York: Simon & Schuster, 2000, p. 262.

237 "The world was his vacation": Author's interview with Terry McAuliffe, Sept. 16, 2003.

238 He frequently: Author's interview with Bill Clinton, Oct. 29, 2004.

238 "He was a man defined": Author's interview with Joe Lockhart, Jan. 7, 2004.

240 Dick Morris, Clinton's pollster: Dick Morris, *Behind the Oval Office: Winning the Presidency in the Nineties*. New York: Random House, 1997, p. 236.

240 "One of the nicest": Bill Clinton interview.

241 In the end: Elizabeth Drew, *On the Edge: The Clinton Presidency*. New York: Simon & Schuster, 1994, pp. 290–292.

241 "Clinton loved his": Drew, p. 292.

242 "I am convinced that we are": Drew, p. 293.

244 "He liked the Vineyard": Author's interview with Joe Lockhart, Sept. 4, 2003.

244 "Things I might have": Author's interview with Bill Galston, Aug. 25, 2003.

245 "Senior staff would regard": Bill Galston interview.

245 "These [bad] moods were": Morris, pp. 242–243.

245 Morris even tested: Morris, p. 237.

245 "This advice was": Morris, p. 238.

246 "I hadn't camped": Hillary Rodham Clinton, *Living History*. New York: Simon & Schuster, 2003, p. 301.

246 In the summer of: Morris, p. 239.

247 "At the outset of his": Alan Brinkley and Davis Dyer, eds., *The American Presidency*. Boston: Houghton Mifflin Company, 2004, essay by Matthew Dickinson, p. 500.

249 He felt that he couldn't: Peter Baker, *The Breach: Inside the Impeachment and Trial of William Jefferson Clinton*. New York: Scribner, 2000, pp. 46–50, 56.

249 To lessen the strain: Baker, p. 56.

250 "The last thing in": Hillary Rodham Clinton, p. 468.

250 "By the time we settled": Hillary Rodham Clinton, p. 469.

250 Clinton recalls: Bill Clinton interview.

251 His wife recalls: Hillary Rodham Clinton, p. 469.

251 His staff "looked around": Baker, p. 55.

251 "All of you know": Baker, pp. 55–56.

252 "By the end of August": Hillary Rodham Clinton, p. 471.

253 At a joint fund-raiser: Katharine Q. Seelye, "For Vacationing Clintons, a Flavor of Old Times," *The New York Times*, Aug. 22, 1999, p. 30.

Chapter Eighteen: George W. Bush and Prairie Chapel Ranch, Texas

254 "There's nothing like": Author's interview with President George W. Bush, Dec. 30, 2003.

255 By August 2004: Compilation by Mark Knoller, CBS News.

255 On May 22, 2004: Deb Riechmann, Associated Press dispatch, May 22, 2004.

257 "Obviously, I love Texas": White House transcript, George W. Bush's roundtable interview with British print journalists, Nov. 12, 2003.

257 First Lady Laura Bush: Author's telephone interview with Laura Bush, Oct. 14, 2003.

257 "I think we get": Laura Bush interview.

258 "We do love to": Laura Bush interview.

258 "Everyone needs": Author's interview with Reed Dickens, Oct. 13, 2003.

258 "First and foremost": Author's interview with Ari Fleischer, Aug. 22, 2003.

258 The Bushes paid: Claudia Feldman, "Crawford," *Texas Magazine of The Houston Chronicle*, Feb. 11, 2001, p. 6.

258 "The Bushes told": Feldman, p. 6.

258 Heymann came up: Laurence McQuillan with Judy Keen, " 'Texas White House' a refuge from stress; Bush family ranch is an eco-friendly 'haven,' " *USA Today*, April 13, 2001, p. A1.

259 "All he really": Feldman, p. 6.

259 "He can be a": Author's interview with Dan Bartlett, Sept. 11, 2003.

261 "The president": David E. Sanger, "When Goals Meet Reality," *The New York Times*, March 31, 2004, p. A1.

262 At 5:30 A.M. the next day: Author's interview with George H. W. Bush and Barbara Bush, Feb. 20, 2004.

262 "I will get Laura coffee": President George W. Bush interview.

263 Improving the property: Author's interview with Scott McClellan, July 31, 2003.

263 "Cutting brush": Mark Leibovich, "Let's Get One Thing Clear; Presidents Brush Up Their Images With This Chore," *The Washington Post*, Aug. 18, 2002, p. F01.

264 "Fundamentally he": Author's interview with Noam Neusner, Aug. 12, 2003.

265 "He likes sweating": Noam Neusner interview.

266 "It's natural for": Author's interview with Anne Lewis, June 19, 2003.

266 "There are only three": Ari Fleischer interview.

270 Bush summed up: President George W. Bush interview.

Chapter Nineteen: Camp David

273 At a cost of about $2 million: Ruth Marcus, "For Clinton, Camp David Is a Rarely Used Retreat," *The Washington Post*, Nov. 25, 1993.

273 "It is a beautiful place": Author's interview with President George W. Bush, Dec. 30, 2003.

273 President Reagan once said he got "a little stir-crazy": Associated Press dispatch, "Presidential View on White House," *The New York Times*, Sept. 27, 1983.

273 "Just as we did": Tehabi Books and the Ronald Reagan Presidential Foundation, *Ronald Reagan: An American Hero*. New York: Dorling Kindersley Publishing, Inc., 2001, pp. 222–223.

273 "Thank God for": Tehabi Books, pp. 218, 224.

274 Roosevelt, whose legs: For more details on the early site, see the excellent account

in W. Dale Nelson, *The President Is at Camp David*. Syracuse University Press, 1995, pp. 6–7.

275 "Reporters who covered": Nelson, p. 95.

275 He routinely stayed in bed: Nelson, p. 10.

275 Few of the 20 buildings: Nelson, p. 16.

276 Shangri-la was run: Robert F. Cross, *Sailor in the White House: The Seafaring Life of FDR*. Annapolis, Md.: Naval Institute Press, 2003, p. 152.

277 Early one Sunday: Cross, pp. 149–150.

277 On one occasion: Nelson, p. 20.

277 Bess Truman, the First Lady: Nelson, p. 23.

278 He had the buildings winterized: Nelson, p. 26.

278 "Like the fictional": David Eisenhower, in Foreword to Nelson, pp. xi–xii.

279 Eisenhower also: Nelson, p. 39.

280 Among the movies: Nelson, p. 39.

280 By 1958: Nelson, p. 35.

280 At first, the bombastic: Nelson, p. 43.

281 At lunch, Khrushchev: Nelson, p. 47.

281 At the end of the visit: Nelson, p. 48.

281 "I have heard this expression": Nelson, p. 49.

283 Sometimes he would tour: Author's interview with Senator Edward Kennedy, April 29, 2004.

283 Lyndon Johnson's first: Nelson, p. 61.

284 "It will ruin us": Nelson, p. 59.

284 He let his beagles: Nelson, p. 64.

285 "In the mountains": Richard Reeves, *President Nixon: Alone in the White House*. New York: Simon & Schuster, 2001, p. 97.

285 Early on, White House Chief: Nelson, p. 70.

285 It turned out: Reeves, p. 96.

285 Even the bomb shelter: Nelson, pp. 83–84.

285 Haldeman said: Nelson, p. 71.

286 For example: Reeves, pp. 98–99.

287 On a weekend in: Richard Nixon, *RN: The Memoirs of Richard Nixon*. New York: Grosset & Dunlap, 1978, p. 504.

287 "One of the reasons": Nelson, p. 75.

287 In August 1972: Jonathan D. Salant, "Tapes: Nixon Called Reagan 'Strange,'" Associated Press dispatch, Dec. 10, 2003.

288 At about the time: Nelson, p. 76.

288 By October: Nelson, p. 86.

288 He took Haldeman: Reeves, pp. 546–547.

289 He also wanted: Stephen E. Ambrose, *Nixon, Volume Three: Ruin and Recovery 1973–1990.* New York: Simon & Schuster, 1991, p. 19.

289 "I find that": Reeves, p. 349. Also see Nelson, p. 77.

289 During this time: Reeves, pp. 552–553, 554.

290 Brezhnev also had: Nelson pp. 80–81.

290 During May 1972: Reeves, p. 593.

291 "When I got": H. R. Haldeman, *The Haldeman Diaries: Inside the Nixon White House.* New York : G. P. Putnam's Sons, 1994, p. 672.

291 "I have to": Haldeman, p. 672.

291 Then the two men: Nixon, p. 847.

291 Next it was Ehrlichman's turn: Reeves, pp. 600–601.

291 "I wish I were" he said: Reeves, p. 602.

292 Nixon later said: Nelson, p. 94.

292 He visited the camp: Nelson, p. 104.

293 One afternoon in July 1978: Rosalynn Carter, *First Lady from Plains.* Fayetteville, Ark.: University of Arkansas Press, 1994, p. 258.

293 "I don't think": Author's interview with President Jimmy Carter, March 7, 2004.

294 Sadat asked: Rosalynn Carter, p. 257.

294 "I am very much": Nelson, pp. 120–121.

294 Carter told me: Jimmy Carter interview.

295 "A president": Nelson, p. 129.

295 In all, Carter would: Nelson, p. 130.

296 On one skiing: Nelson, p. 132.

296 Carter also made secret escapes: Jimmy Carter interview.

298 Reagan would: Author's interview with Ken Duberstein, Feb. 13, 2004.

298 "Ronnie enjoyed": Nancy Reagan, *I Love You, Ronnie: The Letters of Ronald Reagan to Nancy Reagan.* New York: Random House, 2000, pp. 143–144.

299 Reagan visited: Nelson, p. 135.

301 "When I came": George Bush, *All the Best, George Bush: My Life in Letters and Other Writings.* New York, Scribner, 1999, pp. 496–498.

302 Bush later told me: Author's interview with George H. W. Bush, Feb. 20, 2004. See also Barbara Bush, *Barbara Bush: A Memoir.* New York: Charles Scribner's Sons, 1994, p. 343.

302 Bush used an office: Barbara Bush, p. 288.

302 Among the guests: George H. W. Bush interview.

303 In May 1991: Barbara Bush, pp. 410–412.

304 "He wants to": Ruth Marcus, "For Clinton, Camp David Is a Rarely Used Retreat," *The Washington Post*, Nov. 25, 1993.

304 After she went: Author's interview with Mike McCurry, Sept. 11, 2003.

304 "Camp David has the": Author's interview with Joe Lockhart, Sept. 4, 2003.

305 "I don't care what the": Author's interview with Terry McAuliffe, Sept. 16, 2003.

305 "You could go": Joe Lockhart interview.

305 He invited: For a more detailed account of Clinton's efforts, see John F. Harris, "Going for Broke, Coming Up Short; Clinton's Gamble Fails to Yield a Deal," *The Washington Post*, July 26, 2000, p. A22. Also, Douglas Waller, "The Peace Breakdown," *Time*, Aug. 7, 2000, p. 66.

306 As of August 2004: Compilation by Mark Knoller, CBS News.

307 Mike Gerson: Author's interview with Mike Gerson, Jan. 29, 2004.

307 Gerson was invited: Mike Gerson interview.

308 On the morning of: Bob Woodward, *Bush at War*. New York: Simon & Schuster, 2000, pp. 74–75.

308 At one point: Woodward, pp. 80–81.

308 After a break: Woodward, p. 91.

309 "At that point in time": President George W. Bush interview.

309 Laura Bush told me: Author's interview with Laura Bush, Oct. 14, 2003.

310 In Mobile: Author's interview with Noelia Rodriguez, Oct. 9, 2003.

311 "It's where a": Author's interview with Ken Khachigian, March 29, 2004.

BIBLIOGRAPHY

Ambrose, Stephen E., *Nixon: Volume Two, The Triumph of a Politician 1962–1972.* New York: Simon & Schuster, 1989.

Aron, Cindy S., *Working at Play: A History of Vacations in the United States.* New York: Oxford University Press, 1999.

Axelrod, Alan, *When the Buck Stops with You: Harry S. Truman on Leadership.* Portfolio, 2004.

Bellavia, Regina M. and Curry, George W., *Cultural Landscape Report for Sagamore Hill National Historic Site.* Brookline, Mass.: Olmsted Center for Landscape Preservation, 2003.

Bernstein, Carl, and Woodward, Bob, *All the President's Men.* New York: A Touchstone Book published by Simon & Schuster, 1974.

Bernstein, R. B., *Thomas Jefferson.* New York: Oxford University Press, 2003.

Beschloss, Michael R., *The Crisis Years: Kennedy and Khrushchev 1960–1963.* New York: Edward Burlingame Books, 1991.

Black, Conrad, *Franklin Delano Roosevelt: Champion of Freedom.* New York: Public Affairs, 2003.

Brinkley, Alan, and Dyer, Davis, eds., *The American Presidency.* Boston: Houghton Mifflin Company, 2004.

Bullion, John L., *In the Boat with LBJ.* Plano, Tex.: Republic of Texas Press, 2001.

Bunch III, Lonnie G., Crew, Spencer R., Hirsch, Mark G., and Rubenstein, Harry R., *The American Presidency: A Glorious Burden.* Washington and London: Smithsonian Institution Press, 2000.

Bush, Barbara, *Barbara Bush: A Memoir.* New York: Charles Scribner's Sons, 1994.

Bush, Barbara, *Reflections: Life After the White House.* New York: A Lisa Drew Book/Scribner, 2003.

Carter, Jimmy, *Christmas in Plains.* New York: Simon & Schuster, 2001.

Carter, Jimmy, *Keeping Faith: Memoirs of a President.* Fayetteville, Ark.: The University of Arkansas Press, 1995.

Carter, Rosalynn, *First Lady from Plains.* Fayetteville, Ark.: The University of Arkansas Press, 1994.

Clarke, Thurston, *Ask Not: The Inauguration of John F. Kennedy and the Speech That Changed America.* New York: Henry Holt and Company, 2004.

Clinton, Hillary, *Living History.* New York: Simon & Schuster, 2003.

Cormier, Frank, *LBJ: The Way He Was.* Garden City, N.Y.: Doubleday & Company, Inc., 1977.

Cramer, Richard Ben, *What It Takes.* New York: Vintage Books, 1993.

Cross, Robert F., *Sailor in the White House: The Seafaring Life of FDR.* Annapolis, Md.: Naval Institute Press, 2003.

Dallek, Robert, *An Unfinished Life: John F. Kennedy, 1917–1963.* Boston: Little, Brown and Company, 2003.

Dallek, Robert, *Flawed Giant: Lyndon Johnson and His Times 1961–1973.* New York: Oxford University Press, 1998.

Dalton, Kathleen, *Theodore Roosevelt: A Strenuous Life.* New York: Alfred A. Knopf, 2002.

Dalzell, Jr., Robert F., and Dalzell, Lee Baldwin, *George Washington's Mount Vernon: At Home in Revolutionary America.* New York: Oxford University Press, 1998.

Donald, David Herbert, *Lincoln at Home: Two Glimpses of Abraham Lincoln's Family Life.* New York: Simon & Schuster, 1999.

Donovan, Robert J., *Boxing the Kangaroo: A Reporter's Memoir.* Columbia, Mo.: University of Missouri Press, 2000.

Dows, Olin, *Franklin Roosevelt at Hyde Park.* New York: American Artists Group, Inc., 1949.

Duffy, Michael, and Goodgame, Dan, *Marching in Place: The Status Quo Presidency of George Bush.* New York: Simon & Schuster, 1992.

Eisenhower Dwight D., *At Ease: Stories I Tell to Friends.* Eastern National, 2000. Originally published in New York by Doubleday, 1967.

Eisenhower, Dwight D., *Mandate for Change 1953–1956.* Garden City, N.Y.: Doubleday, 1963.

Eisenhower, Susan, *Mrs. Ike: Memories and Reflections on the Life of Mamie Eisenhower.* New York: Farrar, Straus and Giroux, 1996.

Ferris, Gary, *Presidential Places: A Guide to the Historic Sites of U.S. Presidents.* Winston-Salem, N.C.: John F. Blair, 1999.

Ford, Betty, *The Times of My Life.* New York: Ballantine Books, 1978.

Ford, Gerald R., *A Time to Heal: The Autobiography of Gerald R. Ford.* New York: Harper & Row, 1979.

Gallagher, Hugh Gregory, *FDR'S Splendid Deception: The moving story of Roosevelt's massive disability—and the intense efforts to conceal it from the public.* Arlington, Va.: Vandamere Press, 1994.

Gergen, David, *Eyewitness to Power: The Essence of Leadership, Nixon to Clinton.* New York: Simon & Schuster, 2000.

Gluck, Sherwin, *TR's Summer White House: Oyster Bay.* Oyster Bay, N.Y.: Sherwin Gluck, 1997, 1999.

Goodwin, Doris Kearns, *No Ordinary Time: Franklin and Eleanor Roosevelt: The Home Front in World War II.* New York: Simon & Schuster, 1994.

Gould, Lewis L., *The Presidency of Theodore Roosevelt.* Lawrence, Kan.: University Press of Kansas, 1991.

Hagedorn, Hermann, *The Roosevelt Family of Sagamore Hill.* New York: The Macmillan Company, 1954.

Hagedorn, Hermann, and Roth, Gary G., *Sagamore Hill: An Historical Guide.* Oyster Bay, N.Y.: Theodore Roosevelt Association, 1977, 1993.

Halliday, E. M., *Understanding Thomas Jefferson.* New York: HarperCollins, 2001.

Hannaford, Peter, ed., *Recollections of Reagan: A Portrait of Ronald Reagan.* New York: William Morrow and Company, 1997.

Hannaford, Peter, *Ronald Reagan and His Ranch: The Western White House, 1981–1989.* Bennington, Vermont: Images from the Past, 2002.

Hardesty, Von, *Air Force One: The Aircraft That Shaped the Modern Presidency.* San Diego, Calif.: Tehabi Books, 2003.

Harris, Bill, *Homes of the Presidents.* Wayne, N.J.: CLB, 1997.

Harris, Wilhelmina S., *Adams National Historical Park: A Family's Legacy to America.* Washington, D.C.: National Park Service, U.S. Department of the Interior, 1983.

Hartmann, Robert T., *Palace Politics: An Inside Account of the Ford Years.* (New York: McGraw-Hill, 1980.

Hersey, John, *Aspects of the Presidency.* New York: Ticknor & Fields, 1980.

Hersey, John, *Key West Tales.* New York: Vintage Books, 1993.

Horn, Stanley F., *The Hermitage: Home of Old Hickory.* New York: Greenberg, 1950.

Hoyt, Mary Finch, *East Wing.* Philadelphia, Pa.: Xlibris, 2001.

Hunt, Gaillard, ed., *The First Forty Years of Washington Society in the Family Letters of Margaret Bayard Smith.* New York: Frederick Ungar, 1965.

Jackson, Donald, *A Year at Monticello, 1795*. Golden, Colo.: Fulcrum, 1989.

Jackson, Robert H., *That Man: An Insider's Portrait of Franklin D. Roosevelt*. New York: Oxford University Press, 2003.

Jeffers, H. Paul, *An Honest President: The Life and Presidencies of Grover Cleveland*. New York: William Morrow, 2000.

Karabell, Zachary, *Chester Alan Arthur*. New York: Times Books, 2004.

Ladies' Hermitage Association, *Andrew Jackson's Hermitage*. Hermitage, Tenn.: The Ladies' Hermitage Association, 1986.

Leech, Margaret, *Reveille in Washington 1860–1865*. New York: Harper & Brothers, 1941.

Malone, Dumas, *The Sage of Monticello*. Boston: Little, Brown and Company, 1981.

Marton, Kati, *Hidden Power: Presidential Marriages That Shaped Our Recent History*. New York: Pantheon Books, 2001.

McEwan, Barbara, *Thomas Jefferson's Poplar Forest*. Lynchburg, Va.: Warwick House, 1987.

Meacham, Jon, *Franklin and Winston: An Intimate Portrait of an Epic Friendship*. New York: Random House, 2003.

McCullough, David, *John Adams*. New York: Simon & Schuster, 2001.

McCullough, David, *Mornings on Horseback*. Boston: G. K. Hall & Co, by arrangement with Simon and Schuster, 1981.

McCullough, David, *Truman*. New York: A Touchstone Book, 1992.

Morris, Edmund, *Theodore Rex*. New York: Random House, 2001.

Nagel, Paul C., *John Quincy Adams: A Public Life, a Private Life*. Cambridge, Mass.: Harvard University Press, 1997.

Nelson, W. Dale, *The President Is at Camp David*. Syracuse University Press, 1995.

Nixon, Richard, *RN: The Memoirs of Richard Nixon*. New York: Grosset & Dunlap, 1978.

O'Donnell, Kenneth P., and Powers, David F., with McCarthy, Joe, *"Johnny, We Hardly Knew Ye": Memories of John Fitzgerald Kennedy*. Boston: Little, Brown and Company, 1970.

Peterson, Merrill D., *Visitors to Monticello*. Charlottesville, Va.: University Press of Virginia, 1989.

Pierson, Hamilton W., *Jefferson at Monticello*. North Stratford, N.H.: Ayers Company Publishers, 2000.

Pinsker, Matthew, *Lincoln's Sanctuary: Abraham Lincoln and the Soldiers' Home*. New York: Oxford University Press, 2003.

Reagan, Nancy, *I Love You, Ronnie*. New York: Random House, 2000.

Reedy, George, *Lyndon B. Johnson: A Memoir*. New York: Andrews and McMeel, 1982.

Reeves, Richard, *President Kennedy: Profile of Power*. New York: Simon & Schuster, 1993.

Reeves, Richard, *President Nixon: Alone in the White House*. New York: Simon & Schuster, 2001.

Remini, Robert V., *The Life of Andrew Jackson*. New York: Penguin Books USA, 1990.

Roosevelt, Eleanor, *Franklin D. Roosevelt and Hyde Park: Personal Recollections of Eleanor Roosevelt*. National Park Service, U.S. Department of the Interior, 1977.

Roosevelt, Elliott, and Brough, James, *An Untold Story: The Roosevelts of Hyde Park*. New York: G.P. Putnam's Sons, 1973.

Rothman, Hal K., *LBJ's Texas White House: "Our Heart's Home."* College Station, Tex.: Texas A & M University Press, 2001.

Sammon, Bill, *Fighting Back: The War on Terrorism—from Inside the Bush White House*. Washington, D.C.: Regnery, 2002.

Sandburg, Carl, *Abraham Lincoln: Part II, The War Years, 1861–1864*. New York: A Harvest/HBJ Book, 1982.

Sandburg, Carl, *Abraham Lincoln: Part III, The War Years, 1864–1865*. New York: A Harvest/HBJ Book, 1982.

Schlesinger, Arthur M., Jr., *A Thousand Days: John F. Kennedy in the White House*. Boston: Houghton Mifflin, 1965.

Schweizer, Peter, and Schweizer, Rochelle, *The Bushes: Portrait of a Dynasty*. New York: Doubleday, 2004.

Skinner, Kiron K., Anderson, Annelise, and Anderson, Martin, eds., *Reagan: A Life in Letters*. New York: Free Press, 2003.

Smith, Hedrick, *The Power Game: How Washington Works*. New York: Ballantine Books, 1988.

Smith, Sally Bedell, *Grace and Power: The Private World of the Kennedy White House*. New York: Random House, 2004.

Sullivan, George, *Presidents at Play*. New York: Walker and Company, 1995.

Truman, Harry S., *Memoirs by Harry S. Truman, Volume One: Year of Decisions*. Garden City, N.Y.: Doubleday & Company, 1955.

Truman, Harry S., *Memoirs by Harry S. Truman, Volume Two: Years of Trial and Hope, 1946–1952*. Garden City, N.Y.: Doubleday & Company, 1956.

Truman, Margaret, *Harry S. Truman*. New York: Pocket Books, 1974.

Unbylined. *LBJ Country*. Fredericksburg, Tex.: Awani Press, 1970.

Vernon, Laura, ed., *Harry Truman Slept Here: A Glimpse at the Trumans' Private Life in Independence, Missouri*. Independence, Mo: Posy Publications, 1985.

Ward, Geoffrey C., ed., *Closest Companion: The Unknown Story of the Intimate Friendship between Franklin Roosevelt and Margaret Suckley*. Boston: Houghton Mifflin Company, 1995.

Walker, Turnley, *Roosevelt and the Warm Springs Story.* New York: A. A. Wyn, 1953.

Wallace, Chris, *Character: Profiles in Presidential Courage.* New York: Rugged Land, 2004.

Walsh, Kenneth T., *Air Force One: A History of the Presidents and Their Planes.* New York: Hyperion, 2003.

Walsh, Kenneth T., *Feeding the Beast: The White House Versus the Press.* Philadelphia, Pa.: Xlibris, 2003.

Walsh, Kenneth T., *Ronald Reagan: Biography.* New York: Park Lane Press, 1996.

Wead, Doug, *All the Presidents' Children: Triumph and Tragedy in the Lives of America's First Families.* New York: Atria Books, 2003.

Weber, Ralph E. and Weber, Ralph A., eds., *Dear Americans: Letters from the Desk of Ronald Reagan.* New York: Doubleday, 2003.

White, Theodore H., *The Making of the President 1960.* New York: Atheneum House, 1961.

Wiencek, Henry, *An Imperfect God: George Washington, His Slaves, and the Creation of America.* New York: Farrar, Straus, and Giroux, 2003.

Willis, Resa, *FDR and Lucy: Lovers and Friends.* New York: RoutledgeFalmer, 2004.

Wills, Garry, *"Negro President": Jefferson and the Slave Power.* Boston: Houghton Mifflin Company, 2003.

Withey, Lynne, *Dearest Friend: A Life of Abigail Adams.* New York: A Touchstone Book, 2001.

Woodward, Bob: *The Agenda: Inside the Clinton White House.* New York: Simon & Schuster, 1994.

Woodward, Bob, and Bernstein, Carl, *The Final Days.* New York: A Touchstone Book, 1976.

INDEX

ABOUT THE AUTHOR

Kenneth T. Walsh is the chief White House correspondent for *U.S. News & World Report*.

He started reporting and writing about the presidency for the magazine in 1986 and has won the two most prestigious awards for covering the White House: the Aldo Beckman Award and the Gerald R. Ford Prize. He has won the Ford Prize twice.

He appears frequently on a variety of television programs on NBC, MSNBC, Fox, and CNN, among others, and is a guest on numerous radio shows. He lectures widely and is an award-winning adjunct professor of communication at the American University in Washington, D.C.

Walsh is former president of the White House Correspondents' Association and remains on the association's governing board. He holds a B.A. in journalism from Rutgers University and an M.A. in communication from AU. He lives with his wife, Barclay, in Bethesda, Maryland, and Shady Side, Maryland. They have two children, Jean and Chris.